Learning Aid

for use with

Basic Marketing
A Marketing Strategy
Planning Approach

Sixteenth Edition

William D. Perreault, Jr.
University of North Carolina

Joseph P. Cannon
Colorado State University

E. Jerome McCarthy
Michigan State University

Boston   Burr Ridge, IL   Dubuque, IA   Madison, WI   New York   San Francisco   St. Louis
Bangkok   Bogotá   Caracas   Kuala Lumpur   Lisbon   London   Madrid   Mexico City
Milan   Montreal   New Delhi   Santiago   Seoul   Singapore   Sydney   Taipei   Toronto

McGraw-Hill
Irwin

Learning Aid for use with
BASIC MARKETING: A MARKETING STRATEGY PLANNING APPROACH
William D. Perreault, Jr., Joseph P. Cannon and E. Jerome McCarthy

Published by McGraw-Hill/Irwin, an imprint of The McGraw-Hill Companies, Inc., 1221 Avenue of the
Americas, New York, NY 10020. Copyright © 2008 by The McGraw-Hill Companies, Inc. All rights reserved.

1 2 3 4 5 6 7 8 9 0 QPD/QPD 0 9 8 7 6

ISBN: 978-0-07-322283-7
MHID: 0-07-322283-6

www.mhhe.com

The McGraw-Hill Companies

Contents

Introduction

This *Learning Aid is* designed to help you organize and learn all of the material that is presented in *Basic Marketing,* 16th edition. Feedback from marketing instructors--and students--indicates that students who use the *Learning Aid* regularly do tend to learn the material better--and also tend to do better on examinations.

Please note, however, that the *Learning Aid is* intended to be used along with *Basic Marketing. It is not a substitute for reading and carefully studying the text!*

How the Learning Aid Is Organized

The *Learning Aid is* divided into 22 chapters--one chapter for each corresponding chapter in *Basic Marketing.* These are followed by separate chapters for Appendix A: Economics Fundamentals and Appendix B: Marketing Arithmetic.

Each chapter in the *Learning Aid* contains the following five sections:

A. What this chapter is about
B. Important terms
C. True-false questions
D. Multiple-choice questions
E. Application exercises

The purpose of each of these sections is explained below. Please note that some sections are designed to be used *before* you read each chapter in *Basic Marketing.*

What This Chapter Is About

This section provides a brief introduction to each chapter in *Basic Marketing.* It should be read *before* you read the text--to help you focus on the important points in each chapter.

Important Terms

This section lists the important new terms introduced in each chapter of *Basic Marketing*--and the page on which each term first appears. (These terms are shown in red in the text to help you find them.)

You should look over the list of important terms *before* reading each chapter--to help you focus on the key points in the chapter. *After* reading each chapter, you should review the list of important terms to make sure you understand each term. If you have any doubts about what a particular term means, use the indicated page number to find and restudy its definition in the text--or look up the term's definition in the Glossary at the end of the text. Some students even write out the definitions of each important term on 3 x 5 cards--to help them study for exams.

True-False Questions

This section provides a series of *self-testing* true-false questions--to test your understanding of the material presented in *Basic Marketing*. The correct answer for each question is given at the end of the test--along with a page number showing where the correct answer can be found in the text.

After reading each chapter in the text and reviewing the important terms, try to answer all of the true-false questions *before* looking at the correct answers. Then check your answers--and for each question that you answered wrong, review the related text material to find out *why* your answer is wrong. This is an important step! Simply memorizing the correct answers is *not* likely to improve your exam performance!

Multiple-Choice Questions

This section contains a series of *self-testing* multiple-choice questions--to further test your understanding and comprehension of the material presented in *Basic Marketing*. Again, the correct answer for each question is given at the end of the questions--along with a page number showing where the correct answer can be found in the text.

Ideally, you should take the multiple-choice tests only *after* you have read the text, reviewed the important terms, and tried the true-false questions. Again, you should try to answer all of the questions *before* looking at the correct answers--and make sure you review the text material to learn *why* your wrong answers were wrong!

Finally, keep in mind that the self-testing true-false and multiple-choice questions are just a *sample* of what you might expect on an exam. They do not cover every single concept discussed in the text--nor do they cover every possible type of question that might be asked. In other words, *simply answering these self-testing questions is not adequate preparation for exams. You* must also read and study the text!

Application Exercises

This section includes two or more exercises for each of the chapters in *Basic Marketing* (not including the appendices). One of the exercises for each of the first 19 chapters is based on the *Computer-Aided Problem* found at the end of the corresponding chapter in the text. Each exercise is designed to illustrate and apply some of the more important concepts and analytical approaches introduced in the text.

Although these exercises are designed mainly to be discussed in class and/or assigned as homework--you *can still benefit from doing them even if your instructor does not assign them.* Many students find the "Introductions" to each exercise quite helpful in understanding the related text material. And many of the exercises contain short "caselets" which show how concepts discussed in the text can be applied in the "real world. " Doing these exercises will not only improve your understanding of the text material--but will also better prepare you for more advanced marketing and business case courses.

Note: Your instructor has been supplied with suggested answers for each of the application exercises--and with software that can be used to work the computer-aided exercises. So even if the exercises are not formally assigned, you can still do them--and ask your instructor to show you the suggested answers so you can check your answers. Your instructor will surely be impressed by your dedication to learning!

How to Study for Examinations

While no study routine works best for everyone, the following suggestions are based on proven learning principles and should be of benefit to most students. *For every chapter your instructor assigns in Basic Marketing:*

1.   Read the *what this chapter is about* section in the *Learning Aid.*

2.   Look over the *important terms* section in the *Learning* Aid.

3.   Read the learning objectives listed at the beginning of the chapter.

4.   Read the chapter from beginning to end without any interruptions--and *without doing any underlining or note taking.* (Underlining key points while you read interrupts your flow of thought and tends to reduce reading comprehension.)

5.   Read the chapter again--this time underlining key points and/or writing notes in the page margins. Look at the exhibits and illustrations, and think about how they relate to the text material.

6.   Review the *important terms* section in the *Learning* Aid to make sure you can define each term.

7.   Take the self-testing true-false test in the *Learning* Aid--and go back to the text to study any questions you answered wrong.

8.   Take the self-testing multiple-choice test in the *Learning* Aid--and go back to the text to study any questions you answered wrong.

9.   Take detailed classroom lecture notes--and review them *immediately after class to* make sure that they are complete and that you understand everything your instructor said.

10.   Do any *application exercises* that your instructor assigns.

11.   *Optional:* Do the *application exercises* that were not assigned.

12.   Just before the examination--review:

    a.   the points you underlined in the text and/or your notes in the page margins.
    b.   the *important terms* in the *Learning* Aid.
    c.   the self-testing true-false and multiple-choice questions in the *Learning* Aid--especially the questions you answered wrong the first time.
    d.   any *application exercises* that were assigned.
    e.   your lecture notes.

Good luck!

Acknowledgement

We deeply appreciate the ongoing contributions of Ms. Lin Davis. Through several editions she has made valuable contributions in all aspects of preparing this manual. In addition, she independently did the desktop publishing work to prepare the manuscript in final form ready to be duplicated by the printer.

Professor Andrew Brogowicz of Western Michigan University contributed many creative ideas to early editions of this *Learning Aid*. His contributions have continued to influence many of the new, revised, and/or updated exercises.

Chapter 1

Marketing's value to consumers, firms, and society

What This Chapter Is About

Chapter 1 introduces the concept of marketing. First, we show how marketing relates to production—and why it is important to you. Then the text shows that we can view marketing in two ways: from a micro view and from a macro view. The importance of a macro-marketing system in any kind of economy is emphasized. The vital role of marketing functions is discussed. It is emphasized that producers, consumers, *and* marketing specialists perform marketing functions. You will learn that responsibility for performing the marketing functions can be shifted and shared in a variety of ways, but that from a macro viewpoint all of the functions must be performed by someone.

Chapter 1 also shows how important marketing can be within a business firm or a nonprofit organization. In particular, the "marketing concept" and the evolution of firms from a production to a marketing orientation is explained. Then, the importance of understanding the difference between a production orientation and a marketing orientation is discussed. The differences between for-profit and nonprofit organizations are also included. In addition, we covered ways that social responsibility and marketing ethics relate to the marketing concept, and ended with the criticisms of marketing. Macro-marketing was introduced in this chapter, but the major thrust of this book is on managerial (micro) marketing.

Important Terms

production, p. 5
customer satisfaction, p. 5
innovation, p. 6
marketing, p. 6
pure subsistence economy, p. 7
macro-marketing, p. 8
economies of scale, p. 10
universal functions of marketing, p. 10
buying function, p. 10
selling function, p. 10
transporting function, p. 10
storing function, p. 10
standardization and grading, p. 10
financing, p. 10
risk taking, p. 10
market information function, p. 10
intermediary (middleman), p. 10

collaborators, p. 10
e-commerce, p. 11
economic system, p. 12
command economy, p. 12
market-directed economy, p. 12
simple trade era, p. 15
production era, p. 15
sales era, p. 15
marketing department era, p. 15
marketing company era, p. 15
marketing concept, p. 16
production orientation, p. 16
marketing orientation, p. 16
customer value, p. 19
micro-macro dilemma, p. 23
social responsibility, p. 23
marketing ethics, p. 24

True-False Questions

___ 1. According to the text, marketing means "selling" or "advertising."

___ 2. Actually making goods or performing services is called marketing.

___ 3. Marketing plays an essential role in creating customer satisfaction.

___ 4. It is estimated that marketing costs about 50 percent of each consumer's dollar.

___ 5. Marketing discourages the development and spread of new ideas, goods, and services.

___ 6. Marketing is both a set of activities performed by organizations and a social process.

___ 7. Marketing is the performance of activities that seek to accomplish an organization's objectives by anticipating customer or client needs and directing a flow of need-satisfying goods and services from producer to customer or client.

___ 8. Marketing activities should be of no interest to a nonprofit organization.

___ 9. Marketing does not occur unless two or more parties are willing to exchange something for something else.

___ 10. In a pure subsistence economy—when each family unit produces everything it consumes—no marketing is involved.

___ 11. A marketing exchange is a single transaction between a firm and a customer, nothing more.

___ 12. Macro-marketing is a set of activities that direct an economy's flow of goods and services from producers to consumers in a way which effectively matches supply and demand and accomplishes the objectives of society.

___ 13. Macro-marketing emphasizes how the whole system works, rather than the activities of individual organizations.

___ 14. Achieving effective marketing in an advanced economy is simplified by the fact that producers are separated from consumers in only two ways: time and space.

___ 15. "Economies of scale" means that as a company produces larger numbers of a particular product, the cost for each of these products goes down.

___ 16. The "universal functions of marketing" consist only of buying, selling, transporting, and storing.

___ 17. Marketing functions are performed by producers, consumers, and a variety of marketing specialists.

___ 18. Intermediaries specialize in trade and production.

_____ 19. While intermediaries facilitate exchange, their cost makes the whole macro-marketing system less efficient.

_____ 20. Marketing collaborators are any firms that provide the marketing functions of buying and selling.

_____ 21. E-commerce refers to exchanges between organizations (not individuals) and the activities that facilitate those exchanges.

_____ 22. Responsibility for performing the marketing functions can be shifted and shared in a variety of ways, but no function can be completely eliminated.

_____ 23. Not all societies need an economic system.

_____ 24. In a market-directed economy, government officials decide what and how much is to be produced and distributed by whom, when, to whom, and why.

_____ 25. In a market-directed economy, price is a rough measure of how society values particular goods and services.

_____ 26. The American economy is entirely market-directed.

_____ 27. The simple trade era was a time when families traded or sold their "surplus" output to local middlemen who resold these goods to other consumers or distant middlemen.

_____ 28. Marketing departments are usually formed when firms go from the "production era" to the "sales era."

_____ 29. A company has moved into the "marketing company era" when, in addition to short-run marketing planning, the total company effort is guided by the marketing concept.

_____ 30. The marketing concept says that a firm should aim all its efforts at satisfying customers, even if this proves to be unprofitable.

_____ 31. The term "marketing orientation" means making products that are easy to produce and then trying to sell them.

_____ 32. The three basic ideas included in the definition of the marketing concept are: customer satisfaction, a total company effort, and sales as an objective.

_____ 33. There are no functional departments in a firm that has adopted the marketing concept.

_____ 34. The marketing concept was very quickly accepted, especially among producers of industrial commodities like steel and pipe.

_____ 35. In the past two decades, many firms in service industries adopted the marketing concept.

_____ 36. A good or service that doesn't meet a consumer's needs results in low customer value.

_____ 37. In marketing, it is the manager's viewpoint that matters, not the customer's.

___ 38. The text credits L. L. Bean's success to its offering good customer value.

___ 39. Because they don't try to earn a profit, the marketing concept is not very useful for nonprofit organizations.

___ 40. A nonprofit organization does not measure profit in the same way as a firm.

___ 41. Sometimes micro-macro dilemmas arise because what is "good" for some producers and consumers may not be "good" for society as a whole.

___ 42. A firm's obligation to improve its positive effects on society and reduce its negative effects is called fiscal responsibility.

___ 43. The moral standards that guide marketing decisions and actions are called marketing ethics.

Answers to True-False Questions

1. F, p. 4	16. F, p. 10	31. F, p. 16
2. F, p. 5	17. T, p. 10	32. F, p. 16
3. T, p. 5	18. F, p. 10	33. F, p. 17
4. T, p. 5	19. F, p. 10	34. F, p. 17
5. F, p. 6	20. F, p. 10	35. T, p. 17
6. T, p. 6	21. F, p. 11	36. T, p. 19
7. T, p. 6	22. T, p. 11	37. F, p. 19
8. F, p. 6	23. F, p. 12	38. T, p. 21
9. T, p. 7	24. F, p. 12	39. F, p. 21
10. T, p. 7	25. T, p. 12	40. T, p. 22
11. F, p. 7	26. F, p. 13	41. T, p. 23
12. F, p. 8	27. T, p. 15	42. F, p. 23
13. T, p. 8	28. F, p. 15	43. T, p. 24
14. F, p. 9	29. T, p. 15-16	
15. T, p. 10	30. F, p. 16	

Multiple-Choice Questions (Circle the correct response)

1. According to the text:
   a. marketing is much more than selling or advertising.
   b. the cost of marketing is about 25 percent of the consumer's dollar.
   c. marketing affects every single aspect of your daily life.
   d. marketing discourages research and innovation.
   e. all of the above are true statements.

2. The text stresses that:
   a. advertising and selling are not really part of marketing.
   b. marketing is nothing more than a set of business activities performed by individual firms.
   c. marketing techniques have no application for nonprofit organizations.
   d. marketing is a social process and a set of activities performed by organizations.
   e. a good product usually sells itself.

3. *Marketing*:
    a.   is concerned with need-satisfying goods, but not with services.
    b.   involves an attempt to anticipate customer or client needs.
    c.   is primarily concerned with efficient use of resources and fair allocation of output.
    d.   includes activities such as accounting, production, and financial management.
    e.   is the process of selling and distributing manufactured goods.

4. *Macro*-marketing:
    a.   is not concerned with the flow of goods and services from producers to consumers.
    b.   seeks to match homogeneous supply capabilities with homogeneous demands for goods and services.
    c.   refers to a set of activities performed by both profit and nonprofit organizations.
    d.   focuses on the objectives of society.
    e.   All of the above are true statements.

5. In advanced economies:
    a.   mass production with its economies of scale makes the cost of each product higher.
    b.   exchange is simplified by discrepancies of quantity and assortment.
    c.   there is little need for marketing specialists.
    d.   both supply and demand tend to be homogeneous in nature.
    e.   producers and consumers experience a separation of values.

6. Which of the following is *not* one of the "universal functions of marketing"?
    a.   Production
    b.   Standardization
    c.   Financing
    d.   Buying
    e.   Transporting

7. Firms that specialize in providing marketing functions other than buying and selling are known as:
    a.   suppliers.
    b.   intermediaries.
    c.   advisors.
    d.   collaborators.
    e.   agents.

8. Which of the following is a *true* statement?
    a.   Since marketing is concerned with many thousands of different products, there is no one set of marketing functions that applies to all products.
    b.   Responsibility for performing marketing functions can be shifted and shared, but no function can be completely eliminated.
    c.   From a micro viewpoint, every firm must perform all of the marketing functions.
    d.   Marketing functions should be performed only by marketing intermediaries or collaborators.
    e.   Many marketing functions are not necessary in market-directed economies.

9. Which of the following statements about economic decision making is *true*?
   a. In a market-directed economy, the micro-level decisions of individual producers and consumers determine the macro-level decisions.
   b. Government planning usually works best when economies become more complex and the variety of goods and services produced is fairly large.
   c. The United States may be considered a pure market-directed economy.
   d. Command economies usually rely on market forces to determine prices.
   e. All of the above are true statements.

10. A firm that focuses its attention primarily on "selling" its present products in order to meet or beat competition is operating in which of the following "management eras"?
    a. Production era
    b. Sales era
    c. Marketing department era
    d. Marketing company era
    e. Advertising era

11. Based on the following company statements, which company is most likely to be in the marketing company era?
    a. "Our sales force was able to sell middlemen more of our new product than they can resell in all of this year."
    b. "Our marketing manager is coordinating pricing, product decisions, promotion, and distribution to help us show a profit at the end of this year."
    c. "The whole company is in good shape—demand exceeds what we can produce."
    d. "Our long range plan—developed by our marketing manager—is to expand so that we can profitably meet the long-term needs of our customers."
    e. "Our new President previously led our marketing effort as Vice President of Sales."

12. Which of the following best explains what the "marketing concept" means:
    a. Firms should spend more money on marketing than they have in the past.
    b. A firm's main emphasis should be on the efficient utilization of its resources.
    c. All of a firm's activities and resources should be organized to satisfy the needs of its customers—at a profit.
    d. A company's chief executive should previously have been a marketing manager.
    e. A firm should always attempt to give customers what they need regardless of the cost involved.

13. The difference between "production orientation" and "marketing orientation" is best explained as follows:
    a. there are no separate functional department in a marketing-oriented firm.
    b. in a marketing-oriented firm, the total system's effort is guided by what individual departments would like to do.
    c. production-oriented firms usually do not have a marketing manager.
    d. in a marketing-oriented firm, every department's activities are guided by what customers need and what the firm can deliver at a profit.
    e. all major decisions are based on extensive marketing research studies in marketing-oriented firms.

14. Customer value
    a. is greater if benefits exceed costs.
    b. becomes less important as competition increases.
    c. is the same thing as low price.
    d. affects a customer's relationship with a firm before and after a sale.
    e. both a and d are true.

15. Which of the following statements about nonprofits is *false*?
    a. Marketing is being more widely accepted by nonprofit organizations.
    b. The marketing concept is as important for nonprofit organizations as it is for business firms.
    c. In business firms and in nonprofit organizations, support comes from satisfied customers.
    d. A nonprofit organization does not measure profit in the same way as a firm.
    e. The marketing concept provides focus in both business firms and nonprofit organizations.

16. Which of the following is NOT an example of the micro-macro dilemma?
    a. Having a dog or cat can teach a child responsibility, but add expenses to the family budget.
    b. Some people like to smoke cigarettes, but the smell annoys many others.
    c. Aluminum soft-drink cans are convenient, but expensive to pick up along the highway.
    d. Nuclear power may reduce your fuel bill, but worry others.
    e. Driving fast can be fun, but is hazardous to other people.

Answers to Multiple-Choice Questions

1. a, p. 4
2. d, p. 6
3. b, p. 6
4. d, p. 8
5. e, p. 9
6. a, p. 10

7. d, p. 10
8. b, p. 11
9. a, p. 12
10. b, p. 15
11. d, p. 15-16
12. c, p. 16

13. d, p. 16
14. e, p. 19
15. c, p. 22
16. a, p. 23

Exercise 1-1

What is marketing?

Introduction

Society ignored or even criticized the contributions of marketing until the beginning of the 20th century. At that time, economies once marked by a scarcity of goods began to enjoy an abundance of goods. Marketing skills were needed to solve the distribution problems that resulted. Thus, it was not until the early 1900s that the importance of marketing was realized—and that marketing was accepted as a separate academic subject in schools and colleges.

Today, countries that operate with market-directed economies have achieved genuine improvements in standards of living—while most command economies have collapsed or are "on the ropes." Even today, however, many people do not have a very clear understanding of marketing. No one single definition of marketing will satisfy everyone. Many people—including some students and business managers—tend to think of marketing as just "selling" or "advertising." Others see marketing as an all-inclusive social process that can solve all the world's problems. Some critics, meanwhile, seem to blame marketing for most of society's ills!

This exercise is intended to help you see more clearly what marketing is all about. One way to learn about marketing is to study the definitions in the text. Another way is to use these definitions. This is the approach you will follow in this exercise.

Assignment

Listed below are some commonly asked questions about marketing. Answer each of these questions in a way that shows your understanding of marketing.

1.   What activities does marketing involve besides selling?

2.   How would you respond to the criticism "Marketing just adds unnecessary costs to the price of everything we buy"?

3. Is marketing useful for nonprofit organizations? Explain.

4. Why do we need intermediaries? Don't they just add to the cost of distributing products to consumers?

5. How do consumers in a market-directed economy influence what products will be produced and by whom?

6. Why is effective marketing needed in an advanced economy? Isn't mass production—with its economies of scale—the real key to meeting consumer needs at the lowest cost?

Question for Discussion

Should marketing be viewed as a set of activities performed by business and nonprofit organizations, or alternately as a social process? Why is it important to make this distinction?

Exercise 1-2

How marketing functions can be shifted and shared

Introduction

The marketing process does not take place automatically. It requires that certain marketing functions or activities be performed by various marketing institutions—and by *consumers* themselves. The following eight functions are essential to the marketing of all goods: buying, selling, transporting, storing, grading, financing, risk-taking, and market information. No matter how simple or complex the marketing process is, these functions must be performed. Some functions may be performed several times to facilitate the marketing of a given product, while others may be performed only once. At times, the performance of a function may be shifted from one member of a marketing system to another. For example, some modern wholesalers and retailers shift the burden of storing goods back to manufacturers. But, the fact remains that each of the eight functions must be performed by someone at least once before any good can be marketed—none can be eliminated.

Assignment

This assignment illustrates how the performance of marketing functions can be shifted and shared. Read the following case carefully and then answer the questions that follow in the space provided.

HALO MARKET

Aaron and Valerie Bennett are a young couple who work in Seattle and live in a small apartment downtown. They shop for most of their food—including meat—at Halo Market, a small grocery store located near their apartment. The Bennetts inspect the packages of meat and select the amount and type of meat they want for their meals that week. They have always been happy with the quality and selection of meat at Halo Market—and they like the store's "satisfaction or your money back" guarantee.

The Halo Market is too small to have a full butcher department and meat freezer. Instead, the owner, Lorenzo Salazar, buys fresh meat from Choice Cuts, a wholesale butcher. The wholesaler keeps a large quantity of bulk meat in cold storage—and then cuts grade-A stew beef, steaks, roasts, hamburger, and other selections to fill orders from the Halo Market and its other grocery store customers. The wholesaler delivers the meat to Salazar each morning before the store opens. At the end of the month the wholesaler bills Halo Market for its purchases.

This arrangement seems to work well. Although Salazar doesn't keep computerized records, he knows his customers' preferences and he orders carefully. He knows that steaks sell well when the weather allows even apartment dwellers to barbecue on their balconies, but he cuts back on big steaks as soon as cooler weather hits. He packages the meat in convenient serving sizes and makes up more small packages than most grocery stores because many apartment dwellers live alone. With a day or two's notice, he can also handle special requests. As a result, Halo Market can offer a selection that meets most customers' needs. If Salazar orders too much of a certain type of meat and it has not sold within a few days, he marks down the price—to prompt a quicker sale.

Based on your analysis of this description, answer the following questions.

1.   Does the Halo Market help to resolve discrepancies of quantity between food producers and consumers? Briefly explain your answer.

_____

_____

_____

2.   Does the Halo Market help to resolve discrepancies of assortment between food producers and consumers? Briefly explain your answer.

_____

_____

_____

3.   The eight basic marketing functions are listed below. Check Yes or No whether each function is performed by someone in this description. If "Yes," explain *when* and *by whom* each function was performed. If "No," explain why not.

a)   Buying: Yes _____ No _____ Explain.

_____

_____

_____

b)   Selling: Yes _____ No _____ Explain.

_____

_____

_____

c)   Grading: Yes _____ No _____ Explain.

_____

_____

_____

d)   Transporting: Yes _____ No _____ Explain.

_____

_____

_____

e)   Storing: Yes _____ No _____ Explain.

_____

_____

_____

f)   Financing: Yes _____ No _____ Explain.

_____

_____

_____

g)   Market information: Yes _____ No _____ Explain.

_____

_____

_____

h)   Risk-taking: Yes _____ No _____ Explain.

_____

_____

_____

Like most young couples, Aaron and Valerie Bennett are always interested in ways to make their budget stretch further. An article in the Sunday newspaper on cutting grocery costs suggests buying meat directly from downtown wholesalers. According to the article, some meat wholesalers will sell direct to consumers—if the consumer buys a whole side of beef. The article described it this way. The customer calls the meat company and agrees on a price and time to pick up the purchase. The meat packing plant then cuts the side of beef into large pieces and wraps them in freezer paper. The wholesaler requires customers to pay with cash when they pick up the meat. The newspaper article says that on a per pound basis the price is about 25 percent cheaper than the same selection of meat would be at a grocery store.

4. If the Bennetts were to buy meat directly from the wholesaler, they would probably need to perform some of the basic marketing functions themselves. Each of the basic marketing functions is listed below. For each function, check Yes or No to indicate if the Bennetts would need to perform this function. In addition, briefly explain any difficulties you think they might face in trying to perform the function.

a) Buying: Yes _____ No _____ Explain.

_____

_____

_____

b) Selling: Yes _____ No _____ Explain.

_____

_____

_____

c) Grading: Yes _____ No _____ Explain.

_____

_____

_____

d) Transporting: Yes _____ No _____ Explain.

_____

_____

_____

e) Storing: Yes _____ No _____ Explain.

_____

_____

_____

f)   Financing: Yes _____ No _____ Explain.

_____

_____

_____

g)   Market information: Yes _____ No _____ Explain.

_____

_____

_____

h)   Risk-taking: Yes _____ No _____ Explain.

_____

_____

_____

Name a product for which all eight marketing functions do *not* need to be performed by someone somewhere in the marketing system. Explain your thinking about what functions do not need to be performed.

Exercise 1-3

Marketing-oriented vs. production-oriented firms

Introduction

Business firms can be classified as either "production-oriented" or "marketing-oriented," depending on whether they have adopted the "marketing concept." The marketing concept is a modern philosophy that simply states that a firm should aim all its efforts at satisfying its customers--at a profit. This philosophy implies a total management commitment to (1) customer satisfaction, (2) a total company effort, and (3) profit, not just sales, as an objective of the firm. The same idea applies to nonprofits, but some measure of long-term success other than profit may serve as an objective.

In general, a production-oriented organization tries to get customers to buy what the firm has produced, while a marketing-oriented firm tries to produce and sell what customers need. Actually, the terms "production-oriented" and "marketing-oriented" should be viewed as opposite ends of a continuum along which different firms could be placed. But it is often useful to classify a firm as being *mainly* production-or marketing-oriented.

In practice, however, there is no simple way of identifying the two types of firms. Instead, one must look for subtle "clues" to help decide whether a firm is production-oriented or marketing-oriented. These clues can take many forms, such as the attitudes of management toward customers, the firm's organization structure, and its methods and procedures.

Assignment

This exercise gives you some practice in identifying production-oriented and marketing-oriented firms. You will be given pairs of firms--and a "clue" about each firm. On the basis of these clues, you must decide which one of the two firms is more marketing-oriented and which is more production-oriented.

For each pair of firms, print an *M* before the firm that you think is marketing-oriented and a *P* before the firm that is production-oriented--and then briefly explain your answers. (Note: each set should have an *M* and a *P*--you *must* make a choice.) The first pair is answered for you as an example.

Orientation		Clues

1. **P** Firm A: "Our goal is to run at full capacity and sell everything that we make."

    M Firm B: "Our goal is to build customer loyalty by designing products that they want to buy. "

    Firm A is interested in "doing its own thing," while Firm B has focused its efforts on producing what customers want and need.

2. ___ Firm A: "We've given the people in this city one of the finest museums in the world, but hardly anyone attends. It's a case of misplaced social values--and something must be done about it."

    ___ Firm B: "We've got to find out what it is about our museum exhibits that turn people away. It's a case of needing to do a better job of meeting people's needs--rather than sitting back and waiting for people to see the light."

3. ___ Firm A: "We're getting killed by overseas competitors. We need to improve our quality control and do a better job of meeting customers' expectations."

    ___ Firm B: "Overseas producers compete unfairly with cheap labor. We need to have our public relations department lobby for tighter import quotas so that we can make a profit."

4. ___ Firm A: "As sales manager, my job is to hire salespeople who can "move" as many units as we can produce. After all, the higher the sales, the higher the profits."

    ___ Firm B: "As finance manager, my job is to determine how many units it will be profitable for us to sell at the price customers are willing to pay."

5. ___ Firm A: "People today want the convenience of one-stop shopping and we've got to go where the customers are. It will cost us more to construct a building in the shopping center, but we'll attract more regular customers and that's the key to profit for a bank."

___ Firm B: "It would cost us too much to build a bank in the shopping center. We'll locate our bank a few blocks away where the land is cheaper. We can depend on our low prices and good selection to bring the customers to us."

6. ___ Firm A: "How much will it improve our customer service if we buy an additional delivery truck?"

___ Firm B: "How much money will we save if we wait a year before buying an additional delivery truck?"

7. ___ Firm A: "What competitive advantage would the proposed new product have in satisfying consumer needs?"

___ Firm B: "Our competitor's new product is a great idea. Let's see if we can produce and sell it at a lower price."

8. ___ Firm A: "Our sales have dropped. Let's ask our intermediaries why customers have stopped buying our product."

___ Firm B: "Our sales are too low. Perhaps we could use our most persuasive salespeople to recruit some new intermediaries."

9. ___ Firm A: "It helps to have an accountant as president. When she took over the company, she found that it was too expensive for a salesperson to visit many of our smaller customers, and now our sales force concentrates its efforts on satisfying those larger accounts that contribute the most to our profits."

   ___ Firm B: "Our sales have nearly doubled since the sales manager was promoted to president. He's tripled the amount we spend on personal selling and advertising, and he's told the accountants to stick to their balancing the books and leave the marketing budget to him."

10. ___ Firm A: "Sure our inventory costs are high. But how many customers would we lose if we were frequently unable to fill orders immediately?"

    ___ Firm B.: "Our inventory costs are too high. We'll have to reduce our inventory, even if it means that it will take customers longer to get their orders."

11. ___ Firm A: "Our profits have been declining. Perhaps we should search for new opportunities to satisfy unfulfilled needs."

    ___ Firm B: "Our profits have been declining. Perhaps we should search for ways to cut costs and make more efficient use of our resources."

Question for Discussion

If, as the text emphasizes, it is so important that firms be marketing-oriented, how is it that many production-oriented firms are not only surviving but apparently operating profitably?

Exercise 1-4

Ethical challenges in marketing

Introduction

Marketing managers face many challenges—including difficult decisions in areas of social responsibility and ethics. Some guidelines in these areas are provided by the laws of our society. Clearly, a marketing manager must know and obey laws that govern marketing actions. But, there are many decision areas in marketing where laws do not exist, and where the question of what is "right" or "wrong" is not so clear-cut. Usually, these are decision areas where the marketing manager must deal with trade-offs or conflicts—situations where what is good for some customers, stockholders, employees, other channel members, or society in general is not good for someone else. These are situations where the marketing manager must weigh all of the facts—and make a personal judgment about what to do.

Throughout the text, you will be alerted to many of the decision areas where a marketing manager must be sensitive to ethical decisions. This exercise provides an opportunity for you to start thinking about some of these issues. Later in the course you may want to look at your answers again—to see if you've changed your mind about any of them.

Assignment

Listed below are short descriptions of situations that *might* be classified as "ethical" dilemmas. For each situation, identify which person or group has the ethical dilemma and state what action you would recommend in their position—and why. Be sure to write down any assumptions you are making. Keep in mind that different people might have a very different reaction to what is a "correct" or "incorrect" answer for most of the situations in this exercise. So, the objective is for you to analyze the situation—and think about what *you* would do.

1. Silvan Rubber Company has for many years made strong rubber tie-down straps. The straps are very useful for securing loads on large commercial trucks and they are sold directly to large trucking companies and through cash-and-carry wholesalers to smaller firms. Last summer, sales of the straps picked up suddenly and Silvan Rubber found from newspaper articles that they were being used by inner-city youths for a game of "bungee jumping" from overpasses and railroad bridges. Concerned about the possibility of being held liable if any accidents occurred, Silvan Rubber sent a memo to all its customers asking them not to sell the straps to youngsters and the president of the company appeared on TV interview shows expressing his disapproval of using the tie-down straps for anything other than securing loads on trucks. The media attention has only heightened the craze and an influential consumer rights group has written to Silvan Rubber to ask them to withdraw the tie-down straps from the market.

Recommendation (and reason):

2. Raphael Abrams is very flattered to be invited for a second round of interviews for a job as assistant marketing manager with A-1 Designers and Builders. As a new graduate, he's eager to get a position with A-1, which has done well developing new designs for houses aimed at the "executive" market. Abrams has some background in the business because he has worked each summer as a junior salesperson for similar housing developments run by his uncle's company. In fact, on several occasions he has been in direct competition with A-1 to sell customers a home. The managers at A-1 know about his family connection and Abrams has told them that he wants to be hired on his own merits. In the last interview of the day, the president of A-1 asks Abrams: "So what do you think are going to be the "hot" trends in high-end homes this coming year?" Abrams thinks that this is a great opportunity to demonstrate his knowledge, but also worries that the whole interview process may be part of an effort to get inside information about his uncle's marketing plans.

    Recommendation (and reason):

3. Two different advertising agencies were doing the advertising planning work for two competing computer manufacturers—Best Digital Computers and New Day Computing. However, the larger of the two advertising agencies, Over-the-Top Advertising, recently bought out the other agency. The acquired agency had been doing the work for New Day Computing. The president of the newly merged agency wrote a letter to the marketing manager at New Day and said "Because there may be the appearance of a conflict of interest in our handling both your account and Best Digital Computers, the most ethical thing for us to do is resign from your account." The marketing manager at New Day immediately telephoned to say: "Ethical? You're going to leave me high and dry looking for a new agency and in the meantime all the people who used to work on my account will be telling Best Digital Computers the details about my marketing plans."

    Recommendation (and reason):

4. Teresa Westbrook has been shopping for a new leather recliner for her family room and is very impressed with the price quoted by Recliner World for a brand-name recliner she has seen advertised in a decorating magazine. Recliner World is able to offer customers deeply discounted prices on brand-name leather furniture because it sells by phone. It has no warehouse or showroom and has eliminated those costs. Instead, telephone orders are passed along to manufacturers who ship furniture directly to consumers by contract truck carriers. Although the price is good, Ms. Westbrook is reluctant to order the recliner because it might not be as comfortable as it looks. To help close the sale, the Recliner World telephone salesman tells Ms. Westbrook the name of a retailer in Westbrook's area that carries the same chair—and suggests "Why don't you go over there and try the recliner and then call me back to order it if it's what you want."

Recommendation (and reason):

5. A company that sells bottled "pure mineral water" has just found that a problem in its filtering process has resulted in trace amounts of chemicals in some of the bottles it has already shipped. The small levels of chemicals involved are not a health hazard, and no law has been violated. Further, it is very unlikely that anyone else would detect the problem. On the other hand, the company has always promoted its product as "pure and of the highest quality." The only way to correct the problem is to recall all of the bottles that are already in retailer and wholesaler inventories—which would be very costly and also generate bad publicity in a very competitive market. What should the company do?

Recommendation (and reason):

6. A manufacturer that sells telecommunications equipment to foreign governments is working on an important sale in a developing nation. The company's local agent middleman in the country has explained that competitor firms from other countries are paying influential local citizens to serve as "consultants." The agent has pointed out that "this is how business is done here—it's who you know that counts. Without consultants, someone else will definitely get the business." The agent has asked for $50,000 to hire consultants. As director of international sales, Rosa Hassan worries that some of the money paid to consultants might be used to bribe the foreign government officials involved in the purchase. On the other hand, she believes that the company will lose out on the sale if it does not have the help of the local consultants who know how decisions will be made—and by whom.

Recommendation (and reason):

7. A large chain of retail stores is considering opening a store in a small city. The chain's low prices will almost certainly drive many of the existing local retailers out of business. They simply can't buy in large enough quantities to be cost competitive. There are equally profitable opportunities for new stores in other, more competitive markets. On the other hand, if the chain does not move into the small city it is likely that sooner or later some other competitor will—and the market is not large enough for two chains.

Recommendation (and reason):

8. Doctors at Parkview Medical Center were awarded a very large contract to conduct research on the weight-loss effects of a diet supplement. Because the doctors are on the staff of the medical school, all the money from the study goes to a special fund to provide scholarships for needy medical students. When the physicians agreed to the contract, they were pretty sure that sooner or later they'd see their results in an advertisement which would begin: "Doctors at a major research hospital proved that significant weight-loss . . ." So, they were especially careful in their research and set up a controlled study in which the researchers did not know which patients were taking the supplement and which weren't. The results were clear-cut and showed that most patients taking the supplement lost more than 10 pounds during the study. In the final report, the researchers noted that almost all of the patients regained their excess weight when they stopped using the supplement. However, advertisements for the supplement do not mention the weight regain.

Recommendation (and reason):

Question for Discussion

Are the ethical challenges faced by a marketing manager any different—in a basic way—than the challenges faced by businesspeople in other types of jobs? Why or why not?

Exercise 1-5

Revenue, cost, and profit relationships

This exercise is based on computer-aided problem number 1--Revenue, Cost, and Profit Relationships. A complete description of the problem appears on page 29 of *Basic Marketing,* 16th edition.

This is a practice problem—to get you started with the PLUS computer program and help you see how spreadsheet analysis will help you with more complicated problems.

Sue Cline is interested in increasing profits from the notebook line. She knows that she can do this by increasing revenue, by decreasing costs—or, more generally, developing a marketing mix that results in a greater difference between revenue and cost.

1.   Write down the selling price, quantity sold, revenue, cost, and profit as they appear in the notebook column of the initial spreadsheet.

        Price: _____   Cost: _____
        Quantity: _____   Profit: _____
        Revenue: _____

2.   Revenue will increase if a higher price can be charged and the quantity sold remains unchanged. Change the price for a notebook to $2.20 and record the resulting profit.

        Profit: _____

3.   Revenue will increase if a larger quantity can be sold at the same price. Change the price on the spreadsheet back to $2.00, and increase the quantity sold to 6,600. Record the resulting profit.
        Profit: _____

4.   Profit will increase if the same revenue can be achieved at lower cost. Change the quantity sold back to 6,000 and decrease the total cost amount to $7,800. Record the resulting profit.

        Profit: _____

5.   Another possible approach for increasing profits would be to lower prices—if it results in a larger quantity sold. Cline thinks that she might sell 6,500 notebooks at a price of $1.85, 7,200 notebooks at $1.70, or 7,500 notebooks at $1.55. If she is right about these price-quantity relationships, what price would you recommend? Why? (For simplicity here, we'll assume that the total cost is $9,000 regardless of the quantity sold).

6. As another alternative, Cline is thinking of improving the product and charging a higher price—about $2.25 a unit. To improve the product, she will need to use a different supplier who uses better materials—and who would charge $12,250 for a minimum order of 7,000 notebooks. Assuming that she could sell all 7,000 notebooks, approximately what price would she have to be able to charge to make at least as much profit as in the best alternative from the question above. (Hint: change the quantity sold and total cost values on the spreadsheet, and then do a What If analysis. In the What If analysis, select the notebook selling price as the variable to vary and vary it between a minimum of $2.18 and a maximum of $2.28. Select revenue and profit as the values to display. Study the results and compare them to your answer to Question 5.)

Approximate price she would have to charge: _____, which would result in a profit of

_____.

7   If Cline decided that customers would only pay $2.15 for the improved notebook, approximately how many would she have to sell to make some profit (that is, profit greater than O) given a total cost of $12,250? (Hint: change the notebook selling price to $2.15 on the spreadsheet, and then do a What If analysis—selecting quantity as the value to vary and revenue and profit as the values to display; or, try different prices on the spreadsheet until you zero in on the correct answer. If the first What If analysis does not provide an answer, continue with the What If analysis using a large or smaller minimum or maximum value until you get closer to the answer.)

Quantity she would have to sell: _____ units.

Chapter 2

Marketing strategy planning

What This Chapter Is About

The nature of the marketing management process is introduced--and the importance of marketing strategy planning is explained. The four Ps--Product, Price, Place, and Promotion--are introduced as the controllable elements which the marketing manager blends into a marketing mix to satisfy a particular target market. It is very important for you to understand the four Ps--because planning the four Ps is the major concern of the rest of the text.

In this chapter you will learn how alert marketers find attractive market opportunities—ones that enable them to get a competitive advantage. The firm must zero in on the strategy that is best for the firm given its objectives and resources—and taking into consideration its strengths and weaknesses and the opportunities and threats that it faces. Four broad types of marketing opportunities that help in identifying new strategies at home and abroad are discussed. Keep in mind that international marketing is now commonplace and necessary.

This chapter introduces a framework for marketing strategy planning. Study it carefully so you can understand how the material in the following chapters will fit together. And start thinking about marketing opportunities—and how to find your own "breakthrough opportunity."

Important Terms

marketing management process, p. 32
strategic (management) planning, p. 33
marketing strategy, p. 33
target market, p. 33
marketing mix, p. 33
target marketing, p. 34
mass marketing, p. 34
channel of distribution, p. 37
personal selling, p. 37
customer service, p. 37
mass selling, p. 38
advertising, p. 38
publicity, p. 38
sales promotion, p. 38

marketing plan, p. 41
implementation, p. 41
operational decisions, p. 41
marketing program, p. 43
customer equity, p. 43
breakthrough opportunities, p. 48
competitive advantage, p. 48
differentiation, p. 50
S.W.O.T. analysis, p. 51
market penetration, p. 52
market development, p. 52
product development, p. 53
diversification, p. 53

True-False Questions

____ 1. The marketing management process consists of (1) planning marketing activities, (2) directing the implementation of the plans, and (3) controlling these plans.

____ 2. Strategic (management) planning is a managerial process of developing and maintaining a match between the resources of the production department and its product opportunities.

____ 3. Marketing strategy planning is the process of deciding how best to sell the products the firm produces.

____ 4. A marketing strategy specifies a target market and a related marketing mix.

____ 5. A target market consists of a group of consumers who are usually quite different.

____ 6. A marketing mix consists of the uncontrollable variables which a company puts together to satisfy a target market.

____ 7. Target marketing aims a marketing mix at some specific target customers.

____ 8. The mass marketing approach is more production-oriented than marketing-oriented.

____ 9. The terms "mass marketing" and "mass marketer" mean the same thing.

____ 10. The problem with target marketing is that it limits the firm to small market segments.

____ 11. The four "Ps" are: Product, Promotion, Price, and Personnel.

____ 12. The customer should not be considered part of a "marketing mix."

____ 13. The Product area is concerned with developing the right physical good, service, or blend of both for the target market.

____ 14. A channel of distribution must include several kinds of intermediaries and collaborators.

____ 15. Customer service is needed when a customer wants the seller to resolve a problem with a purchase.

____ 16. Personal selling and advertising are both forms of sales promotion.

____ 17. Price is the most important of the four Ps.

____ 18. The marketing mix should be set before the best target market is selected.

____ 19. A marketing plan and a marketing strategy mean the same thing.

____ 20. Implementation means putting the marketing plan into operation.

___ 21. Short-run decisions that stay within the overall guidelines set during strategy planning are called implementation decisions.

___ 22. A marketing program may consist of several marketing plans.

___ 23. A marketing program should lower customer equity.

___ 24. An extremely good marketing plan may be carried out badly and still be profitable, while a poor but well-implemented plan can lose money.

___ 25. The watch industry has become much more marketing-oriented.

___ 26. Attractive opportunities are those that the firm has some chance of doing something about given its resources and objectives.

___ 27. "Breakthrough opportunities" are ones that help innovators develop hard-to-copy marketing strategies that will be very profitable for a long time.

___ 28. A firm with a "competitive advantage" has a marketing mix that the target market sees as better than a competitor's mix.

___ 29. It is useful to think of the marketing strategy planning process as a narrowing-down process.

___ 30. Segmentation is the process a manager goes through to decide which subgroups of customers to select.

___ 31. Differentiation means that the firm's marketing mix is similar to its competitors' mixes.

___ 32. There are usually more different strategy possibilities than a firm can pursue.

___ 33. A S.W.O.T. analysis is one way to zero in on a marketing strategy that is well-suited to the firm.

___ 34. Marketing opportunities involving present markets and present products are called "market penetration" opportunities.

___ 35. A "market development" opportunity would involve a firm offering new or improved products to its present markets.

___ 36. Often, attractive opportunities are fairly close to markets the firm already knows.

___ 37. When it comes to choosing among different types of opportunities, most firms tend to be production-oriented and usually think first of diversification.

1. T, p. 32	14. F, p. 37	27. T, p. 48
2. F, p. 33	15. T, p. 37	28. T, p. 48
3. F, p. 33	16. F, p. 37	29. T, p. 49
4. T, p. 33	17. F, p. 38	30. T, p. 50
5. F, p. 33	18. F. p. 39	31. F, p. 50
6. F, p. 33	19. F, p. 41	32. T, p. 51
7. T, p. 34	20. T, p. 41	33. T, p. 51
8. T, p. 34	21. F, p. 41	34. T, p. 52
9. F, p. 34	22. T, p. 42-43	35. F, p. 52
10. F, p. 34	23. F, p. 43	36. T, p. 53
11. F, p. 35	24. T, p. 45	37. F, p. 54
12. T, p. 35	25. T, p. 45-46	
13. T, p. 36	26. T, p. 48	

Multiple-Choice Questions (Circle the correct response)

1.   Which of the following is one of three basic marketing management jobs?
   a.   To direct the implementation of plans
   b.   To control the plans in actual operation
   c.   To plan marketing activities
   d.   All of the above

2.   The marketing management process:
   a.   includes the on-going job of planning marketing activities.
   b.   is mainly concerned with obtaining continuous customer feedback.
   c.   involves finding opportunities and planning marketing strategies, but does not include the management tasks of implementing and control.
   d.   is called "strategic planning."
   e.   Both a and d are true statements.

3.   A marketing strategy consists of two interrelated parts. These are:
   a.   selection of a target market and implementing the plan.
   b.   selection of a target market and development of a marketing mix.
   c.   selection and development of a marketing mix.
   d.   finding attractive opportunities and developing a marketing mix.
   e.   finding attractive opportunities and selecting a target market.

4.   Marketing strategy planners should recognize that:
   a.   target markets should not be large and spread out.
   b.   mass marketing is often very effective and desirable.
   c.   firms like General Electric, Sears, and Procter & Gamble are too large to aim at clearly defined markets.
   d.   target marketing is not limited to small market segments.
   e.   the terms "mass marketing" and "mass marketers" mean essentially the same thing.

5. A marketing mix consists of:
   a. policies, procedures, plans, and personnel.
   b. the customer and the "four Ps."
   c. all variables, controllable and uncontrollable.
   d. product, price, promotion, and place.
   e. none of the above.

6. Which of the following statements about marketing mix variables is *false?*
   a. "Promotion" includes personal selling, mass selling, and sales promotion.
   b. The term "Product" refers to services as well as physical goods.
   c. A channel of distribution does not have to include any middlemen.
   d. Generally speaking, "Price" is more important than "Place."
   e. The needs of a target market virtually determine the nature of an appropriate marketing mix.

7. A "marketing plan":
   a. is just another term for "marketing strategy."
   b. consists of several "marketing programs."
   c. includes the time-related details for carrying out a marketing strategy.
   d. is a strategy without all the operational decisions.
   e. ignores implementation and control details.

8. Which of the following would NOT require an operational decision for a leading hair color manufacturer?
   a. Solicit orders from any new, financially attractive, salons.
   b. Drop colors that are losing appeal.
   c. Create a fresh ad for each Sunday newspaper.
   d. Set a competitive price if a primary competitor offers a special discount.
   e. Promote the fair price and satisfactory quality of the product.

9. A "marketing program":
   a. is another name for a particular marketing mix.
   b. blends several different marketing plans.
   c. consists of a target market and the marketing mix.
   d. is primarily concerned with all of the details of implementing a marketing plan.
   e. must be set before a target market can be selected.

10. Which of the following statements about customer equity is *false*?
    a. Expected losses depend on customer equity.
    b. If the parts of a firm's marketing program work well together, it should increase the firm's customer equity.
    c. Expected profits depend on customer equity.
    d. If a firm has more than one marketing strategy, it will likely decrease the firm's customer equity.
    e. None of the above is false.

11. The watch industry example in the text serves to illustrate that:
   a.   good implementation and control is usually more important than good planning.
   b.   there are a limited number of potential target markets.
   c.   an effective marketing strategy guarantees future success.
   d.   consumers want only high-quality products.
   e.   a successful strategy often involves a marketing mix that is very different from what competitors have offered.

12. The text's discussion of "death-wish marketing" suggests that
   a.   firms that don't spend more on marketing than their competitors are likely to fail.
   b.   managers who seek big breakthroughs, rather than going after easier to achieve marketing opportunities, face big risks and are likely to fail.
   c.   it is fairly common for marketing efforts to turn out poorly, so to avoid that fate and get better than average results, a good manager needs to use a logical process for marketing strategy planning.
   d.   getting good marketing results is really quite easy as long as the marketing manager focuses on the 4Ps.
   e.   all of the above are good answers.

13. A breakthrough opportunity
   a.   is an opportunity that gives a firm some sort of competitive advantage.
   b.   can usually be achieved by copying the "best practices" of other firms that sell similar products.
   c.   is one that helps an innovator develop a hard-to-copy marketing strategy that will be very profitable for a long time.
   d.   is one that requires the firm to "breakthrough" its current resource limitations to obtain a new type of competitive advantage.
   e.   is usually achieved by making better operational decisions.

14. Breakthrough opportunities:
   a.   are so rare that they should be pursued even when they do not match the firm's resources and objectives.
   b.   seldom occur within or close to a firm's present markets.
   c.   are especially important in our increasingly competitive markets.
   d.   are those which a firm's competitors can copy quickly.
   e.   are best achieved by trying to hold onto a firm's current market share.

15. Differentiation means that
   a.   the firm should aim its efforts at a target market that is different from a target market that a competitor would find attractive.
   b.   a firm's marketing mix is distinct from and better than what is available from a competitor.
   c.   a firm uses its resources in a different way than competitors use their resources.
   d.   a firm should screen out opportunities using different criteria than those used by other firms.
   e.   when a firm's marketing strategy is not going well it should change to a different set of operational decisions.

16. A S.W.O.T. analysis includes:
    a. strengths.
    b. weaknesses.
    c. opportunities.
    d. threats.
    e. all of the above.

17. When a firm tries to increase sales by selling its present products in new markets, this is called:
    a. market penetration.
    b. market development.
    c. product development.
    d. diversification.
    e. market integration.

Answers to Multiple-Choice Questions

1. d, p. 32
2. a, p. 32
3. b, p. 33
4. d, p. 34
5. d, p. 35
6. d, p. 38

7. c, p. 41
8. e, p. 41-42
9. b, p. 43
10. d, p. 43
11. e, p. 45-46
12. c, p. 47-48

13. c, p. 48
14. c, p. 48
15. b, p. 50
16. e, p. 51
17. b, p. 52

Exercise 2-1

Mass marketing vs. target marketing

Introduction

A marketing manager's planning job is to find attractive market opportunities and develop effective marketing strategies. A "marketing strategy" consists of two interrelated parts: (1) a *target market--a* fairly homogeneous group of customers to whom a company wishes to appeal, and (2) a *marketing mix*--the controllable variables which the company puts together to satisfy this target group.

Here, it is important to see the difference between *mass marketing* and *target marketing* in planning marketing strategies.

Production-oriented firms typically assume that everyone's needs are the same. They try to build universal appeals into a marketing mix that--it is hoped--will attract "everyone. " This approach we will call "mass marketing." Marketing-oriented firms, on the other hand, recognize that different customers usually have different needs-so they try to satisfy the needs of some particular group of customers--whose needs are fairly similar--rather than trying to appeal to everyone. This "target marketing" approach--a logical application of the marketing concept--simply means that a marketing strategy should aim at *some* target market.

Assignment

This exercise is designed to illustrate the difference between mass marketing and target marketing. Read each of the following cases carefully, and then (1) indicate in the space provided whether each firm is following a mass-marketing or a target-marketing approach and (2) briefly explain your answers.

1. Green Vision Corp. has just introduced a new type of lawn sprinkler called the "Summer Shower Sprinkler" and it is being promoted as the "ultimate lawn sprinkler--more convenient than rain." According to Green Vision's president, the sprinkler is "absolutely guaranteed" not to leak, rust, or break. Moreover, "it has a unique mechanical timer so that it turns itself off automatically after a set period of time. But when it is turned on, the water pressure makes it 'crawl' along the hose so that different areas get watered without having to touch or move the sprinkler." Available in several models ranging in price from $40 to $70, the "Summer Shower Sprinkler" is expected to sell "in the millions." "This product is so superior," say company officials, "that no household in the United States will want to be without one."

    a)   Mass marketing _____   Target marketing _____

    b)   Comments: _____
         _____
         _____
         _____
         _____
         _____

2. Amir Abdelkader recently retired after 20 years of service as a chef for a luxury cruise line. During his career, he worked on ships that took him to almost every part of the world. In the process, he learned to prepare the favorite dishes of many different countries. Amir and his wife--also an outstanding cook--have decided to use their savings to open an "ethnic" restaurant, but with a difference. Each week they will feature the cuisine of a different region. Amir is sure that their restaurant will be an outstanding success. "We want to be a destination restaurant," he says, "a place where adventurous folks want to come for special meals and service to celebrate special occasions. Our prices won't be cheap, but that will help us afford special promotional mailings to the upscale professionals who live within driving distance of the restaurant."

    a)   Mass marketing _____   Target marketing _____

    b)   Comments: _____
         _____
         _____
         _____
         _____

3. Consumers may eventually enjoy "personalized" cable TV channels--with shows that are tailored to each individual viewer's interests in both entertainment and advertising content. By combining detailed survey information about respondents with AM-PM, Inc.'s computerized cable switching system, producers of news, comedy, and other types of shows may be able to combine them into personalized broadcasts. Every show and ad in these personalized broadcasts will appeal to each reader's self-identified interests. Thus, people who drink beer will see shows with beer ads, but non-beer drinkers never will. And antique collectors can look forward to special shows on antiques, while bicycle racers can look forward to documentaries about the sport. But because of equipment limitations, for the next four or five years the "personalized" broadcasts will be limited to markets with no more than 300,000-500,000 potential viewers.

a)   Mass marketing _____   Target marketing _____

b)   Comments: _____

_____

_____

_____

_____

_____

4. Phoenix Information Systems markets personal computers (PCs) in the U.S. and Canada. The company started out selling fast, sophisticated machines to scientists and enthusiasts. Machines were only assembled on order and were distributed through the company's regional branches. But, recently the company decided to take a different approach after the company had two years of losses. The company's founder made the following announcement: "PCs are now a commodity. From now on, Phoenix will buy computers from whoever can make them cheapest—whether they're in Korea, Singapore, or wherever--and distribute them through any retail store that wants to sell them. We already have contracts with department stores like Sears, electronics stores like Best Buy, office supply stores like Staples, and even discount stores like Wal-Mart. We plan to become the country's leading volume supplier."

a)   Mass marketing _____   Target marketing _____

b)   Comments: _____

_____

_____

_____

_____

_____

Question for Discussion

A marketing strategy should aim at some target market. But does "target marketing" guarantee that a firm's marketing strategy will be successful?

Exercise 2-2

Developing a unique marketing mix
for each target market

Introduction

Developing a marketing strategy consists of two *interrelated* tasks: (1) selecting a target market and (2) developing the best marketing mix for that target market.

Marketing-oriented firms recognize that not all potential customers have the same needs. Thus, rather than first developing a marketing mix and *then* looking for a market to sell that mix to, marketing-oriented firms first try to determine what kind of mix each possible target market may require. Then they select a target market based on their ability to offer a good marketing mix at a profit.

Assignment

This exercise assumes that different groups of customers in a general market area may have different needs and therefore may require different marketing mixes. Three possible target markets and alternative marketing mixes are described below for each of four different product types. For each product type, select the marketing mix which would be best for each target market. *(All alternatives must be used, i. e., you cannot use one alternative for two target markets.)* Indicate your selection by writing the letter of the marketing mix in front of the target market you select.

Note: To make it easier for you, each target market consists of only one individual or family, but it should be clear that each individual or family really represents a larger group of potential customers who have similar needs.

I. Product type: Automobile

Possible Target Markets   *Alternative Marketing Mixes*

____ (1) Middle-aged couple with two children   (a) A five-year-old, "for sale by owner"
           who have just purchased a mountain   Honda Civic listed in the classified
           cabin for use as a family "retreat."   ads of a local newspaper.

____ (2) A manager of a real estate firm who   (b) A Lexus sedan with luxury
           uses his company car to show clients   features--on a one-year lease from the
           the community--and convey a   Lexus dealer in a nearby city.
           successful business image.

____ (3) A student who needs a car to   (c) A Jeep Liberty SUV purchased with
           commute to the college campus--and   financing arranged by the salesman at
           to work a paper route.   a local car dealer--and backed with an
                                                             extended service warranty.

II. Product type: Food

Possible Target Markets   *Alternative Marketing Mixes*

____ (1) Airline pilot who has just arrived   (a) A large pepperoni pizza and some
           from an out-of-town flight at 8:30   Mountain Dews delivered to the
           p.m.   house-purchased at "2.00 off the
                                                            regular price" with a coupon from an
                                                            insert in the newspaper.

____ (2) Middle-aged low-income housewife   (b) Nationally advertised brand of frozen
           concerned with feeding her large   "gourmet" dinner on display in the
           family a well-balanced meal, while   frozen-food case of a "7-Eleven"
           operating on a tight budget.   convenience food store.

____ (3) Young mother who has spent the day   (c) "Market basket" of spaghetti sauce,
           at the office and has to rush to get her   pasta, and garlic bread loaf purchased
           children dinner before going to a   at a large supermarket that advertises
           business dinner.   "low everyday prices."

III.   Product type: Computer

Possible Target Markets

_____ (1)   Young working couple who want their child to learn about computers by using educational game programs.

_____ (2)   Sales rep who wants to keep records of his sales calls and prepare short reports for the home office while he travels.

_____ (3)   A local Savings and Loan that has to constantly update deposit and withdrawal information--and prepare a variety of company records and reports.

Alternative Marketing Mixes

(a)   A laptop computer from Dell with pre-loaded software—sold with an "on-site or on-the-road" service agreement.

(b)   Powerful mini-computer leased from a manufacturer--such as Sun Micro-systems--that uses knowledgeable salespeople to help the customer decide on the right equipment.

(c)   Inexpensive e-Machine computer sold by a mass-merchandiser that advertises its discount prices.

IV.   Product type: Clothing for Vacations

Possible Target Markets

_____ (1)   Wealthy couple planning to go on a winter cruise in the Mediterranean.

_____ (2)   Young college student planning to go to Daytona, Florida for Spring Break.

_____ (3)   Middle-income, family planning to go to Disney World for a week with their two young children.

Alternative Marketing Mixes

(a)   Discount clothier that spends most of its advertising budget on radio spots and features "final markdowns" on last season's fashions.

(b)   Mail-order catalog sent to subscribers of "Architectural Digest" which features high-priced "resort wear" in exotic prints.

(c)   Department store with women's, men's and children's clothing departments with moderate prices that advertises through inserts in the local paper.

V.   Product type: Stereo Equipment

Possible Target Markets

____ (1)   Middle-class married couple who are looking for a stereo that will blend in with their living room furniture.

(a)   Popular brand of an AM/FM console stereo with an attractive wood cabinet purchased on credit at a large department store.

____ (2)   Affluent young executive who wants to install a stereo in her penthouse, but doesn't know much about stereo equipment.

(b)   Expensive component stereo system, manufactured by a firm with a reputation for high quality and sold by a dealer who specializes in stereo equipment.

____ (3)   Do-it-yourself enthusiast who wants to add a stereo to the basement recreation room he has just built.

(c)   Build-it-yourself component stereo kit featured in a catalog published by a large mail-order distributor of electronic equipment.

Question for Discussion

Assuming that a firm cannot satisfy all the needs of all potential customers, what factors should a marketing manager consider before selecting a target market?

Exercise 2-3

Analysis of strengths, weaknesses, opportunities and threats for marketing strategy planning

Introduction

From Chapter 2, you know that a marketing strategy requires decisions about the specific customers the firm will target and the marketing mix the firm will develop to appeal to that target market. However, the idea isn't just to come up with some strategy. After all, there are usually hundreds or even thousands of combinations of marketing mix decisions and target markets (that is, different strategies) that a firm might try. So, the challenge is to zero in on the best strategy.

As suggested by Exhibit 2-11 in the text, it is useful to think of the marketing strategy planning process as a narrowing-down process that starts with a broad look at a market—paying special attention to customer needs, the firm's objectives and resources, and competitors. This helps to identify new and unique opportunities that might be overlooked if the focus is narrowed too quickly. Among the alternative opportunities that may be possible within the broad market, a marketing manager should try to identify a marketing strategy that will give the firm a competitive advantage. A competitive advantage means that a firm has a marketing mix that the target market sees as better than a competitor's mix—which increases the firm's chances for profit or survival.

A useful tool for identifying a competitive advantage and for zeroing in on a feasible strategy is S.W.O.T. analysis, which identifies and lists the firm's own strengths as well as weaknesses and threats and opportunities that may arise because of changes in the market environment. As you move along with the marketing course, you will develop a more in-depth understanding of S.W.O.T. analysis and how it can help in identifying a competitive advantage

Assignment

This exercise is designed to start you thinking about S.W.O.T analysis and to give you some initial practice in applying it. Think about each of the situations described in the following questions and then indicate whether you think that it involves a threat or an opportunity (or a strength or weakness) and then give your reasons.

1. The state highway department has authorized funding for a new highway bypass around a fast-growing city. It will take 5 years to complete the planning and construction of the bypass. For each of the following companies, is this change in the market environment likely to represent an opportunity or a threat? Explain your thinking (including any important assumptions you think you need to make about the company).

    a. A local paving contractor

        _____ a threat   _____ an opportunity

        reasons:

        _____

        _____

        _____

        _____

        _____

    b. An established car dealership that is located downtown in the city and has limited space

        _____ a threat   _____ an opportunity

        _____

        _____

        _____

        _____

        _____

        _____

    c. A national fast-food restaurant chain

        _____ a threat   _____ an opportunity

        _____

        _____

        _____

        _____

        _____

        _____

d. A company that publishes maps

_____ a threat   _____ an opportunity

_____
_____
_____
_____
_____

2. A company that has been developing electronic devices for the military is considering the possibility of developing new products and new markets. It wants to pursue opportunities to market security devices to the increasing number of companies in large cities across the U.S. who have become alarmed about issues of homeland security. Consider each of the following factors and indicate whether you think it would be a strength or a weakness for this company if it chose to pursue this market. Explain your reasons (including any important assumptions you think you need to make about the company).

a. The firm's expertise in developing electronic devices

_____ a weakness   _____ a strength

_____
_____
_____
_____
_____
_____

b. The firm's knowledge of how to promote products it develops

_____ a weakness   _____ a strength

_____
_____
_____
_____
_____
_____

c. The firm's ability to reach customers who are located in many different areas

____ a weakness   ____ a strength

_____
_____
_____
_____
_____
_____

d. The firm's knowledge of likely competitors and its ability to anticipate their reactions to its marketing strategy decisions

____ a weakness   ____ a strength

_____
_____
_____
_____
_____

Question for Discussion

Why do marketing managers for a firm need to consider not only their own firm's strengths and weakness but also those of competitors or likely competitors?

Name: _____   Course & Section: _____

Exercise 2-4

Target marketing

This exercise is based on computer-aided problem number 2--Target Marketing. A complete description of the problem appears on page 57 of *Basic Marketing*, 16th edition.

1. Marko's marketing manager is interested in ways to reduce distribution cost--to increase profits. Marko knows that many customers in the target market want products quickly once they decide to buy. And at present no competitor provides really fast delivery. Marko could switch to air transportation--and that would get products delivered faster and increase the percent of purchasers who would buy its product. But better delivery service would also increase distribution cost per unit sold to $2.50. If Marko were to change to the new distribution system, approximately what share of the target market's purchases would it need to get to earn a total profit of $41,800? (Hint: Set the distribution cost per unit to $2.50 on the spreadsheet, and then do a What If analysis--varying the firm's share of purchases and displaying profit.)

    Firm's Percent (share) of target market purchases
    required to earn a profit of $41,800: _____

2. If Marko won this share of the target market's purchases, how many units would it expect to sell? What would its total cost be? What would its total revenue be?

    Quantity Sold (units)   _____

    Total Cost at this quantity $_____

    Total Revenue at this cost $_____

3. If Marko implemented this strategy, but only won a share of the purchases that was 5 percent less than the percent needed to earn $41,800, what would happen to total profit?

    Profit: _____

4. If Marko were to use air transportation with the mass marketing approach and this added $.50 a unit to distribution cost--resulting in a unit distribution cost of $3.00--approximately what share of purchases would Marko have to win to earn a profit of $41,800? (Hint: change the unit distribution cost on the spreadsheet, and then do a What If analysis as described above. If the first What If analysis does not provide an answer to the question, continue with the What If Analysis using a larger or smaller minimum and maximum value for the share value until you get closer to the answer. In other words, use the What If analysis to help "search" for the answer you need.)

    Firm's Percent (share) of target market purchases
    required to earn a profit of $41,800: _____

5. If Marko implemented this approach, but only won a share of purchases that was 5 percent less than the percent needed to earn about $41,800, what profit would be earned?

    Profit: _____

6. Marko is thinking about doing additional marketing research to help "fine tune" the promotion it is thinking about using with its target marketing strategy. The marketing research will add $4,000 to the total promotion cost, but Marko thinks that the more precisely targeted promotion might increase its share of purchases to 55 percent. If Marko's estimates are correct, would it make sense to spend the extra money on marketing research? Briefly explain the reason for your answer. (Note: do your analysis assuming that distribution cost will be $2.00 per unit, and that other values are as originally planned--that is, as they appeared on the original spreadsheet.)

    _____

    _____

7. If the marketing research above cost $10,000 and Marko managers estimated that the improved promotion might increase their share of market to as much as 56 percent of the market, would it make sense to spend the money on the additional marketing research? Why?

    _____

    _____

8. Marko thinks that it would have to charge an even lower price of $13.75 a unit to win a larger share of the "mass market. " If it charged a price $13.75 and its share of purchases in the mass market increased to 25 percent, what profit would be earned?

    Profit: $_____

9. If other competitors reacted to Marko's price cut with price cuts of their own, and Marko's share of purchases in the mass market fell back to 20 percent, what profit would be earned?

    Profit: $_____

10. Briefly discuss the profit implications of firms trying to compete with each other in the mass market by offering lower and lower prices?

    _____

    _____

Chapter 3

Focusing marketing strategy with segmentation and positioning

What This Chapter Is About

Creatively defining a firm's markets (product-markets) can suggest many possibilities-and how to do this should be studied carefully. The focus is on how you can use market segmentation to identify possible target markets. Segmenting markets is vital to marketing strategy planning--but it is often done poorly, in part because it is easy to fall into the trap of defining markets only in terms of product features. The approaches covered in Chapter 3 will help you avoid this pitfall. You will also see how more sophisticated approaches--like clustering, customer relationship management, and positioning--are used to make better market segmentation decisions.

To improve your understanding, try to apply these approaches to a market in which you actually buy something. Then see how the dimensions in *your* own market segment affect the marketing mix that is offered to you. There is a logic to marketing strategy planning--marketing mixes flow directly from the characteristics of target markets. Try to get a feel for this interaction as you learn how to segment markets.

This chapter makes it clear why it is important to understand markets--and customers. In later chapters, you will build on this base--as you learn more about the demographic and behavioral dimensions of the consumer market and the buying behavior of business and organizational customers.

This is a very important--if difficult--chapter, and deserves careful study. It is difficult because it requires *creative* thinking about markets--but this can also be rewarding.

Important Terms

market, p. 61
generic market, p. 62
product-market, p. 62
market segmentation, p. 65
segmenting, p. 66
market segment, p. 66
single target market approach, p. 67
multiple target market approach, p. 67

combined target market approach, p. 68
combiners, p. 68
segmenters, p. 69
qualifying dimensions, p. 72
determining dimensions, p. 72
clustering techniques, p. 80
customer relationship management, p. 80
positioning, p. 82

True-False Questions

___ 1. A market consists of a group of potential customers with similar needs.

___ 2. A generic market is a market with broadly similar needs and sellers offering various and often diverse ways of satisfying those needs.

___ 3. A product-market is a market with very similar needs and sellers offering various close substitute ways of satisfying those needs.

___ 4. A generic market description looks at markets narrowly--and from a producer's viewpoint.

___ 5. A firm's "relevant market for finding opportunities" should be bigger than its present product-market--but not so big that the firm couldn't expand and be an important competitor in this market.

___ 6. Just identifying the geographic boundaries of a firm's present market can suggest new marketing opportunities.

___ 7. A generic market description should include both customer-related and product-related terms.

___ 8. Effective market segmentation requires a two-step process: (1) naming broad product-markets and (2) segmenting these broad product-markets into more homogeneous submarkets--also called product-markets--for the purpose of selecting target markets and developing suitable marketing mixes.

___ 9. The first step in segmenting product-markets is to name the broad product-market area to be segmented.

___ 10. Naming markets is a disaggregating process.

___ 11. Segmenting is an aggregating process.

___ 12. When segmenting markets, "good" market segments are ones that are heterogeneous within, homogeneous between, substantial, and operational.

___ 13. The multiple target market approach combines two or more homogeneous submarkets into one larger target market as a basis for one strategy.

___ 14. A segmenter is usually attempting to satisfy a submarket with its own unique demand curve--and therefore must settle for a smaller sales potential than a combiner.

___ 15. Demographic segmenting dimensions are always more effective than behavioral dimensions (such as needs, benefits sought, and rate of use).

___ 16. Segmenting approaches cannot be used for business markets.

____ 17.   The determining dimensions may help identify the "core features" which will have to be offered to everyone in the broad product-market.

____ 18.   Segmenting international markets is usually easy because so much good data is available.

____ 19.   The first step in segmenting international markets is to segment by country or region.

____ 20.   The first step in the seven-step approach to market segmentation is to select the broad product-market.

____ 21.   The example in the seven-step approach to market segmentation uses retirement centers in the Sun Belt as its broad product-market.

____ 22.   In the seven-step approach to market segmentation, it is best to form homogeneous submarkets before identifying the needs of all potential customers.

____ 23.   In the example in the seven-step approach to market segmentation, the "family vacationers" and the "resort seekers" should be combined because both groups want fun experiences.

____ 24.   Clustering techniques try to find similar patterns within sets of customer-related data.

____ 25.   Customer relationship management (CRM) is a variation of the clustering approach.

____ 26.   "Positioning" refers to a packaged goods manufacturer's efforts to obtain the best possible shelf or display location in retail stores.

____ 27.   The only way to "reposition" a product is to make some physical change to it.

____ 28.   Positioning analysis is useful for combining but not for segmenting.

____ 29.   Both a firm's manager and its customers are likely to view its marketing mix alike.

Answers to True-False Questions

1. F, p. 61	11. T, p. 66	21. F, p. 75
2. T, p. 62	12. F, p. 67	22. F, p. 75-76
3. T, p. 62	13. F, p. 67	23. F, p. 77-78
4. F, p. 62	14. F, p. 69	24. T, p. 80
5. T, p. 63	15. F, p. 71	25. T, p. 80
6. T, p. 64	16. F, p. 71-72	26. F, p. 82
7. F, p. 64	17. F, p. 73	27. F, p. 82
8. T, p. 65	18. F, p. 74	28. F, p. 84
9. T, p. 65	19. T, p. 74	29. F, p. 84
10. T, p. 65	20. T, p. 75	

Multiple-Choice Questions (Circle the correct response)

1. A market consists of:
    a. a group of potential customers with similar needs who are willing to exchange something of value.
    b. various kinds of products with similar characteristics.
    c. sellers offering substitute ways of satisfying needs.
    d. all the firms within a particular industry.
    e. both a and c.

2. A market in which sellers offer various close substitute ways of satisfying the market's needs is called a:
    a. generic market.
    b. relevant market.
    c   product-market.
    d. central market.
    e. homogeneous market.

3. Which of the following is the best example of a "generic market"?
    a. The expensive ten-speed bicycle market
    b. The U.S. college student creative expression market
    c. The photographic market
    d. The pet food market
    e. The teenage market

4. A generic market
    a. competitor might have only a tiny market share in the generic market but a large share in its product-market.
    b. often includes consumers who will satisfy the same need in quite different ways.
    c. often involves sellers who compete in different product-markets.
    d. All of the above are true.
    e. None of the above are true.

5. A firm's "relevant market for finding opportunities":
    a. should be as large as possible.
    b. should have no geographic limits.
    c. should be no larger than its present product-market.
    d. should always be named in product-related terms.
    e. None of the above is a true statement.

6. Market segmentation:
    a. tries to find heterogeneous submarkets within a market.
    b. means the same thing as marketing strategy planning.
    c. assumes that most submarkets can be satisfied by the same marketing mix.
    d. assumes that any market is likely to consist of submarkets.
    e. All of the above are true statements.

7.   Naming broad product-markets is:
     a.   an assorting process
     b.   a disaggregating process
     c.   a segmenting process
     d.   an accumulating process
     e.   an aggregating process

8.   Segmenting:
     a.   is essentially a disaggregating or "break it down" process.
     b.   assumes that all customers can be grouped into homogeneous and profitable market segments.
     c.   tries to aggregate together individuals who have similar needs and characteristics.
     d.   usually results in firms aiming at smaller and less profitable markets.
     e.   assumes that each individual should be treated as a separate target market.

9.   "Good" market segments are those which are:
     a.   heterogeneous within.
     b.   operational.
     c.   homogeneous between.
     d.   substantial--meaning large enough to minimize operating costs.
     e.   all of the above.

10. Having segmented its market, the Martinez Corp. has decided to treat each of two submarkets as a separate target market requiring a different marketing mix. Apparently, Martinez is following the _____ target market approach.
     a.   single
     b.   combined
     c.   multiple
     d.   separate
     e.   general

11. Segmenting and combining are two alternate approaches to developing market-oriented strategies. Which of the following statements concerning these approaches is *true*?
     a.   Combiners treat each submarket as a separate target market.
     b.   Segmenters try to develop a marketing mix that will have general appeal to several market segments.
     c.   A combiner looks at various submarkets for similarities rather than differences.
     d.   A segmenter assumes that the whole market consists of a fairly homogeneous group of customers.
     e.   Both segmenters and combiners try to satisfy some people very well rather than a lot of people fairly well.

12. Behavioral segmenting dimensions do not include:
     a.   benefits offered.
     b.   kind of shopping involved.
     c.   brand familiarity.
     d.   family life cycle.
     e.   type of problem-solving.

13. When segmenting a product-market, a marketing manager should keep in mind that:
   a. demographic dimensions are usually the best place to start.
   b. qualifying dimensions help identify which customers are in the product-market.
   c. determining dimensions are relevant in business markets, but not consumer markets.
   d. most markets should initially be defined based on features of alternative products available to customers.
   e. its usually best to focus on a single segmenting dimension rather than trying to consider several all at once.

14. Which of the following types of dimensions would be the most important if one were particularly interested in why some target market was likely to buy a particular brand within a product-market?
   a. Primary dimensions
   b. Secondary dimensions
   c. Qualifying dimensions
   d. Determining dimensions
   e. Both a and c above.

15. International marketing:
   a. requires more segmenting dimensions than domestic marketing.
   b. adds just one step to other segmenting approaches.
   c. requires segmenting by country or region first.
   d. usually involves working with data that is less available and less dependable.
   e. All of the above are true statements.

16. In the seven-step approach to market segmentation,
   a. the first step is to select the broad product-market.
   b. determining needs are identified before qualifying needs.
   c. the example is about apartment buildings in cities with large student populations.
   d. submarkets are quickly identified without considering all potential customers' needs.
   e. none of the above.

17. Which of the following statements about clustering techniques is *true?*
   a. Clustering techniques try to find dissimilar patterns within sets of customer-related data.
   b. Computers are usually needed to search among all of the data for homogeneous groups of people.
   c. Computers identify the relevant dimensions and do the analysis.
   d. A cluster analysis of the toothpaste market indicated that most consumers seek the same benefits.
   e. All of the above are true.

18. Which of the following statements about customer relationship marketing (CRM) is *true?*
   a. Instead of segmenting information, CRM uses information on a customer's past purchases.
   b. Amazon.com is a good example of a firm that uses CRM.
   c. Firms that operate on the Internet may be able to communicate with their customers faster than other firms, but the costs of doing so are higher.
   d. CRM is a variation of the positioning approach.
   e. All of the above are true.

19. "Positioning":
   a. involves a packaged-goods manufacturer's attempt to obtain the best possible shelf space for its products in retail outlets.
   b. is useful for segmenting but not combining.
   c. helps strategy planners understand how customers think about various brands or products in relation to each other.
   d. applies only to existing products, not new products.
   e. eliminates the need for subjective decision making in product planning.

20. "Positioning" is concerned with
   a. how current target customers think about the products available from one company.
   b. how customers think about the competing brands in a market.
   c. an analysis of the design strengths and weaknesses of products in a market
   d. the economic factors that affect consumer choices among alternative brands.
   e. None of the above is true.

Answers to Multiple-Choice Questions

1. e, p. 61
2. c, p. 62
3. b, p. 62
4. d, p. 62
5. e, p. 63
6. d, p. 65
7. b, p. 65

8. c, p. 66
9. b, p. 67
10. c, p. 67-68
11. c, p. 68
12. d, p. 71
13. b, p. 72
14. d, p. 72

15. e, p. 74
16. a, p. 75
17. b, p. 80
18. b, p. 81
19. c, p. 82
20. b, p. 82

Exercise 3-1

Product-markets vs. generic markets

Introduction

A practical first step in searching for breakthrough opportunities is to define the firm's present (or potential) markets. Markets consist of potential customers with similar needs and sellers offering various ways of satisfying those needs.

Markets can be defined very broadly or very narrowly--with either extreme being a potential threat to effective strategy planning. For example, defining its market too broadly as "transportation" could result in Toyota seeing itself in direct competition with manufacturers of airplanes, ships, elevators, bicycles, little red wagons, and perhaps even spaceships! On the other hand, a definition such as "the market for six-passenger motor vehicles with gasoline-powered internal-combustion engines" would be too narrow--and doesn't even identify "potential customers."

While there is no simple and automatic way to define a firm's *relevant* market, marketers should start by defining the relevant generic market and product-market using the 3 and 4 part definitions discussed on pages 63-64 of the text and shown below:

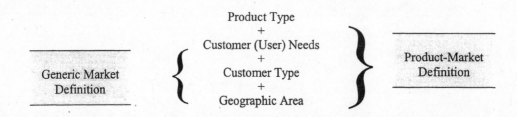

It often requires a lot of creativity to think in terms of generic markets and product-markets--but failure to do so can cause strategy planners to overlook breakthrough opportunities--and leave themselves exposed to new forms of competition. Just ask the manufacturers of kerosene lamps, buggy whips, and mathematical slide rules!

Assignment

This exercise will give you some practice in naming product-markets and generic markets. It will also require you to be creative and apply your marketing intuition.

Listed below are several generic markets and brand-name products. Using the 3 and 4 part definitions of generic markets and product-markets, suggest possible market names in the blanks. Note: There are no "right answers," but they should be logical and consistent. Generic markets should *not* include any product-related terms. A generic market can have several related product-markets. And a product is offered to a product-market that is a part of a larger generic market. Question 1 is answered to help you get started.

1. Generic market: Security for families in the world
   a) Product-market: *Homeowner's insurance for financial security for home-owning families in the United States.*
   b) Product-market: *Guards for physical security for wealthy families in the world*
   c) Product-market: *Smoke alarms for mental security for families in the developed countries.*

2. Generic market: Summer educational (learning) opportunities for preteen kids in large cities like Chicago

   a)   Product-market: _____

   b)   Product-market: _____

   c)   Product-market: _____

3. Generic market: Information exchange by business firms in Europe, North America, and Asia

   a)   Product-market: _____

   b)   Product-market: _____

   c)   Product-market: _____

4. Generic market: Family entertainment for middle and upper income people in the United States

   a)   Product-market: _____

   b)   Product-market: _____

   c)   Product-market: _____

5. Product: The David Letterman TV show

   a)   Product-market: _____

   b)   Generic market: _____

6. Product: Ben and Jerry's Chocolate Fudge Brownie Low-Fat Frozen Yogurt

   a)   Product-market: _____

   b)   Generic market: _____

7. Product: Sony Handycam digital video camera-recorder

   a) Product-market: _____

   b) Generic market: _____

Question for Discussion

How can a firm decide *which* and *how many* markets to enter?

Exercise 3-2

Applying marketing segmentation concepts

Introduction

The development of successful marketing strategies depends to a large extent on the planner's ability to segment markets. Unfortunately, this is not a simple process. Segmenting usually requires considerable management judgment and skill. Those marketers who have the necessary judgment and skill will have a real advantage over their competitors in finding profitable opportunities.

Segmenting is basically a process of gathering individuals into homogeneous market segments on the basis of similar customer needs and characteristics. Although segmenting is often helped by the use of marketing research and computer techniques, such techniques are not always necessary--or economically practical. Further, even if formal research is to be conducted, it may be necessary for a manager to first sharpen the problem-solving focus by developing some preliminary ideas about what market segments might be of particular interest.

Although market segmentation is critically important, too many managers don't really know how to get started-because they have not practiced applying the concepts discussed in Chapter 3. Yet, by using these concepts as part of an organized, integrative approach, the strategy planner can often identify useful segments. This exercise takes you step-by-step through such an approach. It is workable and has been used in the development of successful marketing strategies. *It is especially useful when looking for new market opportunities.*

Thus, in this exercise you will be asked to segment a market and then to think of what products (and whole marketing mixes) might be most appropriate for each segment. Practice this approach by applying the same ideas to other product-markets.

Assignment

Assume you have been asked to segment the following broad product-market: automotive vehicles for transporting families or small groups in the world. Think about the many product offerings in this market and the people who buy them. Then, answer the following questions.

1. *List potential customers needs.* In the space below, list all the needs you can think of that potential customers may have in this product-market area. Be sure to focus on needs rather than product features. (Note: don't limit the list just to needs that might apply to most people-also include needs that may only apply to certain types of people. For example, some people may want a "prestige" image, and for others that may be totally irrelevant-or even a big negative.)

2. *Form "homogeneous submarkets"-i.e., "narrow" product-markets.* Recognizing that some people have different needs than others, on a piece of scratch paper "rough out" at least four different submarkets based on needs. Start by forming one submarket around some typical type of customer-perhaps even yourself. (You want to be able to aggregate similar people into this segment as long as they can be satisfied by the same marketing mix.) For this submarket, write down the most important need dimensions and customer-related characteristics (including demographic dimensions). Continue this process by identifying another "distinct" submarket (that is, one that would be composed of people who are not similar to the first submarket in terms of needs, characteristics, and the type of marketing mix they would want). Continue this process until you have identified the needs and characteristics of at least four submarkets.

Still working on your scratch paper, review the list of need dimensions for each possible submarket and identify the determining dimensions by putting an asterisk beside them. Although the qualifying dimensions are important-perhaps reflecting "core needs" that must be satisfied well-they are not the determining dimensions we are seeking now. To help identify the determining dimensions, think carefully about the needs and attitudes of the people in each possible submarket. At first, those dimensions may not seem very important from market to market, but if they are determining to those people then they *are* determining!

Once you are satisfied that you have identified at least four distinct submarkets, name ("nickname") the product-markets involved. You will probably want to select names by thinking about which of the determining dimensions you have identified as most important for each submarket-perhaps aided by your descriptions of customer characteristics.

Now, review the notes on your scratch paper and make any refinements that help to clarify the ways in which the different submarkets might be dissimilar (and how they might be similar).

3. Summarize the work you did in Question 2 by using the diagram below to draw a picture of the product-market and the subproduct-markets you identified. Vary the size of the submarkets to show what you think might be their estimated market potential. Give each submarket a name.

A diagram of the broad product-market
for automotive vehicles for transporting
families or small groups in the world

4. Now, for the product-markets that you identified in Question 2, show:

a) the name of each submarket.
b) each submarket's important needs.
c) other customer characteristics for each submarket--especially demographic or lifestyle dimensions.
d) the type of products that would appeal to each submarket.

Product-Market 1

a) Name: _____

b) Needs: _____

_____

c) Characteristics: _____

_____

_____

d) Products: _____

_____

_____

_____

Product-Market 2

a)   Name: _____

b)   Needs: _____

_____

c)   Characteristics: _____

_____

_____

d)   Products: _____

_____

_____

_____

_____

Product-Market 3

a)   Name: _____

b)   Needs: _____

_____

c)   Characteristics: _____

_____

_____

d)   Products: _____

_____

_____

_____

_____

Product-Market 4

a)   Name: _____

b)   Needs: _____

        _____

c)   Characteristics: _____

        _____

        _____

d)   Products: _____

        _____

        _____

        _____

        _____

Question for Discussion

If you were a marketing manager, what else would you like to know about possible product-markets before selecting a target market?

Exercise 3-3

Using positioning to evaluate marketing opportunities

Introduction

Finding target market opportunities is a continuing challenge for all marketers. Understanding how customers view current or proposed market offerings is often a crucial part of this challenge. And understanding customer perceptions is more difficult when different segments of the market have different needs and different views of how well current or proposed products meet those needs. Developing insights requires that you try to answer questions such as: Are there customer segments with needs which no existing products are satisfying very well? Could our existing product be modified to do a better job of satisfying the needs of some segment? Could promotion be used to communicate to consumers about aspects of the product--so that target customers would "see" it in a different way?

There are no easy answers to such questions, but *positioning* approaches can help. As explained in the text (pages 82-84), positioning uses marketing research techniques which measure customer views of products or brands according to several product features (e.g., do consumers think of a brand of detergent as "gentle" or "strong" relative to other brands?). Usually, customers are also asked to decide the amount of each feature than would be "ideal" (e.g., how strong a detergent do you want?)

The results are plotted on a two- or three-dimensional diagram--called a "product space. " Each dimension represents a product feature that the customers feel is important. The diagram shows how each product or brand was rated on each of the dimensions. In other words, it shows how the various products or brands are "positioned" relative to each other--and relative to the "ideal" products or brands of different segments of customers. Usually, circles are used to show segments of customers with similar "ideal points" along the dimensions.

The mechanics of how all this is done are beyond the scope of this course. But you should know that positioning research techniques produce a very useful graphic aid to help marketing managers do their job better. Looking at a product space for a market, a marketing planner may see opportunities to "reposition" existing products or brands through product and/or promotion changes. Or he may spot an empty space which calls for the introduction of a new product. Often, he may be quite surprised to see that customer views of market offerings differ a great deal from his own ideas.

Assignment

Figure 3-3 is a fictional "product space" diagram for ready-to-eat breakfast cereal. The diagram shows how target customers rated several brands of cereal along two product dimensions which have been identified only as Dimension A and Dimension B. respectively. The diagram also shows 8 segments of customers grouped together on the basis of similar "ideal points. " For example, customers in segment #8 desire a lot of both attribute A and B.

Study Figure 3-3 carefully and then answer the following questions.

FIGURE 3-3
Product Space for Ready-to-Eat Breakfast Cereal

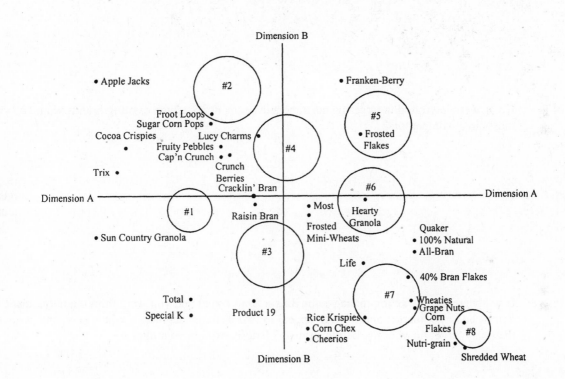

1. a)   Based on your interpretation of Figure 3-3, what product feature does Dimension A appear to represent?

    b)   Based on your interpretation of Figure 3-3, what product feature does Dimension B appear to represent?

2. What opportunities for "repositioning" *existing* products do you see in Figure 3-3? Be specific, and indicate the segment(s) to which you want to target your appeal(s).

3.   What opportunities for introducing *new* products do you see in Figure 3-3? Be specific, and indicate the segment(s) whose needs you would want to satisfy.

4.   If you were interested in targeting customers in segment #6, which existing brands would be your most direct competitors?

5.   If you were the marketing manager for Raisin Bran cereal and you were thinking about using the combined target market approach to appeal to two different segments, which segments would be the likely target for your marketing strategy? Briefly explain your choice.

6.   In Figure 3-3 there are already many competing product offerings in the upper left and lower right quadrants. Why doesn't an innovative producer offer a new product to the far left and bottom of the space--where there is currently no product?

7.   Are the two product dimensions shown in Figure 3-3 the two most important dimensions in choosing a brand of breakfast cereal? If not, what dimensions are most important?

8.   Do all potential customers agree as to which two dimensions are the most important dimensions in choosing a brand of breakfast cereal? If not, what are the implications for using "positioning" as an aid in evaluating market opportunities?

Question for Discussion

Is positioning an art or a science? Why?

Exercise 3-4

Segmenting customers

This exercise is based on computer-aided problem number 3--Segmenting Customers. A complete description of the problem appears on pages 86-87 of *Basic Marketing,* 16th edition.

1.   Audiotronics Software's marketing manager is thinking about the possibility of combining two of the segments into a single target market. He is not certain which segments to combine. But he thinks he will be more successful if the two segments are as similar as possible.

   It occurred to him that the same spreadsheet he used to cluster customers could be used to compute a score showing how similar the segments are to each other. All that would be needed would be to enter the "summary" importance ratings for a segment in the spreadsheet, and then record how similar that segment is to each of the other segments. Complete this analysis for each of the segments and fill in the table below. (Remember that the spreadsheet computes "how far" customers are from the typical segment member, so a *lower* score is more *similar.)*

Summary Importance Rating			Segment	Overall Similarity		
No. of features	*Easy to Use*	*Easy to Learn*		Fearful Typists	Power Users	Prof. Specialists
3	8	9	Fearful			
9	2	2	Power			
7	5	6	Specialist			

2.   Based on this analysis, which pair of segments seem to be most similar (homogeneous) with respect to the importance of different software features?

   _____

   _____

3.   Based on this analysis, which pair of segments seem to be least similar (homogeneous) with respect to the importance of different software features?

   _____

   _____

4. The marketing manager is thinking about developing a product that could be "positioned" to satisfy each of the two most similar segments "pretty well." He thinks that the summary importance ratings for each segment are a good indicator of what each segment's "ideal" product would be like. So, he decided to average the importance ratings for the *two most similar* segments and develop a product that matched that "average need." But, he wants to see how well such a product would meet the needs of the individual segments. To further evaluate this idea, complete the table below.

Importance Factor	Importance First Segment	Importance Second Segment	Sum of Ratings	Average Rating
Features				
Easy to Use				
Easy to Learn				

5. If a product could be developed to match the average ratings above, how well do you think it would satisfy each of the segments? Briefly explain your answer. (Hint: enter the "average" ratings in the spreadsheet, and see how similar the needs met by this "average" product are with the needs of each of the different segments.)

Similarity Score for the "average product"	Fearful Typists	Power Users	Prof. Specialists

Explanation: _____

_____

_____

6. A computer programmer at the company has suggested that they just try to produce a product based on the average needs of all three segments. Use the same approach you used above to evaluate how similar a product based on the average of all three segments would be to the needs of each of the individual segments.

Factor	Fearful	Power	Specialist	Sum	Average
Features					
Easy to Use					
Easy to Learn					
Similarity Score for the "average product"	Fearful Typists		Power Users		Prof. Specialists

7. Based on the "average product similarity scores" you computed in Question 6 above, does it appear that the programmer's idea would provide a good basis for developing a product that would appeal to "the whole market" (i.e., all three segments)? Briefly explain your answer.

_____

_____

_____

Chapter 4

Evaluating opportunities in the changing marketing environment

What This Chapter Is About

In the last chapter, you learned that finding opportunities takes a real understanding of customers. But marketing managers cannot select target markets or plan strategies in a vacuum. The marketing environment affects the attractiveness of possible opportunities. And opportunities need to be carefully evaluated and screened--to identify the really attractive ones.

A company's objectives can guide this process--and its resources may limit the search for opportunities, or alternatively give the firm a competitive advantage.

This chapter treats the competitive environment in some depth (building on the economic concepts reviewed in Appendix A, which follows Chapter 22). The marketing manager can't control competitors--but he can try to avoid head-on competition--or plan for it when it is inevitable.

The economic and technological environment can change rapidly. These shifts may require changes in marketing strategies.

The political and legal environment is given special attention because of its possible impact on the marketing manager in both domestic and international markets. Further, the evolution of legislative thinking is outlined as a foundation for discussion in later chapters.

The cultural and social environment concerns the number of people and how they live and behave. A marketing manager must understand his markets--and cultural and social environments affect the way people buy.

Finding *attractive* opportunities requires screening and evaluation--and various approaches are presented towards the end of the chapter, including a discussion of evaluating opportunities in international markets.

Important Terms

mission statement, p. 92
competitive environment, p. 95
competitor analysis, p. 97
competitive rivals, p. 97
competitive barriers, p. 98
economic and technological
      environment, p. 100
technology, p. 101

Internet, p. 101
nationalism, p. 103
North American Free Trade Agreement
      (NAFTA), p. 104
consumerism, p. 105
cultural and social environment, p. 108
strategic business unit (SBU), p. 114
portfolio management, p. 114

True-False Questions

_____ 1. A business firm's only objective should be to earn enough profit to survive.

_____ 2. Trying to maximize short-run return on investment may not be good in the long run.

_____ 3. A mission statement should focus on just the key goals for the organization.

_____ 4. Winning a larger market share necessarily leads to greater profitability.

_____ 5. Company objectives should lead to a hierarchy of marketing objectives.

_____ 6. Attractive opportunities should make use of a firm's resources and its unique strengths.

_____ 7. A large producer with economies of scale always has a competitive advantage over smaller firms.

_____ 8. A patent owner has a 20-year monopoly to develop and use its new product, process, or material.

_____ 9. Although the marketing manager cannot control the competitive environment, he can choose strategies that will avoid head-on situations.

_____ 10. In a competitor analysis, a current (or planned) target market and marketing mix is compared with what competitors are currently doing (or are likely to do).

_____ 11. Competitive rivals are always easy to identify.

_____ 12. Competitive barriers are the conditions that make it possible for a firm to compete in a market.

_____ 13. The inflation rate experienced by the United States in recent years was just about the highest in the world.

_____ 14. When the dollar is strong in international exchange, it is easier to sell U.S. products in overseas markets.

_____ 15. Technology is the application of voodoo to convert an economy's resources to output.

_____ 16. The Internet is a system for linking computers around the world.

_____ 17. Changes in the technological environment could be rejected by the cultural and social environment--through the political and legal environment--even though such changes might help the economic environment.

_____ 18. Nationalism may affect marketing strategy planning by determining to whom and how much a firm may sell.

_____ 19. Key countries in Europe have moved to the euro, a new unified money system for the European Union.

_____ 20. Because NAFTA is a short-term proposition, its economic impact has already been significant.

_____ 21. The political environment may either block or promote new marketing opportunities.

_____ 22. Consumerism is a social movement seeking to give sellers as much power and legal rights as buyers and consumers.

_____ 23. Businesses and individual managers are subject to both criminal and civil laws.

_____ 24. The Clayton Act deals with tying contracts, exclusive dealing contracts, and price-fixing conspiracies.

_____ 25. Product warranties are regulated by the Magnuson-Moss Act.

_____ 26. Laws such as the Pure Food and Drug Act were passed because pro-competition legislation did not protect consumers very well in some areas.

_____ 27. The Consumer Product Safety Commission tries to encourage safe product design, but the commission has almost no power to deal with unsafe products.

_____ 28. Recent trends indicate a major shift in traditional thinking about buyer-seller relations from "let the seller beware" to "let the buyer beware."

_____ 29. Because the cultural and social environment tends to change slowly, firms should try to identify and work with cultural attitudes rather than trying to encourage big changes in the short run.

_____ 30. Product-market screening criteria should be mainly quantitative in nature, because qualitative criteria are too subjective.

_____ 31. Forecasts of the probable results of implementing whole strategic plans are needed to apply quantitative screening criteria.

_____ 32. The profit potentials of alternative strategic plans can be evaluated at the same time only if the plans are very similar.

33. The General Electric "strategic planning grid" forces company managers to make three-part judgments (high, medium, and low) about the business strengths and industry attractiveness of all proposed or existing product-market plans.

34. The G.E. "stop-light" evaluation method is a very objective approach because G.E. feels there are too many possible errors if it tries to use subjective criteria for judging "attractiveness" or "strength."

35. SBUs are small businesses that try to compete with major divisions of larger multiproduct companies.

36. Portfolio management tends to emphasize current profitability and return on investment, often neglecting the long run.

37. Most industrial products tend to be near the "insensitive" end of the continuum of environmental sensitivity.

38. If the risks of getting into international marketing are difficult to evaluate, it usually is best to start with a joint venture.

Answers to True-False Questions

1. F, p. 91	14. F, p. 100-101	27. F, p. 107
2. T, p. 92	15. F, p. 101	28. F, p. 108
3. T, p. 92	16. T, p. 101	29. T, p. 110
4. F, p. 92-93	17. T, p. 103	30. F, p. 110
5. T, p. 93	18. T, p. 103	31. T, p. 110
6. T, p. 93	19. T, p. 104	32. F, p. 112
7. F. p. 94	20. F, p. 104	33. T, p. 112
8. T, p. 94	21. T, p. 105	34. F, p. 113
9. T, p. 95	22. F, p. 105	35. F, p. 114
10. T, p. 97	23. T, p. 105	36. T, p. 114
11. F, p. 97	24. F, p. 106	37. T, p. 115
12. F, p. 98	25. T, p. 106	38. F, p. 116
13. F, p. 100	26. T, p. 106	

Multiple-Choice Questions (Circle the correct response)

1. Which of the following objectives of a business is the *most* important?
   a. To engage in some specific business activity which will perform a socially and economically useful function.
   b. To develop an organization to carry on the business and implement its strategies.
   c. To earn enough profit to survive.
   d. All three of the above are equally important, because a failure in any one could lead to a total failure of the business.
   e. Both b and c are more important than a.

2.   Of the following, the *last* objectives that a firm should specify are its:
     a.   company objectives.
     b.   marketing objectives.
     c.   promotion objectives.
     d.   advertising objectives.
     e.   price objectives.

3.   A first step in evaluating marketing opportunities is to:
     a.   decide which markets the firm wishes to enter.
     b.   consider the objectives and resources of the firm.
     c.   hire a "futurist" as a marketing consultant.
     d.   estimate market and sales potentials.
     e.   find out if potential competitors are larger.

4.   Which of the following statements about the competitive environment is *false?*
     a.   Competition-free environments are rare.
     b.   Marketing managers should choose strategies that avoid head-on competition.
     c.   A firm that has a marketing mix that its target market sees as better than its competitors' has a competitive advantage.
     d.   Over the long run, most product-markets tend toward monopolistic competition.
     e.   In a competitor analysis, the firm's first step should be to identify all potential competitors.

5.   Which of the following is *not* an example of how the economic and technological environment may affect marketing strategy planning?
     a.   The price of bicycles is rising because of inflation.
     b.   Bicycle manufacturers are finding it difficult to sell from websites because shipping an individual bike is very expensive.
     c.   Because of exchange rates, imported bikes are cheaper than those made in the United States.
     d.   Computer-controlled assembly lines can turn out a new bike every three and one-half seconds.
     e.   The demand for bikes is increasing because consumers are becoming more health conscious.

6.   With the "unification of Europe":
     a.   many of the taxes and rules that have limited trade among member countries of the European Union were eliminated.
     b.   the need to adjust strategies to reach submarkets of European consumers disappeared.
     c.   firms operating in Europe have harder access to large markets.
     d.   consumer prices rose.
     e.   All of the above are true statements.

7.   NAFTA is:
     a.   a free-trade pact between the U.S., Canada, and Mexico.
     b.   a short-term proposition.
     c.   trying to eliminate most trade barriers with Mexico in the next five years.
     d.   all of the above.
     e.   none of the above.

8. President Kennedy's "Consumer Bill of Rights" did *not* include the right to:
   a. a clean and safe environment.
   b. safety.
   c. be informed.
   d. choose.
   e. be heard.

9. The Sherman Act is primarily designed to:
   a. prevent monopolies or conspiracies in restraint of trade.
   b. stop the flow of foreign products into the United States.
   c. prevent unfair or deceptive acts or practices in commerce.
   d. reduce price discrimination by manufacturers.
   e. eliminate deceptive selling practices.

10. The Federal Trade Commission Act of 1914 is primarily concerned with:
    a. deceptive warranties.
    b. price-fixing agreements.
    c. conspiracies in restraint of trade.
    d. mergers which might substantially lessen competition.
    e. unfair methods of competition.

11. The Clayton Act is *not* concerned with:
    a. product warranties.
    b. price discrimination by manufacturers.
    c. exclusive dealing contracts.
    d. tying contracts.
    e. encouraging competition.

12. A firm that discriminates in price on goods of "like grade and quality" may be in violation of the
    _____ Act.
    a. Sherman
    b. Robinson-Patman
    c. Wheeler-Lea
    d. Magnuson-Moss
    e. Antimerger

13. The Consumer Product Safety Commission is responsible for:
    a. developing and enforcing safety standards for bicycles.
    b. developing and enforcing environmental protection standards.
    c. preventing the distribution and sale of adulterated or misbranded foods, drugs, and cosmetics.
    d. All of the above.
    e. None of the above.

14. The Consumer Product Safety Commission
    a. does not have any power--it can only advise the FTC.
    b. protects small business from large business, rather than protecting consumers.
    c. was created by the Pure Food and Drug Act.
    d. has no effect on marketing strategy planning until a product is on the market and proved to be dangerous by a government agency.
    e. has broad power to set safety standards and penalties for violation of these standards.

15. The recent interest in physical fitness has forced producers of food, clothing, and other products to reconsider their marketing strategies. Which of the following does this trend illustrate?
    a. economic and technological environment.
    b. cultural and social environment.
    c. existing business situation.
    d. political and legal environment.
    e. resources and objectives of the firm.

16. In the short run at least, which of the following is usually *beyond* the control of the marketing manager?
    a. political and legal environment.
    b. economic and technological environment.
    c. cultural and social environment.
    d. competitive environment.
    e. All of the above.

17. Product-market screening criteria should be:
    a. quantitative.
    b. qualitative.
    c. realistic and achievable.
    d. all of the above.
    e. all of the above *except* b.

18. Which of the following is a quantitative screening criteria?
    a. increase sales by $100,000.
    b. earn 25 percent return on investment.
    c. cover all start-up costs in the first year.
    d. all of the above are quantitative criteria.
    e. all of the above are qualitative criteria.

19. General Electric's "strategic planning grid":
    a. substitutes precise quantitative estimates for management judgment and intuition.
    b. places too much emphasis on industry attractiveness, almost ignoring the firm's own business strengths.
    c. emphasizes market share and market growth rate.
    d. is oversimplified in that it assumes all opportunities must be either "good" or "bad."
    e. None of the above is a true statement.

20. GE's Planning Grid approach to evaluating proposed and existing plans and businesses:
    a. considers how profitable opportunities are likely to be.
    b. reflects the corporation's objectives.
    c. helps managers see why some ideas are supported and others are not
    d. can use quantitative data but it is basically a qualitative approach.
    e. All of the above are true.

21. Organizational units within a larger company which focus their efforts on selected product-markets and are treated as separate profit centers are called:
   a.   portfolios.
   b.   strategic business units.
   c.   BTUs.
   d.   functional departments.
   e.   basing points.

22. According to the "continuum of environmental sensitivity":
   a.   industrial products usually need to be adapted to foreign markets more than consumer products.
   b.   faddy or high-style consumer products are easily adaptable to foreign markets and thus involve very little risk in international marketing.
   c.   it is extremely risky to market basic commodities in international markets.
   d.   some products are more adaptable to foreign markets than others--and thus may be less risky.
   e.   All of the above are true statements.

Answers to Multiple-Choice Questions

1. d, p. 91	9. a, p. 106	17. d, p. 110
2. d, p. 93	10. e, p. 106	18. d, p. 110-11
3. b, p. 93	11. a, p. 106	19. e, p. 112-13
4. d, p. 95	12. b, p. 106	20. e, p. 112-13
5. e, p. 100	13. a, p. 107	21. b, p. 114
6. a, p. 104	14. e, p. 107	22. d, p. 115
7. a, p. 104	15. b, p. 108	
8. a, p. 105	16. e, p. 108	

Exercise 4-1

How marketing environment variables affect strategy planning

Introduction

Marketing managers are not free to choose *any* marketing strategy they please. On the contrary, their choice of strategies is usually affected by variables related to the:

1. Objectives and resources of the firm
2. Competitive environment
3. Economic and technological environment
4   Political and legal environment
5. Cultural and social environment

These variables are sometimes called "uncontrollable" because, in the short run, they are beyond the control of marketing managers--although in the long run, marketing managers may be able to influence some or all of these variables.

In the short run, at least, these marketing environment variables may force marketing managers to change their present strategies--or even to choose less-than-ideal strategies. On the other hand, trends in the marketing environments often create new opportunities for alert marketing strategy planners.

Assignment

This exercise is intended to stimulate your thinking about how the marketing environment variables *might* affect marketing strategy planning. Read each of the following situations carefully and answer the questions that follow each situation.

1. In recent years, various federal and local agencies, environmental groups, and consumer advocates have been promoting greater concern for the environmental impact of solid waste, especially disposable products and packaging. Consequently, many communities now have active "recycling" programs, and some consumers have begun to switch from products or packages that are not biodegradable. What effect do you think these trends might have on the marketing efforts of a consumer packaged goods company like Unilever?

    _____

    _____

    _____

2. The rapid growth of ethnic groups--including Hispanics, Blacks, and Asian-Americans--and the increasing share of income going to these consumers is influencing the marketing strategy of many firms, especially in geographic areas where ethnic subgroups are most concentrated. How would this increasing cultural diversity impact a manufacturer of children's clothing that is interested in increasing its market share among Hispanic consumers who live in California?

_____

_____

_____

3. The North American Free Trade Agreement has spurred American and Japanese auto companies to build new assembly plants and parts factories in Mexico. The market in Mexico is growing but in addition many of the cars that are produced in Mexico will be exported to other Latin American countries. How do these free trade changes affect marketing opportunities for Ford? For Honda?

_____

_____

_____

4. The three major TV networks, ABC, CBS, and NBC, used to split almost all the audience for "prime time" TV. But the wide penetration of cable television means that viewers can now tune in a wide variety of cable shows--ranging from sports and comedy to news and weather. And advertisers can select from more channels too. The result is a very large number of TV advertising outlets each of which delivers a smaller number of viewers. How do these changes in the competitive, economic, and technological environments affect the marketing strategies of the major networks?

_____

_____

_____

5. Computerized scanners at checkout counters can provide retailers, wholesalers, and producers with instant data on the sales on a wide variety of packaged goods. How would this technological advance affect a retailer such as Best Buy stores?

_____

_____

_____

6. For years, Intel enjoyed explosive growth in the demand for its Pentium processors as the demand for PCs grew. Although other companies offered processors at lower prices, they took only a small share of the market because their processors operated at a slower speed. However, in recent years the growth in demand for personal computers has been in low-end units intended for home use--and almost every manufacturer has introduced home models with price tags under $500. Because home computers typically don't require as much processing speed, and because the price of the processor is a major portion of a low-price computer, Intel's competitors have very rapidly taken away market share. How do you think the competition Intel faces has affected its marketing strategy for its current and new chips?

_____

_____

_____

Question for Discussion

How can marketers deal effectively with changing trends and developments in their marketing environments?

Exercise 4-2

Analyzing competitors' strategies

Introduction

The competitive environment affects the number and types of competitors a marketing manager must face--and how the competitors may behave. Although a marketing manager usually can't control what a competitor does, it is possible to plan for competition--and where possible to avoid head-on competition by finding new or better ways to satisfy customers' needs. Thus, the search for a breakthrough opportunity--and some sustainable competitive advantage--requires an understanding not only of customers but also of competitors. That's why marketing managers often turn to competitor analysis to evaluate the strengths or weaknesses of competitors' marketing strategies.

As discussed on pages 97-99 of the text, competitor analysis is simply a logical extension of the marketing strategy planning framework that focuses on identifying a target market and the marketing mix to meet that market's needs. It also considers competitive barriers--conditions that may make it difficult or impossible for a firm to compete in a market. A careful competitor analysis may help a marketing manager see opportunities to serve new markets--ones which play to a firm's strengths while avoiding its weaknesses, including competitive weaknesses.

Doing a complete competitor analysis is a real challenge. You will be better equipped to take on that challenge at the end of the course when you know more of the details of marketing strategy planning. But, this exercise gets you started with this type of thinking.

Assignment

The following case describes a retail hardware store and its competitive environment. Read and analyze the case carefully--to better understand the company's marketing strategy strengths and weaknesses. Then, complete the competitor analysis table and answer the questions--being sure to support your ideas with facts from the case.

Teague's Ace Hardware

Teague's Ace Hardware is located in an affluent suburb of a medium-sized city. The store is in a neighborhood shopping center that also includes a grocery store, drugstore, dry cleaners and a pet store. It is between two of the city's largest private schools--and the area is favored as a place to live by doctors, lawyers, and other high-income families.

Maria Teague bought the store five years ago in partnership with her brother, Armando Teague. Maria quit her job as a financial advisor with Vanguard Investments to try her hand at retailing, and Armando had retired after 20 years in the U.S. Air Force. When the Teagues took it over, the store had been in business for ten years. At first they made few changes except that Maria used acquired skills to computerize inventory and ordering.

Teague's is a typical Ace Hardware with more than 15,000 items kept regularly in stock. Almost all the stock is ordered through the regional Ace Hardware warehouse, which is about three hours away. With computer links and UPS delivery, most items can be restocked within two days to a week. Because the store is small, Teague's often orders in small quantities.

To meet customers' needs, Teague's has added more decorating items than many similar stores. One employee is regularly assigned to a van that will go to customers' houses to measure and install blinds and match existing paint colors. Over the years, the Teagues have also added locksmithing, glass cutting, and lawnmower engine repair to the services they offer.

The Teagues found that most customers tend to come to the store at the beginning or end of the day and that mid-day business is very slow. Two full-time employees operate cash registers at the front of the store but most of the sales staff are part-timers. The Teagues hired several retired tradesmen to work a three-hour shift in the morning. In the afternoon and on week-ends, high-school students assist customers. The Teagues try to have enough salespeople "on the floor" to greet almost all customers as soon as they enter the store and help them find and select what they need.

Until recently, Teague's competition came from Town & Country, a builders' supply house and lumber yard, and from another neighborhood hardware store, Apex Sentry Hardware, which is on a country road about three miles away. Last year, however, Home Improvement Depot--a subsidiary of a national retailer--opened a large warehouse store. It is located on an abandoned railroad switching yard two miles towards the center of town. The Home Improvement Depot is huge--more than 5 times the size of the local builders' supply and more than 20 times the size of Teague's.

When Home Improvement Depot opened, Armando Teague said: "This'll probably be the end of us. There's hardly an item that we sell that the warehouse store doesn't sell--and at a deep discount too. There's no way we can match their prices! When they sell lawnmowers, they bring in a truckload." But after a year, Maria was not so pessimistic. As she said to Armando, "We've had our best year ever. I wish I understood it. I hear that the Sentry Hardware is about to close its doors--and one of our part-timers says that Town & Country Builders Supply is like a ghost town."

Concisely complete the table on the following page--with specific emphasis on aspects of Teague's strategy that is different from its competitors. Some of the blanks have been filled in for you.

	Teague's Ace Hardware	Town & Country Builders' Supply	Home Improvement Depot
Target Market (Who are the customers; how do they shop)		Builders and contractors; some walk-in homeowner business; most customers are probably knowledgeable and know specifically what they want	
Product (focus of product line, including service; branding; guarantees			Very broad product line of hardware and lumber; Some well-known brands; Mainly self-service with some help available at front-desk
Place (channel relationships with suppliers; transportation and storing considerations	Tied to Regional Ace Hardware Wholesaler		National purchasing; truck-load direct deliveries from manufacturers
Price (price level; credit terms; special sales; etc.)	High compared to competition	Discounts to big customers or on large orders, and free delivery for large items	Very low everyday prices; delivery available at extra cost; modest discounts and credit to contractors who are regular customers
Promotion		Ads in newspaper & in local real estate magazine; Yellow pages; some telemarketing and personal selling (out of store) to big developers and contractors	National TV ads and local newspaper inserts; special sales desk for contractors to place special orders
Competitive Barriers			Chain's large volume purchases give it a cost advantage; large facility supports product availability

1.   What are some of the key ways that the Ace Hardware wholesaler might help Teague's to compete with the other competitors?

2.   Do you think that Teague's competes most directly with Town & Country or with Home Improvement Depot? Explain your reasons.

3.   Why do you think that Teague's could have a profitable year even when Apex Sentry Hardware and Town & Country are having real problems?

4.   Is there anything that Teague's could do if another local hardware store were to open nearby (or if Apex Sentry Hardware were to make changes) and offer a similar marketing mix designed to serve the same target customers?

Question for Discussion

If head-on competition makes it more difficult to develop a successful marketing strategy, why do so many firms continue to compete in markets that are characterized by pure (or nearly pure) competition?

Exercise 4-3

How the legal environment affects marketing strategy planning

Introduction

Even in a "free enterprise" economy like the one in the United States, a marketing strategy planner faces many legal constraints. These laws are often confusing--and may even appear contradictory. Further, the laws are frequently written vaguely by legislators--to allow the courts to interpret and apply them. But the interpretation may vary depending on the current political environment. In spite of these problems, it is critical that marketing managers make every effort to understand the political-legal environments--because business must operate and develop its marketing strategies within these environments.

Assignment

The following cases describe marketing activities that might be judged illegal. Study each case carefully and determine the law (or laws) which appear to be *most relevant* to each situation. Then state why you answered as you did. You should refer to the following list of laws in completing this exercise:

Sherman Antitrust Act	Wheeler-Lea Act
Clayton Act	Antimerger Act
Federal Trade Commission Act	Consumer Product Safety Act
Robinson-Patman Act	Magnuson-Moss Act

Note: Most of these laws are discussed in this chapter and summarized in Exhibit 4-4 on page 106 of the text--and this is the depth of understanding expected here. Most are discussed later--see subject index--but here we want to get a "big picture" feel for the likely impact of legislation.

The first case is answered for you as an example--but try to answer it yourself before looking at the suggested answer! [Note: You do not have to decide on legality, but merely indicate what law(s) *might* be involved or be most relevant in the situation.]

1. Industrial Drill Press (IDP)--a large manufacturer of industrial drill presses with an estimated 45 percent share of the U.S. market--wanted to diversify its product line. After investigating several possibilities, IDP decided to enter the rapidly growing market for industrial band saws--which are used to cut metal bars and tubes. The company felt it would take too long to develop its own manufacturing and distribution facilities, and therefore chose to diversify by buying firms already in the band-saw business.

Over a two-year period, IDP bought out three leading producers of band saws. Some observers have predicted that IDP will dominate the market for industrial band saws within another three years.

a)   Federal legislation: *Antimerger Act*
b)   Reason: *The firm is engaged in mergers which may tend to substantially lessen competition in the band-saw industry.*

2.   Georgia Spence purchased a "boom box"—with a CD player that would play MP3 music files or regular CDs--from a mail-order retailer after seeing the retailer's ad in the Sunday *New York Times*. Georgia was attracted by the low price--and was assured by the "full one-year warranty" highlighted in the ad. Three months after the unit arrived, the CD unit stopped working. Georgia called the retailer's toll-free number to find out how to get warranty service. The salesperson who answered Georgia's call said that he would email her a copy of the manufacturer's written warranty and service instructions.   To Georgia's surprise, the manufacturer's "full one-year warranty" read as follows:

"The manufacturer warranties this high quality stereo unit against all possible defects for a period of one full year, except for the motor on the CD player, which is covered for 30 days, and except for all plastic parts, which are not covered at all. Should this unit fail to operate during this period, it should be shipped at the purchaser's expense in the original carton to: Repair Depot, 1716 Rushmore Road, Ithaca, NY. A certified check for $49.95 should be enclosed to cover handling charges. This is the only warranty provided by the manufacturer, and all other express or implied warranties are hereby excluded. This warranty does not cover damage caused by improper handling or abuse. The manufacturer shall be the sole judge of whether any parts are defective or whether they were damaged through improper handling or abuse."

a)   Federal legislation: _____

b)   Reason: _____

_____

_____

_____

_____

3.   Advantage Skis, Inc. has just discovered that some of its high performance fiberglass water skis were manufactured with a faulty fastener which could cause the adjustable rubber "shoe" on the ski to pop off under stress--such as might occur when skiing at high speed or performing spins or other tricks. Company officials estimate that no more than 5 percent of the 10,000 pairs of skis manufactured and sold during the past year were defective. Rather than engage in an expensive recall, Advantage Skis, Inc. has notified its retailers to repair the skis at no cost to the owner whenever a defective model is discovered.

        a)   Federal legislation: _____

        b)   Reason: _____

        _____

        _____

        _____

        _____

4.   Lean-n-Mean Exercise Corporation, a firm located in Santa Monica, CA, advertised *its Body Shaper,* "an amazing new isometric exercise device" in the *Los Angeles Times.* According to the ad, "individual results vary, but through only 5 minutes a day of effortless exercise you can expect to add up to 2 inches to your biceps and up to 3 inches to your chest while losing up to 4 inches from your waistline and up to 10 pounds from your present weight during an average 14-day period." The ad stated that the body shaper could be purchased by mail for only $14.95 and added "Try the Body-Shaper risk free. If you are not completely satisfied, return the Body Shaper within 30 days and the purchase price will be promptly refunded."

        The ad caught Timothy Lukach's eye and he ordered the exerciser--enclosing a money order for the specified amount. About a month later, he received a package containing a hard rubber cable about 2 feet long, and a small pamphlet describing various diet plans. Believing he had been cheated, he demanded that his money be refunded as advertised. Shortly afterwards, he received a form letter from the firm stating that his request for a refund had been denied on the grounds that "more than thirty days has passed since you placed your order."

        a)   Federal legislation: _____

        b)   Reason: _____

        _____

        _____

        _____

        _____

5.　MacGregor Paint Co. has been selling its products only through paint and hardware retailers, but recently the company decided to try to sell its spray paints through supermarket chains. To encourage the food chains to purchase in large quantities, MacGregor offered them a special 12 percent quantity discount. MacGregor does not plan to offer quantity discounts to its paint and hardware retailers. Several food chains have already agreed to carry the spray paints, but one large national chain--whose business MacGregor really wants--has refused to stock the paints unless MacGregor agrees to give the chain an additional 3 percent "advertising allowance."

a)　Federal legislation: _____

b)　Reason: _____

_____

_____

_____

_____

6.　Fuel-oil producers were caught by surprise when December temperatures dropped unexpectedly. Because of inadequate fuel-oil reserves, most producers had trouble quickly filling orders from their distributors across the country. In a number of areas across the country, fuel-oil prices shot up by as much as 60 percent more than normal. During the shortage, the three fuel-oil distributors in Bear Creek, a mountain area on the North Carolina and Tennessee border, kept their delivery trucks running 24 hours a day to ensure that customers did not find themselves without heat. By mid-January, the shortages had begun to let up. About that time, the owners of the three distributorships saw each other at a monthly civic club luncheon. As they were discussing the added costs of all of the "overtime" deliveries, one of the men suggested that they all keep their prices at the current level "until the February peak demand period is over. " The other two agreed that this would help improve profits.

a)　Federal legislation: _____

b)　Reason: _____

_____

_____

_____

_____

Question for Discussion

Marketing-related legislation has often had different objectives and varying degrees of interpretation and enforcement. Why? What is the current trend? In which direction does the political and legal environment appear to be moving?

Exercise 4-4

Competitor analysis

This exercise is based on computer-aided problem number 4--Competitor Analysis. A complete description of the problem appears on page 118 of *Basic Marketing,* 16th edition.

1. Mediquip has focused on lowering costs because the market appears to be price-sensitive. But Mediquip sees that there may be other ways to take advantage of its company strengths. Laser Tech already has parts it could use in producing the laser scalpel, but that may reduce its flexibility. Mediquip product designers think they can develop a product that better meets a doctor's needs if Mediquip spends $50,000 for front-end design costs, but they wonder if a profit can still be earned with a product that costs $7,400 to produce. Mediquip's marketing manager thinks that the firm could get a 70 percent share of the market--leaving only a 30 percent share for Laser Tech--if it could develop this product and still set a price to meet what Laser Tech will have to charge. Based on this situation, what would Mediquip's average cost per machine be, and what price would it have to charge to earn a $1,000 profit per machine? Based on these estimates, would you recommend that Mediquip move ahead with the idea of improving the product? Why?

    Average cost per machine: $ _____   Price: $ _____

    _____

    _____

    _____

    _____

    _____

2. Mediquip can keep its product development plans secret until it enters the market. But Mediquip is wondering about what Laser Tech might do if Mediquip does keep its plans secret. For example, Laser Tech might think that it would be able to capture 70 percent share of the market and set its price to cover its costs based on that quantity. In this case, what would Laser Tech estimate as its likely average cost per machine? What price would it set if it expected each unit to contribute $1,000 to profit?

    For Laser Tech:

    Average cost per machine: $ _____

    Price (at 70 percent share): $ _____

3. If these events occur, each firm would enter the market with a price that had been set assuming that it would win 70 percent of the market. Clearly, it's not possible for each firm to have 70 percent share of the market. If Mediquip developed the improved product but only captured 40 percent of the market, its sales, costs, and profits might look quite different than it had planned. Assume Mediquip spent the extra money on product design and unit product costs, but then only won 40 % of the market. For this case, fill in the information requested below.

    For Mediquip:

    Price (at 70 percent share) $ _____

    Less, Average Total Cost per Machine
              (at 40 percent share,) $ _____

    = Profit (or Loss) per Machine $ _____

4. In the space provided below, calculate what profit (or loss) Mediquip would earn in this situation:

    Actual total revenue = quantity actually sold X price set

    Quantity sold (at 40 percent share)   _____

    Price set (assuming 70 percent share) $ _____

    Actual total revenue $ _____

    Less, Total Design, Production
              and Selling Costs (at 40%) $ _____

    = Total Profit (or Loss) Contribution $ _____

5. Drawing on this analysis, briefly explain several important reasons why a marketing manager should understand the competitive environment when planning a marketing strategy.

    Reason number 1: _____

    Explanation: _____

    _____

    _____

    Reason number 2: _____

    Explanation: _____

    _____

    _____

Chapter 5

Demographic dimensions of global consumer markets

What This Chapter Is About

Marketing-oriented managers must understand their customers--and Chapter 5 is the first of a group of three chapters about customers and their buying behavior. Actually, we know a great deal about potential customers. Therefore, there is no reason to rely on erroneous stereotypes or vague generalizations.

In this chapter you will see why demographic dimensions are important in selecting target markets. You'll start with an introduction to the demographics of global consumer markets--that will help you understand why so many firms are looking for international marketing opportunities. You will also see how the U.S. population is changing--and why these changes are vital to marketing strategy planning. You will see how the age distribution is shifting--and how consumer spending patterns vary considerably by age, stage in family life cycle, ethnic group, and other dimensions.

Really understanding the material in this chapter will help you to deepen your skills in segmenting markets and evaluating market opportunities. So don't just memorize a lot of "facts." Instead, try to get a "feel" for relationships. Demographic relationships are enduring--and a good understanding of these relationships will help you avoid mistakes when decisions about the size or attractiveness of potential markets must be made quickly.

Important Terms

gross domestic product (GDP), p. 125
birthrate, p. 134
Metropolitan Statistical Area (MSA), p. 139
real income, p. 140

disposable income, p. 142
discretionary income, p. 143
empty nesters, p. 144
senior citizens, p. 145

True-False Questions

___ 1. Very little information is available on the demographic dimensions of consumer markets in other parts of the world.

___ 2. The population of the United States is about 15 percent of the world's population.

___ 3. With the exception of a few densely populated cities around the world, most of the world's population is fairly evenly distributed in rural areas.

4. One widely used measure of national income is gross domestic product (GDP).

5. The gross national income is a limited measure of the output of the economy since it considers the total market value of goods, but not services, produced in a year.

6. The gross domestic product (GDP) does not include foreign income earned in a country.

7. An analysis of literacy in various countries shows that only one tenth of the world's population can read and write.

8. Based on population alone, the Northeast United States looks like a more attractive market than the West Coast.

9. Several of the Western states are experiencing huge increases in population in this decade while some of the Northeastern states are experiencing only small increases.

10. In spite of declining birthrates, it seems certain that the U.S. population will continue to grow because of immigration.

11. The birthrate--the number of babies born per 1,000 people--has continued to decline for the last fifty years.

12. Despite a declining birthrate, the average age of the population will continue to decrease for some time due to the effects of the post-World War II baby boom.

13. During this decade, there will be big increases in the 45-64 age group, but that growth will slow in the next decade.

14. The decline in the number of senior citizens will continue in the next decade.

15. Over 50 percent of all households consist of married couples with children under 18.

16. Single-adult households account for over 27 percent of all households in the United States.

17. About 15 percent of all Americans live and work on farms in rural areas.

18. A Metropolitan Statistical Area (MSA) is an integrated economic and social unit having a population nucleus of at least one million people.

19. Consolidated Metropolitan Statistical Areas, the largest MSAs, have 1 million or more in population.

20. About 13 percent of all Americans move each year.

21. The distribution of income in the United States has changed drastically in the last 50 years, moving a greater proportion of the families into the middle and upper income levels.

22. More than 40 percent of the total U.S. income goes to the well-to-do households with incomes over $173,640--the top 5 percent.

___ 23. Disposable income is the income remaining after taxes and savings have been subtracted.

___ 24. Most discretionary income is spent on necessities.

___ 25. While income has a direct bearing on spending patterns, other demographic dimensions--such as age and stage in family life cycle--may be just as important to marketers.

___ 26. "Empty nesters" are an important group of highly mobile individuals who do not maintain a regular place of residence and thus are a very difficult group to track.

___ 27. Many firms cater to the senior citizen market--although about half of these older people are below the poverty level.

___ 28. In the U.S., about 1 in 5 families speaks a language other than English at home.

___ 29. In the U.S., nearly 35 percent of Black families have an income of $50,000 or more.

___ 30. The largest and fastest-growing ethnic group in the U.S. is Asian-Americans.

Answers to True-False Questions

1. F, p. 123	11. F, p. 134-35	21. T, p. 139-40
2. F, p. 124	12. F, p. 135-36	22. F, p. 142
3. F, p. 125	13. T, p. 136	23. F, p. 142
4. T, p. 125	14. F, p. 136	24. F, p. 143
5. F, p. 125,130	15. F, p. 137	25. T, p. 143
6. F, p. 130	16. T, p. 138	26. F, p. 144
7. F, p. 132	17. F, p. 138	27. F, p. 145
8. T, p. 132	18. F, p. 139	28. T, p. 146
9. T, p. 133	19. T, p. 139	29. T, p. 146
10. T, p. 134	20. T, p. 139	30. F, p. 147

Multiple-Choice Questions (Circle the correct response)

1. Which of the following statements is true?
   a. The United States makes up less than five percent of the total world population.
   b. In general, less-developed countries experience a faster rate of population growth than developed countries.
   c. There is a worldwide trend toward urbanization.
   d. The world population is now over 6 billion people.
   e. All of the above are true.

2. Which of the following countries has the *highest* GNI per capita?
   a. United States
   b. India
   c. Switzerland
   d. Saudi Arabia
   e. Venezuela

3. Which of the following countries has the *lowest* GNI per capita?
   a. India
   b. Kuwait
   c. Italy
   d. Mozambique
   e. Brazil

4. The state with the largest percentage increase in population between 2000 and 2010 is:
   a. New York
   b. Nevada
   c. Illinois
   d. South Dakota
   e. Michigan

5. U.S. population trends suggest that:
   a. the U.S. will grow at a faster rate during the next 25 years than it did during the last 50 years.
   b. the U.S. population has started to decline because the birthrate has been declining for the past 50 years.
   c. the dominant population will continue to be senior citizens.
   d. the U.S. has finally reached "zero population growth."
   e. the average age of the U.S. population will continue to rise for many years.

6. Which of the following is *not* an accurate statement about consumer markets in the United States?
   a. There are already over 309 million people in the United States.
   b. The average age of the U.S. population is rising.
   c. The number of people in the 65+ age group will decline very substantially in the next decade.
   d. Less than a fourth of U.S. households consist of husband, wife, and children under 18.
   e. More than a fourth of U.S. households are single-adult.

7. Which of the following statements about the U.S. population is *true*?
   a. Between 1950 and the present, the population doubled in every state in the nation.
   b. The U.S. population will stop growing by the year 2010.
   c. Our population is getting younger despite decreasing birthrates.
   d. Less than 2 percent of the population now live and work on farms.
   e. All of the above are true statements.

8. Which of the following statements is *true?*
    a. A Metropolitan Statistical Area generally centers on one urbanized area of 50,000 or more in population and includes bordering "urban" areas.
    b. Some national marketers sell only in the largest Metropolitan Statistical Areas.
    c. Metropolitan Statistical Areas are a more useful classification method for marketers than political boundaries.
    d. All of the above are true statements.
    e. None of the above are true statements.

9. Mobility has an important bearing on marketing planning. Approximately what percent of Americans move each year?
    a. 3 percent
    b. 13 percent
    c. 36 percent
    d. 50 percent
    e. 63 percent

10. The income distribution in the United States
    a. makes little difference to marketing decisions, since it can't be controlled by the marketing manager.
    b. has stayed about the same for 50 years.
    c. now has a larger percent of people at the lower levels.
    d. shows that higher income people still receive a very large share of the total income.
    e. none of the above are true.

11. With respect to income, government data indicate that:
    a. the top 5 percent get more than 40 percent of total income.
    b. most Americans are still at the bottom of the income pyramid.
    c. middle-income families are enjoying huge increases in real income and no longer need to pinch their pennies.
    d. there are only a few families in the United States with incomes over $60,000.
    e. None of the above is a true statement.

12. Disposable income is defined as:
    a. total market value of goods and services produced.
    b. gross national product per capita.
    c. income available after taxes.
    d. income available before taxes.
    e. income available after taxes and "necessities."

13. Lila Wright's salary as a sales rep for a computer software firm was $25,000 last year. She earned an additional $10,000 in sales commissions. Her tax bill was $9,000 and bills covering other necessities such as food, housing, and transportation amounted to $10,000. What was Lila's disposable income last year?
    a. $35,000.
    b. $26,000.
    c. $25,000.
    d. $19,000.
    e. $16,000.

14. Which of the following statements is true?
    a. The majority of senior citizens have income below the poverty level.
    b. Singles and young couples are more willing to try new products.
    c. Empty nesters are frequently big spenders.
    d. All of the above are true statements.
    e. b and c are true statements, but not a.

15. Which of the following is *not* an accurate statement about ethnic groups in the United States?
    a. People from different ethnic groups may be influenced by different cultural variables.
    b. One in five families speaks a language other than English at home.
    c. African-Americans outnumber Hispanics in the U.S. by two to one.
    d. Ethnic groups are growing at a faster rate than the population as a whole.
    e. Asian-Americans tend to be a diverse group in terms of language, religion, culture, and country of origin.

Answers to Multiple-Choice Questions

1. e, p. 124-25
2. c, p. 128-29
3. d, p. 128-29
4. b, p. 134
5. e, p. 134-35

6. c, p. 133-38
7. d, p. 138
8. d, p. 139
9. b, p. 139
10. d, p. 139-42

11. e, p. 140-42
12. c, p. 142
13. b, p. 142
14. e, p. 143-45
15. c, p. 146-47

Exercise 5-1

Strategy planning for international markets: Consumer products

Introduction

Many brand names are recognized worldwide and firms with successful products in their domestic markets frequently turn to international markets for rapid growth and new profit opportunities. Marketing strategy planning is, in essence, no different for international markets than for domestic markets. The firm should choose a target market and develop a marketing mix to satisfy the needs of that target market.

But in practice, international marketing strategy planning can be much more difficult, however. Strategy planners often must deal with unfamiliar marketing environment variables. And there may be big differences in language, customs, beliefs, religion and race, and even income distribution from one country to another. Even identical products may differ in terms of which needs they satisfy, the conditions under which they are used, and people's ability to buy them. In addition, new and unfamiliar competitors are likely to be encountered.

Also, reliable data for market analysis may be harder to obtain when a firm moves into international markets. The wealth of published data which American marketers tend to take for granted may not exist at all. And consumers in some countries are far less willing to take part in market research studies than most Americans.

This exercise shows how some market analysis might be done for international markets—and shows some of the common pitfalls a marketer is likely to make in planning international marketing strategies.

Assignment

Read the following case and answer the questions that follow:

ELITE BEVERAGES CORPORATION

Elite Beverages Corporation recently developed a new beverage named "Devine Mocha," a chocolate-coffee flavored drink targeted to people who take their lunch to work. The flavorful combination is packaged in aseptic "drink boxes" which have a long shelf life and don't require refrigeration. Devine Mocha met with success when introduced for sale in the United States a year ago. Although the product had been formulated to be consumed cold, research showed a very large market for people who drink Devine Mocha warm, by microwaving it in its original carton. A majority of lunchrooms and cafeterias have one or more microwave ovens available.

When Elite Beverages commissioned extensive survey data in the U.S., the company found that the new drink appealed to different groups of consumers, depending on their previous lunchtime drink habit. According to the survey, Devine Mocha had a favorable rating with 40 percent of the U.S. coffee drinkers, a 30 percent favorable rating with those who usually drank soft drinks, and a 10 percent favorable rating with those whose typical lunchtime drink was tea. Sales and survey data show that among those that like the taste, about 10 percent of purchasers actually switch to Devine Mocha. Little acceptance was achieved among wine, milk, and water drinkers.

Encouraged by the success of Devine Mocha, Elite Beverages Corporation decided to expand its market coverage overseas. The following four countries are being considered as potential new markets: United Kingdom, France, Spain, and Germany. Because limited funds for expansion are available, only *one* of these countries will be selected for the first international market for Devine Mocha. The marketing manager of Elite Beverages was asked to decide which of the four countries would offer the highest dollar sales potential.

As a start, the manager obtained the market data shown in Table 5-1 by looking up the populations of the four countries (use the population figures from Exhibit 5-3 on pages 128-29 of the text), and then asking a market research firm to estimate the average per capita expenditures in these countries for tea, coffee, and soft drinks.

TABLE 5-1
Estimated Average Annual per Capita Expenditures on
Selected Meal-Time Beverages in Four Countries

Country	Population	Per Capita Beverage Expenditures		
		Coffee	Soft Drink	Tea
United Kingdom	61,285,000	$40	$12	$80
France	61,638,000	$20	$40	$15
Spain	40,549,000	$15	$40	$30
Germany	82,283,000	$60	$80	$25

The manager got an initial estimate of dollar sales potential for Devine Mocha in each country based on the experience in the U.S. with each of the three segments identified by the present drink choice. For example, based on U.S. experience, 40 percent of the coffee drinkers in a country can be expected to like Devine Mocha, and of those, 10 percent are likely to switch their beverage purchases to Devine Mocha. So Devine Mocha can be expected to pick up 4 percent (that is, 40 percent times 10 percent) of coffee drinkers' per capita beverage purchases. Looking at Table 5-1, we see that in the U.K., per capita coffee purchases were $40, so Devine Mocha could expect $1.60 (that is 4 percent of $40) expenditure. This result is entered into the table that follows, and the calculations for the U.K. have been completed.

1. a. Determine the per capita dollar sales potential for Devine Mocha in France, Spain, and Germany by completing the table.

Percent who like taste of Devine Mocha	Former Drink Preference			Total Potential per Capita Expenditure for Devine Mocha
	Coffee	**Soft Drink**	**Tea**	
	40	30	10	
Country	Per Capita Potential Expenditure On Devine Mocha, by Segment			
	Coffee	**Soft Drink**	**Tea**	
United Kingdom	$1.60	$0.36	$0.80	$2.76
France				
Spain				
Germany				

(Top header of table: U.S. Experience)

b. Now calculate the total sales potential by country. Again, the U.K. has been completed as an example.

Country	Population	Calculated per capita sales of Devine Mocha	Total Sales Potential
United Kingdom	61,285,000	$2.76	$169,146,600
France	61,638,000		
Spain	40,549,000		
Germany	82,283,000		

2. Based on your estimates in the table above, which one of the four countries would offer the highest dollar sales potential for Devine Mocha?

3.   What do the above calculations assume about the Elite Beverages Corporation's potential target markets for Devine Mocha?

4.   Will Elite Beverages Corporation have to change its marketing mix when it expands overseas? Why or why not?

Question for Discussion

The per capita beverage expenditures shown in Table 5-1 are just imaginary--but an actual market research study would no doubt show that beverage expenditures do in fact vary considerably among these and other countries. Should a firm's marketing strategy planning be based solely on such data and U.S. experience--or would further study or even test marketing be desirable.

Exercise 5-2

How demographic trends affect marketing strategy planning

Introduction

A common approach to identifying markets uses "demographic" characteristics of customers--such as age, sex, race, education, occupation, geographical location, income, marital status, and family size. The popularity of demographics is due to the fact that such characteristics are easily measured, easily understood, and readily available in published form. Demographic characteristics are very useful for identifying market segments, planning appropriate marketing mixes and estimating market potential.

This exercise will stress another major use of demographics--to monitor changes and trends in the uncontrollable cultural and social environments to help find new marketing opportunities.

We will focus on four major demographic trends:
1.   People in the "baby boom" generation are entering their peak earning--and saving--years.
2.   The increasing life spans of senior citizens.
3.   The trend toward smaller family units and a larger number of "single adult" households.
4.   The growing number of ethnics and how their culture will shape society and markets.

You will be asked to evaluate the likely positive or negative effects of these four trends on three major industries.

Assignment

Listed below are three major industries in the United States. In the space provided, discuss the likely positive and/or negative effects of the above-mentioned demographic bends on *each* of the three industries. Base your answers on the text discussion and your general knowledge--DO NOT DO ANY LIBRARY OR FIELD RESEARCH. Use your head instead--to apply what you already know!

Industries

Leisure Time	Cosmetics	Restaurants

1.   Industry: Leisure Time

    a)   Effects of baby boom generation's peak earnings and saving years.

    b)   Effects of longer life span of senior citizens.

    c)   Effects of smaller family units and more "single adult" households.

    d)   Effects of growing ethnic culture on society and markets.

2. Industry: Cosmetics

   a) Effects of baby boom generation's peak earnings and saving years.

   b) Effects of longer life span of senior citizens.

   c) Effects of smaller family units and more "single adult" households.

   d) Effects of growing ethnic culture on society and markets.

3.   Industry: Restaurants

   a)   Effects of baby boom generation's peak earnings and saving years.

   b)   Effects of longer life span of senior citizens.

   c)   Effects of smaller family units and more "single adult" households.

   d)   Effects of growing ethnic culture on society and markets.

Question for Discussion

Name some other important demographic trends. How might these trends affect the three industries discussed in the exercise?

Exercise 5-3

Marketers must know their markets

Introduction

The "golden rule" of marketing is: "Know thy market!" Firms that live by this rule are generally more successful than those that do not. And the fact that *most* new businesses and products fail is ample proof that many firms do *not* know their markets.

Some marketers pay close attention to government statistics--anxious to take advantage of any new opportunities such data may reveal. Surprisingly, however, many marketers seem to be almost totally unaware of how much valuable demographic data is already available. So, this exercise has a twofold purpose. First, it will help you see how much you know about the U.S. market. If you are like most people, some of your views will be grossly inaccurate. That explains our other purpose--to familiarize you with the kinds of demographic data that are usually available in published form.

Every marketer should be an expert on sources of marketing information. You will learn about several valuable sources (see pages 132 and 216-18 in particular in the text, but also pages 198 and 203). Now, we will look in depth at just one source--the *Statistical Abstract of the United States*. Issued annually by the U.S. Department of Commerce, the *Abstract* contains about 1,500 summary tables of statistics describing social, political, and economic trends in the United States and world markets. Each issue also contains a list of sources (Appendix III) which--together with detailed footnotes--can guide you to more specific sources of information. The *Abstract is* probably the best starting point for locating statistical data--and an invaluable reference book (also available in electronic form on the Internet at www.census.gov) for any marketer who wishes to keep informed of demographic trends. Keep in mind that some government statistics are published with a considerable "lag" and some figures are estimates.

Assignment

The following list of questions is designed to compare your "best guess" about the U.S. market with actual government statistics. First of all, look at the questions and write down your estimate for the demographic data in question. *Do not try to look up the correct answer in any reference source until you have completed this part!* There is no penalty for being wrong!

After you have completed the first column, go to a library (or go to the Census Bureau website at www.census.gov) and obtain the *most recent* available edition of the *Statistical Abstract of the United States*. (The *Statistical Abstract is* usually published late in each year, so the most recent edition may not have the current year's date.) Use the *Abstract* to look up the correct answers to each question and write the answers in the adjacent column. Note the date of the most recent data available and the units of measurement. The answers to all of these questions can be found in the *Abstract* through careful use of the index. Take the opportunity to browse through the other kinds of information available and remember that the *Abstract is* constructed from a very large number of U.S. government reports and that additional detail is available in the original documents.

Q.	Date of *Abstract* used _____	Your Estimate	Answer from Abstract, /units (date)
1.	What is the total population of the USA?		
2.	What is the U.S. birthrate?		
3.	What is the median age of the U.S population?		
4.	What percentage of all people over 25 years old in the U.S., a. Did not finish high school? b. Have completed at least 4 years of college?		
5.	What is the median income of married-couple families, a. Wife in paid labor-force? b. Wife not in paid labor-force? c. Male householder, no wife present? d. Female householder, no husband present?		
6.	What are the annual U.S. total personal consumptions in the following categories: a. Food and tobacco? b. Clothing, accessories, and jewelry? c. Transportation? d. Medical care? e. Recreation? f. Education? g. Housing?		
7.	What is the U.S. annual *per capita* consumption of the following: a. Sugar? b. Red Meat? c. Cheese? d. Fresh bananas? e. Broccoli? f. Beer? g. Coffee? h. Milk? i. Carbonated soft drinks?		
8.	What percentage of U.S. households have: a. Television? b. Cable? c. VCR? d. Computer? e. Internet connection? f. Broadband Internet connection?		
9.	What percentage of public schools have instructional classrooms with: a. Internet access? b. Internet access using broadband connection? c. Internet access using wireless connection?		
10.	For each instructional computer with Internet access (in public schools), how many students must share it?		

Question for Discussion

Identify which of your estimates was closest to the mark, and which was farthest away from the data; what are the implications for marketing strategy planning?

Exercise 5-4

Demographic analysis

This exercise is based on computer-aided problem number 5--Demographic Analysis. A complete description of the problem appears on page 149 of *Basic Marketing,* 16th edition.

1. a. The estimate of the growth rate for the 45-59 age segment in part depends on guessing the number of people who will move into or out of the areas served by Stylco's retailers. That may vary considerably due to regional shifts, employment trends, and other social factors. However, Naomi Davis realizes that her marketing mix will be more profitable if she has good distribution in areas where her target market is living. If she can realign distribution so that she is represented in boutiques in retail markets serving 75 percent of her 45-59 year-old target market (rather than the current boutiques, that reach only 60 percent of that market), what would happen to total profits by the year 2010?

Total profit from 45-59 age group in year 2010 with 75 % penetration _____

b. If Davis works on building distribution in the wrong retail markets, she might end up with stores that serve a smaller--rather than larger--percent of her target market. If she made changes and the percentage of Black population (age 45-59) served by the retailers fell from 60 percent to 40 percent, what would happen to profits?

c. What are the implications of this pattern of results?

2. Davis is also considering another type of change in her approach for reaching consumers in the 45-59 age group. Currently, her retailers are in markets that include about 60 percent of the Black consumers in that age range. However, a chain that is doing a very good job of attracting consumers with the highest incomes has approached Davis about carrying her lines. The chain's stores are in markets that include about 35 percent of Black consumers in the 45-59 age range, but most of the consumers it reaches are in the higher income range and they are willing to spend more on clothes. So, the chain would like to be the *exclusive* distributor of a higher priced line of styles for the 45-59 age group. Davis figures that the profit per unit on the new line would be $15, in part because of lower selling costs and in part because of higher prices. Further, the chain is expanding rapidly and it is estimated that by the year 2010 it will reach 35 percent more customers than it did in 2005. Finally, because the chain enjoys such strong loyalty from its target market, Davis believes that the ratio of unit sales to market size might increase to .010.

If Davis decides to make the required changes and to work exclusively with the retail chain to reach the 45-59 age target customers, would she earn greater profits?

2010 Profit from the line for the 45-59 age range customers using the chain _____

2010 Total profit from both lines _____

Would working with the chain increase profits? _____

3. Davis is concerned that if she gives the chain store an exclusive on the line for the 45-59 age group then the boutiques that have been carrying her products will switch to another supplier for the 35-44 age range line. In other words, the profit contribution from the 35-44 age range product line would drop to 0 by the year 2010. If that were to happen, what would be the impact on total profits?

Total profit from both lines in year 2010   _____

less Profit contribution expected in 2010   – _____
        from the 35-44 product line

Profit without the 35-44 line: _____

4. What do you think about the proposition of going with the chain store? Give your reasons.

Chapter 6

Final consumers and their buying behavior

What This Chapter Is About

Chapter 6 focuses on the contribution of the behavioral sciences to our understanding of consumer behavior. As we saw in Chapter 5, demographic analysis does not fully explain *why* people buy or *what* they buy.

The importance of considering several behavioral dimensions at the same time is stressed. This is not easy because there are many psychological and sociological theories. Nevertheless, marketing managers must make decisions based on their knowledge of potential target markets. They must do their best to integrate the various theories and findings. This chapter is intended to get you started.

At the beginning of the chapter, a model of consumer behavior is presented to help organize your thinking. Later in the chapter, an expanded model of consumer behavior is presented. Try to find a way of integrating these models together for yourself. Behavioral science findings can be a great help, but you still must add your own judgment to apply the various findings in particular markets. These findings coupled with "market sense" can take you a long way in marketing strategy planning.

Important Terms

economic buyers, p. 152
economic needs, p. 152
needs, p. 154
wants, p. 154
drive, p. 155
physiological needs, p. 155
safety needs, p. 155
social needs, p. 155
personal needs, p. 155
perception, p. 157
selective exposure, p. 157
selective perception, p. 157
selective retention, p. 157
learning, p. 158
cues, p. 158
response, p. 158

reinforcement, p. 158
attitude, p. 159
belief, p. 159
expectation, p. 162
psychographics, p. 162
lifestyle analysis, p. 162
social class, p. 164
reference group, p. 165
opinion leader, p. 165
culture, p. 166
extensive problem solving, p. 169
limited problem solving, p. 169
routinized response behavior, p. 169
low involvement purchases, p. 169
dissonance, p. 169
adoption process, P. 170

True-False Questions

_____ 1. Because demographic analysis isn't of much value in predicting which specific products and brands will be purchased, many marketers have turned to the behavioral sciences for insight and help.

_____ 2. Economic needs include things such as convenience, efficiency in operation or use, dependability in use, and economy of purchase or use.

_____ 3. Economic needs affect many buying decisions, but for some purchases the behavioral influences are more important.

_____ 4. A drive is a strong need that is learned during a person's life.

_____ 5. The PSSP needs are power, security, social acceptance, and prestige.

_____ 6. Motivation theory suggests that people have hierarchies of needs, and that they never reach a state of complete satisfaction.

_____ 7. Consumers select varying ways to meet their needs because of differences in perception.

_____ 8. Selective perception refers to a person's ability to screen out or modify ideas, messages, or information that conflict with previously learned attitudes and beliefs.

_____ 9. Learning is a change in a person's thought processes caused by prior experience.

_____ 10. Reinforcement of the learning process occurs when a cue follows a response and leads to a reduction in the drive tension.

_____ 11. An attitude is a person's point of view towards something.

_____ 12. Advertising is so powerful that changing consumers' negative attitudes is usually the easiest part of the marketing manager's job.

_____ 13. An expectation is an outcome or belief that a person likes to remember.

_____ 14. Personality traits have been very useful to marketers in predicting which products or brands target customers will choose.

_____ 15. Lifestyle analysis refers to the analysis of a person's day-to-day pattern of living--as expressed in his activities, interests, and opinions.

_____ 16. Social influences are concerned with how an individual interacts with family, social class, and other groups who may have influence on the buying process.

_____ 17. Buying responsibility and influence within a family vary greatly--depending on the product and the family.

___ 18. People with the same income level may be in different social classes.

___ 19. The U.S. class system is far less rigid than the class system in India.

___ 20. The social class system in the United States is usually measured in terms of income, race, and occupation.

___ 21. A person normally has several reference groups.

___ 22. "Opinion leaders" are generally higher income people and better educated.

___ 23. The attitudes and beliefs that we usually associate with culture tend to change slowly.

___ 24. Different purchase situations may require different marketing mixes--even when the same target market is involved.

___ 25. A homemaker doing weekly grocery shopping is more likely to use extensive problem solving than limited problem-solving or routinized response behavior.

___ 26. Low involvement products are products that are seldom purchased by the target market.

___ 27. Dissonance might cause a consumer to pay more attention to automobile advertisements after a new car is purchased than before the purchase.

___ 28. Post-purchase regret is an even bigger problem than dissonance.

___ 29. In the adoption process, the evaluation step usually comes before the trial step.

___ 30. Knowing how a target market handles the decision-making process, the adoption process, and learning can aid marketing strategy planning.

___ 31. Using your intuition in developing marketing mixes for international markets is generally a safe way to proceed.

Answers to True-False Questions

1. T, p. 152	12. F, p. 160	23. T, p. 166
2. T, p. 153	13. F, p. 162	24. T, p. 167
3. T, p. 153-54	14. F, p. 162	25. F, p. 169
4. F, p. 155	15. T, p. 162	26. F, p. 169
5. F, p. 155	16. T, p. 163	27. T, p. 169
6. T, p. 156	17. T, p. 164	28. T, p. 170
7. T, p. 157	18. T, p. 164	29. T, p. 170
8. T, p. 157	19. T, p. 164	30. T, p. 171-72
9. T, p. 158	20. F, p. 164	31. F, p. 172
10. F, p. 158	21. T, p. 165	
11. T, p. 159	22. F, p. 165	

Multiple-Choice Questions (Circle the correct response)

1. According to the text, the economic-buyer theory:
   a. says that most consumers do not know the economic value of products they purchase.
   b. explains why people behave the way they do.
   c. includes psychological variables and social influences.
   d. is too simplistic to explain consumer behavior.
   e. assumes that consumers always buy the lowest price alternative.

2. Which of the following is *not* a psychological variable?
   a. Social class
   b. Motivation
   c. Perception
   d. Attitudes
   e. Learning

3. A good marketing manager
   a. knows that only a few basic needs explain almost all consumer product choices.
   b. doesn't have to understand consumer needs if his product has some design improvements over his competitor's product.
   c. should find ways to create internal drives in consumers.
   d. knows that consumer needs in product-markets are probably much more specific than those in a related generic market.
   e. will make fewer strategy planning mistakes if he uses the economic-buyer theory.

4. According to motivation theory, the *last* needs a family would usually seek to satisfy would be:
   a. safety needs.
   b. personal needs.
   c. physiological needs.
   d. social needs.

5. Psychological theories of motivation and needs suggest that:
   a. lower-level needs must be completely satisfied before higher-level needs become important.
   b. a particular good or service might satisfy different levels of needs at the same time.
   c. all consumers satisfy needs in the same order.
   d. self-esteem is an example of a social need.
   e. All of the above are true statements.

6. When consumers screen out or modify ideas, messages, and information that conflict with previously learned attitudes and beliefs, this is called:
   a. selective retention.
   b. selective exposure.
   c. selective perception.
   d. selective dissonance.
   e. selective cognition.

7.   A change in a person's thought processes caused by prior experience is called:
     a.   learning
     b.   attitude change
     c.   belief change
     d.   response
     e.   reinforcement

8.   Which of the following is not a major element in the learning process?
     a.   Drive
     b.   Cues
     c.   Dissonance
     d.   Reinforcement
     e.   Response

9.   An attitude:
     a.   is easily changed.
     b.   is a person's point of view toward something.
     c.   is the same as opinion and belief.
     d.   is a reliable indication of intention to buy.
     e.   All of the above are true statements.

10. The AIO items used in lifestyle analysis include:
     a.   activities, interests, and opinions.
     b.   attitudes, interests, and opinions.
     c.   activities, intentions, and opinions.
     d.   attitudes, intentions, and opinions.
     e.   attitudes, income, and opinions.

11. Which of the following is *not* a social influence?
     a.   Culture
     b.   Social class
     c.   Family
     d.   Reference group
     e.   Personality

12. Which of the following statements about social class is NOT true?
     a.   The various classes tend to have different beliefs and feelings.
     b.   The various classes tend to prefer to shop in different stores.
     c.   The various classes tend to want different types of treatment by salespeople.
     d.   In the U.S., the social class system is less rigid than in most other countries.
     e.   In the U.S., the system for measuring social class is based mainly on a person's income.

13. According to the text, social class in the U.S. is usually measured in terms of:
     a.   income.
     b.   occupation, education, and housing arrangements.
     c.   income, occupation, and education.
     d.   race, religion, and occupation.
     e.   income, occupation, and religion.

14. For which of the following products would reference group influence probably be *least important?*
   a. Clothing
   b. Cigarettes
   c. Furniture
   d. Canned peaches
   e. Wine

15. Opinion leaders are:
   a. usually better educated.
   b. usually reference group leaders.
   c. not necessarily opinion leaders on all subjects.
   d. usually wealthy, middle- or upper-class people.
   e. All of the above are true statements.

16. Behavioral scientists recognize different *levels* of consumer problem solving. Which of the following is *not* one of these levels?
   a. Routinized response behavior
   b. Limited problem solving
   c. Rational problem solving
   d. Extensive problem solving
   e. All of the above are recognized levels of problem solving.

17. Dissonance is:
   a. a type of cue.
   b. a form of laziness commonly observed among low-income consumers.
   c. a type of positive reinforcement.
   d. tension caused by uncertainty about the rightness of a decision.
   e. none of the above.

18. Which of the following gives the proper *ordering* of the steps in the "adoption process"?
   a. Awareness, interest, trial, evaluation, decision, dissonance
   b. Awareness, interest, trial, decision, evaluation, confirmation
   c. Awareness, interest, evaluation, trial, decision, confirmation
   d. Interest, awareness, trial, decision, evaluation, dissonance
   e. Awareness, interest, evaluation, decision, trial, confirmation

19. In developing marketing mixes for consumers in international markets, marketing managers should:
   a. generalize from one culture to another.
   b. use their intuition.
   c. know about the specific social and intrapersonal variables.
   d. follow their beliefs.
   e. all of the above.

20. The present state of our knowledge about consumer behavior is such that:
   a. the behavioral sciences provide the marketing manager with a complete explanation of the "whys" of consumer behavior.
   b. a marketing manager usually must blend intuition and judgment with findings from the behavioral sciences to explain and predict consumer behavior.
   c. relevant market dimensions can be easily identified and measured using "psychographics."
   d. marketing research can't tell us much more about specific aspects of consumer behavior.
   e. All of the above are true statements.

Answers to Multiple-Choice Questions

1. d, p. 153
2. a, p. 154
3. d, p. 153-54
4. b, p. 155-56
5. b, p. 157
6. c, p. 157
7. a, p. 158

8. c, p. 158
9. b, p. 159
10. a, p. 162
11. e, p. 163
12. e, p. 164
13. b, p. 164
14. d, p. 165

15. c, p. 165
16. c, p. 169
17. d, p. 169
18. c, p. 170-71
19. c, p. 172
20. b, p. 173

Exercise 6-1

Psychological variables and social influences affect consumer buying behavior

Introduction

To plan good marketing strategies, marketing managers must try to improve their understanding of buying behavior. Ideally, marketers would like to know *how* and *why* individual consumers buy the way they do. Then it might be possible to group individual consumers with similar needs and buying behavior into homogeneous market segments for which suitable marketing mixes could be developed.

This is easier said than done, however, because human behavior is very complex. Traditional demographic analysis, for example, can be used to study basic trends in consumer spending patterns, but it is of little use in explaining *why* people like, choose, buy, and use the products and brands they do.

For this reason, many marketers have turned to the behavioral sciences for help in understanding how and why consumers behave as they do. However, there is no "grand theory" available right now which ties together all the behavioral theories and concepts in a way which will explain and predict all aspects of human behavior. Therefore, marketers must try to understand the various behavioral theories and concepts. Then they can put them together into a model of consumer behavior that works in their own particular situation.

Hopefully, the complex decision-making processes that take place within the buyer behavior model are clearer to you after reading Chapter 6 of the text. Although the model presented in the text can't explain or predict consumer behavior, it does provide a useful framework that identifies the major variables that influence consumer behavior.

This exercise should improve your understanding of various psychological (*intra*personal) variables and social (*inter*personal) influences that may affect a consumer's behavior. You will recall from Chapter 6 that psychological variables focus on the individual while social influences involve relations with others.

Assignment

In the short cases that follow, a variety of psychological variables and social influences are operating to influence a consumer's response. For each case, identify the relevant psychological variables and social influences and briefly explain how each item is illustrated in the case. The first case has been completed for you as an example.

1.   Carlos and Faith Gumucio and their two children are considering the purchase of a recreational vehicle. Carlos is enthusiastic because, he argues, the RV would be perfect for family camping trips, as well as fishing trips with his friends. Faith is less in favor of the purchase. She is nervous about camping in remote locations--and wonders how they would get help in emergencies. She also remembers a report that RVs get low gas mileage and are, therefore, expensive to run. Carlos is quick to point out that the same report described the large potential savings of a weeklong vacation in an RV compared to staying at a hotel or motel.

a.   Psychological variables
   1)   *PSSP hierarchy*   Explanation: *Faith is afraid of being isolated--safety needs.*
   2)   *Selective Processes* Explanation: *Faith only remembers the part of the report that supports her viewpoint.*

b.   Social influences
   1)   *Family*   Explanation: *Carlos wants to take family on camping vacations, but Faith is concerned about the family's safety.*
   2)   *Reference Group*   Explanation: *Carlos wants to take his friends on a fishing trip in "his" RV.*

2.   Eli Hahn has had a cold--and all of the typical symptoms that come with it--for almost a week. At first he hadn't taken any medicine. He had always felt that there wasn't anything you could do about a cold. However, while he was playing cards at the home of some friends they kidded him about his runny, red nose. When they offered him an Advil cold and flu tablet, he figured it wouldn't hurt to try it. To his surprise, he felt much better after taking the tablet. The next morning, he stopped at a drugstore on his way to work and bought a package of the medicine. Eli had never heard of Advil before, but while driving home from work that evening he noticed a large billboard for Advil.

a.   Psychological variables

   1) _____ Explanation: _____

   _____

   2) _____ Explanation: _____

   _____

   3) _____ Explanation: _____

   _____

b.   Social Influences

1) _____ Explanation: _____

_____

2) _____ Explanation: _____

_____

3.   Melodye Hadley just returned from a year in Japan as an exchange student. To see her old friends, she is planning a dinner party with a traditional Japanese menu. As she is grocery shopping, she recalls her first experience with sushi--a raw fish delicacy she plans to serve at her party. When her host family first served it to her, she was not sure she would be able to eat it. Nothing in her American upbringing had prepared her to eat raw fish. However, she did not want to offend her hosts, so she smiled bravely and downed the sushi. To her amazement it was delicious, and she now enjoys sushi frequently. She is sure she will have a lot of fun persuading her friends to try it too.

a.   Psychological variables

1) _____ Explanation: _____

_____

2) _____ Explanation: _____

_____

3) _____ Explanation: _____

_____

b.   Social Influences

1) _____ Explanation: _____

_____

2) _____ Explanation: _____

_____

4.   Portia Begay is planning to buy a DVD recorder, but is unsure where she wants to shop or what brand she wants to buy. She has asked her boss, who is an "electronics nut," for his advice, and she has started looking at websites to find out about the features of different brands. She is most interested in a Sony brand unit that is compatible with all major DVD formats (many recorders work with only a subset of the formats), including the one used by the DVD drive in her computer. The Sony unit also comes with a wireless receiver that allows her to transfer video from her digital video camera without hooking up any cables. An added plus is that the DVD recorder's remote control unit would also work with her Sony TV, which she has had for a year and found very satisfactory. In addition, her boyfriend thinks that the Sony offers "a good value for the price," although it is more expensive than what she had originally expected to spend.

a.   Psychological variables

1) _____ Explanation: _____

_____

2) _____ Explanation: _____

_____

3) _____ Explanation: _____

_____

b.   Social Influences

1) _____ Explanation: _____

_____

2) _____ Explanation: _____

_____

5. Seth and Elsa Robbins are trying to decide where to go on a vacation trip. Seth had been interested in going to the Florida Keys, but they rejected that alternative based on reports from friends that it wasn't that interesting. They briefly considered a trip to Aruba, but Elsa didn't like the idea of "leaving the country." Two very expensive resorts in Palm Beach were also considered, but rejected because both Seth and Elsa were afraid they would feel out of place at such "fancy" accommodations. Finally, they settle on a moderate-priced motel near Disneyland and Epcot Center, where they have previously enjoyed relaxing visits.

    a.   Psychological variables

        1) _____ Explanation: _____

        _____

        2) _____ Explanation: _____

        _____

        3) _____ Explanation: _____

        _____

    b.   Social Influences

        1) _____ Explanation: _____

        _____

        2) _____ Explanation: _____

        _____

Question for Discussion

Which items--psychological variables or social influences--have the most influence over consumer behavior and thus are more important for the marketing strategy planner?

Exercise 6-2

Consumer decision process

Introduction

While consumer behavior may often appear to be quite irrational to the casual observer, most behavioral scientists agree that consumers are *problem solvers* seeking to relieve tension caused by their unsatisfied needs. How an individual consumer goes about solving problems depends on the intrapersonal and interpersonal variables that affect that individual. In general, however, most consumers tend to follow a five-step decision process (see Exhibit 6-10 on page 171 of the text):

1. Becoming aware of need.
2. Gathering information about choices.
3. Setting criteria and evaluating alternatives--perhaps trying some out.
4. Deciding on the solution.
5. Evaluating the purchase experience.

The length of time it takes to complete the decision process and how much attention is given to each of the five steps depends, of course, on the nature of the problem and how much experience an individual has had in trying to solve this particular kind of problem. To understand the process better, it helps to recognize three levels of problem solving: *extensive problem solving, limited problem solving,* and *routinized response behavior.* See Exhibit 6-9 on page 169 of text.

The purpose of this exercise is to illustrate the three levels of consumer problem solving by relating them to *your* consumer decision experiences in the marketplace.

Assignment

Think of *three* recent purchases that *you* made that involved extensive problem solving, limited problem solving, and routinized response behavior. For each of these purchases, outline the decision process that you used. You may wish to follow the five-step process listed above, indicating how you went about performing each of the five steps.

1.   Routinized response behavior: Product _____

        Explanation:

2.   Limited problem-solving: Product _____

        Explanation:

3.   Extensive problem-solving: Product _____

        Explanation:

Question for Discussion

Which of the three levels of problem solving offers marketers the most opportunity? The least opportunity? Why?

Exercise 6-3

Selective processes

This exercise is based on computer-aided problem number 6--Selective Processes. A complete description of the problem appears on page 175 of *Basic Marketing*, 16th edition.

1. Submag's marketing manager analyzed the response of a previous mailing to customers on the first mailing list. She found that 3,105 subscriptions were received from a total mailing of 25,000 promotion pieces.

    What percent of the people who received the initial mailing subscribed? _____

2. By analyzing subscription orders from the first list by zip code area, she found that the orders from people who lived in large cities averaged $4.00, substantially higher than their "country cousins." She concluded that city residents were more interested in her magazines. The company that provided the first mailing list said that it could use a computer to sort future lists so that Submag only got names and addresses of people who live in large cities. This service would cost an extra $.02 per name (mailing). Would it make sense for Submag to target its promotion at people who live in large cities and spend more (i.e., by using the sorted mailing list)? Explain your answer.

    _____

    _____

    _____

3. Submag's marketing manager thinks that people who live in large cities are also less likely to miss the point of the ads. This would result in losing fewer potential customers due to selective perception. Assuming 25,000 mailings, do an analysis that shows how the number of subscribers and expected profit change as the percent of consumers lost due to selective perception varies between 50 percent to 70 percent, and then answer the questions below. (Note: remember that city dwellers are likely to spend an average of $4.00 per subscription, and that it will cost $.34 per mailing).

In this situation, how many subscribers would be required to earn a profit of $8,060?

_____ number of subscribers

At a profit of $8,060, what percent of potential customers would be lost due to selective perception?

_____ percent

If the percentage of customers lost due to selective perception were reduced from the above percent to 52 percent, what would the difference in expected profits be?

$ _____.00 profit at 52 percent lost due to selective perception

- 8.060.00

$_____ difference in profit if selective perception is reduced

4. The supplier of the first list has told Submag's marketing manager that other direct mail marketers have found that people in large cities are more likely to open the envelope and read a mailing if the name is printed directly on the envelope (instead of on an adhesive mailing label) or if the name and address is printed on the letter itself. It would cost Submag an extra 2 cents per mailing to add this personalizing. This would probably reduce the number of people who threw out the mailings without opening them. If using the sorted mailing list and personalizing the letters reduced the percentage of potential customers lost due to selective exposure to 4 percent, would it make sense for Submag to go to the extra expense of personalizing the letters? Explain your answer.

_____

_____

_____

_____

_____

_____

Chapter 7

Business and organizational customers and their buying behavior

What This Chapter Is About

Chapter 7 discusses the buying behavior of the important business and organizational customers who buy for resale or for use in their own businesses. They buy more goods and services than final customers! There are many opportunities in marketing to producers, to intermediaries, to government, and to nonprofit organizations--and it is important to understand how these organizational customers buy.

Organizations tend to be much more economic in their buying behavior than final consumers. Further, some must follow pre-set bidding and bargaining processes. Yet, they too have emotional needs. And sometimes a number of different people may influence the final purchase decision. Keep in mind that business and organizational customers are problem solvers too. Many of the ideas in Chapter 6 carry over, but with some adaptation.

This chapter deserves careful study because your past experience as a consumer is not as helpful here as it was in the last few chapters. Organizational customers are much less numerous. In some cases it is possible to create a separate marketing mix for each individual customer. Understanding these customers is necessary to plan marketing strategies for them. Try to see how they are both similar and different from final customers.

Important Terms

business and organizational customers, p. 178
purchasing specifications, p. 181
ISO 9000, p. 181
purchasing managers, p. 181
multiple buying influence, p. 182
buying center, p. 183
vendor analysis, p. 183
requisition, p. 185
new-task buying, p. 186
straight rebuy, p. 186
modified rebuy, p. 186

just-in-time delivery, p. 189-90
negotiated contract buying, p. 191
outsource, p. 191
reciprocity, p. 192
competitive bids, p. 194
North American Industry Classification System
(NAICS) codes, p. 198
open to buy, p. 201
resident buyers, p. 202
Foreign Corrupt Practices Act, p. 203

_____ 1. Business and organizational customers are wholesalers or retailers, but not buyers who buy to produce other goods and services.

_____ 2. Since sellers usually approach each business or organizational customer directly through a sales representative, it is possible that there can be a special marketing strategy for each individual customer.

_____ 3. Specific business customs vary little from country to country.

_____ 4. ISO 9000 assures a customer that the supplier has effective quality checks in place.

_____ 5. A salesperson usually must see the organizational buyer or purchasing manager first, before any other employee in the firm is contacted.

_____ 6. A buying center consists of all the people who participate in or influence a purchase.

_____ 7. Multiple buying influence makes the promotion job easier.

_____ 8. "Vendor analysis" involves a formal rating of suppliers on all relevant areas of performance.

_____ 9. Emotional needs are often quite relevant for the different people involved in the purchase decision, and therefore a marketing mix should satisfy both the needs of the customer company and the individual needs of those who influence the purchase.

_____ 10. A requisition is a request to buy something.

_____ 11. Strong multiple buying influence is most likely to be involved when there is new-task buying.

_____ 12. When the majority of a company's purchases involve straight rebuy buying, these purchases occupy most of an effective buyer's time.

_____ 13. Many firms are increasing the number of suppliers with whom they work—and expecting less cooperation from them.

_____ 14. "Just-in-time" delivery means reliably getting products there before or very soon after they are needed.

_____ 15. Negotiated contracts commonly are used for products that can be described sufficiently well that suppliers know what is wanted and can submit definite prices or bids.

_____ 16. Even if a supplier has developed the best marketing mix possible and cultivates a close relationship with the customer, that customer may not give all of its business to that one supplier.

_____ 17. Purchasing managers tend to resist reciprocity, but it may be forced on them by their sales departments.

___ 18. Transaction costs usually increase with B2B e-commerce.

___ 19. Competitive bids are the terms of sale offered by different suppliers in response to the purchase specifications posted by the buyer.

___ 20. Competitive bidding over the Internet is slow and inconvenient.

___ 21. Reverse auction sites foster competition among sellers.

___ 22. Auction sites foster competition among buyers.

___ 23. Organizational buyers typically do not even see a sales rep for straight rebuys since e-commerce order systems now automatically handle those orders.

___ 24. Buyers who delegate routine buying to a computer often will be more impressed by a new company's offer of an attractive marketing mix, perhaps for a whole line of products, rather than just one individual product.

___ 25. Manufacturers tend to be concentrated by geographic location and industry, and the majority of them are quite small.

___ 26. Two-digit NAICS code breakdowns start with broad industry categories, but more detailed data may be available for three-digit and four-digit industries.

___ 27. Compared to manufacturers, services firms are more numerous, smaller, and more spread out.

___ 28. Most retail and wholesale buyers see themselves as selling agents for manufacturers.

___ 29. Committee buying by retailers will probably force better strategy planning by wholesalers and manufacturers, instead of relying just on persuasive salespeople.

___ 30. The large number of items bought and stocked by wholesalers and retailers makes it imperative that inventories be watched carefully.

___ 31. The retail buyer is "open-to-buy" whenever his cost of merchandise is less than his forecasted sales.

___ 32. Resident buyers are employees of retail stores whose job it is to reach the many small manufacturers in central markets who cannot afford large sales departments.

___ 33. The government market is the largest customer group in the United States—accounting for about 30 percent of the U.S. gross domestic product.

___ 34. All government customers are required by law to use a mandatory bidding procedure that is open to public review.

___ 35. Government buyers avoid the use of negotiated contracts whenever there are a lot of intangible factors.

___ 36. The Internet is not a very effective way to locate information on potential government target markets.

___ 37. In international markets, it is legal to make small grease money payments--if they are customary in that country.

Answers to True-False Questions

1. F, p. 178	14. F, p. 189-90	27. T, p. 199-200
2. T, p. 180	15. F, p. 191	28. F, p. 200
3. F, p. 180	16. T, p. 192	29. T, p. 201
4. T, p. 181	17. T, p. 192	30. T, p. 201
5. T, p. 181	18. F, p. 192	31. F, p. 201
6. T, p. 183	19. T, p. 194	32. F, p. 202
7. F, p. 183	20. F, p. 194	33. T, p. 202
8. T, p. 183	21. T, p. 194	34. F, p. 202
9. T, p. 184	22. T, p. 194	35. F, p. 203
10. T, p. 185	23. T, p. 195	36. F, p. 203
11. T, p. 186	24. T, p. 196	37. T, p. 203
12. F, p. 186	25. T, p. 196-97	
13. F, p. 187	26. T, p. 198-99	

Multiple-Choice Questions (Circle the correct response)

1. Which of the following is a business or organizational customer?
   a. producers of goods and services.
   b. a retailer.
   c. a wholesaler.
   d. a government agency.
   e. All of the above are business and organizational customers.

2. In comparison to the buying of final consumers, the purchasing of organizational buyers:
   a. is strictly economic and not at all emotional.
   b. is always based on competitive bids from multiple suppliers.
   c. leans basically toward economy, quality, and dependability.
   d. is even less predictable.
   e. Both a and c are true statements.

3. Today, many agricultural commodities and manufactured items are subject to rigid control or grading. As a result, organizational buyers often buy on the basis of:
   a. purchasing specifications.
   b. negotiated contracts.
   c. competitive bids.

4. In a buying center, multiple buying influences can include:
   a. users.
   b. buyers.
   c. gatekeepers.
   d. deciders.
   e. all of the above.

5. A large manufacturer is about to purchase a large supply of an unfamiliar chemical that will be used in the production of an important new product. What kind of buying would the company be most likely to do?
   a. New-task buying
   b. Straight rebuy buying
   c. Modified rebuy buying

6. Close buyer-seller relationships in business markets can
   a. lower total costs because of shared tasks.
   b. reduce flexibility because of long-term commitments.
   c. provide customers with inventory exactly when it's needed.
   d. involve changes in a firm's product and procedures to satisfy just one customer.
   e. all of the above.

7. Today, when a buyer can't specify all of the details of what it will need in the future, the relationship with a supplier is most likely to involve:
   a. a reverse auction.
   b. a procurement site.
   c. negotiated contracts.
   d. competitive bids.
   e. all of the above.

8. An automobile manufacturer's practice of buying some of its raw materials from other manufacturers who in turn buy from it is an example of:
   a. a procurement site.
   b. vendor analysis.
   c. specification buying.
   d. being "open to buy."
   e. reciprocity.

9. People from sales, production, quality control, and finance are working with the purchasing department to select a new supplier. The sales manager wants to select a supplier that is also a customer for some of the firm's own products. The sales manager
   a. is a gatekeeper.
   b. is more likely to get his way if his company is located in Japan instead of the U.S.
   c. is trying to use vendor analysis to his advantage.
   d. is not a member of the buying center, so he can be ignored.
   e. none of the above.

10. B2B e-commerce sites include:
    a. online marketplaces.
    b. catalog sites.
    c. collaboration hubs.
    d. procurement sites.
    e. all of the above.

11. Which of the following NAICS codes would provide the most specific information about a sub-category of an industry?
   a.   31
   b.   315
   c.   3152
   d.   Cannot be determined without additional information.

12. If you obtain a customer's four digit NAICS code, you should know that:
   a.   this firm might be manufacturing quite different products than other firms with the same number.
   b.   the firm may also have a five digit code.
   c.   a number of other firms probably have the same code.
   d.   the firm may also have a six digit code.
   e.   All of the above are true.

13. As contrasted with manufacturers, producers of services are:
   a.   more geographically spread out.
   b.   growing fast domestically and internationally.
   c.   more numerous.
   d.   All of the above.
   e.   None of the above.

14. Which of the following statements about retail buying is *false?*
   a.   In most retail operations, a "resident buyer" runs his own department--and his decision is final.
   b.   Most retail buyers see themselves as purchasing agents for their target customers.
   c.   Retail buyers make most purchases as straight rebuys.
   d.   A retail buyer is usually "open to buy" only when s/he has not spent all of the budgeted funds.
   e.   Resident buyers are independent buying agents who help producers and middlemen reach each other inexpensively.

15. Which of the following statements about bidding for government business is *true?*
   a.   Government buying needs are hard to identify--and their primary concern is with finding the lowest price.
   b.   Government buyers avoid using negotiated contracts since they must purchase at a pre-set price.
   c.   A government buyer may be forced to accept the lowest bid that meets the specifications.
   d.   The biggest job of the government buyer is to locate enough potential suppliers so the bidding procedure works effectively.
   e.   All of the above are true statements.

16. The Foreign Corrupt Practices Act:
   a.   prohibits U.S. firms from paying bribes to foreign officials.
   b.   levies stiff penalties against people who pay bribes.
   c.   exempts managers whose agents secretly pay bribes.
   d.   was amended to allow small grease money payments if they are customary in that country.
   e.   All of the above.

1. e, p. 178
2. c, p. 179-80
3. a, p. 181
4. e, p. 182-83
5. a, p. 186
6. e, p. 187-91

7. c, p. 191
8. e, p. 192
9. b, p. 192
10. e, p. 193-94
11. c, p. 198-99
12. e, p. 198-99

13. d, p. 199-200
14. a, p. 200-202
15. c, p. 202
16. e, p. 203

Exercise 7-1

Analyzing organizational buying behavior

Introduction

Some people see organizational buying and consumer buying as two very different processes. Organizational buying is thought of as "economic," while consumer buying is seen as "emotional." In fact, closer study of buying processes suggests that organizational and consumer buying may be quite similar in many ways. For example, like consumers, organizational buyers are *problem solvers*. And while their problems may be very different, both consumer and organizational buyers seem to use three levels of problem solving. In Chapter 6, we saw that consumer buyers do extended, limited, and routinized problem solving. Similarly, organizational buyers do *new-task, straight rebuy, and modified rebuy buying.*

Recognition of the three levels of problem solving by organizational buyers *and* the different problem solving steps they pass through has important implications for market analysis. It suggests that organizational markets can be segmented not only in terms of product-related needs, industry categories, and geographic location--but also in terms of similarities and differences in buying behavior. *Each level of problem solving may require a different marketing* mix--especially in regard to the promotion variable--even when identical goods or services are involved. Knowing the nature of buying behavior at each level helps to determine the proper ingredients for a marketing mix.

This exercise shows how knowledge of organizational buying behavior can improve marketing strategy planning--in three "case" situations. You will be asked to identify the problem-solving level for a business product. Then you will discuss likely buying behavior and how this might affect a firm's marketing strategy planning.

Assignment

Assume the role of marketing manager for a large firm that produces stain-resistant fabrics that are used by furniture companies to upholster chairs, sofas, and love seats. Similar fabrics are typically available to the furniture producers from several competing suppliers, including some larger and some smaller firms. While some slight differences in patterns and colors may exist, all of the suppliers produce fashionable fabrics that meet the quality and style standards set by the customers' production and marketing departments. In fact, most of the competing suppliers use the exact same method to treat fabrics so that they will resist stains. And, with few exceptions, the prices charged by all suppliers tend to be almost identical.

Recently, you learned--from your sales force--of three potential customers whose needs might be satisfied by the fabric you sell. Read each of the three buying situations described below, and then:

a) Determine which level of problem solving--new-task buying, straight rebuy, or modified rebuy--applies to each situation.

b) Discuss in detail the probable nature of the firm's buying behavior in each situation. Which of the five decision-making steps in Chapter 6 (page 171) would be most important in each situation? Why? Which is the next most important? Why? How important would multiple buying influence be in each situation?

c) Explain how your firm might vary its marketing mix to satisfy the potential customer's needs in each situation.

Situation 1:

The potential customer has been selling a very successful line of upholstered furniture for a number of years. The company has not been using a stain-resistant fabric. But, furniture retailers have recently been complaining that the furniture gets soiled very easily. The potential customer thinks that your stain-resistant fabric could possibly be used instead of the fabric it gets from its current supplier.

a) Level of problem solving: _____

b) Nature of buying behavior:

c) Marketing mix:

Situation 2:

The customer has been purchasing a similar fabric from one of your firm's competitors for several years, but is dissatisfied with its present supplier's delivery service and technical support.

a)   Level of problem solving: _____ _____

b)   Nature of buying behavior:

c)   Marketing mix:

Situation 3:

The customer has been purchasing all of its fabric from one of your competitors on a regular basis for several years. No change in this procedure is expected.

a)   Level of problem solving: _____

b)   Nature of buying behavior:

c)   Marketing mix:

Question for Discussion

In which of the three buying situations would emotional needs be most important? Least important? To what extent does this depend on the overlap between individual buyer needs and company needs?

Exercise 7-2

Using NAICS codes to analyze business markets

Introduction

Compared to the final consumer market, business markets have a smaller number of customers and much of the buying potential is concentrated among a relatively few large firms. Further, firms within the same industry often cluster together by geographic location. For these reasons, it may be less difficult to analyze business markets than consumer markets.

Much published data is available to help the marketing manager analyze business markets. The most important source of information is the federal government--that regularly collects data on the number of establishments, their sales volumes, and number of employees for a large number of industry groups. The data is reported for North American Industry Classification System (NAICS) code industries. NAICS is a unique, all-new system for classifying business establishments. It is the first economic classification system that groups together economic units that use like processes to produce goods or services. NAICS includes some 350 new industries being separately recognized for the first time. NAICS replaces the old SIC system and reflects the structure of today's economy in the U.S., Canada, and Mexico, including the emergence and growth of the service sector and new and advanced technologies. It is a flexible system that allows each country to recognize important industries in more detail.

NAICS groups the economy into 20 broad sectors, up from the 10 divisions of the old SIC system. NAICS industries are identified by a 6-digit code, in contrast to the 4-digit SIC code. The first two digits designates a major Economic Sector (such as Manufacturing, 33, in this exercise). The third digit designates an Economic Subsector (such as Electrical Manufacturing, Equipment, and Supplies, 335, in this exercise). The fourth digit designates an Industry Group and the fifth digit the NAICS Industry. The international NAICS agreement fixes only the 1st five digits of the code. The sixth digit identifies subdivisions in individual countries. Thus, six-digit U.S. codes may differ from counterparts in Canada or Mexico, but at the five-digit level they are standardized.

Assignment

Reliable Manufacturing Company produces a line of electrical products for business markets. Reliable's recently-appointed marketing manager is currently in the process of reevaluating the firm's marketing strategy for an important product, "electric widgets," which he suspects may not be realizing its full sales potential. In particular, he feels that Reliable has been following a "mass-marketing" approach for this product and has neglected to identify which markets the product appeals to and their relative importance.

The marketing manager began his analysis by attempting to determine which six-digit NAICS industries may have some need for electric widgets. First, he analyzed past sales records for the product and assigned NAICS codes to previous and present customers. Next, he asked his sales manager to go through the NAICS manual and check off the six-digit industries that he believed would be relevant for the product. Finally, to make sure that other potential customers were not being overlooked, he conducted a survey of companies falling under other NAICS categories to find out whether they might have any possible use for the product. As a result of this analysis, a total of 12 industries were identified as potential target markets for electric widgets. These industries are listed in columns 1 and 2 of Table 7-1.

Having identified 12 potential target markets for electric widgets, the marketing manager then conducted another survey of a sample of firms belonging to each industry to determine the market potential for each industry. Included in the data he collected were the amount of each firm's annual dollar purchases for the product and the number of production workers employed. This data is summarized in columns 3 and 4 of Table 7-1. From the sample data for each NAICS industry, the marketing manager then calculated the average dollar purchases per production worker. The results are shown in column 5.

1. Complete column 5 of Table 7-1 by calculating the average dollar purchases per worker for NAICS industry #335311- transformers. Show your calculations below.

In order to project the sample data to the entire U.S. market, Reliable's marketing manager turned to the *Annual Survey of Manufacturers* to find the national total of production workers employed by each industry. From this data, shown in column 6, he was then able to estimate the national market potential for each NAICS industry by multiplying column 6 by column 5. These estimates are shown in column 7.

2. Complete column 7 of Table 7-1 by calculating the national market potential for NAICS industry #335311. Show your calculations below.

Finally, because Reliable's sales territories were aligned according to states, the marketing manager proceeded to estimate the market potential for each industry in each state. For example, he again turned to the *Annual Survey of Manufacturers* to determine the number of production workers employed in the state of Illinois for those industries that operated in Illinois. From this data, shown in column 8, he was then able to estimate the market potential for each NAICS industry within Illinois. The results, computed by multiplying column 8 by column 5, are shown in column 9.

3. Complete column 9 of Table 7-1 by calculating the market potential in Illinois for NAICS industry #335311. Show your calculations below.

TABLE 7-1
Calculation of Market Potential for "Electric Widgets" Using Market Survey Approach for National and Illinois Markets

NAICS Code	Manufacturing Potential "Industry" Target Markets	Market Survey Results			National Market Number of Production Workers (1,000)	Estimated National Market Potential ($1,000)	Illinois Market Number of Production Workers ($1,000)	Estimated Illinois Market Potential ($1,000)
		Product Purchases	Number of Production Workers	Average Purchases per Worker				
(1)	(2)	(3)	(4)	(5)	(6)	(7)	(8)	(9)
334513	Electric measuring instruments	$11,250	3,700	$3.04	45.1	$137.1	3.1	$9.4
335311	Transformers	50,150	4,616	$___	37.6	$___	3.8	$___
335312	Motors and generators	28,400	10,896	2.61	78.3	204.4	3.0	7.8
335314	Industrial controls	40,100	4,678	8.57	30.8	264.0	3.2	27.4
335221	Household cooking appliances	2,600	2,104	1.24	16.9	21.0	3.9	4.8
335222	Household refrigerators and home freezers	149,600	5,215	28.69	40.2	1,153.3	–	–
335224	Household laundry equipment	35,200	3,497	10.07	17.8	179.2	–	–
335211	Electric housewares and fans	1,200	3,208	0.37	40.3	14.9	3.7	1.4
335212	Household vacuum cleaners	1,875	402	4.66	7.5	35.0	–	–
335228	Other appliances	600	912	0.66	4.9	3.2	–	–
335121	Residential lighting	65,500	6,451	10.15	101.6	1,031.2	–	–
334111	Computers	132,100	6,889	19.18	185.7	3.561.7	7.5	143.8
	TOTAL	$518,575				$7,013.3		$235.9

Column:

(1),(2) Six-digit NAICS industries making up the industrial market for "electric widgets."

(3) Dollar value, classified by industries, of purchases of electric widgets as reported by those firms included in the survey.

(4) Number of production workers as reported by those firms included in the survey.

(5) Average dollar value of "electric widget" purchases per production worker for each NAICS industry. Computed by dividing column 3 by column

(6) Number of production workers for the entire U.S. market for the given NAICS industries.

(7) The resultant estimated national market potential for the total market. Computed by multiplying column 6 by column 5.

(8) Number of production workers for Illinois trading area for the given NAICS industries. Note: Blanks in column 8 indicate either that there are no firms in Illinois for a particular NAICS industry, or that there are only a few firms and the Census Bureau has deleted the information to avoid disclosure.

(9) The resultant estimated Illinois are market potential. Computed by multiplying column 8 by column 5.

4. a) *For all industries combined,* what percentage of the total national market potential for electric widgets is represented by the state of Illinois? Show your work below.

    b) *For NAICS industry #335311 only,* what percentage of the national market potential for electric widgets is represented by the state of Illinois? Show your work below.

5. Suppose Reliable's marketing manager learned that actual sales of his firm's electric widgets to NAICS industry #335312 amounted to about 20 percent of its national market potential for that industry--while sales to the other 11 industries ranged from 5-10 percent. Suppose further that he then decided that the firm should aim at achieving 20 percent of its national market potential in *each* of the 12 NAICS industries--and set his sales quotas accordingly. Is it likely that Reliable could achieve these sales quotas? Why or why not? Comment on this approach to marketing strategy planning.

6. Which of the 12 NAICS industries would you select as your target market(s) for the electric widgets if you were Reliable's marketing manager? Why?

    a) For the national market:

    b) For the Illinois market:

Question for Discussion

After selecting its target market(s), how could Reliable then go about identifying and reaching those firms that make up the target market(s)? What other information would be needed and how could the information be obtained?

Exercise 7-3

Vendor analysis

This exercise is based on computer-aided problem number 7--Vendor Analysis. A complete description of the problem appears on page 205 of *Basic Marketing,* 16th edition.

1. Supplier 2 is thinking about adding U.S. wholesalers to its channel of distribution. The supplier would ship in large, economical quantities to the wholesaler and the wholesaler would keep a stock of chips on hand. The wholesaler would charge CompuTech a higher price--$1.90 a chip. But with the chips available from a reliable wholesaler CompuTech's inventory cost as a percent of its total order would only be 2 percent. In addition, the cost of transportation would only be $.01 per chip. Assuming CompuTech planned to buy 84,500 chips, what would its total costs be with and without the wholesaler? Should CompuTech encourage the supplier to add a wholesaler to the channel?

    Total Costs for Vendor Supplier 2, buying direct   _____

    Total Costs for Vendor Supplier 2, using wholesaler   _____

    _____

    _____

    _____

2. Supplier 2 has explored the idea of adding wholesalers to the channel, but has found that it will take at least another year to find suitable wholesalers and develop relationships. As a result, if CompuTech deals with Supplier 2 its inventory cost as a percent of the total order would remain at 5.4 percent, and transportation cost would remain at $.03 per chip. But the supplier is still interested in improving its marketing mix now--so it can develop a strong relationship with CompuTech. Based on an analysis of CompuTech's needs, Supplier 2 has developed a new design for the electronic memory chips.

    The redesigned chips would have a built-in connector, so CompuTech would not have to buy separate connectors. In addition, the new design would make it faster and easier to replace a defective chip. The supplier estimates that with the new design it would cost CompuTech only $1.00 to replace a bad chip.

    The supplier has not yet priced the new chip, but it would cost the supplier an additional $.06 to produce each chip. If the supplier set the price of the chip at $1.93 each (the old price of $1.87 plus the additional $.06), how much would the new design cost CompuTech on an order of 84,500 chips. (Hint: compute CompuTech's total cost for the current design based on an order quantity of 84,500 chips, and then compute the total cost assuming the new price, the reduced cost of replacing a defective chip, and no cost for a connector.)

For Supplier 2:

Total Cost for Vendor, old version of chip _____

Total Cost for Vendor, redesigned chip _____

Change in total cost _____

3. The supplier is thinking about pricing the new design at a price higher than $1.93--so it can make more profit than it would have made with the old design. But the supplier also wants CompuTech's total cost to be lower than it would have been with the old design. What price would you recommend? Explain the reason for your recommendation. (Hint: set the values on the spreadsheet to correspond to CompuTech's costs if it buys the new design, but vary its cost--the supplier's price--for the chips and display CompuTech's total vendor cost.)

Price Supplier 2 should charge for the new chips _____

Explanation: _____

_____

_____

_____

_____

_____

Chapter 8

Improving decisions with marketing information

What This Chapter Is About

Marketing managers need information to plan effective marketing strategies. Chapter 8 stresses that getting good information for marketing decisions involves much more than just surveys.

Many managers now rely on marketing information systems and intranets to help meet their recurring information needs. But marketing managers must also deal with ever-changing needs in dynamic markets. So you should understand how marketing research can help marketing managers solve problems--and make better decisions.

A scientific approach to marketing research is explained and illustrated. This approach can help marketing managers solve problems--not just collect data.

This chapter also shows that the text's strategy planning framework is especially helpful in identifying marketing problems. This framework, along with a "scientific approach," can be very helpful in solving real problems. Often, small bits of information available *now* are far more valuable than an extensive research report that cannot be available for several months.

Try to understand how to go about a scientific approach to problem solving--just finding the right problem is sometimes half the job. This is something you should be able to do by the end of the text--even though you do not have all the tools and skills needed to do a formal research project. Specialists can be hired to do that part of the job if you--as the marketing manager--have correctly identified what information is needed to make the marketing strategy decisions.

Important Terms

marketing research, p. 208
marketing information system (MIS), p. 208
intranet, p. 211
data warehouse, p. 211
decision support system (DSS), p. 211
search engine, p. 211
marketing model, p. 212
scientific method, p. 213
hypotheses, p. 213
marketing research process, p. 214
situation analysis, p. 215
secondary data, p. 216
primary data, p. 216

research proposal, p. 218
qualitative research, p. 219
focus group interview, p. 219
quantitative research, p. 220
response rate, p. 221
consumer panels, p. 223
experimental method, p. 224
statistical packages, p. 226
population, p. 227
sample, p. 227
confidence intervals, p. 228
validity, p. 228

True-False Questions

____ 1. Marketing research is best defined as a set of techniques applied by specialists in survey design or statistical methods.

____ 2. The key advantage in using an MIS is that it makes information continually available and accessible.

____ 3. A marketing information system is an organized way of using "one-shot" research projects to gather, access, and analyze information that will help marketing managers make better decisions.

____ 4. Marketing research details may be handled by staff or outside specialists, but the marketing manager must know how to promote communication and cooperation in getting the information required.

____ 5. Intranets are common in firms of all sizes.

____ 6. A decision support system (DSS) is a computer program that makes it easy for a marketing manager to get and use information as he or she is making decisions.

____ 7. Marketing managers who have decision support systems probably don't need search engines also.

____ 8. Decision support systems that include marketing models allow the manager to see how answers to questions might change in various situations.

____ 9. The scientific method is a decision-making approach that focuses on being objective and orderly in testing ideas before accepting them.

____ 10. Hypotheses are statements of fact about relationships between things or what will happen in the future.

____ 11. The marketing research process is a five-step application of the scientific method that includes: defining the problem, analyzing the situation, getting problem-specific data, interpreting the data, and solving the problem.

____ 12. Defining the problem is usually the easiest job of the marketing researcher.

____ 13. Developing a list that includes all possible problem areas is a sensible start to the situation analysis step.

____ 14. Gathering primary data about the problem area is part of analyzing the situation.

____ 15. Secondary data is information that is already collected or published.

____ 16. Much secondary data can be found on the Internet.

___ 17. Even though there's a lot of secondary data on the Internet, there are no good tools for finding it.

___ 18. Standard website search engines can miss important databases.

___ 19. Almost all U.S. government data is available online and in inexpensive publications.

___ 20. The *Statistical Abstract of the United States* is a good source of primary data.

___ 21. The *Statistical Abstract of the United States* is an excellent source of secondary data in print form, but unfortunately it is not yet available on the Internet.

___ 22. A written research proposal is a plan that specifies what marketing research information will be obtained and how.

___ 23. Misunderstandings between marketing managers and technical experts can be avoided by using written research proposals.

___ 24. The two basic methods for obtaining information about customers are questioning and observing.

___ 25. Qualitative research seeks in-depth, open-ended responses.

___ 26. A focus group interview involves interviewing 6 to 10 people in an informal group setting.

___ 27. Focus groups are now being held online as well as in person.

___ 28. Focus groups are popular in consumer markets, but not business markets.

___ 29. Focus groups are a way to gather primary data quickly and at a relatively low cost.

___ 30. Focus groups are a way to gather secondary data quickly and cheaply.

___ 31. It is typical to use quantitative research in preparation for doing qualitative research.

___ 32. Quantitative research seeks structured responses that can be summarized in numbers --like percentages, averages, or other statistics.

___ 33. A common quantitative research approach is to use survey questionnaires with simple fill-in-a-number questions.

___ 34. The response rate is the percent of people contacted who complete a questionnaire.

___ 35. Mail, e-mail, and online surveys are economical per questionnaire--if a large number of people respond.

___ 36. A mail survey is the best research approach if you want respondents to expand on particular points and give in-depth information.

___ 37. With the observation method, the researcher avoids talking to the subject.

38. Customers' use of online shopping services on the Internet allow retailers to observe customers' behavior without talking to them.

39. A device called the "people meter" provides observation of television audiences.

40. The use of computer scanners to observe what customers actually do is changing research methods for many firms.

41. A consumer panel is a group of consumers who provide information occasionally --whenever a meeting of the group is called.

42. With the experimental method, the responses of groups that are similar, except on the characteristic being tested, are compared.

43. The experimental method is used in test-marketing of new products (for example, when a company tries variations of its marketing mix in different geographic areas).

44. Syndicated research is an economical approach for collecting research data needed by many different firms.

45. About 40 percent of marketing research spending is for syndicated research.

46. One should always seek to obtain as much marketing information as possible before making a decision.

47. Statistical packages are easy-to-use computer programs that help analyze data.

48. In regard to marketing research, *population* means the total group that responds to a survey.

49. In most marketing research studies, only a sample--a part of the relevant population--is surveyed.

50. With random samples, researchers can narrow confidence intervals by increasing sample sizes.

51. Validity concerns the extent to which data measures what it is intended to measure.

52. Conducting and interpreting a marketing research project should be left entirely to the researcher because most marketing managers have no training in this area.

53. Marketing managers are of less importance in international marketing research efforts because of the greater need for local experts.

1. F, p. 208	19. T, p. 217	37. T, p. 222
2. T, p. 208	20. F, p. 218	38. T, p. 223
3. F, p. 208	21. F, p. 218	39. T, p. 223
4. T, p. 209	22. T, p. 218	40. T, p. 223
5. T, p. 211	23. T, p. 219	41. F, p. 223
6. T, p. 211	24. T, p. 219	42. T, p. 224
7. F, p. 211	25. T, p. 219	43. T, p. 225
8. T, p. 212	26. T, p. 219	44. T, p. 226
9. T, p. 213	27. T, p. 219	45. T, p. 226
10. F, p. 213	28. F, p. 219	46. F, p. 211,226
11. T, p. 214	29. T, p. 220	47. T, p. 226
12. F, p. 214	30. F, p. 220	48. F, p. 227
13. T, p. 215	31. F, p. 220	49. T, p. 227
14. F, p. 216	32. T, p. 220	50. T, p. 228
15. T, p. 216	33. T, p. 221	51. T, p. 228
16. T, p. 216	34. T, p. 221	52. F, p. 228
17. F, p. 216	35. T, p. 221	53. F, p. 229
18. T, p. 216	36. F, p. 222	

Multiple-Choice Questions (Circle the correct response)

1. In small companies,
   a. there is no need for marketing research.
   b. there should be a marketing research department--or there will be no one to do marketing research.
   c. the emphasis of marketing research should be on customer surveys.
   d. salespeople often do what marketing research gets done.
   e. there usually isn't enough money for a manager to use a search engine.

2. Marketing research:
   a. requires a market research department in the company.
   b. consists mainly of survey design and statistical techniques.
   c. should be planned by research specialists.
   d. can be used by nonprofits as well as for-profit organizations.
   e. All of the above are true.

3. Which of the following statements about marketing information systems is *true?*
   a. Marketing information systems are used to gather, access, and analyze data from intracompany sources, while marketing research deals with external sources.
   b. Decision support systems allow managers to see how answers to questions might change in different situations.
   c. Computerized marketing information systems tend to increase the quantity of information available for decision making but not without some corresponding decrease in quality.
   d. The value of decision support systems is limited because the manager can't use them while he is actually making his decisions.
   e. All of the above are true statements.

4. The scientific method is important in marketing research because it:
   a. forces the researcher to follow certain procedures, thereby reducing the need to rely on intuition.
   b. develops hypotheses and then tests them.
   c. specifies a marketing strategy which is almost bound to succeed.
   d. Both a and b are correct.
   e. All of the above are correct.

5. The most difficult step of the marketing research process is:
   a. analyzing the situation.
   b. collecting data.
   c. observation.
   d. defining the problem.
   e. interpreting the data.

6. A small manufacturing firm has just experienced a rapid drop in sales. The marketing manager thinks that he knows what the problem is and has been carefully analyzing secondary data to check his thinking. His next step should be to:
   a. conduct an experiment.
   b. develop a formal research project to gather primary data.
   c. conduct informal discussion with outsiders, including middlemen, to see if he has correctly defined the problem.
   d. develop a hypothesis and predict the future behavior of sales.
   e. initiate corrective action before sales drop any further.

7. When analyzing the situation, the marketing analyst:
   a. sizes up the situation by talking with executives in competitive companies.
   b. searches the Internet for information that is already available in the problem area.
   c. begins to talk informally to a random sample of customers.
   d. talks to experts in data analysis at trade association meetings.
   e. All of the above.

8. Popular search engines for locating secondary data on the Internet can be found at the websites for:
   a. Google.
   b. Ask.
   c. Yahoo.
   d. All of the above.
   e. None of the above.

9. Which of the following is a good source for locating secondary data:
   a. a focus group interview.
   b. personal interviews with customers.
   c. the *Statistical Abstract of the United States*.
   d. a marketing research survey.
   e. none of the above.

10. A research proposal
   a. should be written by the marketing manager--not the researcher--since the manager knows what needs to be done.
   b. usually can't provide much information about how data will be collected, since it is hard to tell until the research is started.
   c. might lead a marketing manager to decide that the proposed research will cost more than it is worth.
   d. is a plan developed during the problem definition stage of research.
   e. All of the above are true.

11. A marketing analyst would *not* use which of the following research methods when gathering primary data?
   a. Observation
   b. Experiment
   c. Mail survey
   d. Library search
   e. Personal interviews

12. With regard to getting problem-specific data:
   a. the observation method involves asking consumers direct questions about their observations.
   b. surveys distributed by e-mail are declining in popularity.
   c. focus group interviews are usually more representative than a set of personal interviews.
   d. telephone surveys are limited to short, simple questions—they don't allow the interviewer to learn what a respondent is really thinking.
   e. None of the above is a true statement.

13. To be effective, marketing research should be:
   a. quantitative.
   b. qualitative.
   c. either or both--depending on the situation.

14. A marketing researcher wants to do in-depth research on business customers' experiences with the company's products. She is MOST likely to get what she wants if she uses
   a. an e-mail survey.
   b. the focus group approach.
   c. the observation approach.
   d. personal interviews.
   e. None of the above is very useful for getting in-depth information about business customers' attitudes.

15. Experimental method research:
   a. is often used in test-marketing of new products.
   b. can use either questioning or observing.
   c. compares the responses of two or more groups that are similar EXCEPT on the characteristic being tested.
   d. is used to compare groups for differences.
   e. all of the above.

16. Which of the following statements about marketing research is *false?*
    a. A low response rate may affect the accuracy of results.
    b. Managers never get all the information they would like to have.
    c. Getting more or better information is not always worth the cost.
    d. Because of the risks involved, marketing managers should never base their decision on incomplete information.
    e. A marketing manager should evaluate *beforehand* whether research findings will be relevant.

17. A statistical package is most likely to be used for a marketing research project that:
    a. used focus group interviews.
    b. relied on secondary data.
    c. included a mail, e-mail, or online survey.
    d. consisted of open-ended questions in a personal interview.
    e. was based on qualitative research.

18. At the step when data are interpreted, a marketing manager should:
    a. leave it to the technical specialists to draw the correct conclusions.
    b. realize that statistical summaries from a sample may not be precise for the whole population.
    c. know that quantitative survey responses are valid, but qualitative research may not be valid.
    d. be satisfied with the sample used as long as it is large.
    e. All of the above are correct.

Answers to Multiple-Choice Questions

1. d, p. 208
2. d, p. 209
3. b, p. 211
4. d, p. 213
5. d, p. 214
6. c, p. 215

7. b, p. 216
8. d, p. 216
9. c, p. 218
10. c, p. 218
11. d, p. 219
12. e, p. 219-23

13. c, p. 219
14. d, p. 222
15. e, p. 224-25
16. d, p. 211,226
17. c, p. 226
18. b, p. 227-28

Exercise 8-1

Controlling an Internet or intranet search for secondary data

Introduction

Marketing managers often fail to take full advantage of all the information that is available to help them make effective decisions. While time and cost factors usually prevent a manager from obtaining perfect information, there is often much more information--already collected and readily available--than managers actually use.

On the other hand, too many marketers tend to be "survey researchers" who feel they must always rush out to gather original data--i.e., *primary data*--whenever some problem arises. They tend to overlook the large amount of *secondary data* that is already available for free--or for a fee--that is usually far less than the cost of a "start from scratch" effort to obtain primary data. Information that is relevant to a problem or decision often is available in the firm's internal records, in various published sources, or from a variety of online sources that often can be tapped from a manager's desktop computer.

Most managers sooner or later turn to a search engine to help find information available from websites on the Internet or from their firms' own intranets. Using a search engine can really help to speed up a search and zero in on the right information. However, sometimes a search for a simple term will return hundreds or even thousands of links--many of which are not directly relevant to the manager's interest but which take time to review.

Most search engines allow the user to control the search and make it more specific--by entering the search term using special formats. Knowing how to use this sort of feature helps the user zero in on the right information--and screen out information that is not useful--more quickly and efficiently. So, the purpose of this exercise is to give you a feel for the different ways that you can control a search. For this exercise, we will focus on the search term formats used by Yahoo (www.yahoo.com). However, Google and many other search engines offer the same features and often they are based on exactly the same formatting approaches ("search syntax"). This is a pencil and paper exercise and you do NOT need to have an Internet connection or use Yahoo to complete it. However, you'll immediately see the advantages of what you're learning if you try a search (on a topic of interest to you) and experiment with the different search formats discussed below.

Assignment

In this assignment, several different marketing management decision-making situations are briefly described. In each case, there is a description of the type of information that is of interest to the manager. Your job is to provide search terms that would help the search engine focus the search on finding links to information that is most relevant to the manager's problem. You are also asked to provide a brief explanation of what you are trying to accomplish with each search term. Table 8-1 (below) summarizes some of the special formatting approaches that you can use to focus a search, and gives an example of how each of them might be used. Study the table and then use it as a guide to developing the search terms and explanations you provide for each case. The first case is completed for you as an example.

Table 8-1
Tips for Better Searching with the Yahoo Search Engine*

What You Are Trying to Do, *and* *How To Do It*	Example	Search Term You Would Enter
Get a list of links to web pages where a particular word is found: *Simply type the word*	Search for references to the allergy drug, *Allegra*	Allegra
Get a list of links to web pages where *any* of several words are found: *Type one search word, then a space, then the next word, and continue for as many words as you want.*	Search for references to the allergy drug *Allegra* or for the allergy drug *Claritin*	Allegra Claritin
Search for words that are part of a phrase: *Put quote marks around the whole phrase*	Search for references to the phrase *allergy symptoms*	"allergy symptoms"
Get a list of links to web pages that must include certain words: *Attach a + in front of words that must appear in the results document*	Search for references that include both the word *allergy* and the word *symptoms*, but not necessarily together as a phrase.	+allergy +symptoms
Specify a word that must *not* appear in the results list: *Attach a – in front of word that must not appear in the results*	Find references to the allergy drug *Allegra* but exclude references to the rock band, *Allegra Rocks*	Allegra -Rocks
Combine any of the above into a single request: *Type one formatted term and then a space and then the next formatted term and so on until they are all entered*	Find references to the term *allergy symptoms* and the allergy drug *Allegra* but not the *Allegra Performing Arts Center*	+ "allergy symptoms" +Allegra -"Performing Arts Center"

1.   Rosita Perez has just been appointed product manager at Lubricant Technology, Inc. after a number of years in field sales and customer support positions. She is now responsible for strategy planning for the firm's SiLube brand of silicon-based machine lubricants. However, because the previous product manager left the company before she was appointed, she feels that she needs a lot more background on her new brand and her new job responsibilities. Her first thought is to do a search on her firm's intranet to see what she can find that's relevant.

Search term: *SiLube "marketing plan"*

Explanation: *This search should find all pages on the fimn's intranet that reference the word* SiLube *or the phrase* marketing plan *(but not pages that just include a reference the word marketing or the word plan by themselves).*

2.   Ms. Perez tried the searches given in the example above, but each search has returned a report with hundreds of links. To help narrow things down for an initial look, she has decided to try to find only marketing plans that actually reference the SiLube brand.

Search term: _____

Explanation: _____

_____

_____

3.   Ms. Perez was talking with another manager about trying to improve the new-product development process for SiLube brands. Her colleague said, "I got a flyer on a new-product development conference that's going to be San Antonio, or maybe it was Dallas, next month. It might be a good place to get ideas. But, I don't remember the details about the conference and unfortunately I threw the flyer away."

Search term: _____

Explanation: _____

_____

_____

4.   Jacob Mann is the marketing manager for a biotech startup firm that is developing a new medicine for treatment of respiratory disorders. Its first product is showing promising results in first stage clinical trials with patients, but it will be some time before the firm will be able to get approval from the Food and Drug Administration to release the drug. Mann has learned from a contact at the American Lung Association that another firm, United Therapeutics, is working on several products in the same area. Mann is interested in finding out anything he can about United Therapeutics or its LungRx subsidiary.

Search term: _____

Explanation: _____

_____

_____

5.   Greta Cheney is evaluating the market for various types of household appliances and wants to see if there is Census Bureau data available on the Internet for how many households have microwave ovens, air conditioners, trash compactors, and dishwashers.

Search term: _____

Explanation: _____

_____

_____

6.   Ira DeBerry is the sales manager for Midwest Ford, a large Ford dealership with facilities in a number of cities. In the past, the Ford Taurus was one of the firm's best selling models, but since the Taurus was redesigned and the list price was raised, sales have been slow. DeBerry's salespeople have complained that they keep losing sales to the Toyota Camry. DeBerry wants to prepare a sales kit to give his sales reps a lot more information about the Taurus, including information based on what favorable product reviews have said. He did an initial search of the Internet to look for automobile reviews. His search on the word Taurus produced many thousands of links, but as he started reviewing the links in detail he found that most of them were to web pages concerned with astrology (where Taurus was usually referenced as one of the astrological "signs.")

Search term: _____

Explanation: _____

_____

_____

7.   DeBerry (case above) has decided to refine his search to see if he can find web pages that discuss both the Taurus and the Camry and that discuss crash tests.

Search term: _____

Explanation: _____

_____

_____

Question for Discussion

With so much *secondary* data readily available from the Internet and from other sources, why is there ever a need for a marketing manager to gather *primary* data?

Exercise 8-2

Evaluating marketing research

Introduction

Marketing managers need good information to develop effective marketing strategies. They need to know about the marketing environment variables, about possible target customers, and about the marketing mix decisions they can make.

Sometimes the only way to get needed information is with marketing research. When this is the case, the manager can sometimes get help--perhaps from marketing research specialists in the firm or from outside specialists. But, marketing managers must be able to explain what their problems are--and what kinds of information they need. They should also know about some of the basic decisions made during the research process--so they know the limitations of the research. They need to be able to see if the results of a research project will really solve the problem!

It is true that marketing research can involve many technical details--that is why specialists are often involved. But, often a marketing manager can use "common sense"--and knowledge of marketing strategy planning--to improve marketing research.

Assignment

In this exercise you are presented with short cases that involve marketing research. You are asked to identify and comment about the possible limitations of the research. The cases are accompanied by questions that will help to get your thinking started.

You will need to know about the marketing research ideas discussed in Chapter 8 to evaluate the cases. But, remember that the idea here is *not* just to memorize the points from the text. Rather, you should really think about the *problem,* and use common sense along with the information in the book to evaluate the case situation.

A sample answer is provided to the first case--to give you an example of the type of thinking that might be helpful. But--before you read the answer--think about how you would answer the question yourself.

1.   A marketing manager for a big industrial equipment company wanted to get ideas about new products he should develop. A salesman suggested that they conduct a few focus group interviews with a few "friendly" customers--to get some ideas. This seemed like a good idea, so an outside marketing specialist was hired to set up and videotape two focus group sessions.

    After the sessions, the specialist presented a short summary report. His main conclusion was that 40 percent of the participants wanted a certain type of machine, and urged the company to develop one quickly "since the market will be large." He also said that from watching the tapes he was certain that the customers were unhappy with the products they had been getting from the firm. This left the marketing manager quite concerned and wondering what to do.

a) Is a focus group interview a good basis for drawing the type of conclusions offered by the outside researcher? Why or why not?

Sample Answer: The conclusion probably is not justified. A focus group interview includes relatively few customers, and they may not be representative. Also, trying to provide quantitative summaries of the qualitative results might be really misleading. The new product might be a good idea, but just because a few people in a focus group mentioned it does not mean that there will be a large market. That will require more study.

b) Should the manager hire the marketing research firm to do a large survey to see if customers are really unhappy, as he suggests based on the focus groups? Why or why not?

Sample Answer: It is too early to be thinking about rushing out to do a big expensive survey. After all, conclusions reached by watching a focus group interview can vary a lot depending on who watches it. As a start, the marketing manager might watch the tapes of the focus groups and see if he draws the same conclusions. Other views might be sought as well. Even if the conclusion seems correct, it would be best to define the problem more specifically, and do a situation analysis to get a better idea about what research is needed.

2. A marketing manager for a BMW dealership is trying to decide how many cars to order during the coming year--to be sure to have enough on hand to meet demand. He decides that it would be useful to do a survey of customers to whom he has sold this brand in the last year. He wants to know how satisfied they are with their current car, and he wants to know how many want to buy another BMW from him in the coming year. He would also like to know if they could afford another expensive car so soon. He decides to have salesmen call the customers and ask the following questions:

(1) How do you feel about the car you bought from us? Are you very satisfied, or only moderately satisfied?

(2) Do you plan to buy another BMW from us during the coming year? Yes, you plan to buy; or no, you don't plan to buy.

(3)   I have one final question, and your response will be strictly confidential and used only in statistical summaries with answers from other respondents. Would you please tell us your annual income? $_____

   a)   Do you think that customers will give a valid response to the second question? Why or why not?

   b)   Do you think that customers will give a valid response to the last question? Why or why not?

   c)   What is there about the way that the first question is worded that might keep the manager from getting valid information about how satisfied a customer really is? *(Hint:* Read the whole question several times carefully from the point-of-view of different customers.)

3.   A marketing manager for Bank of America wants to survey potential customers to see if they know about the bank's new investment services. An outside marketing research specialist tells the manager that for $5,000 the research firm can send out a mail survey to 500 people, tabulate the results, and present a report. He explains that the bank will need to provide a computer mailing list of people who have accounts at the bank--to save costs in developing the sample. He concludes by pointing out that the research will be quite inexpensive: "We will give you results from a representative sample of 500 people, at only $10 per respondent. And you can be confident with a sample of 500 that the statistics are accurate."

   a)   Is the proposed sample well-suited to the manager's problem? Why or why not?

   b)   Is the researcher's concluding statement misleading? *(Hint:* Think about the response rate issue.) Why or why not?

4. A marketing manager for Isaac's, an expensive men's clothing store, is concerned that profits have dropped, and he has noticed that many customers who once were "regulars" are not coming back anymore. He decides to send out a questionnaire to a sample of old customers, using addresses from his mailing list. He wrote a letter asking customers to respond to his questionnaire. He also provided a postage paid envelope for return of the completed forms. The instructions on the short questionnaire were:

(1) Please discuss the things you liked most about this store the last time you purchased clothing here?

(2) Please explain what you like least about this store. Please discuss anything that bothers you.

(3) Please tell us at what other men's clothing stores you shop, and what it is about each store that you like?

   a) Is a mail survey useful for questions like these? Why or why not?

   b) What would you recommend if the manager asked you for ideas on how to get better information about his problem?

Question for Discussion

How do the limitations of qualitative research differ from the limitations of quantitative research?

Exercise 8-3

Marketing research

This exercise is based on computer-aided problem number 8--Marketing Research. A complete description of the problem appears on pages 232-33 of *Basic Marketing,* 16th edition.

1. Texmac asked firms that had the old machine if they would replace it with their new product if it were priced at $10,000. Forty percent said that they would buy the new equipment. Texmac asked another question of the respondents who said that they would not buy the new equipment at $10,000. Specifically it asked if they would buy the new machine if it were priced at $9,750. Another 25 firms said that they would buy the new machine at the lower price. Texmac figures that those who said that they would buy the machine at the higher price would also buy it at the lower price.

    Based on this information and information from the spreadsheet for the problem (assuming that there are 5,000 firms), calculate what percent of the sample would buy the machine at the lower price:

    _____ percent who would buy only at the $9,750 price.

    plus   _____ percent who would buy at either price.

    equals _____ total percent who would buy at lower price.

2. Now, use the spreadsheet to compute what results the firm would expect based on the lower price ($9,750) and the total percent who would buy at the lower price. Fill in the table below to compare these results with the results that would be expected at the higher price ($10,000).

	Price $10,000	Price $9,750
Expected quantity of replacements:	_____	_____
Total expected revenue:	_____	_____
Expected contribution to profit:	_____	_____
Recommended price	_____	

Explanation: _____

_____

_____

3.   The marketing manager at Texmac wants more detail about what might happen at the price you are recommending. He knows that the number of "old machines" reported by the 500 sample firms may not be exactly representative of the total population. But, marketing research specialists at the firm say that he can be 95 percent confident that the estimate of the number of old machines per 500 firms is probably accurate within a confidence interval of plus or minus 20 machines. Thus, the marketing manager wants to know how your estimate of contribution to profit might change if the actual number of old machines per 500 in the market varies over the range of the confidence interval. To provide this information, do a "What If" analysis and complete the table below. (Note: use the price and percent who would buy based on your recommendation from the previous page).

Estimated Number of Old Machines	Expected Profit
200 (minimum)	_____
204	_____
208	_____
212	_____
216	_____
220	_____
224	_____
228	_____
232	_____
236	_____
240 (maximum)	_____

4.   Texmac's marketing manager says that the market opportunity will be less attractive than it looks if the actual number of textile producers in the population is smaller than the company thinks. Indicate if you agree or disagree with his statement. Briefly discuss why.

_____

_____

_____

Chapter 9

Elements of product planning for goods and services

What This Chapter Is About

Chapter 9 introduces the idea of a "product"—that may be a physical good or a service or (often) a blend of both.

Then, the idea of product classes—and how they relate products to marketing mix planning is explained. Two sets of product classes—for consumer products and business products—are introduced. Notice that the same product might be classified in two or more ways at the same time—depending on the attitudes of potential customers.

These product classes should be studied carefully. They are an important thread linking our discussion of marketing strategy planning. In fact, these product classes can be a shorthand way of describing how customers look at Products—and this has a direct bearing on Place (how the Product will get to them) and Promotion (what the seller should tell them).

Chapter 9 also discusses other important aspects of Product—branding, packaging, and warranties.

Branding is concerned with identifying the product. A good brand can help improve the product's image and reinforce the firm's effort to increase the product's degree of brand familiarity. A respected name builds brand equity.

The advantages and disadvantages of both dealer and manufacturer branding should be studied carefully. They will help you understand the "battle of the brands"—and why some markets are so competitive.

Packaging involves promoting, protecting, and enhancing the product. It can actually improve a product—perhaps making it more appealing and/or protecting it from damage. Packaging can also complement promotion efforts by making the whole product more attractive or carrying a promotion message. A firm's commitment to recycling has become an important packaging issue.

Warranties are also important in strategy planning. Some consumers find strong warranties particularly attractive.

By the end of the chapter you should see that wise decisions on packaging and branding can improve any marketing mix—and may help a firm avoid extremely competitive—or even pure competition— situations.

Important Terms

product, p. 237
quality, p. 237
service, p. 239
product assortment, p. 240
product line, p. 240
individual product, p. 240
consumer products, p. 241
business products, p. 241
convenience products, p. 241
staples, p. 241
impulse products, p. 242
emergency products, p. 242
shopping products, p. 242
homogeneous shopping products, p. 242
heterogeneous shopping products, p. 243
specialty products, p. 243
unsought products, p. 243
new unsought products, p. 243
regularly unsought products, p. 244
derived demand, p. 244
expense item, p. 245
capital item, p. 245
installations, p. 245
accessories, p. 246
raw materials, p. 246
farm products, p. 246
natural products, p. 246
components, p. 247

supplies, p. 248
professional services, p. 248
branding, p. 248
brand name, p. 248
trademark, p. 248
service mark, p. 248
brand familiarity, p. 249
brand rejection, p. 249
brand nonrecognition, p. 250
brand recognition, p. 250
brand preference, p. 250
brand insistence, p. 250
brand equity, p. 251
Lanham Act, p. 252
family brand, p. 253
licensed brand, p. 253
individual brands, p. 253
generic products, p. 253
manufacturer brands, p. 254
dealer brands, p. 254
private brands, p. 254
battle of the brands, p. 254
packaging, p. 255
universal product code (UPC), p. 255-56
Federal Fair Packaging and Labeling Act, p. 256
warranty, p. 257
Magnuson-Moss Act, p. 257

True-False Questions

_____ 1. Quality refers to the ability of a product to satisfy a customer's need.

_____ 2. The more features a product has the higher-quality product it is.

_____ 3. A "product" may not include a physical good at all.

_____ 4. It's usually harder to balance supply and demand for services than for physical goods.

_____ 5. It is usually easier to achieve economies of scale when the product emphasis is on a service rather than a good.

_____ 6. A product line should be thought of as a firm's product assortment.

_____ 7. An individual product is a particular product within a product line and is usually differentiated by brand, level of service, size, price, or some other characteristic.

_____ 8. Consumer product classes are based on how consumers think about and shop for a product.

_____ 9. Convenience products are products a consumer needs but isn't willing to spend much time or effort to shop for.

_____ 10. Because customers are not willing to spend much time or effort shopping for staples, they are not bought very often.

_____ 11. Impulse products are items that the customer decides to purchase on sight, may have bought the same way many times before, and wants "right now."

_____ 12. The distinctive aspect of emergency products is that they are only purchased when the consumer is in danger.

_____ 13. Shopping products are those products that a customer feels are worth the time and effort to compare with competing products.

_____ 14. If customers see a product as a homogeneous shopping product, they will base their purchase decisions on the one variable they feel is or can be different--price.

_____ 15. Price matters more than quality and style for products that the customer sees as heterogeneous shopping products.

_____ 16. Specialty products are expensive and unusual products that customers insist upon having and generally have to travel far to find.

_____ 17. Unsought products are those products that have no potential value for customers.

_____ 18. A consumer product must be either a convenience product, a shopping product, or a specialty product--it cannot be all three.

_____ 19. In times of recession, a good marketing mix aimed at business and organizational customers may not be very effective unless it has some impact on final consumer demand, because the demand for final consumer products derive from the demand for business products.

_____ 20. The fact that the demand for most business products is derived means that industry demand will be fairly elastic, although the demand facing individual firms may be extremely inelastic.

_____ 21. For tax purposes, the cost of a business expense item is spread over a number of years.

_____ 22. Since business products buyers do relatively little shopping compared to consumer products buyers, the business products classification system is determined by how buyers think about the products and how they will be used.

_____ 23. Installations include only buildings and land rights--such as factories, farms, stores, office buildings, mining deposits, and timber rights.

24. If a customer purchases an installation, it is a capital item, but if it is leased the lease payments are an expense item.

25. Although accessory equipment are capital items, purchasing agents usually have more say in buying accessories than in buying installations.

26. Raw materials become part of a physical good--and they are expense items.

27. Component parts and materials are capital items that have had more processing than raw materials.

28. Unlike farm products, components are usually bought using purchasing specifications.

29. A product originally considered a component part when it was sold in the OEM market might become a consumer product in the after market--and probably would require a different marketing mix.

30. Supplies are commonly described as MRO items, meaning that "More Rational Ordering" procedures are normally followed for them.

31. Maintenance supplies are similar to consumers' convenience products--and branding may become important for such products.

32. Some important operating supplies that are needed regularly and in large volumes are purchased at global exchanges on the Internet.

33. Professional services are expense items, and often the cost of buying them outside the firm is compared with the cost of having company personnel do them.

34. The terms branding, brand name, and trademark all mean about the same thing—and can be used interchangeably.

35. Service mark is a legal term that refers to a service offering.

36. Branding is advantageous to producers--but not to customers.

37. Despite the many advantages of branding, a marketing manager would probably be wise to avoid spending large amounts on branding unless the quality can be easily maintained.

38. A firm whose products have reached the brand insistence stage will enjoy a more inelastic demand curve than a firm whose products have achieved brand preference.

39. A respected brand name lowers brand equity.

40. The Lanham Act specifies what types of trademarks can be protected by law and makes provisions for registration records--but it does not force registration.

41. Counterfeiting is illegal everywhere in the world.

42. A licensed brand is a well-known brand that different sellers pay a fee to use.

___ 43. Generic products are products which have no brand at all other than identification of their contents and the manufacturer or middleman.

___ 44. The major disadvantage of manufacturer brands is that manufacturers normally offer lower gross margins than the middleman might be able to earn with his own brands.

___ 45. Eventually, dealer-branded products may win the "battle of the brands," perhaps because dealers are closer to customers and they can control shelf space.

___ 46. While packing is concerned with protecting the product, packaging refers only to promotion.

___ 47. Packaging plays no role when the product emphasis is on service.

___ 48. Better protective packaging is more important to final consumers than to manufacturers and middlemen.

___ 49. A firm should adopt a more expensive package only when the overall effect will be to reduce the total distribution cost for its product.

___ 50. Large supermarket chains have been eager to use the universal product code system—to speed the checkout process and eliminate the need for marking the price on every item.

___ 51. If enforced, the Federal Fair Packaging and Labeling Act of 1966 would all but eliminate a manufacturer's control over the packaging of its products.

___ 52. A warranty explains what a seller promises about its product.

___ 53. The Magnuson-Moss Act requires all manufacturers to offer consumers written warranties for all products.

1. T, p. 237	19. F, p. 244	37. T, p. 249
2. F, p. 237	20. F, p. 245	38. T, p. 250
3. T, p. 238	21. F, p. 245	39. F, p. 251
4. T, p. 240	22. T, p. 245	40. T, p. 252
5. F, p. 240	23. F, p. 245	41. F, p. 252-53
6. F, p. 240	24. T, p. 246	42. T, p. 253
7. T, p. 240	25. T, p. 246	43. T, p. 253
8. T, p. 241	26. T, p. 246	44. T, p. 254
9. T, p. 241	27. F, p. 247	45. T, p. 254
10. F, p. 241	28. T, p. 247	46. F, p. 255
11. T, p. 242	29. T, p. 247	47. F, p. 255
12. F, p. 242	30. F, p. 248	48. F, p. 255
13. T, p. 242	31. T, p. 248	49. F, p. 255
14. T, p. 242-43	32. T, p. 248	50. T, p. 256
15. F, p. 243	33. T, p. 248	51. F, p. 256
16. F, p. 243	34. F, p. 248	52. T, p. 257
17. F, p. 243	35. T, p. 248	53. F, p. 257
18. F, p. 244	36. F, p. 248-49	

Multiple-Choice Questions (Circle the correct response)

1. According to the text, the term "product" means:
   a. any tangible item that satisfies needs.
   b. goods but not services.
   c. the need-satisfying offering of a firm.
   d. any item that is mass produced by a firm.
   e. all of the above.

2. Regarding quality:
   a. the best credit card may not be the one with the highest credit limit.
   b. the best clothing may not be a pair of slacks, but a pair of jeans.
   c. the best computer may not be the most powerful one.
   d. All of the above are true.
   e. None of the above is true.

3. Marketing mix planning for services
   a. is easier than for physical goods because services don't need to be stored.
   b. is more likely to be influenced by economies of scale.
   c. must consider where the service is produced.
   d. All of the above are true.
   e. None of the above is true.

4. The set of all products a firm sells is called its:
   a. product line.
   b. individual products.
   c. product assortment.
   d. tangible products.

5.   The text's consumer product classes are based upon:
      a.   methods of distribution.
      b.   NAICS codes.
      c.   the nature of the products.
      d.   the way people think about and buy products.
      e.   the way firms price their products.

6.   Which of the following is *not* included as a product class in the classification system for consumer products given in the text?
      a.   Convenience products
      b.   Staple products
      c.   Specialty products
      d.   Shopping products
      e.   Durable products

7.   As Mona Begay was doing her weekly supermarket shopping, she walked down the cat food aisle to pick up her usual six cans of brand "X." However, she came upon a special display of a new, highly advertised brand and decided to try it instead. In this case, the cat food she bought is:
      a.   an impulse product.
      b.   a specialty product.
      c.   an unsought product.
      d.   a homogeneous shopping product.
      e.   a staple product.

8.   You are stranded in your automobile during a snowstorm. You decide to walk to the closest service station for tire chains. In this case you would consider the tire chains as:
      a.   emergency products.
      b.   staple products.
      c.   impulse products.
      d.   shopping products.
      e.   specialty products.

9.   Mr. Tomas feels that most people are too emotional and status-minded concerning their automobile purchases. "An automobile's only function is transportation," he says, "and those high-priced 'chrome-wagons' can't do anything that most lower priced cars won't do." Tomas only considers Fords, Chevrolets, and Dodges when he looks around for a new car and he feels all these cars are alike. For him automobiles are:
      a.   a specialty product.
      b.   a homogeneous shopping product.
      c.   a convenience staple product.
      d.   a heterogeneous shopping product.
      e.   a staple product.

10.   Specialty products would be best described as having:
      a.   brand insistence and inelastic demand.
      b.   brand preference and inelastic demand.
      c.   brand insistence and elastic demand.
      d.   brand preference and elastic demand.
      e.   a relatively high price and durability.

11. Which of the following statements about consumer products is *true*?
    a. Convenience products are those that customers want to buy at the lowest possible price.
    b. Shopping products are those products for which customers usually want to use routinized buying behavior.
    c. Specialty products are those that customers usually are least willing to search for.
    d. Unsought products are not shopped for at all.
    e. None of the above statements is true.

12. Motels are a good example of:
    a. convenience products.
    b. shopping products.
    c. specialty products.
    d. unsought products.
    e. Could be any of the above.

13. Which of the following is *not* a general characteristic of most business products?
    a. From a tax perspective, all purchases of business products are written off in the year in which the purchase is made.
    b. Their demand is derived from the demand for final consumer products.
    c. Industry demand may be inelastic while each company's demand may be elastic.
    d. Buying is basically concerned with economic factors.
    e. All of the above are characteristics for most business products.

14. Tax regulations affect business buying decisions because:
    a. expense items are depreciated.
    b. capital items are written off over several years.
    c. installations are expensed in one year.
    d. capital items are expensed in one year.

15. The business product classes discussed in the text are based on:
    a. how sellers think about products.
    b. how buyers think about products.
    c. how the products are to be used.
    d. all of the above.
    e. both b and c.

16. Which of the following is *not* one of the business product classes discussed in the text?
    a. Professional services
    b. Farm products
    c. Component parts
    d. Accessory equipment
    e. Fabrications

17. Which of the following business products to be purchased by a firm is *most* likely to involve top management in the buying decision?
    a. Raw materials
    b. Accessory equipment
    c. Operating supplies
    d. Installations
    e. Component parts

18. Which of the following would *not* be classified as accessory equipment?
    a.   Office typewriters
    b.   Filing cases
    c.   Portable drills
    d.   All of the above might be accessory equipment.
    e.   None of the above is likely to be accessory equipment.

19. Raw materials are usually broken down into two broad categories which are:
    a.   domestic animals and crops.
    b.   farm products and natural products.
    c.   forest products and mineral products.
    d.   maintenance materials and operating materials.
    e.   farm products and chemicals.

20. Which of the following would *not* be considered as a component part by an auto manufacturer?
    a.   Automobile batteries
    b.   Steel sheets
    c.   Automobile jacks
    d.   Tires
    e.   All of the above can be considered component parts, except when they are sold in the replacement market.

21. A marketing manager for a firm that produces component parts should keep in mind that:
    a.   most component buyers prefer to rely on one reliable source of supply.
    b.   the after market for component parts generally requires the same marketing mix as the one used to serve the original equipment market.
    c.   any product originally sold as a component part becomes a consumer product when sold in the after market.
    d.   the original equipment market and the after market for component parts should be viewed as separate target markets.
    e.   All of the above are true statements.

22. Supplies may be divided into three main categories. Lubricating oils and greases for machines on the production line would be classified as:
    a.   maintenance items.
    b.   production items.
    c.   operating supplies.
    d.   repair supplies.
    e.   accessories.

23. A "brand name" is:
    a.   any means of product identification.
    b.   a word used to identify a seller's products.
    c.   the same thing as "branding."
    d.   the same thing as a "trademark".
    e.   All of the above.

24. Which of the following conditions would *not* be favorable to branding?
   a. Dependable and widespread availability is possible
   b. Economies of scale in production
   c. Fluctuations in product quality due to inevitable variations in raw materials
   d. Product easy to identify by brand or trademark
   e. Demand is strong so the price can be high enough to be profitable

25. What degree of brand familiarity has a manufacturer achieved when the firm's particular brand is chosen out of habit or past experience, even though various "name" brands are available?
   a. Brand rejection
   b. Brand preference
   c. Brand recognition
   d. Brand insistence
   e. Nonrecognition of brand

26. Which of the following statements about the Lanham Act is *true?*
   a. It spells out what kinds of brand names can be protected.
   b. Registration under the Lanham Act only applies to licensed brands.
   c. The Lanham Act makes registration of a brand name mandatory.
   d. Registering under the Lanham Act does not help protect a trademark to be used in foreign markets.
   e. All of the above are true statements.

27. A firm that has decided to brand all its products under one label is following a policy of:
   a. dealer branding.
   b. generic branding.
   c. family branding.
   d. manufacturer branding.
   e. None of the above.

28. Which of the following statements about manufacturer or dealer brands is *true?*
   a. Dealer brands are distributed only by chain-store retailers.
   b. Dealer brands may be distributed as widely or more widely than many manufacturer brands.
   c. Dealer brands are the same as "licensed brands."
   d. Manufacturer brands are sometimes called private brands.
   e. All of the above are true.

29. A wholesaler might develop a dealer brand because it:
   a. permits the wholesaler to raise prices.
   b. usually leads to faster turnover of products.
   c. usually leads to less inventory carrying costs.
   d. usually cuts his promotion costs.
   e. protects against channel changes by manufacturers.

30. Which of the following statements regarding the "battle of the brands" is *true?*
    a. It is pretty well over as the dealers now control the marketplace.
    b. Middlemen have no real advantages in the battle of the brands.
    c. If the present trend continues, manufacturer brands will disappear.
    d. Manufacturer brands have been losing ground to dealer brands.
    e. The battle of the brands has increased the differences in price between manufacturer brands and dealer brands.

31. Which of the following statements about the strategic importance of packaging is *false?*
    a. A package may have more promotional impact than a firm's advertising efforts.
    b. A new package can become the major factor in a new marketing strategy by significantly improving the product.
    c. Packaging is concerned with promoting, protecting, and enhancing.
    d. Better packaging always raises total distribution costs.
    e. A package should satisfy not only the needs of consumers but also those of business and organizational customers.

32. The Federal Fair Packaging and Labeling Act:
    a. suggests voluntary informative labeling of food products with respect to their nutrients, weight, and volume.
    b. mandates that companies clearly show the fat content of foods.
    c. encouraged each firm to use a different size package, so consumers would have more choice.
    d. prohibits the use of universal product codes as a substitute for marking prices on retail products.
    e. basically requires that consumer products be clearly labeled in understandable terms.

33. The Magnuson-Moss Act requires that:
    a. all firms provide written warranties for all products.
    b. a warranty must be clearly written, if one is offered.
    c. all warranties be strong warranties.
    d. all warranties be for at least one year.
    e. all of the above.

Answers to Multiple-Choice Questions

1. c, p. 237	12. e, p. 244	23. b, p. 248
2. d, p. 237	13. a, p. 245	24. c, p. 249
3. c, p. 239-40	14. b, p. 245	25. b, p. 250
4. c, p. 240	15. e, p. 245	26. a, p. 252
5. d, p. 241	16. e, p. 246	27. c, p. 253
6. e, p. 242	17. d, p. 245	28. b, p. 254
7. e, p. 241	18. d, p. 246	29. e, p. 254
8. a, p. 242	19. b, p. 246	30. d, p. 254
9. b, p. 242-43	20. b, p. 247	31. d, p. 255
10. a, p. 243	21. d, p. 247	32. e, p. 256
11. d, p. 243	22. c, p. 248	33. b, p. 257

Exercise 9-1

Classifying consumer products

Introduction

Consumer product classes are based on *how consumers think about and shop for products*. However, different groups of potential customers may have different needs and buying behavior for the same product. Thus, the same product could be placed in two or more product classes--depending on the needs and behavior of target customers. Therefore, product planners should focus on specific groups of customers (i.e., market segments) whose needs and buying behavior are relatively homogeneous.

This exercise will give you some practice in using consumer product classes. As you do the exercise, you will see that the product classes have very little meaning unless they are related to specific target markets.

Assignment

The buying behavior of several customers or potential customers is described below for Kodak disposable cameras. (A disposable camera is basically a "box" of film with a built-in lens; after the roll of film in the camera is used up, the customer turns in the whole camera to have the prints processed). Assume in each situation that the customer being described is representative of a particular group of customers--all possessing the same needs and exhibiting similar buying behavior. Then: (a) indicate in which consumer product class the product should be placed based on the characteristics of each group of customers and (b) state *why* you placed the product in this class. Use the following classes, which are described on pages 241-44 in the text.

Staple convenience product	Heterogeneous shopping product
Impulse convenience product	Specialty product
Emergency convenience product	New unsought product
Homogeneous shopping product	Regularly unsought product

The first situation has been answered for you as an example.

1. Ingrid Stevenson, a college student, decided to take her boyfriend to a "water amusement park" as a birthday present. She also wanted to take pictures so that he'd remember the day, but didn't want her expensive digital camera to get wet near the pools, slides, and water rides. So, she decided she would also give him a disposable camera at the start of the day--although she didn't want to spend more than $20 on top of what the park tickets cost. Ingrid didn't know much about disposable cameras, but she went in the University Camera Shop and asked the salesperson for advice about what to buy that would meet her budget, make pictures of reasonable quality, and hopefully work in the water. He recommended that she buy a waterproof Kodak model that came with high speed film and would even work for underwater shots.

    Product Class: *Heterogeneous shopping product.*

Reason: *Customer spends time and effort to compare quality and features, has little concern for brand, and is not too concerned about price as long as it's within her budget.*

2.   Jeremy Bower walked into a CVS drugstore and told the clerk at the camera counter that he wanted to buy a disposable camera with a built-in flash. The clerk said the store carried several such cameras, including ones with the Kodak, Fuji, and CVS brands. "I'll take the one with the lowest price," Jeremy told the clerk.

Product Class: _____

Reason:

3.   Dawn Brady was at her cousin's house and saw some photographs that her cousin had taken with a Kodak disposable camera. She was so surprised by the quality of the pictures that she decided to purchase the same camera. The next day she went to a nearby camera store and found that the store did not have the Kodak in stock--although it did have other brands in stock at about the same price. The salesperson in the store assured her that the others were just as good. But Dawn ignored this advice and tried two other stores that were also out of stock. Getting frustrated, Dawn was ready to drive across town to a Target store. However, when she stopped for gas at a convenience store, she came upon a display of Kodak disposable cameras. She quickly bought one--even though she felt the price would be lower at Target.

Product Class: _____

Reason:

4. While deep-sea fishing off the coast of Hawaii, Toby Rosso caught a large swordfish. He decided that his friends back home would never believe his "fish story" if he didn't have pictures. But he did not have a camera. As soon as the boat got back to the dock, Toby went to a nearby tourist shop. He was pleased to see a display of Kodak disposable cameras, but was sorry to see a much higher price than the same camera sold for in his hometown. He bought one anyway, because he wanted to take some pictures right away before the fish was taken away to the fish market.

Product Class: _____

Reason:

5. Wesley Pierce teaches high school science courses. He spends most of his leisure time doing amateur photography. In fact, he enjoys photography so much that for several years he has volunteered to teach the advanced photography workshop offered by the city recreation department. He has won several awards for his photographs of mountain landscapes. Wesley has even earned extra cash by selling some of his photos to companies that print postcards. Several of his friends have encouraged him to turn professional, but he prefers using his talents mainly as a hobby.

Product Class: _____

Reason:

6. While Hope Jekubovich was shopping in her local supermarket, she came upon an end-of-aisle display with several different types of Kodak disposable cameras. At first, she doubted the product quality because the cameras all had plastic lenses. But remembering the Kodak advertisements she had seen on television and in magazines, she decided to buy one so that her grandchildren, who were visiting for the week, could take pictures during their stay.

Product Class: _____

Reason:

Question for Discussion

What implications do your answers to the above exercises have for Kodak when planning its marketing strategies? Be specific?

Exercise 9-2

Classifying business products

Introduction

Compared to consumer products buyers, business products buyers do relatively little shopping. The accepted practice is for the seller to come to the buyer. This means that business product classes based on shopping behavior are *not* useful. The business product classes are determined by *how buyers think about products* and *how the products will be used.*

The business product classes may be easier to use than consumer product classes, because business and organizational buyers tend to have similar views of the same products. Another reason is that the way a purchase is treated for tax purposes affects its classification. The treatment is determined by the Internal Revenue Service rather than the buyer--so little variation is possible.

However, it is possible that a product may be placed in different classes by two buyers because of how they view the purchase. A "small" truck might be classified as an "accessory" by a large manufacturer, while a small manufacturer would view the same truck as an important "installation." Thus, how the customer sees the product is the determining factor--and it will affect marketing mix planning!

Assignment

This exercise focuses on the essential differences between business product classes. After carefully reading the following cases, indicate which type of business product each case is *primarily* concerned with. Use the following classes:

Installations	Component materials
Accessories	Supplies
Raw materials	Professional services
Component parts	

Then explain your answers, taking into consideration the various characteristics of each type of product as explained in the text on pages 245-48. The first case is answered for you as an example.

1. **Jill Jessup** manages airplane maintenance for a major airline. As chief mechanic she knows which **parts often** need replacing and orders seals, O-rings, and gasket kits in large quantities so she will **always** have them on hand.

    a) Product Class: *Supplies (repair items)*

    b) Reason: *Although the engine parts are components parts when a plane is manufactured, Jessup keeps these replacement parts on hand so they are supplies--just like oil and grease. They are not raw materials because they are not further processed for sale to consumers.*

2. Genesis Research is a marketing research company that helps clients improve their management and marketing decision making--through data collection and evaluation. The firm employs specialists in consumer, industrial, transportation, medical, and government research. It offers clients national field surveys, consumer mail panels, test marketing facilities, shopping center interviews, group interviewing facilities, and a telephone interviewing center--in addition to sophisticated computer and data analysis programs.

    a) Product Class: _____

    b) Reason:

3. Van Wallace is the marketing manager for First Security, Inc., a company that makes expensive rigid camera cases and equipment like tripods for independent film production companies. He is currently planning to introduce a lightweight, flexible tripod for use with professional video cameras.

    a) Product Class: _____

    b) Reason:

4. Gracie Joffe's company makes rechargeable power supplies for use with portable computers. The power supplies are designed to make it fast and easy for manufacturers of notebook size computers to install them as the computer is moving down an assembly line.

    a) Product Class: _____

    b) Reason:

5. The office staff for *Sima's Old Car Buying Guide* are debating whether to add a computerized voice-mail system. One advocate of the idea argues that "all the other car magazines are using voice-mail to take classified ads. The customer can leave the ad--along with a credit card number--whenever it's convenient. Clearly, it's the wave of the future." Paul Sima, who inherited the business from his grandfather has a different opinion: "These systems cost too much. And they won't bring in any more ads--they'll just encourage people to call in ads at the last minute right at our deadline."

    a) Product Class: _____

    b) Reason:

6. Leah Jakeway runs a company that makes electronic connectors. Manufacturers use them in computers and a wide range of electronic equipment to join groups of wires to internal components. Some manufacturers contract for purchase directly with Jakeway, but because these connectors must all conform to worldwide standards, they are also sold "off the shelf" by many wholesale distributors.

   a) Product Class: _____

   b) Reason:

7. Southern Nuts Company buys pecans from hundreds of small pecan growers in South and North Carolina. The pecans are accumulated, sorted, and stored until they are sold to candy companies, bakeries, and other food processing firms.

   a) Product Class: _____

   b) Reason:

Question for Discussion

Which types of products would most likely be associated with the following kinds of buying: (a) new-task buying, (b) straight rebuy, (c) modified rebuy? Why? Illustrate with examples from Exercise 9-2.

Exercise 9-3

Achieving brand familiarity

Introduction

In hopes of developing a strong "customer franchise," American firms spend billions of dollars annually to promote brands for their products. Nevertheless, many brands are, for practical purposes, valueless because of their *nonrecognition* among potential customers. And while obtaining *brand recognition* may be a significant achievement--given the many nondescript brands on the market--this level of brand familiarity does not guarantee sales for the firm. To win a favorable position in monopolistic competition, a firm may need to develop *brand preference* or even *brand insistence* for its products.

Why are some firms more successful than others in their branding efforts? The reasons are not always clear. Unfortunately, brand loyalty, like many aspects of buying behavior, remains a rather mysterious phenomenon. In general, a firm probably must produce a good product and continually promote it, but this alone may not ensure a high level of brand familiarity--particularly if the firm does not direct its efforts toward some specific target market.

This exercise gets at some important problems in branding--such as conditions favorable to branding--and the difficulty of achieving brand familiarity for certain types of products. As you do the exercise, you may begin to wonder if brands are really relevant for some product classes. You may also wish to speculate about how much effort is spent promoting brands to consumers who have no use for the product in question--or for whom brand names are meaningless.

Assignment

1. List from *memory* (DO NOT DO ANY "RESEARCH") up to five brand names for each of the following product types. List the first brands that come to mind. If you cannot think of *any* brands for a particular product type, write "none" in the Brand 1 column.

Product	Brand 1	Brand 2	Brand 3	Brand 4	Brand 5
Bottled Water					
Frozen Yogurt					
Roofing Shingles					
Mattresses					
Crayons					
Trash Compactors					

2.   What level of brand familiarity do you think exists among the majority of consumers for each of the following products?

Product Types   Level of Brand Familiarity

a)   Bottled Water: _____

b)   Frozen Yogurt: _____

c)   Roofing Shingles: _____

d)   Mattresses: _____

e)   Crayons: _____

f)   Trash Compactors: _____

3.   From the product types listed in Questions 1 and 2, indicate for which one branding would be *most appropriate* and explain what conditions make branding so favorable for that product type.

Product type: _____

Conditions:

4.   From the product types listed in Questions 1 and 2, indicate for which one branding would be *least appropriate* and explain what conditions make branding so unfavorable for that product type.

Product type: _____

Conditions:

Question for Discussion

Why would a firm want to "license" the use of another firm's brand name?

Exercise 9-4

Comparing branded product offerings

Introduction

Most manufacturers of consumer products use *manufacturer brands* (often called "national brands") to try to develop a loyal group of customers for their products. At the same time, more and more wholesalers and retailers are offering consumers *dealer brands* (sometimes called "private brands") to try to develop channel and store loyalty. As a result, millions of dollars are spent each year for promotion in a "battle of the brands."

The "battle of the brands" takes many forms--and attitudes toward brands vary a lot both among consumers and marketers. Some retailers tend to stock mainly manufacturer brands. Meanwhile, some manufacturers--particularly in the shoe industry--have opened up their own retail outlets to promote their own brands.

To add to the "battle of the brands," some food retailers also carry *generic products*--unbranded products in plain packages (or unpackaged!)--to appeal to price-conscious consumers. This gives consumers even more products to choose from--but may make it more difficult and confusing to determine the "best buy." This exercise is designed to give you additional insight into the "battle of the brands." You are asked to make price comparisons between manufacturer brands and dealer brands--and then decide which is the "better buy."

Assignment

1.   Visit a large chain supermarket and record the prices of the items listed on the next page. For each item, select one manufacturer brand and one dealer brand. Record the name of the manufacturer brand and then its price. If no dealer brand is available, write the price of the generic product in the dealer column. If the store carries neither a dealer brand nor a generic product, write the price of the manufacturer brand in that column also. Completely fill in all columns so that you can compare the totals.

2.   Which do you think is the "better buy"--manufacturer brands or dealer brands? Why? What factors did you take into consideration in deciding that is the better buy?

PRICE COMPARISON CHART			
Store Visited:			Date:
Item/Size	Name of Manufacturer Brand	Price of Manufacturer brand	Price of Dealer Brand
Spaghetti Sauce/26 oz.			
Ketchup/24 oz.			
Mayonnaise/32 oz.			
Chick. Noodle Soup/10.75 oz.			
Ground Coffee/13 oz.			
Coffee Creamer/22 oz.			
Peanut Butter/18 oz.			
Toasted Oats Cereal/15 oz.			
Sliced Peaches, can/15 oz.			
Sweet Corn, can/15.25 oz.			
Stuffing Mix/6 oz.			
Bacon, Sliced/16 oz.			
Popcorn, Microwave/10.5 oz.			
Fudge Brownie Mix/21 oz.			
Sugar/5 lb.			
Canola Oil/48 oz.			
Orange Juice/64 oz.			
Yellow Mustard/8 oz.			
Cola/2 liter			
Dog Food/20 lb.			
Paper Towels/Big Roll			
Aluminum Foil/75 sq. ft.			
Plastic Sandwich Bags/100 ct.			
Bathroom Tissue/4-pack			
Trash Bags, kitchen/20 count			
Macaroni and Cheese/7.25 oz.			
Liquid Bleach/96 oz.			

Question for Discussion

Why would a manufacturer be willing to produce dealer brands for a supermarket if it already is producing and advertising a similar product with its own brand name?

Exercise 9-5

Branding decision

This exercise is based on computer-aided problem number 9--Branding Decision. A complete description of the problem appears on page 261 of *Basic Marketing*, 16th edition.

1. After some thought, Wholesteen's marketing manager has concluded that there might be a side effect of the FoodWorld proposal which she had not considered earlier. Specifically, she had not planned on reducing her promotion spending if she accepted the FoodWorld proposal. Yet, FoodWorld would be doing some of its own promotion for the FoodWorld brand. As a result, Wholesteen could reallocate some of its promotion money to attract new customers in areas where it had not been doing promotion. She is interested in evaluating this idea more closely, and would like to know how much sales (in cases) of the Wholesteen brand would have to increase (beyond the 90,000 cases she was expecting from the proposed arrangement) to make the same profit the firm makes at present. (Hint: use the What If analysis to vary the total number of cases of the Wholesteen brand in the right hand column and display the total profit for the current situation and the proposed situation. Repeat the process with new minimum and maximum quantity values until you find a quantity that produces about the same profit.)

    Total Profit earned under current arrangement   _____

    Number of cases to make about the same Profit   _____

    Less, number of cases expected under current proposal   90,000

    Equals, increase in number of cases needed   _____

    Explanation: _____

    _____

    _____

2. Even if Wholesteen were able to attract some new customers, the marketing manager knows that it might take awhile. In the meantime, she is worried about profits. One idea she has is to make a counterproposal of her own. She is thinking about accepting the proposal if FoodWorld is willing to pay a higher price for the cases produced under the FoodWorld brand. She would like to set a price for those cases so that her firm's total profits would stay about the same as now. What price per case for the FoodWorld brand would result in about the same profits as at present? (Hint: use the What If analysis to vary the price per case for the FoodWorld brand and display the total profit for the current situation and the proposed situation. Repeat the process with new minimum and maximum price values until you find a price that produces about the same profit.)

    Target price for FoodWorld brand per case   _____

List some factors that will affect whether FoodWorld might agree or disagree with this price:

_____

_____

_____

_____

_____

Chapter 10

Product management and new-product development

What This Chapter Is About

Chapter 10 introduces product life cycles--and shows the need for managing products and developing new products.

Modern markets are dynamic--and the concepts introduced in this chapter should deepen your understanding of how and why markets evolve. Product life cycles should be studied carefully--to see how marketing strategies must be adjusted over time. In later chapters you will get more detail about how the marketing mix typically changes at different stages of the life cycle. So now is the time to build a good base for what is to come.

This chapter is one of the most important in the text, because new products are vital for the continued success of a business. Yet, a large percentage of new products fail. Such failures can be avoided by using the new-product development process discussed in the text. Think about this process carefully, and try to see how you could help develop more satisfying and profitable products. Creativity in product planning--perhaps seeing unsatisfied market needs--could lead to breakthrough opportunities!

Important Terms

product life cycle, p. 264
market introduction, p. 266
market growth, p. 266
market maturity, p. 266
sales decline, p. 267
fashion, p. 270
fad, p. 271

new product, p. 275
Federal Trade Commission (FTC), p. 275
Consumer Product Safety Act, p. 279
product liability, p. 280
concept testing, p. 280
product managers, p. 284
brand managers, p. 284

True-False Questions

___ 1. The product life cycle is divided into four major stages: market introduction, market growth, market maturity, and market saturation.

___ 2. A firm's marketing mix usually must change--and different target markets may be appealed to--as a product moves through the different stages of its life cycle.

_____ 3. Industry sales and profits tend to rise and fall together as a product moves through its life cycle.

_____ 4. The market introduction stage is usually extremely profitable due to the lack of competitors.

_____ 5. Industry profits tend to reach their peak and start to decline during the market growth stage--even though industry sales may be growing rapidly.

_____ 6. Industry profits decline throughout the market maturity stage because aggressive competition leads to price cutting and increased expenditures on persuasive promotion.

_____ 7. During the sales decline stage, new products replace the old--and all firms remaining in the industry find themselves operating at a loss.

_____ 8. In general, product life cycles appear to be getting longer due to a decline in product innovation.

_____ 9. A fashion is the currently accepted or popular style.

_____ 10. A fad is an idea that is fashionable only to certain groups who are enthusiastic about it--but these groups are so fickle that a fad is even more short-lived than a regular fashion.

_____ 11. Once a firm introduces a product to a market, it has no other choice but to watch its product move through the remaining stages of the product life cycle.

_____ 12. Strategy planning can sometimes extend product life cycles, delaying the move from market maturity to sales decline.

_____ 13. The same product may be in different life cycle stages in different markets.

_____ 14. While a lot of strategy planning is necessary to introduce a new product, no strategy is required to get rid of a dying product.

_____ 15. According to the text, a new product is one that is new in any way for the company concerned.

_____ 16. Six months is the longest time that any product may be called "new" according to the Federal Trade Commission.

_____ 17. Since new products are vital to the survival of most firms, the objective of the new-product development process should be to approve as many new-product ideas as possible.

_____ 18. Product planners should consider long-term welfare in addition to immediate satisfaction--and therefore should offer "pleasing products" instead of "desirable products."

_____ 19. The Consumer Product Safety Commission tries to encourage firms to design safe products--but it has no real power to effectively deal with unsafe products.

___ 20. Product liability means the legal obligation of sellers to pay damages to individuals who are injured by defective or unsafe products.

___ 21. Concept testing is done before any tangible product has been developed--and involves marketing research to determine potential customers' attitudes towards the new-product idea.

___ 22. The development step (in new-product development) involves the testing of physical products as well as test marketing--something that must be done for all products prior to commercialization.

___ 23. The specific organization arrangement for new-product development may not be too important--as long as there is top-level support.

___ 24. Product managers sometimes have profit responsibilities and much power, but often they are "product champions" who are mainly involved in planning and getting promotion done.

Answers to True-False Questions

1. F, p. 264-65	9. T, p. 270	17. F, p. 277
2. T, p. 265	10. T, p. 271	18. F, p. 278-79
3. F, p. 265	11. F, p. 273	19. F, p. 279
4. F, p. 266	12. T, p. 273	20. T, p. 280
5. T, p. 266	13. T, p. 273	21. T, p. 280
6. T, p. 266	14. F, p. 275	22. F, p. 281-82
7. F, p. 267	15. T, p. 275	23. T, p. 283
8. F, p. 269	16. T, p. 275	24. T, p. 284-85

Multiple-Choice Questions (Circle the correct response)

1. The product life cycle has four stages. Which of the following is *not* one of these?
   a. Market introduction
   b. Market growth
   c. Market maturity
   d. Economic competition
   e. Sales decline

2. During the *market introduction* stage of the product life cycle:
   a. considerable money is spent on promotion while place development is left until later stages.
   b. products usually show large profits if marketers have successfully carved out new markets.
   c. most potential customers are quite anxious to try out the new-product concept.
   d. funds are being invested in marketing with the expectation of *future* profits.
   e. product and promotion are more important than place and price.

3. Which of the following statements regarding the *market growth* stage of the product life cycle is *false*?
   a. Innovators still earn profits--but this stage is less profitable for them than the previous stage.
   b. This is the time of peak profitability for the industry.
   c. Many competitors enter the market resulting in much product variety.
   d. The sales of the total industry are rising fairly rapidly as more and more customers buy.
   e. Monopolistic competition is common during this stage.

4. Regarding product life cycles, good marketing managers know that:
   a. all competitors lose money during the sales decline stage.
   b. they are getting longer.
   c. industry sales reach their maximum during the market growth stage.
   d. firms earn their biggest profits during the market introduction stage.
   e. industry profits reach their maximum during the market growth stage.

5. An industry with oligopolistic competition faces falling profits and its sales growth is slow. Demand for individual products has become quite elastic--as consumers see competing products as almost homogeneous. Several firms have dropped out. What is the life cycle stage?
   a. Market maturity
   b. Sales decline
   c. Market growth
   d. Market introduction
   e. Product renewal

6. Marketing managers should recognize that:
   a. product life cycles appear to be getting longer.
   b. every segment within a market has the same product life cycle.
   c. the product life cycle describes the sales and profits of individual products, not industry sales and profits.
   d. firms that enter mature markets have to compete with established firms for declining industry profits.
   e. None of the above is a true statement.

7. In planning for different stages of the product life cycle, strategy planners must be aware that:
   a. losses can be expected during the market introduction stage.
   b. the life cycles of mature product-markets can be extended through strategic product adjustments.
   c. offering the product to a new market segment may start a whole new life cycle.
   d. products can be withdrawn from the market before the sales decline stage--but even here a phase-out strategy is usually required.
   e. All of the above are true statements.

8. Which of the following statements about "new products" is *false?*
   a. In order for it to be advertised as new, there should be a functionally significant change in the product--according to the FTC.
   b. A product should be considered "new" by a particular firm if it is new in any way for that company.
   c. The FTC considers six months as the maximum time that a product should be called "new."
   d. According to the FTC, a product may be called "new" (for example, in advertising) as long as the firm has made at least some minor change in the package or product.
   e. A marketing manager should consider a product "new" if it is aimed at new markets.

9. Regarding the new-product development process,
   a. screening criteria should be mainly quantitative--because qualitative criteria require too much judgment.
   b. concept testing tries to see how the new product works in the hands of potential customers.
   c. it tries to "kill" new ideas that are not likely to be profitable.
   d. market tests should be conducted for all new product ideas before commercialization.
   e. All of the above are true.

10. Which of the following types of products provide low immediate satisfaction but high long-run consumer welfare?
    a. Salutary products
    b. Pleasing products
    c. Desirable products
    d. Deficient products
    e. Generic products

11. The Consumer Product Safety Commission can:
    a. order costly repairs of "unsafe products."
    b. back up its orders with fines.
    c. order returns of "unsafe products."
    d. back up its orders with jail sentences.
    e. All of the above are true.

12. Product or brand managers are commonly used when a firm:
    a. has several different kinds of products or brands.
    b. wants to eliminate the job of the advertising manager.
    c. has one or a few products--all of which are important to its success.
    d. wants to eliminate the job of sales manager.
    e. wants one person to have authority over all the functional areas that affect the profitability of a particular product.

Answers to Multiple-Choice Questions

1. d, p. 264-65	5. a, p. 266-67	9. c, p. 277
2. d, p. 266	6. d, p. 267	10. a, p. 279
3. a, p. 266	7. e, p. 266-75	11. e, p. 279
4. e, p. 266	8. d, p. 275	12. a, p. 284

Exercise 10-1

Identifying a product's stage in the product life cycle

Introduction

This exercise is designed to improve your understanding of the product life cycle--a valuable model for marketing strategy planning. For example, the product life cycle can help decide if and when it will be to a company's advantage to add, change, or drop a given product. Further, where a product is in its life cycle suggests a workable blend of the "four Ps."

Assignment

Read the following five cases carefully and for each one:

a)   Decide which stage of the product life cycle best describes the situation in the case--considering the relevant product-market.

b)   Briefly explain your answer, including such factors as profitability, number of competitors, place, promotion, and pricing.

1.   Adam Lightfoot, legendary founder of Silver Dollar Database Company, has announced that his company will no longer develop and sell database software. Instead, the company will focus its effort on developing a new generation of high performance "data mining" software that will be used to identify complex relationships in data. For example, the data mining software might be used to predict stock market trends, identify target customers for cross-selling promotions, or even isolate genes that predispose a person to a particular disease. Some experts applaud Lightfoot's decision to focus on software which takes advantage of the explosive growth in computing power and the information technology revolution that creates enormous quantities of hard-to-analyze data. However, other firms, like SAS Institute and SPSS, Inc. that helped create the market for this sort of analytical software already have a formidable head start.

a)   Stage of product life cycle: _____

b)   Explanation: _____

_____

_____

2. Opti Lenses Corporation has announced that it will no longer produce *hard contact lenses*. A spokesman for the company said that the firm's share of the market for hard contact lenses had grown in each of the last 5 years, but that the overall market was shrinking as more consumers were switching to other alternatives--including disposable contacts, gas permeable lenses, and laser surgery. Opti Lenses' management has indicated that its decision was motivated by the need to pursue more profitable opportunities. The firm's sales manager also said that the decision was hastened by the fact that several other firms serving this market had begun to focus on "ill-conceived price promotions" that were eroding what profit might be possible from serving those consumers who still prefer the old-style hard lenses.

a) Stage of product life cycle: _____

b) Explanation: _____

_____

_____

_____

3. Straight Up Systems is just entering the fast-growing, but increasingly competitive market for "home theater" systems. Like other available systems, the Straight Up line creates excellent 6-speaker audio that is like what you hear in a movie theater, but it is built into the HDTV unit. The Straight Up marketing manager is confident that he can capture a profitable share of the market because his firm's system has an integrated control unit that automatically coordinates the settings for various components--say, the HDTV monitor, the audio system, a cable box, and a Digital Video Recorder (DVR)--even if they are from different manufacturers. All the user has to do is press the "on" button on the remote control and set the volume. Well-known competitors like Pioneer and Sony don't yet have anything to match the ease-of-use of the Straight Up model. In addition, to attract support from traditional retailers of home electronics products, Straight Up is offering a very low wholesale price. Even at the very low suggested retail price, this will make the Straight Up receiver very profitable for retailers. Straight Up's marketing manager says that this very aggressive pricing will pay off. He predicts that in the next decade home theater systems will replace standard stereo receiver systems--and that already prices of the surround sound systems are dropping rapidly. He says that this will stimulate even faster growth in the home theater market.

a) Stage of product life cycle: _____

b) Explanation: _____

_____

_____

4. Pyramid, Inc., one of the nation's largest producers of personal care products, has just announced plans to sell a new shampoo-conditioner called Tangle Free. The company is spending heavily on magazine and TV ads that will promote Tangle Free as "The shampoo-conditioner that nourishes the hair and that everyone can use daily. No other shampoo is as gentle on your hair or provides as clean and natural a scent." Free samples of Tangle Free will be attached to packages of other Pyramid products, and magazine ads will include cents-off coupons. Despite intense competition, Pyramid expects its new product to capture a 5 percent share of the slowly growing shampoo market.

    a)   Stage of product life cycle: _____

    b)   Explanation: _____

    _____

    _____

5. One of the largest food manufacturers is testing a new product for the large soft-drink market--a patented plastic cup coated with a secret formula. All the consumer has to do is add water and it becomes a carbonated beverage! It is no longer necessary to carry home six-packs or eight-packs. There are no empty bottles or cans to return, and less storage space is needed. The product can also be distributed through normal wholesale channels rather than requiring the special distribution networks now used by the bottling industry. Therefore, the product offers economy as well as convenience.

    a)   Stage of product life cycle: _____

    b)   Explanation: _____

    _____

    _____

Question for Discussion

What alternatives should a firm consider when it finds some or all of its products in the market maturity stage of the product life cycle?

Exercise 10-2

New-product development process

Introduction

The product life cycle shows us that markets and competition are dynamic. Over time old products are replaced with new ones. And as markets mature, firms usually face increasing price competition and erosion of their profit margins. To succeed in spite of these pressures, firms must constantly look for new market opportunities--and that often means identifying and developing new product ideas--and effective strategies to go with them.

While the new-product development process is crucial to the survival and success of most firms, it is also a challenge. Even the best-run companies sometimes "miss" opportunities that--after the fact--seem obvious. And too often companies go ahead and introduce new products that turn out to be costly failures. Marketing managers can increase the odds of success in this area by really understanding the steps of the new-product development process--and what it takes to generate and screen new-product ideas.

This exercise is intended to help develop your skills in this area.

Assignment

The short descriptions that follow provide information about different companies. In each case, there is at least one major problem with the way the company is currently approaching the new-product development process. Read and evaluate each statement carefully, and then explain:

    a)   your diagnosis of the problem, and

    b)   your recommendation for what the company should do as a substitute for what is described in the case situation.

1. Caliber Cycles, Inc. has been successful producing and marketing high performance motorcycles. In searching for new product opportunities, the company became interested in small size, four-wheel all-terrain vehicles (ATVs) designed for children in the 10- to 15-year age group. The head design engineer for the company thought that the company's expertise in designing motorcycles would apply directly to this popular new product. In addition, many of the dealers who carry the firm's motorcycles are interested in the idea. However, one of them noted that there have been many accidents involving four-wheel ATVs--and suggested that the company check into product liability insurance. When this was discussed back at the firm, the engineer said that he did not see a big problem. "After all," he said, "our ATVs will be as safe as others that are available. And in addition the accidents that occur are invariably the fault of the user. We can't be held responsible for user-errors if the product is properly designed and manufactured."

    a)   the problem:

    b)   your recommendation:

2. Superior Wire, Inc. produces and sells special types of wire used in a variety of telecommunication applications. The firm's initial growth came from sales of a new wire that was used by cellular telephone service companies when setting up transmission stations. However, growth in that market has slowed. Moreover, at present, most of the other products offered by the firm are similar to those available from a variety of other suppliers. Angelina Stowe, the marketing manager for the company, recently scheduled a meeting with the company president to discuss problems of falling profits. Stowe expressed concern that the company did not have a specific person responsible for identifying new products. The president pointed out that few other firms in their industry had such a position--and generally argued that new-product thinking was the responsibility of everyone in the firm. After further discussion, the president agreed to let Stowe send out a memo to all company employees encouraging them to be alert to new product ideas--and to submit any ideas to the research and development department for analysis of their technical feasibility.

    a)   the problem:

    b)   your recommendation:

3.   Assurance Drug Company has developed a promising new nonprescription tablet to relieve the symptoms of allergy sufferers. The idea has successfully passed the screening and idea evaluation stages of the company's new-product development process. The company has also completed concept tests and produced some tablets. Now, the head of the new-product development group has sent the following memo to the marketing department. "Our laboratory tests have satisfied the Food and Drug Administration criteria and we are ready to move ahead with a final test market prior to commercialization. I want you to start thinking about this now. If the product does well in the test market, we will need to develop the rest of the marketing mix. We will want to come up with an attention-getting package design--one that will really stand out on a drugstore shelf. We will also need to decide on the brand name we would use in a national distribution. For now, we will just price the product in test market at the same price as our cold tablets. So final pricing decisions will also need to be made. And, of course, we will need to decide what type of promotion to use--and what message we want to get across to potential customers. I wanted to alert you to these exciting developments so that you could be getting your ideas together. We want to be ready to move quickly into commercialization if the test market is successful."

a)   the problem:

b)   your recommendation:

4.   Total Medical Supplies Corporation produces a variety of sterile storage containers used in hospital operating rooms. Recently, large companies like Johnson & Johnson have been aggressive in this market, and they seem to have had better success in identifying new-product opportunities. The sales manager at the company recently sent a memo to the firm's salespeople outlining problems related to the firm's weak financial position. He ended the memo with a plea: "To increase our profits in coming years, we must move ahead aggressively with new-product ideas. The president of the company fully backs this thrust. He has established a new-product screening committee with members from different departments of the firm. You are in contact with the customer--and we need for you to submit your ideas. We promise to carry forward with marketing research on every good idea that comes in. Our objective is to really get behind your ideas--and turn them into products."

a)   the problem:

b)   your recommendation:

Question for Discussion

The text emphasizes that many of the new products that are developed and introduced prove to be expensive failures. Who pays the cost of these failures? Is it just the owners of the companies that introduced them?

Exercise 10-3

Grown stage competition

This exercise is based on computer-aided problem number 10--Growth Stage Competition. A complete description of the problem appears on page 287 of *Basic Marketing*, 16th edition.

1. As competition increases over time, AgriChem is likely to get a reduced share of the market. But, at the same time, the overall market will be growing. What market share, unit sales, and profit is AgriChem's marketing managers expecting in the current year and each of the next five years-- assuming that the overall market grows at a rate of 200,000 units a year? What will AgriChem's long run profit be (that is, the sum of the profit for the current year and profits for each of the next five years)?

Year	Share (percent)	Unit Sales	Profit
0	_____	_____	_____
1	_____	_____	_____
2	_____	_____	_____
3	_____	_____	_____
4	_____	_____	_____
5	_____	_____	_____

    Long Run (Total) Profit _____

2. AgriChem's marketing manager knows that competitors will force prices down over time, and he expects to lose market share as competitors enter the market. But, he also thinks that lower prices will stimulate demand and contribute to growth in the market. In fact, he is thinking about cutting his price to $12.50 now--to try to spur more growth in market demand while he still has a larger share. He thinks that if he cuts his price to $12.50 this year that the annual growth in sales might increase to 280,000 units a year for the current year and each of the next five years. But a price cut now would probably also drive prices down even faster during the next five years. He wants to evaluate the effect of this potential price change on AgriChem's expected long-run profits. Complete the table on the next page to evaluate this situation. (Hint: set the current price on the spreadsheet to $12.50, and set expected unit growth each year to 280,000. Then use the What If analysis to vary years in the future from a minimum of 0 to a maximum of 5 and display AgriChem's price for each year, its unit sales, and its profit.)

Year	Price	Unit Sales	Profit
0	$12.50	_____	_____
1	_____	_____	_____
2	_____	_____	_____
3	_____	_____	_____
4	_____	_____	_____
5	_____	_____	_____

Long Run (Total) Profit _____

3. How do profits for the current year and the first year in the future compare for the two different pricing/growth situations?

_____

_____

_____

_____

4. How do long-run profits (say, for the current year and next five years) compare for the two different pricing/growth situations?

_____

_____

_____

_____

5. Drawing on your analysis, discuss why it is important for a marketing manager to try to anticipate how the market will change over the product life cycle.

_____

_____

_____

_____

Chapter 11

Place and development of channel systems

What This Chapter Is About

Chapter 11 introduces the strategy decisions in Place--and considers how and why channel systems develop the way they do. These ideas will help you understand the Place-related materials that follow in the next three chapters.

"Ideal" Place objectives are explained--to emphasize the relevance of potential customers' behavior to Place planning. These ideal Place objectives are related to the product classes introduced in Chapter 9.

Whether a producer handles the whole distribution itself or works with intermediaries is an important strategy decision. You'll see that channel specialists often develop to help adjust discrepancies of quantity and assortment or to reduce separations between producers and customers. Later, various types of indirect channel systems are explained--so you will have a better understanding of how channel members work together.

This chapter emphasizes that marketing strategy must consider the whole channel--and that channel management is an ongoing, dynamic process. As you learn about these Place decisions, think about why a channel captain can play such an important role in leading the channel toward a common product-market commitment.

Important Terms

True-False Questions

_____ 1. The Place part of the marketing mix is concerned with building channels of distribution and making goods and services available in the right quantities and locations when customers want them.

_____ 2. A channel of distribution is any series of firms or individuals who participate in the flow of goods and services from producer to final user or consumer.

_____ 3. Product classes help solve Place problems and in particular how much market exposure will be needed in each geographic area.

_____ 4. A marketing manager's decisions on Place have long-range effects and are usually harder to change than Product, Price, and Promotion decisions.

_____ 5. Although seldom used, direct-to-user channels are almost always better than channels that use middlemen.

_____ 6. The Internet makes it easier for firms to have direct access to customers.

_____ 7. Most consumer products are sold through intermediaries.

_____ 8. There is no difference between _direct distribution_ and _direct marketing_.

_____ 9. A direct instead of indirect channel is probably a better choice for a producer with limited financial resources.

_____ 10. Discrepancies of quantity exist because producers specialize in making one or a few items—while customers want many items and probably would prefer not to shop at different stores for each item.

_____ 11. Because few customers can consume a big part of any producer's output, the large quantities that mass production makes possible generally cause a discrepancy of assortment.

_____ 12. Collecting larger quantities of similar products, the accumulating process, creates a discrepancy of quantity but permits economies of scale.

_____ 13. Bulk-breaking involves dividing larger quantities into smaller quantities as products get closer to the final market.

_____ 14. The sorting process is usually handled by middlemen--when they put together a variety of products to give a target market what it wants.

_____ 15. The assorting process means sorting products into the grades and qualities desired by different target markets.

_____ 16. Marketing specialists should develop to adjust discrepancies of quantity and assortment only if these discrepancies must be adjusted.

___ 17. A channel system can work well only if its members have accepted a common product-market commitment and are all strongly market-oriented.

___ 18. In a traditional channel system the various channel members make little or no effort to cooperate with each other.

___ 19. Clearly, a producer should always act as "channel captain"--because he is in the best position to help direct the channel as an integrated system of action.

___ 20. Vertical marketing systems are channel systems in which the whole channel focuses on the same target market at the end of the channel.

___ 21. Corporate channel systems involve corporate ownership all along the channel.

___ 22. In regard to the development of the channel system, vertical integration means acquiring firms which operate at different levels of channel activity.

___ 23. Any administered channel system--by definition--is also a contractual channel system.

___ 24. Because of the importance of Place in a firm's marketing mix, marketing managers should always seek maximum market exposure for their products.

___ 25. Ideal market exposure makes a product widely enough available to satisfy the target customers' needs--but not exceed them.

___ 26. An intensive distribution policy refers to the marketing manager's desire to sell through all responsible and suitable wholesalers or retailers.

___ 27. Since it is not necessary to obtain 100 percent coverage of a market to justify or support national advertising, some firms now using intensive distribution might be wise to switch to selective distribution and use only the better middlemen to distribute and promote their products.

___ 28. Exclusive distribution is likely to be used by a producer--to help control prices and the service offered in a channel.

___ 29. Following a 1977 Supreme Court ruling, horizontal or vertical arrangements that limit sales by customer or territory may be legal if it can be shown that there are good reasons for such relationships.

___ 30. Multichannel distribution occurs when a manufacturer uses several competing channels to reach the same target market--perhaps using several middlemen in addition to selling directly itself.

___ 31. Reverse channels are used to retrieve products that customers no longer want.

1. T, p. 290	12. T, p. 297	23. F, p. 303
2. T, p. 290	13. T, p. 297	24. F, p. 305
3. T, p. 291	14. F, p. 297	25. T, p. 305
4. T, p. 291	15. F, p. 298	26. T, p. 305
5. F, p. 293-94	16. T, p. 298	27. T, p. 306
6. T, p. 293	17. F, p. 298	28. T, p. 306
7. T, p. 294	18. T, p. 298	29. F, p. 307
8. F, p. 294-95	19. F, p. 301	30. T, p. 308
9. F, p. 295	20. T, p. 301	31. T, p. 309
10. F, p. 296	21. T, p. 302	
11. F, p. 296	22. T, p. 302	

Multiple-Choice Questions (Circle the correct response)

1. A channel of distribution:
    a. is any series of firms or individuals who participate in the flow of goods and services from producer to final user or consumer.
    b. must include a middleman.
    c. must have at least three members--a manufacturer, a wholesaler, and a retailer.
    d. can't include use of direct distribution from a website.
    e. None of the above is a true statement.

2. The "Place" variable deals with:
    a. choosing the type of channel that's needed to meet customer needs.
    b. forming channels of distribution.
    c. managing relations among channel members to reduce conflict and improve cooperation.
    d. picking the desired level of market exposure.
    e. All of the above.

3. Marketing specialists develop to adjust "discrepancies" in the marketplace. Which of the following best explains the concept of "discrepancies"?
    a. There are many more consumers than there are producers.
    b. The assortment and quantity of products wanted by a customer may be different than the assortment and quantity of products normally produced by a manufacturer.
    c. Supply and demand is no longer determined by market forces because "big business" is more powerful than the individual consumer.
    d. Price is not always a reliable measure of a product's quality.
    e. Although most manufacturers claim to be marketing-oriented, most firms would rather produce what they want to sell rather than what customers want to buy.

4. Discrepancies of quantity occur because:
   a. some consumers have more money than others.
   b. individual producers tend to specialize while individual consumers want a broad assortment of products.
   c. consumers demand more product variety than producers can make.
   d. to obtain economies of scale, individual producers often make larger quantities of products than individual consumers normally want to buy.
   e. there are many more consumers than producers.

5. If you were a retailer attempting to supply a wide variety of products for the convenience of your customers, which of the following "regrouping activities" would you be *most* involved in?
   a. Sorting
   b. Accumulating
   c. Bulk-breaking
   d. Assorting
   e. Breaking bulk

6. When a channel has a "product-market commitment":
   a. all members focus on the same target market at the end of the channel.
   b. its members attempt to share the various marketing functions in appropriate ways.
   c. there is no need for a channel captain to develop.
   d. all of the above.
   e. a and b above--but not c.

7. In "traditional channel systems"
   a. the producer is usually responsible for assorting.
   b. only one middleman is used at each level of the channel.
   c. it is easy to coordinate the necessary marketing functions.
   d. members at each level of the channel often have a very different view of who the competitors are.
   e. the producer sets the objectives for all channel members.

8. Ideally, a "channel captain":
   a. has sufficient market power to force his policies on other channel members.
   b. is a manufacturer.
   c. is a strong retailer or wholesaler.
   d. is assigned this role by majority vote among channel system members.
   e. earns that "position" by effective leadership.

9. If Wal-Mart were to purchase the Zenith Radio Corporation, this would be an example of:
   a. vertical integration.
   b. internal expansion.
   c. horizontal integration.
   d. an administered channel system.

10. Which of the following statements about channel systems is *true?*
   a. Some administered channel systems have achieved the advantages of vertically integrated systems while retaining more flexibility.
   b. All vertical marketing systems are also contractual channel systems.
   c. The independence of firms in traditional channel systems has led to channel efficiencies because of greater freedom of decision making.
   d. Indirect channel systems seem to be generally more effective than direct channels.
   e. Corporate channel systems are competitively superior to administered channel systems.

11. The best level of market exposure for a product
   a. always costs more, but the higher costs lead to higher sales and profits.
   b. is the level which will result in the highest level of attention by middlemen.
   c. is the one which minimizes distribution costs.
   d. is intensive distribution.
   e. makes a product available widely enough to satisfy target customers' needs but NOT exceed them.

12. A manufacturer that tries to sell a product through any *responsible* and *suitable* wholesaler or retailer who will stock or sell the product is seeking what degree of market exposure?
   a. Exclusive distribution
   b. Intensive distribution
   c. Selective distribution

13. Which of the following statements about "ideal" market exposure is *true?*
   a. A manufacturer should aim for maximum market exposure.
   b. As a firm moves from intensive to exclusive distribution, it loses more and more control over price and service.
   c. A selective distribution policy may be necessary to avoid dealing with middlemen who buy too little compared to the cost of working with them.
   d. Intensive distribution refers to the desire to sell through any and every retail outlet.
   e. All of the above are true statements.

14. Marketing managers should know that:
   a. a Supreme Court ruling prohibits exclusive distribution.
   b. vertical arrangements between manufacturers and middlemen which limit sales by customer or territory may be legal according to a recent Supreme Court ruling.
   c. horizontal arrangements among competing manufacturers or middlemen which limit sales by customer or territory are generally considered legal.
   d. vertical arrangements between manufacturers and middlemen which limit sales by customer or territory are always illegal.
   e. both c and d are true statements.

15. Although some middlemen may resent this approach, a manufacturer may have to use "multichannel distribution" because:
   a. present channel members are doing a poor job.
   b. the firm desires to reach different target markets.
   c. big retail chains want to deal directly.
   d. antitrust regulations prohibit relying on just one channel system.
   e. both a and c above.

1. a, p. 290	6. e, p. 298	11. e, p. 305
2. e, p. 290	7. d, p. 298	12. b, p. 305
3. b, p. 296	8. e, p. 300	13. c, p. 306
4. d, p. 296	9. a, p. 302	14. b, p. 307
5. d, p. 298	10. a, p. 303	15. e, p. 308

Exercise 11-1

Evaluating the costs of adjusting discrepancies of quantity and assortment in channel systems

Introduction

If market segmentation were carried to its extreme, every customer would have a set of "tailor-made" goods and services. From an economic standpoint, this normally wouldn't be practical, of course. And fortunately, it isn't necessary--since it's often possible to find reasonably sized groups of consumers having relatively homogeneous needs. This often leads to "economies of scale"--that lower costs to customers.

By their very nature, however, mass production and mass consumption cause discrepancies of quantity and assortment. So, activities for adjusting these discrepancies are needed. The *regrouping activities* are: accumulating, bulk-breaking, sorting, and assorting. These activities can be carried out by the manufacturer or the consumer. Like many activities, however, they are generally performed best by specialists. This is why marketing intermediaries develop--and often become important members of channels of distribution.

Assignment

The following case shows the role of marketing intermediaries (particularly wholesalers) in creating and adjusting discrepancies of quantity and assortment. Questions appear at various points through the case--to test your understanding of the material. Read the case carefully and answer the questions *as they appear*. It is important that you understand the concepts involved, even though the case has been simplified to aid analysis. So think about the implications for a highly developed economy such as the United States.

MOONBEAM REPUBLIC

The Moonbeam Republic is a small developing country that recently experienced an industrial revolution. The country's 100 basic commodities are produced by 100 specialized firms, each of which makes only one product. All of the products are in turn sold through a network of 2,000 equal-sized retailers who are scattered all around the country.

The Constellation Company produces sunstars (a consumer staple) for the Moonbeam Republic. Due to large fluctuations in demand, the sunstars cannot be manufactured in large quantities--and therefore cost $12.50 each to produce. Each week Constellation's salespeople have to call on all of the retailers to solicit their orders for sunstars. This results in a relatively high selling cost of $2.00 per each unit sold. Since orders are generally quite small, order processing costs amount to about 50 cents per unit. Finally, the necessity of shipping many small orders to retailers results in transportation costs of $1.00 per unit. The price Constellation charges for each unit is determined by adding on 50 percent of the *total* unit cost of producing, selling, and delivering the sunstars. Each retailer, then, takes a 40 percent markup on the cost they are charged by Constellation.

1.   How much do consumers in the Moonbeam Republic pay for sunstars? Show your work (and label your numbers). The retail price of sunstars is _____

2.   What discrepancies of quantity and assortment exist in the Moonbeam Republic? Be specific.

Consumers in the Moonbeam Republic complained about the high prices they were being asked to pay for sunstars and other commodities. They blamed retailers for the high prices--demanding that government officials take some action to reduce the retailers' high markups. However, retailers in turn blamed the high prices on the operating practices of manufacturers. Manufacturers acknowledged inefficiencies in their operations, but contended that such problems were unavoidable given the country's present distribution system.

After thinking over the situation quite carefully, the country's economic advisers concluded that the best solution would be to change the nation's distribution system. They recommended that 10 wholesale establishments be added to facilitate the distribution of manufactured commodities. The welfare minister protested, however, that the addition of more intermediaries would only serve to *raise* prices instead of lowering them. Here, the economists countered with the following list to show the advantages of employing wholesalers in the Moonbeam Republic:

a) The presence of wholesalers would tend to stabilize demand for manufacturers, allowing them to take advantage of mass production techniques. It was estimated that manufacturing costs could be cut in half by producing products in larger quantities.

b) Since manufacturers would only have to deal with 10 wholesalers who buy in large quantities instead of 2,000 retailers, their unit selling costs would decrease by 60 percent. Furthermore, since each wholesaler would only be required to sell to 200 retailers, the wholesale selling costs would amount to only about 25 cents per unit for most commodities.

c) Order processing costs would decrease 50 percent for manufacturers, because wholesalers would order in large quantities. However, it will still cost wholesalers about 25 cents per unit to process each order from the retailers.

d) By shipping bulk quantities to the wholesalers, the manufacturers could take advantage of carload freight rates, thereby cutting their shipping costs to about 50 cents per unit. Also, since their orders would travel shorter distances, the wholesalers could ship products at a rate of 30 cents per unit.

e) Because they deal in large quantities of merchandise, the wholesalers would operate with only a 20 percent markup on total unit cost. Moreover, retailers could cut their markups down to 25 percent, since they would each be dealing with only one wholesaler rather than with 100 manufacturers--and therefore would have lower costs.

3. Assuming that the economist's estimates are accurate, calculate the new retail price for sunstars if Constellation were to distribute them through wholesalers. Show your work (and label your numbers).

The new retail price for sunstars would be _____.

4. Should the Moonbeam Republic adopt the plan to use wholesalers in its distribution system? ___ Yes or No? Why?

5.   Explain how the addition of wholesalers would serve to adjust discrepancies of quantity and assortment in the Moonbeam Republic. Be specific.

Question for Discussion

Which marketing functions were added or eliminated with the addition of wholesalers to the Moonbeam Republic's macro-marketing system?

Exercise 11-2

Determining market exposure policies

Introduction

Once a producer decides to use intermediaries (wholesalers and retailers) to help distribute its products, it must decide what degree of market exposure will be best: *exclusive distribution, selective distribution,* or *intensive distribution.* Contrary to popular opinion, maximum exposure is not always desirable. The ideal market exposure should meet--but not exceed--the needs of target customers. As one moves from exclusive distribution to intensive distribution, the total marketing cost may increase--and the quality of service provided by intermediaries may actually decline.

When deciding about the desired market exposure, a marketing manager should consider the functions which intermediaries will be asked to perform and the product class for his product. The product classes summarize some of what is known about the product--including what the target customers think of it, their willingness to shop for it, and the amount of personal attention and service they want. The product class often determines the "ideal" market exposure.

Of course, there sometimes is a difference between a product's *ideal* market exposure and the exposure which it can achieve. Intermediaries are not always willing to carry a new product, especially when several similar products are already on the market. Similarly, intermediaries who are interested in carrying a product may not have the opportunity, unless the producer wants them as a channel partner.

Assignment

This exercise will give you some practice in determining the "ideal" degree of market exposure for a company. Six cases are presented below--with the first serving as an example. Read each case carefully and then indicate (a) the product class which is involved, and (b) the degree of market exposure (intensive, selective, or exclusive) which you think would be "ideal." Then in part (c), explain *why* you think the indicated degree of market exposure would be ideal. State any assumptions that you have made. *Note:* "Ideal" here means the degree of market exposure which will satisfy the target customers' needs (but not exceed them) *and also* will be achievable by the producer. For example, a new producer of "homogeneous" cookies might desire intensive distribution, but agree to sell to only a few food chains because it knows it will not be able to obtain intensive distribution with its undifferentiated cookies. So its "ideal" is selective distribution, and it will adjust the rest of its marketing mix accordingly.

Note: Exhibits 9-3 and 9-4 on pages 242 and 246 of the text may be helpful in completing this exercise.

1. Hart Dinettes, Inc. manufactures a wide line of kitchen dinette sets for sale throughout the United States. The products are distributed through retail outlets. Retailers are supposed to stock a large assortment of dinette sets, along with a large inventory of replacement parts. The tables and chairs are usually shipped to the retailers unassembled. According to a recent cost study, 30 percent of Hart's retailers account for about 80 percent of the company's sales.

a) Product class: *Heterogeneous shopping products*

b) "Ideal" market exposure: *Selective distribution*

c) Why? *The recent cost study shows that a small percentage of retailers are producing most of the business. These middlemen might do an even better job if given more assistance and less direct competition from retailers carrying the same products. Since customers are willing to shop around, reducing the number of outlets would be possible--and might benefit consumers through larger retail inventories and increased customer service.*

2. James River Paper (JRP) recently introduced Absorb, a new double-thick paper towel aimed at families with children. Primarily an industrial products manufacturer, JRP had produced paper towels for a few large grocery chains to sell as their own dealer brand. But Absorb was its first attempt at marketing a consumer product under its own brand. So far, results are not encouraging. Only a few wholesalers have taken on the line. Most are very reluctant to handle Absorb, claiming that retail shelves are already overcrowded with paper towels.

a) Product class: _____

b) "Ideal" market exposure: _____

c) Why? _____

_____

_____

_____

_____

_____

3. Ciao Footwear designs and manufactures a high-quality line of fashionable shoes that are popular among young professional women. The line is quite expensive--and it is sold through specialty shops that handle only this type of fashion shoe (including competing brands). Ciao will only work with retailers who agree to stock a large variety of sizes and colors of Ciao shoes. They also must agree to promote the Ciao line very aggressively. In return, Ciao agrees not to distribute its line to other retailers within the specialty shop's immediate trading area. Since continuing promotion seems to be necessary in this highly competitive market, advertisements for Ciao shoes appear regularly in fashion magazines targeted at professional women and on select cable TV broadcasts, including broadcasts of women's tennis tournaments.

a)   Product class: _____

b)   "Ideal" market exposure: _____

c)   Why? _____

_____

_____

_____

_____

4.   EconoStore, Inc. makes and sells a low-priced line of file cabinets for use in offices. One style of cabinets is designed to store standard size business papers, and another style is designed for computer output. The files are sold directly to universities and other institutions--and indirectly through wholesalers to office equipment dealers. EconoStore's files sell to final customers (not the intermediaries) at prices ranging from about $90 to $300. Most dealers handle several competing brands of file cabinets, including some "high-quality" brands that sell for as much as $1,000.

      a)   Product class: _____

      b)   "Ideal" market exposure: _____

      c)   Why? _____

_____

_____

_____

_____

5.   International Tractor, Inc. (ITI) manufactures a full line of farm machinery--including tractors, graders, and materials-handling equipment. ITI famm products are distributed through over 500 independent dealers scattered throughout the United States. Typically, there is only one ITI dealer near any rural community, although there may be several other dealers who sell competing equipment. Many of ITI's dealerships are quite small, and the company lacks adequate dealers in several key market areas. To further complicate matters, price wars between dealerships are becoming common as industry sales continue to decline. In fact, some ITI dealers often find themselves competing directly with other ITI dealers--since many farmers travel 100 miles or more to purchase new equipment.

      a)   Product class: _____

      b)   "Ideal" market exposure: _____

c) Why? _____

_____

_____

_____

_____

6. Domicile Designs, Ltd. manufactures decorative items for the home. It recently added beaded bamboo curtains to its product line. Designed for use in open doorways or as room dividers, the curtains are available in several colors and can be mounted easily on curtain rods. They are priced at $20 per set and measure six feet long by three feet wide. Like most of the company's products, the curtains are sold in gift shops, hobby shops, and specialty shops such as "Pier-to-Pier" franchise outlets. Initial sales for the curtains have been quite promising. The product seems to have good "eye appeal," according to one shop owner. Apparently, the early customers hadn't planned to buy anything like bamboo curtains, but once they saw them displayed in the store, they couldn't resist buying them.

a) Product class: _____

b) "Ideal" market exposure: _____

c) Why? _____

_____

_____

_____

_____

Question for Discussion

How do you think each firm should try to achieve the "ideal" degree of market exposure you discussed above? Are there any legal constraints they should consider?

Exercise 11-3

Intensive vs. selective distribution

This exercise is based on computer-aided problem number 11--Intensive versus Selective Distribution. A complete description of the problem appears on page 311 of *Basic Marketing,* 16th edition.

1. Hydropump's marketing manager thinks that the type of channel relationship possible with selective distribution would make it possible to get a large share (40 percent) of the pumps sold by its hot-tub dealers. But he realizes that the actual percent might vary. He thinks that the percent could be as low as 35 percent, or go as high as 45 percent. He wants to evaluate the effect that this might have on expected profits. Do a What If analysis, based on the selective distribution alternative, varying Hydropump's percent of dealer unit sales between 35 percent and 45 percent and displaying Hydropump's unit sales and profit, and then complete the missing numbers in the table below.

Percent of Dealer Unit Sales	Expected Unit Sales	Expected Profit
35	_____	_____
37	_____	_____
_____	9,880	193,200
43	_____	_____
44	_____	_____
45	_____	_____

2. How important is it that Hydropump win at least a 40 percent share of the dealers' unit sales? Explain your reasons.

    _____

    _____

    _____

    _____

    _____

3. Hydropump's marketing manager thinks that the hot-tub dealers will pay more attention to the company's product if they get a higher than normal level of attention and help from Hydropump sales reps. However, a sales rep would only be able to spend the extra time with each dealer if he is responsible for fewer accounts. If each rep is assigned only 47 dealers, instead of 70, how many more sales reps would be needed, and how much would personal selling costs increase?

    number of sales reps needed at 47 dealers per rep _____

    personal selling cost for this number of sales reps _____

    less, personal selling cost for 4 sales reps $72,000

    equals, increase in personal selling cost _____

4. With this change in the sales force, Hydropump's manager is confident that the firm will get at least 40 percent--and perhaps as high as 50 percent--of the pumps sold by the dealers. Evaluate Hydropump's likely profit in this situation--and then compare it with your previous analysis (above). Would you recommend that Hydropump add the extra sales reps? Discuss your reasons.

    _____

    _____

    _____

    _____

    _____

    _____

    _____

    _____

Chapter 12

Distribution customer service and logistics

What This Chapter Is About

Chapter 12 is concerned with what is often the "invisible" part of marketing--the physical movement and storing of products--and its not so invisible outcome, the customer service level customers get. Decisions in the logistics area may also have a very significant impact on the cost of a marketing strategy.

This chapter covers some important details concerning logistics and distribution customer service. But the major focus is on integrating transporting and storing into one coordinated effort--not only within an individual firm but also *among firms* in the channel--to provide customers with the appropriate physical distribution customer service level at the lowest total cost. You'll see how and why many firms are adopting approaches such as just-in-time delivery and electronic data interchange (EDI) to improve coordination of logistics in the channel.

The total cost approach to physical distribution, the physical distribution concept, and customer service levels are all important ideas which have significantly improved some companies' marketing strategy planning. But they are not yet well accepted. Try to see why. Helping to apply these ideas may offer a breakthrough opportunity for you.

Important Terms

logistics, p. 314
physical distribution (PD), p. 314
customer service level, p. 315
physical distribution (PD) concept, p. 318
total cost approach, p. 319
supply chain, p. 322
electronic data interchange (EDI), p. 323
transporting, p. 324

containerization, p. 328
piggyback service, p. 328
freight forwarders, p. 329
storing, p. 330
inventory, p. 330
private warehouses, p. 332
public warehouses, p. 332
distribution center, p. 333

True-False Questions

____ 1. Logistics—that is the transporting, storing, and handling of goods within individual firms and along channel systems—accounts for half the cost of marketing.

____ 2. Physical distribution is just another word for logistics.

____ 3. Customer service level is a measure of how rapidly and dependably a firm can deliver what customers want.

____ 4. Marketing managers should be careful to avoid offering customers a level of physical distribution service that might increase storing or transporting costs.

____ 5. According to the physical distribution concept, a firm might lower its total cost of physical distribution by selecting a higher cost transportation alternative.

____ 6. The total cost approach to PD involves evaluating each possible PD system—and identifying all of the costs of each alternative.

____ 7. When a firm decides to minimize total costs of physical distribution, it may also be settling for a lower customer service level and lower sales and profits.

____ 8. A higher physical distribution service level may mean both higher costs and higher profits.

____ 9. Just-in-time shifts more responsibility for PD activities to the supplier.

____ 10. A supply chain involves more firms than a channel of distribution.

____ 11. Electronic data interchange sets a standard for communication between different firms' computer systems.

____ 12. XML is a newer alternative to EDI and relies on exchanging data via the Internet.

____ 13. Transporting is the marketing function of storing goods.

____ 14. The value added to products by moving them should be greater than the cost of the transporting, or there is little reason to ship in the first place.

____ 15. In general, the trend has been toward much more government regulation over transporting.

____ 16. In contrast to railroads which are best suited for moving heavy and bulky freight over long distances, the flexibility of trucks make them especially suitable for moving small quantities of goods short distances.

____ 17. Trucking rates are roughly one-third of airfreight rates.

____ 18. Water transportation is very important to international trade, but it plays a small role within the U.S. market.

___ 19. An important advantage of using airfreight is that the cost of packing and unpacking goods for sale may be reduced or eliminated.

___ 20. The fact that rates on less-than-full carloads or truckloads are often much higher than those on full carloads or truckloads is one reason for the development of wholesalers.

___ 21. Even though freight forwarders usually do not own their own transporting facilities, they can obtain low transporting rates by combining small shipments into more economical quantities.

___ 22. When a firm's small shipments have to be moved by varied transporters, it probably should consider employing the services of freight forwarders.

___ 23. Storing is the marketing function of moving goods.

___ 24. Inventory means the amount of goods being stored.

___ 25. Most channel members provide the storing function for some length of time.

___ 26. Unless a large volume of goods must be stored regularly, a firm should probably choose public over private warehouses--even though public warehouses do not provide all the services that could be obtained in the company's own branch warehouses.

___ 27. The distribution center concept is based on the assumption that reducing storage and increasing turnover will lead to bigger profits.

Answers to True-False Questions

1. T, p. 314	10. T, p. 322	19. T, p. 328
2. T, p. 314	11. T, p. 323	20. T, p. 329
3. T, p. 315	12. T, p. 323	21. T, p. 329
4. F, p. 316	13, F. p. 324	22. T, p. 329
5. T, p. 318	14. T, p. 324	23. F, p. 330
6. T, p. 319	15. F, p. 325	24. T, p. 330
7. T, p. 319	16. T, p. 326	25. T, p. 330
8. T, p. 319	17. T, p. 327	26. F, p. 332
9. T, p. 322	18. F, p. 327	27. T, p. 333

Multiple-Choice Questions (Circle the correct response)

1. Logistics activities include:
   a. transporting, storing, and handling of physical goods.
   b. transporting and selling physical goods.
   c. selling of services.
   d. storing and selling of physical goods.
   e. transporting of services.

2. The physical distribution customer service level is important because:
    a.   it is a measure of how rapidly and dependably a firm delivers what its customers want.
    b.   it may result in lost sales if it is too low.
    c.   it may result in higher costs (and thus lower profits) if it is too high.
    d.   All of the above.
    e.   None of the above.

3. According to the "physical distribution concept":
    a.   transporting, storing, and product-handling are independent activities.
    b.   all transporting, storing, and product-handling activities of a business and a whole channel system should be coordinated as part of one system.
    c.   inventories should be based on production requirements.
    d.   the production department should be responsible for warehousing and shipping.
    e.   the lowest-cost distribution system is the best alternative.

4. Which of the following statements best reflects a marketing-oriented approach to physical distribution?
    a.   "We should create a position of inventory manager and give that person authority to coordinate all physical distribution activities to minimize the total cost of distribution."
    b.   "We should aim to keep our customers fully satisfied 100 percent of the time as this will increase our sales and give us a competitive advantage."
    c.   "We should replace our warehouses with distribution centers to speed the flow. of products and eliminate all storage."
    d.   "We should choose the physical distribution alternative that will minimize the total cost of achieving the level of customer service our target market requires."
    e.   All are equally "marketing-oriented."

5. The "total cost approach" to physical distribution management:
    a.   emphasizes faster delivery service and thus favors the use of airfreight over railroads.
    b.   often ignores inventory carrying costs.
    c.   might favor a high-cost transportation mode if storage costs are reduced enough to lower total distribution costs.
    d.   seeks to reduce the cost of transportation to its minimum.
    e.   All of the above are true.

6. A marketing-oriented physical distribution manager would *insist* that:
    a.   the storage function be eliminated to reduce inventory costs.
    b.   efficiency in physical distribution can be best achieved by minimizing costs.
    c.   emphasis must be on maximizing the customer service level.
    d.   both customer service level and total distribution costs be considered.
    e.   none of the above.

7. Just-in-time systems:
    a.   usually reduce PD costs for business customers.
    b.   usually increase PD costs for suppliers.
    c.   usually shift less responsibility for PD to business customers.
    d.   shift more responsibility for PD to suppliers.
    e.   All of the above.

8. A supply chain:
   a. includes a broader network of firms than a channel of distribution.
   b. shifts and shares logistics functions.
   c. utilizes outside experts and computer models.
   d. shifts and shares logistics costs.
   e. all of the above.

9. Electronic data interchange:
   a. puts information in a standardized format.
   b. makes inventory information more accessible.
   c. is common in both domestic and international communication.
   d. all of the above.
   e. both a and b, but not c.

10. Transporting costs
    a. are usually more than the value added by shipping, but the products are shipped anyway as there is no choice.
    b. do not vary much as a percentage of the final price of products, since big items are shipped by inexpensive means and small items are shipped by more expensive approaches.
    c. usually do not add much to the final cost of products which are already valuable relative to their size and weight.
    d. usually are not large enough to limit the target market that a marketing manager can serve.
    e. None of the above is true.

11. Which of the following transportation modes is "best" regarding "number of locations served"?
    a. Rail
    b. Water
    c. Truck
    d. Pipeline
    e. Air

12. Berry Bros. wants to ship a somewhat bulky, high-valued commodity a short distance--and it is seeking low-cost and extremely fast service. Berry should use:
    a. airfreight.
    b. railroads.
    c. inland waterways.
    d. trucks.
    e. None of the above.

13. Compared to other forms of transportation, airfreight may result in:
    a. a lower total cost of distribution.
    b. less damage in transit.
    c. higher transportation rates.
    d. lower packing costs.
    e. All of the above.

14. Grouping individual items into an economical shipping quantity and sealing them in protective containers for transit to the final destination is called:
   a. containerization
   b. carload service
   c. freight forwarding
   d. piggyback service
   e. all of the above

15. Freight forwarders:
   a. are not very active in international shipping because they are unwilling to handle all the paperwork necessary in overseas shipments.
   b. generally own their own transportation facilities--including pickup and delivery trucks.
   c. can be especially helpful to the marketing manager who ships in large quantities.
   d. accumulate small shipments from shippers and then reship them in larger quantities to obtain lower transportation rates.
   e. All of the above are true statements.

16. Storing:
   a. is related to Place--but has no effect on Price.
   b. is necessary because production does not always match consumption.
   c. must be performed by all members of a channel system.
   d. decreases the value of products.
   e. All of the above are true statements.

17. A manufacturer having irregular need for regional storage of bicycles should use which one of the following?
   a. a private warehouse to be sure of adequate space
   b. public warehouses to provide flexibility and low unit cost
   c. a distribution center
   d. direct distribution
   e. railroads, because they are slow and the bicycles are being stored while they're on the train

18. A distribution center is designed to:
   a. stockpile goods for long periods and avoid rising prices.
   b. buy low and sell high.
   c. reduce inventory turnover.
   d. speed the flow of goods and avoid unnecessary storing.
   e. all of the above.

Answers to Multiple-Choice Questions

1. a, p. 314
2. d, p. 315-17
3. b, p. 318
4. d, p. 318-19
5. c, p. 319-20
6. d, p. 319-20

7. e, p. 322
8. e, p. 322
9. d, p. 323
10. c, p. 325
11. c, p. 326
12. d, p. 326

13. e, p. 328
14. a, p. 328
15. d, p. 329
16. b, p. 330
17. b, p. 332
18. d, p. 333

Exercise 12-1

Evaluating physical distribution alternatives

Introduction

Within the framework of marketing strategy planning, logistics managers seek to provide the level of customer service that satisfies the needs of the firm's target market. Given some specified level of customer service, it is also the logistics manager's job to provide that service at the lowest cost possible. This total cost approach is based on the idea of "tradeoffs" among parts of the distribution system.

For example, a logistics manager may be making a tradeoff when he or she decides to lower transportation costs, because such a move usually results in larger inventory costs. Following the total cost approach, you would not try to minimize with transportation *or* inventory costs. Instead, you would design and operate the physical distribution system in a way that would *minimize the total cost of offering the desired customer service level*. The following exercise will illustrate this idea in greater detail.

Assignment

Read the following case and answer the questions that follow.

CROSSROADS COMPANY

The Crossroads Company is studying its physical distribution system to see if the system needs to be remodeled. Currently, Crossroads' industrial component product is manufactured at the firm's plant in Pittsburgh and then shipped by train to several branch warehouses across the United States. When an order is received at the Pittsburgh plant, the order is relayed to the branch warehouse closest to the customer. The products are then shipped directly to the customer by truck. Crossroads tries to maintain a 70 percent customer service level--that is, it tries to deliver 70 percent of its orders to the customer within three days after the orders are received.

Recently, several company managers have expressed dissatisfaction with the present distribution system. Crossroads' sales manager feels that the 70 percent service level is inadequate--and should be increased to at least 90 percent by adding more warehouses. The production manager wants to cut the service level to 20 percent, to even out his production schedule--although the traffic manager claims this will increase transportation costs too much. Finally, the finance manager has suggested that the firm try to minimize its total distribution costs by providing whatever level of customer service it can while operating at the lowest possible total cost.

To help resolve this conflicting advice from his top managers, Crossroads' president asked his assistant to analyze the relationship between alternative customer service levels and physical distribution costs. The results of this analysis are shown in Figure 12-1.

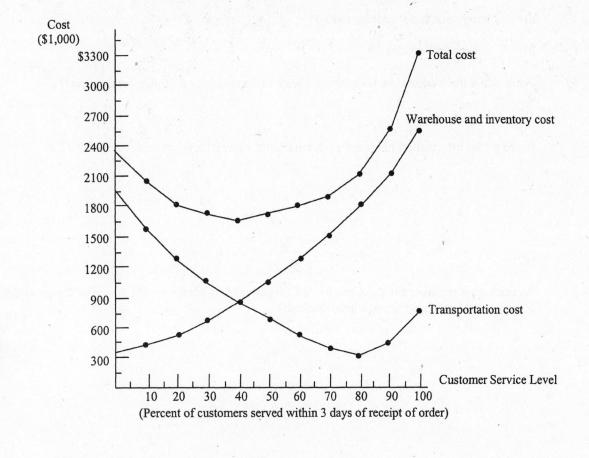

FIGURE 12-1
Distribution Costs at Different Customer Service Levels

1. At what customer service level would the total cost of distribution be *minimized* as the finance manager suggests? What would the minimum total cost be?

    Customer service level _____%   Total cost $ _____

2. According to Figure 12-1, what is Crossroads' total cost of physical distribution at its present 70 percent customer service level?
    $_____

3. What would the total cost be if a 90 percent service level were adopted, as the sales manager desires?
    $_____

4. What would the total cost be if a 20 percent service level were adopted, as the production manager has suggested?

    $ _____

5. What would the *total cost* be if Crossroads attempted to *minimize* its:

    a) warehouse and inventory costs $ _____

    b) transportation costs $ _____

6. What would the total cost be if Crossroads were to *maximize* its customer service level?

    $ _____

7. Based on the information in Figure 12-1, what is the optimal level of customer service?

8. As marketing manager for the Crossroads Company, what advice would you give the president concerning the customer service level decision?

Question for Discussion

What determines the level of service that customers expect?

Exercise 12-2

Integrating physical distribution

Introduction

Successful marketers must pay attention to the distribution customer service they provide their customers. They also must worry about the cost of the service they provide--because ultimately the price of a product should cover the cost. Deciding on the right balance between the distribution customer service level and the costs of transporting and storing is sometimes difficult--and identifying how best to achieve that balance can be even more of a challenge. The job of integrating all of the logistics activities is even more complicated when it requires coordination among different firms in a channel. But the job must be done and done well. One firm can't just reduce its own PD costs if that raises costs somewhere else in the channel--or reduces the service level. For example some business customers may demand just-in-time delivery or expect the convenience and speed of electronic data interchange (EDI)--because that is what is required to make the whole channel more competitive.

Many marketing managers know about the physical distribution concept, but it's easy to fall into the trap of just accepting 'a firm's PD system as "the way it's always been"--never even bothering to think about how to improve it. This exercise gives you practice in analyzing different PD situations--and in applying the concepts discussed in Chapter 12 to improve a marketing strategy.

Assignment

Read each of the following situations carefully. Identify the major PD problem(s) and then make specific suggestions about how you might improve the strategy. State any assumptions that you think are important to your recommendation. In your answer, be sure to show that you understand the various concepts--including the different storing and transporting alternatives--discussed in the text. The first problem is answered for you as an example of the approach to take. But keep in mind that there may be more than one "correct" answer in each situation. The solution will depend, in part, on your creativity!

1.   Capital Orthopedics is a partnership of surgeons who treat broken bones for patients who live in a medium-size town. Most patients need to be in a cast for four to six weeks, and after that many must wear a removable brace for a few more weeks--until the bone is strong. Recently, Capital Orthopedics contracted to provide care to members of a local Health Maintenance Organization, and they agreed that the HMO could do a survey to evaluate patient satisfaction. The doctors were surprised to find that many patients gave them a low rating--primarily because of the inconvenience involved in being fitted for braces. Hospitals in a large city keep a complete assortment of braces on hand, but that is not feasible for a small clinic with limited space. So Capital Orthopedics orders braces from a wholesaler by phone the day a patient's cast is removed, and then the patient schedules another appointment to come back the next day--after the wholesaler delivers the brace-to have it fitted.

Problem: *Fitting of the braces may not be the most important part of what the doctors do, but the unavailability of braces when patients (customers) expect them results in a breakdown in satisfaction with the service. The anxiety of a day without the brace probably doesn't help.*

Recommendation: *Although it may not be possible to stock <u>all</u> of the different types and sizes of braces, the clinic might try to stock one each of the most frequently used braces. Even a "less-than-complete" inventory might avoid many of the problems. Further, and perhaps more important, the timing of the demand for a particular size and type of brace does not arise as a surprise. Most patients have had a cast on for a number of weeks before they come in for the appointment to have it removed. It should be a simple matter for the clinic to order needed braces several days before each patient's cast-removal appointment. Earlier ordering could solve the problem--and increase satisfaction.*

2. Circle City Bakeries makes a variety of sugar-free cookies that are sold by several large supermarket chains in the Midwest. Data from the stores' checkout computers is automatically linked to the Circle City Bakeries in Chicago so that each day's production run, and the shipments to each store, can exactly match the assortment needed to refill each store's display. This reduces inventory costs and also results in fresh cookies. While studying sales figures, the Circle City Bakeries marketing manager noticed that during the previous two months there had been no sales of Almond cookies at one store. On investigation, the manager discovered that a case of Almond cookies were crushed in transit. The shattered cookies--clearly visible through their plastic bags--had been placed on the rack by a stock clerk. Because no customers were buying the damaged cookies, none passed through the checkout scanners, and no replacements were ordered.

    a)   Problem:

    b)   Recommendation:

3.   Select Motor Works (SMW) is a manufacturer of family automobiles and has enjoyed real success in serving a small, but profitable, segment of the U.S. market. SMW's vehicles are renown for safety and durability. But this success brings problems. SMW must provide dealers with repair parts for five different models, many of which have changed significantly over the years. Yet, the success of SMW's strategy depends on strong service from dealers--to keep customers happy, word-of-mouth favorable, and repeat sales strong. The company operates 10 U.S. parts warehouses and ships to dealers by common carrier truck. As the number of older models still in service has increased, dealers have begun to complain about the long re-stock time *and* the large number of parts they must keep in stock to handle the discontinued models. Some customers face a long wait for parts before the dealer can fix a car.

a)   Problem:

b)   Recommendation:

4.   Above & Beyond Designs is the second largest producer of high quality coated fabrics used for outdoor awnings for fine homes, restaurants, and hotels, and in other applications--including boat covers. Above & Beyond Designs sells fabric directly to the thousands of awning fabricators who serve customers in their local markets. Once a consumer selects a fabric from a sample and tells a fabricator what to make, the fabricator calls the regional Above & Beyond Designs sales rep and places an order. Each week's orders are then processed through the home office and the bulky fabric is shipped by truck to the fabricator from either the company's east coast or west coast warehouse. This approach reduces transportation costs and makes it easier to manage the inventory in the warehouse. Although many fabricators are loyal to Above & Beyond Designs fabric, a new competitor from Europe has been taking a share of the market, apparently in large part because it is able to fill orders within a week rather than the three weeks it takes, on average, for Above & Beyond Designs. The Above & Beyond Designs marketing manager does not expect the new competitor to be able to survive, however, because its delivered prices are about 10 percent higher.

a)   Problem:

b)   Recommendation:

5.   Paragon Furniture makes a wide variety of stylish upholstered sofas and chairs. Over time, an increasing share of the company's business has come from special orders which consumers place through furniture stores, most of which handle a number of competing lines. As special orders increased, Paragon slowly increased the choices among upholstery fabrics--and the firm now offers more than 250 colors and patterns. Some customers seem to be delighted with this unique array of choices. Even so, sales have slowly tapered off--and at a recent dealer meeting, several retailers complained that not many customers were willing to wait eight to twelve weeks for Paragon to produce and deliver a custom order. Paragon's sales manager urged the retailers to carry more chairs and sofas in stock, so that they could sell more Paragon furniture "off the display floor."

a)   Problem:

b)   Recommendation:

Question for Discussion

Given the difficulties of coordinating physical distribution activities in a channel, wouldn't it be easier and cheaper for most manufacturers to make all the important PD decisions--and then deal only with middlemen who will accept those decisions.

Exercise 12-3

Total distribution cost

This exercise is based on computer-aided problem number 12--Total Distribution Cost. A complete description of the problem appears on page 335 of *Basic Marketing,* 16th edition.

Tom Phillips, Proto Company's product manager, has heard that a major supplier on the opposite side of the country has dropped its line of charge card blanks. Phillips is trying to decide what distribution system to use to compete for these new target customers. Although he is concerned about the total cost of distribution, he is also concerned about the physical distribution (PD) customer service level. Better customer service may cost more--but it may also help to win customers in this distant market. And these customers may be willing to pay a higher price for a marketing mix with better service.

1. Proto can enter the new market and fill 95 percent of all orders within 7 days using a PD system involving railroad transportation. The shipping cost would be $2.00 a box, and the new market would require 1 warehouse at $26,000 per year. Inventory carrying costs for this PD system are 10 percent. What is the total cost of physical distribution in the new market--if Proto expects to sell 5,000 boxes per year at a price of $40.00 a box? What is the total revenue from the additional sales? How much money is left after the total cost of distribution is subtracted from revenue?

    For the new target market:

    Total revenue $ _____

    less, Total Cost-PD $ _____

    equals Net Revenue after PD costs $ _____

2. If Proto Company uses airfreight it will have to lease space in 2 public warehouses at $9,600 per year each. Airfreight will cost $7.50 a box, and inventory carrying costs will be 5 percent--but Proto could deliver 95 percent of all orders within 3 days. What is the total cost of distribution in the new market--if Proto expects to sell 5,000 boxes per year and keep the price at $40.00 a box? For the new market, what is the total revenue? How much is left after the distribution cost is subtracted from revenue?

    Total revenue $ _____

    less, Total Cost-PD $ _____

    equals Net Revenue after PD costs $ _____

3. How do the two distribution alternatives (described in questions 1 and 2 above) compare in terms of total cost? In terms of customer service level?

    _____

    _____

    _____

    _____

4. The comparisons in question 3 assume that all customers will be charged the same price. But marketing research suggests that customers might pay more for a marketing mix with better customer service. Approximately how high a price would customers have to be willing to pay for Proto to make more money from the airfreight system than by using the railroad system?

    Price at which airfreight system
    would be more profitable: $ _____

Chapter 13

Retailers, wholesalers, and their strategy planning

What This Chapter Is About

Chapter 13 looks at the many changes that have been taking place in retailing and wholesaling.

Try to understand why and how retailers behave--because retailing probably will continue to change in the future. In particular, try to see why there are so many different types of retailers--and why some seem to be doing well while others have serious problems. Note the differences in retailing in different nations.

Don't just memorize the definitions of the various types of retailers. Instead, study what each is doing for some group of target customers. A diagram is presented later in the chapter to help organize your thinking.

It is useful to think of retailers from their point of view--rather than only as outlets for manufacturers' products. Most retailers see themselves as buyers for their customers, rather than selling arms of manufacturers. Try to look at retailing the way they do. This should increase your understanding of this vital part of our marketing system.

Chapter 13 also discusses various kinds of specialized wholesalers who have developed to provide "wholesaling functions"--really just variations of the basic marketing functions. You should become familiar with the various types: what they do, and roughly what they cost.

Wholesalers are not guaranteed a place in channel systems. Some have been eliminated. Others probably will be. And other wholesalers have been making a "comeback" in part because of the Internet.

Like other firms, wholesalers must develop market-oriented strategies. But wholesalers are channel specialists--so think of them as members of channel systems--rather than as isolated firms. This will help you see why wholesalers are very important members of *some* channel systems--while they are not used at all in other channels.

The Internet is impacting retailing and wholesaling in significant ways. This is a trend that will continue. Try to understand why and how.

Important Terms

retailing, p. 339
general stores, p. 342
single-line stores, p. 342
limited-line stores, p. 342
specialty shop, p. 342
department stores, p. 343
mass-merchandising concept, p. 343
supermarkets, p. 344
discount houses, p. 344
mass-merchandisers, p. 345
supercenters (hypermarkets), p. 346
convenience (food) stores, p. 347
automatic vending, p. 347
door-to-door selling, p. 347
telephone and direct-mail retailing, p. 347
wheel of retailing theory, p. 351
scrambled merchandising, p. 352
corporate chain store, p. 353
cooperative chains, p. 354
voluntary chains, p. 354
franchise operation, p. 354
wholesaling, p. 355
wholesalers, p. 355

manufacturers' sales branches, p. 357
merchant wholesalers, p. 358
service wholesalers, p. 358
general merchandise wholesalers, p. 358
single-line (or general-line) wholesalers, p. 359
specialty wholesalers, p. 359
limited-function wholesalers, p. 359
cash-and-carry wholesalers, p. 359
drop-shippers, p. 360
truck wholesalers, p. 360
rack jobbers, p. 360
catalog wholesalers, p. 360
agent middlemen, p. 361
manufacturers' agent, p. 361
export agents, p. 361
import agents, p. 361
brokers, p. 361
export brokers, p. 362
import brokers, p. 362
selling agents, p. 362
combination export manager, p. 362
auction companies, p. 362

True-False Questions

_____ 1. Retailing covers all of the activities involved in the sale of products to final consumers.

_____ 2. About three-fourths of all new retailing ventures fail during the first year in the U.S.

_____ 3. A consumer's choice of a retail store appears to be based almost entirely on emotional needs--economic needs have almost no influence.

_____ 4. A hundred and fifty years ago, general stores--that carried anything they could sell in reasonable volume--were the main retailers in the United States.

_____ 5. A limited-line store will typically carry a broader assortment than a single-line store.

_____ 6. Limited-line stores may carry several lines of merchandise--but with a very limited assortment of products within each line.

_____ 7. A specialty shop is a type of limited-line store that usually is small, has a distinct personality, and aims at a carefully defined market segment by offering knowledgeable salespeople, better service, and a unique product assortment.

8. Department stores are becoming less important and their share of retail business has declined continuously since the 1970s.

9. Conventional retailers believe in a fixed demand for a territory and have a "buy-low and sell-high" philosophy.

10. The mass-merchandising concept says that retailers should offer low prices to get faster turnover and greater sales volumes--by appealing to larger markets.

11. A well-managed supermarket can generally count on a net profit level of only about 1 percent of sales.

12. While discount selling generally involves price cutting on a limited assortment of products, many modern discount houses are fast-turnover, price-cutting operations that offer full assortments, better locations, and more services and guarantees.

13. The average mass-merchandiser has a store that is about the same size as an average supermarket.

14. Supercenters are simply large mass-merchandisers that carry many more shopping products.

15. Single-line mass-merchandisers attract large numbers of customers with their large assortment and low prices in a single product category.

16. Convenience food stores limit their assortment to those "pickup" or "fill-in" items that are needed between trips to a supermarket, and thus earn smaller profits as a percent of sales.

17. Automatic vending has low operating costs because labor costs are very low.

18. Although it's an expensive method of selling--door-to-door retailers may be especially useful for the sale of unsought products.

19. Telephone and mail-order retailing grew for a while, then declined, but the Internet is helping to turn things around again.

20. Cable TV channels devoted to home shopping are holding their own and may never decide to open websites on the Internet.

21. The Internet is JUST another aspect of how low-margin mass-merchandisers appeal to large target markets with discount prices.

22. Retail sales on the Internet are expected to grow rapidly.

23. The Internet makes it harder to do comparison shopping of products and prices.

24. All major retailing developments can be explained by the "Wheel of Retailing" theory—that describes a recurring retail cycle from low cost and low prices to higher cost and higher prices.

25. "Scrambled merchandising" is a way of describing the activities of modern retailers who are willing to carry "unconventional" assortments of products—anything they can sell profitably.

26. Only about 11 percent of all retail stores have annual sales of $5 million or more—but these stores account for almost 70 percent of all retail sales.

27. One of the incentives to corporate chain development is the availability of economies of scale.

28. Voluntary chains are formed by independent retailers in their efforts to compete with corporate chains—while cooperative chains operate similarly except that they are sponsored by wholesalers.

29. Franchising is more popular with goods retailing than with services retailing.

30. Franchise holders now account for about half of all retail sales.

31. Around the world, mass-merchandising is more popular in less-developed nations because they need the lower prices more.

32. E-commerce is making it easier for producers and consumers to connect without the use of wholesalers.

33. Many manufacturers and retailers have realized that wholesaling functions are not always necessary, so wholesalers have been eliminated at an increasing rate since the 1970s.

34. Most modern wholesalers have become more streamlined in their operations, more computerized in controlling their inventories, and more selective in their distribution policies.

35. Recent trends in wholesaling indicate that wholesaling will survive, even though some wholesalers may disappear.

36. All wholesalers perform the following functions for their customers: anticipate needs, regroup products, carry stocks, deliver products, grant credit, provide information and advisory service, provide part of buying function, and own and transfer title to products.

37. The typical merchant wholesaler's operating expenses amount to about 25 percent of sales.

38. The fact that many manufacturers have set up their own sales branches suggests that the use of wholesalers usually make distribution costs unnecessarily high.

39. A producer who uses a direct channel system normally is also considered a wholesaler--because he must take over the wholesaling functions that an independent wholesaler might provide.

_____ 40. Merchant wholesalers don't necessarily provide all of the wholesaling functions, but they do take title to the products they sell.

_____ 41. Service wholesalers provide all of the wholesaling functions--while limited-function wholesalers provide only certain functions.

_____ 42. A general merchandise service wholesaler may represent many different kinds of manufacturers and supply many different kinds of retailers.

_____ 43. Even though cash-and-carry wholesalers are limited-function wholesalers, they operate like service wholesalers, except that the customer must pay cash.

_____ 44. Drop-shippers own the products they sell--but do not actually handle, stock, or deliver them.

_____ 45. Truck wholesalers' operating costs are relatively high because they provide a lot of service relative to how much they sell.

_____ 46. Rack jobbers are limited-function wholesalers, with relatively high operating costs, who help retailers offer a more attractive assortment of products--especially nonfood items.

_____ 47. Catalog wholesalers should probably be classified as retailers--since they sell out of catalogs.

_____ 48. A manufacturer who has the capability of operating its own distribution facilities but lacks customer contacts should consider the use of agent middlemen to facilitate the buying and selling functions.

_____ 49. Agent middlemen are less common in international trade than in U.S. markets because merchant wholesalers can both sell products and handle the financing.

_____ 50. The key role of manufacturers' agents is to provide well-established customer contacts for new products--while assuming all the risks of taking title to the products they handle.

_____ 51. A broker's "product" is information about what buyers need--and what supplies are available.

_____ 52. A small manufacturer with limited financial resources whose only skills are in production should probably consider contracting with a selling agent to act, in effect, as the firm's marketing manager.

_____ 53. The primary advantage of auction companies is that they facilitate buying by description.

1. T, p. 339	19. T, p. 347	37. F, p. 357
2. T, p. 340	20. F, p. 347	38. F, p. 357-58
3. F, p. 341	21. F, p. 347	39. F, p. 357
4. T, p. 342	22. T, p. 347	40. T, p. 357
5. F, p. 342	23. F, p. 350	41. T, p. 357
6. F, p. 342	24. F, p. 352	42. T, p. 358
7. T, p. 342	25. T, p. 352	43. T, p. 359
8. T, p. 343	26. T, p. 353	44. T, p. 360
9. T, p. 343	27. T, p. 353	45. T, p. 360
10. T, p. 343	28. F, p. 354	46. T, p. 360
11. T, p. 344	29. F, p. 354	47. F, p. 360
12. T, p. 345	30. T, p. 354	48. T, p. 361
13. F, p. 345	31. F, p. 355	49. F, p. 361
14. F, p. 346	32. T, p. 355	50. F, p. 361
15. T, p. 346	33. F, p. 355	51. T, p. 362
16. F, p. 347	34. T, p. 356	52. T, p. 362
17. F, p. 347	35. T, p. 356	53. F, p. 362
18. T, p. 347	36. F, p. 356	

Multiple-Choice Questions (Circle the correct response)

1.   Which of the following best describes what "retailing" involves?
   a.   The sale of consumer products to wholesalers, retailers, or final consumers.
   b.   The performance of all merchandising activities except promotion and pricing.
   c.   The sale of both business and consumer products.
   d.   The sale of products to final consumers.
   e.   All of the above describe what retailing involves.

2.   Which of the following would be considered a *limited-line* retailer?
   a.   Supermarket
   b.   Gas station
   c.   Mass-merchandiser
   d.   Drugstore
   e.   Bakery shop

3.   Specialty shops:
   a.   generally try to become well known for the distinctiveness of their line and the special services offered.
   b.   generally carry complete lines--like department stores.
   c.   carry specialty products almost exclusively.
   d.   generally use a mass-marketing approach.
   e.   All of the above are true.

4.	Department stores:
	a.	are often frowned upon by the retailing community because they provide too many customer services.
	b.	normally are large stores which emphasize depth and distinctiveness rather than variety in the lines they carry.
	c.	are very popular with some consumers--and thus may be the only way to reach these market segments.
	d.	are still growing rapidly in number, average sales per store, and share of retail sales.
	e.	All of the above are true statements.

5.	The idea underlying the mass-merchandising concept is that:
	a.	A big profit on each item sold won't earn much if sales volume is low.
	b.	Inventory is a big cost, so everything you stock should be out on a shelf where it can be seen by the mass market.
	c.	A retailer must "buy low and sell high" if it's going to make an attractive profit.
	d.	It is better to sell more at the same price--since total revenue will increase.
	e.	All of the above are true.

6.	Which of the following are *not* "conventional retailers" according to the text?
	a.	General stores
	b.	Single-line stores
	c.	Supermarkets
	d.	Limited-line retailers
	e.	All of the above

7.	Which of the following statements about supermarkets is *true*?
	a.	Supermarkets should be classified as "conventional retailers."
	b.	Net profits after taxes in supermarkets usually run about 1 percent of sales--or less.
	c.	Annual sales for supermarkets average about $50 million.
	d.	They typically carry 15,000 product items.
	e.	All of the above are true statements.

8.	Large departmentalized retail stores that are larger than supermarkets and follow the discount house's philosophy of emphasizing lower margins to achieve faster turnover are called:
	a.	department stores.
	b.	mass-merchandisers.
	c.	category killers.
	d.	specialty shops.
	e.	box stores.

9.	A "supercenter":
	a.	is just another name for a mass-merchandiser.
	b.	essentially refers to large department stores which have adopted supermarket-style operating procedures and methods.
	c.	is concerned with providing all of the customer's routine needs at a low price.
	d.	is another name for a "category killer."
	e.	All of the above are true.

10. The modern convenience (food) stores are successful because they offer:
    a.   wide assortments.
    b.   low prices.
    c.   expanded customer service.
    d.   the right assortment of "fill-in" items.
    e.   All of the above.

11. Which of the following statements about direct-mail retailing is *true?*
    a.   It is hard to target customers using direct-mail retailing.
    b.   Mail-order retailers tend to have lower operating costs than conventional retailers.
    c.   All mail-order retailers offer both convenience products and shopping products.
    d.   Shoplifting is a big problem for mail-order retailers.
    e.   Mail-order retailers place their primary emphasis on low-price merchandise.

12. Electronic shopping via cable TV or computer:
    a.   is expected to grow even faster with the availability of new interactive cable services.
    b.   has come on strong on cable TV where whole channels are devoted to it.
    c.   allows shoppers to order almost any kind of product from their home by phone or online.
    d.   All of the above are true statements.
    e.   None of the above are true statements.

13. Which of the following statements is *false?*
    a.   All types of retailers are now establishing a presence on the Internet.
    b.   Shopping on the Internet is easier when you know exactly what you're looking for.
    c.   The economic impact of the Internet has been phenomenal but is now on the decline.
    d.   Shopping on the Internet makes it easy to compare products and prices.
    e.   None of the above is false.

14. The "Wheel of Retailing" theory suggests that:
    a.   retail stores do not have life cycles.
    b.   retailing profits tend to be cyclical.
    c.   only the largest retailers have a chance to survive in a fast-moving economy.
    d.   new types of retailers enter as low-price operators and eventually begin to offer more services and charge higher prices.
    e.   only discounters can survive in the long run.

15. Which of the following concepts is best illustrated by a retail bakery that sells wristwatches?
    a.   The "superstore"
    b.   Scrambled merchandising
    c.   Time-sharing
    d.   The "wheel of retailing" theory
    e.   Mass-merchandising

16. Census data indicate that:
    a.   only about 11 percent of all retail establishments have annual sales of $5 million or more.
    b.   there are more manufacturers and wholesalers than there are retailers in the United States.
    c.   the large number of small retailers make working with them inexpensive.
    d.   the really large retailers account for a rather small percentage of total retail sales.
    e.   all of the above are true.

17. A group of retailers banding together to establish their own wholesaling organization would be known as a:
   a. cooperative chain.
   b. voluntary chain.
   c. consumer cooperative.
   d. corporate chain.
   e. franchise.

18. Franchisors:
   a. leave it to franchisees to carry out the strategy in their own units.
   b. often help franchisees by providing purchasing power and promotion support.
   c. usually receive fees and commissions from the franchise holder.
   d. reduce the risk of starting a new retailing business because a good strategy has already been developed and tested.
   e. All of the above are true statements.

19. The development of new, more efficient retailers around the world is dependent upon:
   a. the political and legal environment.
   b. the technological environment.
   c. the social and cultural environment.
   d. the economic environment.
   e. all of the above.

20. Which of the following is *least likely* to occur in retailing in the future?
   a. Conventional retailers will continue to feel a profit squeeze.
   b. Scrambled merchandising will decline.
   c. There will be more vertical arrangements between producers and retailers.
   d. There will be an increase in in-home shopping.
   e. Stores will continue to make shopping more convenient.

21. Which of the following is *not* a typical wholesaling function?
   a. provide market information to a producer.
   b. grant credit to customers.
   c. supply capital to pay the cost of carrying inventory.
   d. all of the above are typical wholesaling functions.
   e. none of the above is a typical wholesaling function.

22. Which of the following statements is *least relevant* in explaining how wholesalers are changing with the times?
   a. The Internet is helping many innovative wholesalers to increase their business.
   b. Wholesalers are encouraging their salespeople to be more aggressive in using high-pressure selling techniques.
   c. Many wholesalers have become more selective in their choice of customers--as many small retailers were clearly unprofitable.
   d. Many wholesalers no longer require each customer to pay for all of the services they provide *some* customers.
   e. Wholesalers have streamlined their operations to cut costs and improve profits.

23. Which of the following types of wholesalers has the *highest* operating expenses as a percent of sales?
   a. Manufacturers' agents
   b. Manufacturers' sales branches
   c. Brokers
   d. Drop-shippers
   e. Merchant wholesalers

24. Manufacturers' sales branches:
   a. have very low sales per branch.
   b. are mainly used in weak market areas, where there is not enough business for other types of wholesalers.
   c. operating costs would be even lower than they are now if manufacturers didn't "charge" them with extra expenses.
   d. handle about 30 percent of all wholesale sales.
   e. serve the same basic needs as do brokers.

25. The two basic types of merchant wholesalers are:
   a. single-line and specialty.
   b. service and limited-function.
   c. service and general merchandise.
   d. single-line and limited-function.
   e. agents and brokers.

26. Regarding merchant wholesalers, which of the following statements is TRUE?
   a. They own (take title to) the products they sell.
   b. Merchant wholesalers are the most numerous wholesalers and handle over 60 percent of all wholesale sales.
   c. General merchandise wholesalers of consumer products handle a broad variety of nonperishable items, including both convenience and shopping products.
   d. A specialty wholesaler generally would offer a narrower range of products than a single-line wholesaler.
   e. All of the above are true.

27. Which of the following types of wholesalers do *not* carry stocks for their customers?
   a. Cash-and-carry wholesalers.
   b. Rack jobbers.
   c. Truck wholesalers.
   d. Drop-shippers.
   e. Catalog wholesalers.

28. Which of the following statements about rack jobbers is *true?*
   a. Rack jobbers specialize in hard-to-handle assortments of products.
   b. Rack jobbers provide retailers with specialized information about consumer preferences.
   c. Rack jobbers are practically full-service wholesalers.
   d. Rack jobbers apply their knowledge of local retail preferences in many stores.
   e. All of the above are true statements.

29. A type of middleman that does *not* take title to the products is known as:
   a. an agent middleman.
   b. a limited-function wholesaler.
   c. a rack jobber.
   d. a merchant wholesaler.
   e. a drop-shipper.

30. Which of the following statements *is false?*
   a. Agent middlemen generally provide fewer functions than limited function wholesalers.
   b. Manufacturers' agents usually represent noncompeting manufacturers.
   c. Brokers are often used because of the seasonal nature of production or demand.
   d. Manufacturers' agents generally have more authority over prices and terms of sale than do selling agents.
   e. Agent middlemen are very common is international trade.

31. Turgo, Inc. has just developed a new convenience product for which it wants intensive distribution nationally. It expects a low initial demand and wants to keep selling costs as low as possible while keeping control of marketing. This is Turgo's first product and working capital is small. Which of the following channels would be best?
   a. Turgo's own sales force direct to retailers.
   b. Manufacturers' agents to merchant wholesalers to retailers.
   c. Brokers to consumers.
   d. Turgo's own sales force direct to merchant wholesalers to retailers.
   e. Selling agents to merchant wholesalers to retailers.

32. The principal function of a broker is to:
   a. transport acquired products.
   b. facilitate inspection of products.
   c. establish a central market.
   d. bring buyers and sellers together.
   e. distribute grocery products.

33. The Jory Co. handles the entire output of several small clothing manufacturers on a national basis. The firm has almost complete control of pricing, selling, and advertising. In addition, Jory often provides working capital to the producers, who have very limited financial resources. In return, Jory is paid a substantial commission on all sales. The Jory Co. is a:
   a. selling agent.
   b. full-service wholesaler.
   c. manufacturers' agent.
   d. broker.
   e. none of the above.

1. d, p. 339
2. e, p. 342
3. a, p. 342
4. c, p. 343
5. a, p. 343
6. c, p. 343
7. b, p. 344
8. b, p. 345
9. c, p. 346
10. d, p. 347
11. b, p. 347

12. d, p. 347
13. c, p. 347
14. d, p. 351
15. b, p. 352
16. a, p. 353
17. a, p. 354
18. e, p. 354
19. e, p. 354-55
20. b, p. 352
21. d, p. 355
22. b, p. 355-56

23. e, p. 356-57
24. d, p. 357
25. b, p. 357
26. e, p. 357-59
27. d, p. 360
28. e, p. 360
29. a, p. 361
30. d, p. 362
31. b, p. 361
32. d, p. 361
33. a, p. 362

Exercise 13-1

Identifying and analyzing retail stores

Introduction

Retailing involves the sale of products to final consumers. There are 1,115,906 retailers in the United States. However, as discussed in the text, there are many different types of retailers and they vary both in size and method of operation. Marketing managers of consumer products at all channel levels must understand retailing--for if the retailing effort is not effective, the products may not be sold and *all* members of the channel will suffer. Likewise, consumers must be concerned with retailing--because their standard of living is partly dependent on how well retailing is done.

The purpose of this exercise is to focus your attention on the retailers who serve *your* community. What types of stores are there? How do they operate? Who are their target customers? Why might there be different types of retailers selling *basically* the same kinds of products?

Assignment

Listed below are several types of retail stores that were discussed in the text. For each type:

a)   Give the name and address of a store in your community that illustrates this type.

b)   Briefly describe the store in terms of its *width* and *depth* of assortment. Is it a single-line or limited-line store or a "scrambled merchandiser"? Does the store stress high turnover or low turnover products?

c)   Briefly describe the store in terms of its price/service blend (is the store price-oriented or service-oriented) and estimate whether the store's gross margin is in the *low range* (below 20 percent), *medium range* (20-35 percent), or *high range* (over 35 percent).

Note: If your community does not have a particular store type, write "none" under part (a) and then answer parts (b) and (c) in terms of how you *think* that type of store would operate.

1. *Limited-Line "Conventional " Retailer*

   a)   Store name and address: _____

   b)   Assortment: _____

   c)   Price/Service blend: _____

   Gross margin range: _____

2. *Department Store*

   a)   Store name and address: _____

   b)   Assortment: _____

   c)   Price/Service blend: _____

   Gross margin range: _____

3. *Supermarket*

   a)   Store name and address: _____

   b)   Assortment: _____

   c)   Price/Service blend: _____

   Gross margin range: _____

4. *Mass-Merchandiser*

   a)   Store name and address: _____

   b)   Assortment: _____

   c)   Price/Service blend: _____

   Gross margin range: _____

5. *Single-Line Mass-Merchandiser*

   a)   Store name and address: _____

   b)   Assortment: _____

   c)   Price/Service blend: _____

   Gross margin range: _____

6.   *Convenience (Food) Store*

   a)   Store name and address: _____

   b)   Assortment: _____

   c)   Price/Service blend: _____

   Gross margin range: _____

7.   *Internet Merchant (does not need to be based in your community, but can be)*

   a)   Name and web address: _____

   b)   Assortment: _____

   c)   Price/Service blend: _____

   Gross margin range: _____

Question for Discussion

Why are there so many different types of retailers in the United States? What implications does this have for marketing strategy planning?

Exercise 13-2

Choosing the right kind of wholesaler

Introduction

Wholesalers are less dominant than they once were, but they are still a very important part in our economy. Wholesalers have become more specialized, so a marketing manager who must select a wholesaler must be concerned not only with finding a "good one," but also finding the right *type* of wholesaler.

There are two important types of wholesalers--*merchant wholesalers* and *agent middlemen*. The most important difference between the two types is that merchant wholesalers take title to (own) the products they handle, while agent middlemen do not. There are several types of merchant wholesalers and agent middlemen-and each performs different tasks. A marketing manager should select the type best suited to his marketing strategy. The various types of wholesalers are:

A.   *Merchant Wholesalers*

      1.   *Service Wholesalers*--including general merchandise, single-line and specialty whole-salers.

      2.   *Limited-Function Wholesalers*--including cash and carry, drop-shippers, truck whole-salers, catalog wholesalers, and rack jobbers.

B.   *Agent Middlemen*--including auction companies, brokers, manufacturers' agents, and selling agents.

Assignment

This exercise will give you some practice in choosing the right type of wholesaler. Each of the following cases describes a situation in which a buyer or seller *might* want to use one or more types of merchant wholesalers or agent middlemen. Read each case carefully and then indicate which type(s) of wholesaler(s) would be most appropriate for each situation. Then explain your answer.

The first case is answered for you as an example.

1. San Felipe Food Company was started in Los Angeles in 1960 by a Mexican immigrant. Over the years, the company's spicy corn chips have become a snack food favorite in the greater Los Angeles metropolitan market. In fact, San Felipe's chips have become so popular that the company is now planning to open new plants in Dallas and Phoenix and to expand its market coverage across the whole Southwest. However, the marketing manager for the company doubts that San Felipe can afford to set up the same plant-to-retailer delivery service in the new market areas as it now operates in the Los Angeles area.

   a) Type of Wholesaler: *Merchant wholesaler--truck wholesaler*

   b) Explanation: *The perishability of these products and the wide variety of outlets suggests the need for wholesalers who specialize in carrying stock and delivering on a frequent basis. There might be some specialty wholesalers willing to do this job--but truck wholesalers have specialized in this area for some years and might better understand the needs of the appropriate target markets. There still might be a problem in "selling" them on taking on this company's line.*

2. Sonya Jemez has been managing a frame shop that she owned with her husband. That seemed like an interesting thing to do when she graduated from college, but now she wants to start her own business. She thinks that the growing interest in health food opens up some interesting opportunities. With money borrowed from her father, she made a down payment on a bakery which formerly belonged to a local cookie manufacturer. As her first product, she decided to produce a unique honey and bran muffin. She "discovered" the recipe for this tasty product while traveling in Switzerland, and she is certain that it can be a profitable item if she can distribute it through health food stores and nutrition centers. A number of the health food stores in her area have already expressed interest in carrying the muffins. But Jemez knows that she needs to obtain wider distribution--i.e., outside her present area--to be successful. One of the problems with expanding distribution, however, is that the muffins use no preservatives--so they are perishable.

   a) Type of Wholesaler: _____

   b) Explanation: _____

   _____

   _____

3.   Absolute Corporation--a large manufacturer of backup ("uninterruptable") power supplies and battery packs for computer systems--has decided to produce and sell a new line of automobile batteries. The company deliberately avoided the highly competitive consumer replacement market in the past--but now feels that it has a product that is much longer lasting than any battery currently on the market. Absolute plans to distribute its new batteries through gasoline service stations, automotive stores, hardware stores, and mass-merchandisers. At the present time, the company has very limited financial resources--due to the cost of expanding its manufacturing facilities to produce the new line of batteries.

   a)   Type of Wholesaler: _____

   b)   Explanation: _____

   _____

   _____

4.   Smart Windows produces a line of insulated windows that are used for residential and commercial construction and remodeling. It supplies lumberyards, large glass contractors, and home-builders throughout a three-state area. Smart uses its own trucks for deliveries within a hundred miles--and ships carload quantities by railroad. Currently, five sales reps call directly on its present customers. The company is faced with large swings in demand, however, and has had difficulty finding new customers.

   a)   Type of Wholesaler: _____

   b)   Explanation: _____

   _____

   _____

5.   Neal Jamison recently developed a patented recycling process for diseased trees. Officials from nearby cities--lacking any ecologically acceptable alternatives for disposing of trees that have been cut down--have agreed to deliver their trees free of charge to Jamison's plant. There, the trees are processed and converted into products such as wood chips for landscaping, bark mulch, railroad ties, and patio blocks. However, Jamison has little marketing experience and know-how. Usually buyers come to him by word of mouth--and then he is not sure how to price his products. The firm is in trouble financially and may have to declare bankruptcy unless Jamison can locate a steady and sizable market for his products. But, he has no funds to hire a sales rep or to promote his products.

   a)   Type of Wholesaler: _____

   b)   Explanation: _____

   _____

   _____

6. Specialty Coatings, Inc. (SCI) offers a full line of custom paint pigments, rust preventive coatings, and polishing compounds to a variety of industrial customers. Recently, a manufacturer of fiberglass hot-tubs asked SCI to develop a special polishing compound that could remove small scratches and blemishes from its new tubs. The polish worked so well that SCI decided that it might do well in the consumer market--not only for hot-tubs but also for standard fiberglass tubs and shower enclosures. A test market in Dallas, Texas--that relied on distribution through select hardware stores, hot-tub outlets, and even some mass-merchandisers--proved quite successful. Now, SCI has decided to sell the polish in other large cities--including New York, Detroit, Chicago, San Francisco, Houston, Atlanta, and Miami. SCI has the financial resources to manufacture the product and handle physical distribution to these areas. However, the company does not have any established contacts with the relevant retailers in these markets. Further, SCI is reluctant to hire new sales reps to promote its only consumer product.

a) Type of Wholesaler: _____

b) Explanation: _____

_____

_____

7. Consuelo Duffy is marketing manager for Hilltop, Inc., a firm that processes and markets premium grade frozen and canned vegetables. In recent years, Duffy has been expanding distribution of the Hilltop brand. She does not expect more sales growth this year, but large increases are expected over the next few years. The company had planned to expand production capacity as it was needed, but that plan changed when several small vegetable processing plants came on the market. Hilltop got the processing plants at a very low price because they had not been able to find enough business at profitable prices and were near bankruptcy. Duffy is glad to know that the company now has the capacity to serve expanding market opportunities, but in the meantime she is looking for some way to quickly "get rid of" fairly large quantities of processed peas, corn, and other vegetables that were acquired with the processing plants.

a) Type of Wholesaler: _____

b) Explanation: _____

_____

_____

8.   Delia Garrett is the owner and president of ConnectIt, Inc. Her father started the firm after immigrating to the U.S. in 1960, and it became a respected supplier of brass electrical connectors. Most of the firm's business in the early years came from a relatively small number of electric power companies who placed large orders as they expanded their service in fast-growing areas of the South. After her graduation from an electrical engineering program in 1986, Garrett encouraged her father to shift the firm's focus to making specialized connectors used by firms that assemble electronic parts. In the past, the firm relied primarily on a network of manufacturers' agents who called on customer firms all over the U.S. But now that Garrett has taken over the reins of the firm, she wants to do a better job of reaching overseas markets. There are many thousands of small and large companies in countries all over the world that might use her very specialized connectors. Many of these firms don't have local suppliers but instead order the wide variety of supplies and parts they need from wholesalers in the U.S. These wholesalers attract the firms' business with websites and print materials that describe in detail the thousand and thousands of products that they carry.

a)   Type of Wholesaler: _____

b)   Explanation: _____

_____

_____

Question for Discussion

Why are there so many different types of wholesalers?

Exercise 13-3

Analyzing channels of distribution

Introduction

A channel of distribution consists of different people performing different functions. They are linked together by a common interest in marketing products that someone needs and wants. At one end of the channel are producers and at the other end are customers, and often there are "middlemen" in between.

Most products are *not* distributed directly from the manufacturer to the consumer or final user. The Internet is opening up new possibilities in the area, but middlemen will play an important role in many channels long into the future. In fact, the variety of middlemen has actually increased over the years. Middlemen exist because they perform some necessary functions--often more efficiently and economically than could either manufacturers or consumers.

This exercise focuses on several important types of middlemen. The objective is to determine what specific functions and activities each middleman performs--and to understand the role each plays in the distribution channel. Further, the exercise illustrates that while one type of middleman can sometimes be substituted for another--in other situations different types of middlemen perform complementary functions. Thus, while one channel may be longer than some others, it may also be faster, more economical, or more effective.

Assignment

The activities of several types of middlemen are described below in five cases. For each middleman described:

A.   Identify the *general type* of middleman (a full-service merchant wholesaler, a limited-function merchant wholesaler, or an agent middleman) *and* the *specific type* of middleman (rack jobber, broker, etc.).

B.   Diagram the channel or *channels* of distribution that are described in the case, using the following letters.

(M)   for Manufacturers   [A]   for Agent Middelemen

<R>   for Retailers   [W]   for Full-Service Wholesalers

(C)   for Consumers or   [L]   for Limited-Function Middlemen
       Final Users

The first case has been completed as an example.

1. Patrick Tysor sells carload quantities of chemicals to industrial users--for several chemical manufacturers. Tysor takes title to the products he sells. But he does not take physical possession of them, although he often arranges for transporting the products. One part of his business that is costly is the frequent need to provide credit to small customers.

    a) General Type: *Tysor is a limited-function merchant wholesaler.*

        Specific Type: *drop-shipper*

    b) Diagram of the Channel:

    ```
          ( M )
            |
            v
          [ L ]
            |
            v
          ( C )
    ```

2. TripleA Textiles, Inc., is the manufacturer of TripleA brand acrylic fabrics. TripleA is the leading brand of fabric used in manufacturing waterproof awnings for stores, hotels, and homes. There are about 5,000 "fabricators" around the country who use TripleA brand fabrics to produce custom awnings for their clients. The fabricators order TripleA fabrics from distributors. The distributors maintain inventories (usually at a number of different branch locations) so that they can provide fast delivery. The distributors also offer the fabricators credit, and they carry a complete assortment of grommets, zippers, snaps, metal poles, and other items the fabricators need to make awnings. TripleA Textiles has six salespeople who call on the distributors.

    a) General Type: _____

        Specific Type: _____

    b) Diagram of the Channel:

3. Recently, TripleA Textiles has developed new fabric designs for use in making cushions for outdoor furniture. However, TripleA's traditional distributors have not done a very good job of seeking out orders from the hundreds of small manufacturers who produce outdoor furniture. As a result, TripleA has turned to people like Cecily Burch for additional help in reaching this market. Burch, who also represents producers of a number of other noncompeting lines, aggressively promotes TripleA to manufacturers of outdoor furniture in her region. Burch earns a commission of 6 percent on all of the sales she generates. When Burch calls in an order, TripleA ships the fabric directly to the furniture manufacturer.

    a)   General Type: _____

            Specific Type: _____

    b)   Diagram of the Channel:

4. Dynamo Distributors is a hardware wholesaler who sponsors a voluntary chain of independent hardware retailers. In addition to the usual wholesaling functions, Eagle provides special services for its affiliated stores: its own "dealer brand" products at very competitive prices, free-standing advertising inserts for distribution in the retailer's local newspaper, other merchandising assistance, employee training programs, store location and design assistance, and accounting aid. Merchandise economies are achieved through group buying, and a modern distribution center is used to lower operating costs.

Some retailers who handle only small assortments of hardware items are too small to benefit from membership in the chain. Dynamo operates a subsidiary to provide a smaller assortment of household items (such as extension cords, spray paint, screw drivers) for these "unaffiliated" customers. Retailers must provide their own transportation. The products are priced attractively--considering the small order quantities--but no credit is offered.

    a)   General Type: _____

            Specific Type: _____

    b)   Diagram of the Channel:

5.   Bluestone Pottery, a small company in Seagrove, North Carolina, produces handcrafted pottery plates, cups, bowls, and vases. The owners of Bluestone Pottery want to focus on designing and producing pottery, not on the administrative and financial responsibilities of the business. As a result, they have worked out an arrangement with ClayWorks, Inc., a wholesaler that basically operates as a "marketing manager" for Bluestone Pottery. ClayWorks finds retail gift shops to carry the pottery--and handles pricing, selling, advertising, and all paperwork on orders, including billing and collections. ClayWorks earns a large commission on all sales, but Bluestone's owners like the arrangement because all they need to do is arrange transportation to get the pottery to the retailers.

a)   General Type: _____

Specific Type: _____

b)   Diagram of the Channel:

6.   ElectroNet is an Internet-based firm that works with manufacturers of a wide variety of electronic parts and components and helps them quickly liquidate excess or obsolete inventory. ElectroNet does not actually buy the inventory; rather, it sells the inventory (usually as a complete "lot") on a commission basis by putting a detailed description of what is for sale on its web site and then selling it to the highest bidder. For example, Advance, Inc., manufactures circuit boards used to control electric motors. Current models of Advance circuit boards are usually sold to distributors who supply manufacturers of various types of electronic equipment. However, when Advance introduces a new model, it turns to ElectroNet to sell off its remaining inventory of the discontinued model. Many of the firms that bid on the products listed on ElectroNet's website are in developing nations where there is demand for the products, even if they are not on the cutting edge of technology.

a)   General Type: _____

Specific Type: _____

b)   Diagram of the Channel:

Question for Discussion

Are salespeople middlemen? Where are salespeople shown in channel diagrams?

Exercise 13-4

Selecting channel intermediaries

This exercise is based on computer-aided problem number 13--Selecting Channel Intermediaries. A complete description of the problem appears on page 365 of *Basic Marketing,* 16th edition.

After further discussion, the owner of Giftware Distributing--the merchant wholesaler--says that he might take on some, or even all, of the responsibility for advertising the Art Glass items to gift stores--if Art Glass will sell to him at a lower price--to help cover the advertising expense. Art Glass is considering this idea--and trying to decide what type of arrangement makes the most sense.

1.   Art Glass' marketing manager has decided that it will help him analyze the decision if he first figures out how much Giftware will earn under the current arrangement--assuming that Giftware sells 4,500 units. Although he did not include this calculation in the spreadsheet, he can calculate the total dollar markup because he knows how much Giftware would pay for each item and Giftware's selling price. What is the total dollar markup (contribution to profit) for Giftware?

   Giftware's selling price per item: $ _____

   less, Art Glass' price to Giftware: $ _____

   equals, Giftware's markup per unit: $ _____

   multiplied times the total units sold: 4,500

   equals total $ markup (contribution to to
   profit) earned by Giftware: $ _____

2.   Since Art Glass is considering spending $8,000 on advertising to support Giftware's marketing effort, and since Giftware is expected to sell about 4,500 units, what is the expected advertising cost per unit?

   Advertising expenditure per unit: $ _____

3. Use the spreadsheet to calculate the profit contribution to Art Glass if it sells to Giftware at $10.25 a unit, and Giftware does the advertising needed to sell 4,500 units (that is, so that Art Glass has no advertising expense). Would this be a better arrangement for Art Glass than what it was originally considering? Briefly explain why or why not?

Art Glass' Total Contribution to Profit with this plan: $ _____

Explanation: _____

_____

_____

_____

4. Art Glass' marketing manager thinks that Giftware would be more likely to agree to an arrangement in which Art Glass pays for some of the "up front" advertising expense. He is thinking about offering to pay half of the proposed $8,000 advertising expense. If this plan is used (and Giftware sells 4,500 units), what price should Art Glass charge to enable it to make the same profit contribution as it would if it paid for all of the advertising and sold to the wholesaler at the $12.00 price? (Hint: change the advertising expense on the spreadsheet, and use the What If analysis to vary Art Glass' selling price).

Art Glass' selling price to make about the same contribution if it pays for only half of the advertising expense:

Art Glass' price to Giftware $ _____

Total profit contribution to Art Glass $ _____

5. At Art Glass' price in question 4, how much would Giftware have left as a "contribution to profit" if it sold 4,500 units and paid $4,000 for advertising expense? (Please show your calculations below. Please label the numbers you use.)

Giftware's "contribution to profit" $ _____

6. Art Glass' marketing manager wants to know how this advertising cost-sharing arrangement would compare to the original proposal (that is, with Art Glass paying all of the advertising expense but getting a higher price from Giftware) if Giftware were able to sell 5,000 units, rather than the expected 4,500.

Art Glass' contribution to profit:

from 5,000 units sold at $12.00 with $8,000 ad expense: $ _____

from 5,000 units sold at $ _____ with $4,000 in ad expense: $ _____

7. Would Giftware be motivated to work harder at selling Art Glass' products under the proposed ad cost-sharing arrangement than it would if it bought at the higher price but with Art Glass paying all the advertising expense)? Briefly explain why or why not?

_____

_____

_____

_____

_____

_____

_____

Chapter 14

Promotion—Introduction to integrated marketing communications

What This Chapter Is About

Chapter 14 introduces Promotion--the topic of Chapters 14-16. Be sure to see that Promotion is only one of the four Ps--*not* the whole of marketing. Promotion tries to carry out promotion objectives--just as the other Ps have their own specific objectives.

This chapter looks at promotion objectives and methods from a strategic viewpoint--with emphasis on developing a good promotion blend. Early in the chapter, much attention is given to the communication process and the adoption of new ideas. These theoretical concepts should be studied carefully. They provide a solid base for strategy planning of personal selling (Chapter 15) and advertising (Chapter 16). The concepts of pushing and pulling are also discussed.

Although some of the material appears theoretical, it is important because not all promotion decisions are "just common sense." Poor decisions here could lead to "mass marketing" and the use of a "shotgun" rather than a "rifle" approach to Promotion. This chapter should help you bring a rifle to promotion planning--to practice "target marketing."

Important Terms

promotion, p. 368
personal selling, p. 369
mass selling, p. 370
advertising, p. 370
publicity, p. 370
sales promotion, p. 371
sales managers, p. 372
advertising managers, p. 372
public relations, p. 372
sales promotion managers, p. 372
integrated marketing communications, p. 372
AIDA model, p. 375
communication process, p. 376
source, p. 376
receiver, p. 376
noise, p. 376

encoding, p. 376
decoding, p. 376
message channel, p. 377
pushing, p. 382
pulling, p. 383
adoption curve, p. 385
innovators, p. 385
early adopters, p. 386
early majority, p. 387
late majority, p. 388
laggards, p. 388
nonadopters, p. 388
primary demand, p. 388
selective demand, p. 389
task method, p. 391

___ 1. Promotion is communicating information between seller and potential buyer or others in the channel to influence attitudes and behavior.

___ 2. Advertising is any form of nonpersonal presentation of ideas, goods, or services.

___ 3. Sales promotion refers to activities such as personal selling, advertising and publicity.

___ 4. All sales promotion is aimed at final consumers or users.

___ 5. In total, personal selling is more expensive than advertising.

___ 6. To avoid conflicts, it is usually best for sales promotion to be handled by a firm's advertising manager and sales manager--not by a sales promotion specialist.

___ 7. Planning of promotion blends can be best accomplished by placing specialists in charge of each promotion method; for example, the firm might appoint a sales manager, an advertising manager, and a sales promotion manager to weigh the pros and cons of the various approaches and come up with an effective blend.

___ 8. An effective blending of all of the firm's promotion efforts should produce integrated advertising communications.

___ 9. All of a firm's different communications to a target market should be consistent.

___ 10. The overall objective of promotion is to affect behavior.

___ 11. The three basic objectives of promotion are to inform, persuade, and/or remind.

___ 12. The AIDA model consists of four promotion jobs: attention, information, desire, and action.

___ 13. Much of what we call promotion is really wasted effort because it does not really communicate.

___ 14. A major advantage of personal selling is that the source can get immediate feedback to help direct subsequent communication efforts.

___ 15. The term "noise" refers only to distorting influences within the message channel which reduce the effectiveness of the communication process.

___ 16. If the right message channel is selected, problems related to encoding and decoding in the communication process will be avoided.

___ 17. The communication process is complicated by the fact that receivers are usually influenced not only by the message but also by the source and the message channel.

___ 18. Direct marketing is direct communication between a seller and an individual customer using a promotion method other than face-to-face personal selling.

___ 19. Unfortunately direct-response promotion is limited to mail.

___ 20. A firm that wants to send a specific message to a clearly identified target market probably should seriously consider using integrated direct marketing.

___ 21. Firms who use direct-response promotion need to be very sensitive to ethical and environmental concerns.

___ 22. Interactive information technologies are changing the traditional communication process to a customer-initiated process.

___ 23. In customer-initiated interactive communication, action is more immediate than in the traditional communication process.

___ 24. There is no one right promotion blend for all situations.

___ 25. Salespeople should usually be expected to do all the promotion to middlemen.

___ 26. One reason personal selling is important in promotion to middlemen is that marketing mixes often have to be adjusted from one geographic territory to another.

___ 27. Promotion to employees is especially important in service-oriented industries where the quality of the employees' efforts is a big part of the product.

___ 28. "Pulling a product through the channel" means using normal promotion effort to help sell the whole marketing mix to possible channel members.

___ 29. The large number of potential customers practically forces producers of consumer products and retailers to emphasize advertising and sales promotion.

___ 30. Since business customers are much less numerous than final consumers, it is more practical to emphasize mass selling in the promotion blends aimed at these markets.

___ 31. The adoption curve focuses on the process by which an individual accepts new ideas.

___ 32. Publicity in technical journals is likely to be a more effective method of promotion than personal selling for reaching extremely innovative business firms.

___ 33. The late majority are influenced more by other late adopters—rather than by advertising.

___ 34. Situations that may affect the promotion blend are the stage in the product life cycle and the nature of competition.

___ 35. During the market introduction stage of product life cycles, promotion must pioneer acceptance of the product idea--not just the company's own brand—to stimulate primary demand.

36. In the market growth stage of the product life cycle, promotion emphasis must begin to shift from stimulating selective demand to stimulating primary demand for the company's own brand.

37. In the market maturity stage, the promotion blend of consumer products firms rely almost exclusively on advertising to consumers.

38. Budgeting for marketing expenditures as a percentage of either past or forecasted sales leads to larger marketing expenditures when business is good and sales are rising--and to reduced spending when business is poor.

39. The most sensible approach to budgeting marketing expenditures is the "task method."

Answers to True-False Questions

1. T, p. 368	14. T, p. 376	27. T, p. 383
2. F, p. 370	15. F, p. 376	28. F, p. 383
3. F, p. 371	16. F, p. 377	29. T, p. 384
4. F, p. 371	17. T, p. 377	30. F, p. 384
5. T, p. 371	18. T, p. 378	31. F, p. 385
6. F, p. 372	19. F, p. 378	32. T, p. 386
7. F, p. 372	20. T, p. 378	33. T, p. 388
8. F, p. 372	21. T, p. 379	34. T, p. 388
9. T, p. 372	22. T, p. 380	35. T, p. 388
10. T, p. 374	23. T, p. 381	36. F, p. 389
11. T, p. 374	24. T, p. 382	37. F, p. 389
12. F, p. 373	25. F. p. 382	38. T, p. 390
13. T, p. 376	26. T, p. 383	39. T, p. 391

Multiple-Choice Questions (Circle the correct response)

1. Promotion does *not* include:
   a. personal selling.
   b. advertising.
   c. publicity.
   d. sales promotion.
   e. Promotion includes all of the above.

2. Personal selling is more appropriate than mass selling when:
   a. the target market is large and scattered.
   b. there are many potential customers and a desire to keep promotion costs low.
   c. flexibility is not important.
   d. immediate feedback is desirable.
   e. All of the above are true.

3.   Sales promotion activities:
     a.   try to stimulate interest, trial or purchase.
     b.   always involve direct face-to-face communication between sellers and potential customers.
     c.   usually take a long time to implement.
     d.   are usually a good substitute for personal selling and advertising.
     e.   All of the above.

4.   Sales promotion can be aimed at:
     a.   final consumers or users.
     b.   middlemen.
     c.   the company's own sales force.
     d.   all of the above.
     e.   only a and b above.

5.   Deciding on the appropriate promotion blend is a job for the firm's:
     a.   advertising agency.
     b.   marketing manager.
     c.   advertising manager.
     d.   sales manager.
     e.   sales promotion manager.

6.   Which basic promotion objective should be emphasized by a firm whose product is very similar to those offered by many competitors?
     a.   Communicating
     b.   Persuading
     c.   Reminding
     d.   Informing
     e.   Reinforcing

7.   The AIDA model's four promotion jobs are getting:
     a.   awareness, interest, demand, action.
     b.   attention, interest, desire, action.
     c.   action, interest, desire, acceptance.
     d.   awareness, interest, decision, acceptance.

8.   Which of the following is *not* one of the basic elements in the communication process?
     a.   Feedback
     b.   Receiver
     c.   Encoding
     d.   Dissonance
     e.   Message channel

9.   Communication is *most difficult* to achieve when:
     a.   the source and the receiver are not in face-to-face contact with each other.
     b.   immediate feedback is not provided.
     c.   any trace of "noise" remains in the message channel.
     d.   the source and the receiver do not have a common frame of reference.
     e.   the encoder does not do the decoding.

10. Direct response promotion may include:
   a. Telephone
   b. Print
   c. E-mail
   d. Internet
   e. All of the above

11. To communicate a very specific message to a very select, well-identified group of consumers, one probably should use:
   a. magazines aimed at special-interest groups.
   b. newspapers.
   c. television.
   d. integrated direct-response promotion marketing.
   e. radio.

12. ValCorp will soon introduce a new product, so the marketing manager is having the sales force call on distributors to explain its unique features and how the distributors can best promote it. This illustrates
   a. integrated marketing communications.
   b. a "pulling" policy.
   c. direct response promotion.
   d. a "pushing" policy.
   e. noise in the communication process.

13. Which of the following statements about the *target of promotion* and promotion blends is *true?*
   a. There is no one right promotion blend for all situations.
   b. Promotion to middlemen emphasizes personal selling.
   c. Promotion to employees involves pushing.
   d. Promotion to final consumers is usually a combination of pushing and pulling.
   e. All of the above are true.

14. Regarding planning a promotion blend, a good marketing manager knows that:
   a. the job of reaching all the people in a "buying center" is made easier by their low turnover.
   b. there is not much chance of economies of scale in promotion.
   c. it is seldom practical for salespeople to carry the whole promotion load.
   d. salespeople can be very economical since they devote almost all of their time to actual selling activities.
   e. None of the above is true.

15. Lauren Diaz is strongly influenced by her peer group--and she often adopts a new product only after they have pressured her to try it. She makes little use of mass media and salespeople as sources of information. In terms of the adoption curve, she is
   a. a laggard
   b. a late majority
   c. an early adopter
   d. an innovator
   e. an early majority

16. During the market introduction stage of the product life cycle, the basic objective of promotion is to:
    a. spend more money on promotion than competitors.
    b. remind customers about the firm and its products.
    c. inform the potential customers of the product.
    d. stimulate selective demand.
    e. persuade the early majority to buy the product.

17. Which of the following is the most sensible approach to budgeting for marketing expenditures?
    a. Budget expenditures as a percentage of either past or forecasted sales.
    b. Set aside all uncommitted sales revenue--perhaps including budgeted profits.
    c. Base the budget on the amount required to reach predetermined objectives.
    d. Match expenditures with competitors.
    e. Set the budget at a certain number of cents or dollars per sales unit--using the past year or estimated year ahead as a base for comparison.

Answers to Multiple-Choice Questions

1. e, p. 369
2. d, p. 369
3. a, p. 371
4. d, p. 371
5. b, p. 372
6. b, p. 374

7. b, p. 375
8. d, p. 376
9. d, p. 376
10. e, p. 378
11. d, p. 378
12. d, p. 382

13. e, p. 382-84
14. c, p. 384
15. b, p. 388
16. c, p. 388
17. c, p. 391

Exercise 14-1

The traditional communication process in promotion

Introduction

Promotion must communicate effectively--or it's wasted effort. Yet it is often difficult to achieve effective communication. The communication process can break down in many different ways.

Understanding the whole communication process can improve promotion. As discussed in more detail in the text (see pages 376-78 and Exhibit 14-4), the major elements of the traditional communication process include:

> a source,
> encoding,
> a message channel,
> decoding,
> a receiver,
> feedback, and
> noise.

Each of these different elements can influence the effectiveness of a firm's promotion effort--so marketing managers need to consider each element when planning or modifying their promotion. The whole promotion effort may fail because of a failure in just one element.

This exercise is designed to enhance your understanding of the traditional communication process in promotion planning. The focus here is on specific elements of the process.

Assignment

Listed below are several descriptions of different promotion situations. In each case, there is a problem with the promotion effort. For some reason, communication has not been effective. You may see different elements of the promotion process that may be related to the problem. But, the focus of each situation is on a specific element of the process. So, for each situation, write down *one* element (from the list above) that you think is the major problem. Then, briefly explain why you think that element is a problem, and how the communication process might need to be changed to correct the problem. (Note: your recommendation may include changing one or more elements of the traditional communication process other than the one that you noted as the major problem.)

1.   A company that produces expensive leather briefcases for business executives wants to expand its sales in overseas markets. In the U.S., the company's ads--placed in business magazines—show a group of well-dressed men and women executives preparing for a meeting. Each executive has a briefcase, and the headline for the ad says "If you want respect, it's as important to look professional as it is to act professional." The company adapted this same copy thrust to a Japanese ad that featured Japanese models. But, the effort was a failure. In Japan, there are still very few women in high executive positions, and for many target customers the ad did not help to create a "prestige" image for the company's products.

a)   Problem element of the communication process: _____

b)   Explanation:

2.   A vitamin company has been doing advertising for its line of weight-loss diet supplements. The supplements are targeted to overweight, middle-aged men and women. The company's ads appear on TV exercise programs that are viewed by the same target market. In the ad, a trim professional model explains the product and how safely and effectively it works. But the ads do not seem to be effective. Apparently the overweight viewers don't believe that a trim model really knows about the difficulties of losing weight.

a)   Problem element of the communication process: _____

b)   Explanation:

3.　An insurance company has a list of customers whose policies are about to expire. The company has hired sales reps to telephone these customers and ask them if they would like to renew their policies. Research shows that most customers appreciate this service--since it means that there will not be a lapse in their policy. The company has screened and hired sales reps carefully. Each salesperson has been trained concerning the prices for different policies. The company leaves it to each sales rep to decide what to say--so that the presentation will be as natural as possible. But, the inexperienced salespeople have trouble getting the conversation started and often the customer hangs up before the point of the call is clear.

a)　　Problem element of the communication process: _____

b)　　Explanation:

4.　A student newspaper on a college campus wants to increase revenues by attracting more faculty subscriptions. Very few faculty members currently subscribe. A study by students in a marketing research course found that many faculty members don't subscribe because they think that the price of a subscription is much higher than is actually the case. The subscription manager has placed large ads in the newspaper that clearly show how little it actually costs to subscribe, but so far faculty response has been very disappointing.

a)　　Problem element of the communication process: _____

b)　　Explanation:

5.   Line Drive Life Insurance Company has equipped its sales agents with notebook computers so they can quickly do a detailed, personalized analysis of a prospect's needs and present the results with on-screen graphs--while working with the prospect. The company thought that the computers would be especially helpful for presentations about its combined insurance and retirement-savings products--which are targeted at retired professionals who are interested in leaving a "nest-egg" for their grandchildren. However, since the agents started using the on-screen presentations, their ratio of "closes" (signed contracts) to sales calls has dropped for the retiree market segment. One of the retirees commented to the salespeople that "we old people don't want all this razzle-dazzle, we just want to hear what you have to say about the plan." But most of the agents continue to use the notebook computers anyway--because of its powerful presentation graphics.

a)   Problem element of the communication process: _____

b)   Explanation:

Question for Discussion

Does a marketer who has set up a website on the Internet to enable interactive communications initiated by customers need to worry about the elements of the traditional communication process? Explain your thinking.

Exercise 14-2

Using the adoption curve to develop promotion blends

Introduction

We have continually stressed that each of the "four Ps" should be matched with the needs and characteristics of target markets. But marketing mix planning can get more complicated in the promotion area. Even though a target market may have fairly homogeneous needs--*groups of people within this market may differ considerably in their sources of information and how quickly they adopt new products.* Therefore, marketing managers may need to use several promotion blends--over time--to communicate effectively with this target market.

Promotion blend planning should use the adoption curve--which shows when different groups accept ideas. Five adopter groups are commonly used: innovators, early adopters, the early majority, the late majority, and laggards.

As outlined in the text (see pages 385-88), a unique pattern of communication exists within and between each of these adopter groups. Therefore, each may require its own promotion blend.

Assignment

This exercise is designed to show how an understanding of the adoption curve can be helpful when planning promotion blends. Read the following case and then *develop a promotion blend for each adopter group* within the firm's target market. Outline in detail what kind of mass selling, personal selling, and sales promotion you would use, if any, to reach each adopter group. Be specific. For example, if you decide to advertise in magazines, give examples of the magazines you would use. Above all, be creative-- it's expected of you!

After you outline your promotion blend for each adopter group, explain *why* you chose that particular blend in the space marked "Comments." Here, you should consider some of the important characteristics of each adopter group--as discussed in the text.

Note that you are only being asked to focus *on promotion to final consumers*. The firm would also have to do some promotion work in the channels-just to obtain distribution--and adoption curve thinking should be applied to middleman adoption too. But all of this promotion activity should be ignored here--because we want to focus on the way that final consumers would accept the product and its impact on promotion planning.

Mediamax, Ltd.--one of the world's largest manufacturers of electronics equipment--has just announced the introduction of a revolutionary new device called the Ultimedia. Aimed primarily at the "serious consumer" market, the Ultimedia features a fascinating combination of features and capabilities. It can record and play two hours of very high resolution digital video (or audio). It is small--about the size of an Altoids breath mint tin--so it fits easily in the user's pocket. Yet, it has a fold-out 4" high resolution display screen. It is powered by a revolutionary "100 year" battery. It also has built-in software and wireless capabilities to transfer compressed audio or video over the Internet, or to store high-definition movies on a computer harddrive. With its built-in cell phone, it can even be used for portable video conferencing. One electronics magazine described the Ultimedia as "the technical leap that will ultimately bring digital video into every aspect of life."

The quality of the Ultimedia's digital audio and video is exceptional. In the past, this quality of video could only be achieved with expensive video cameras that were ten times as large and required tapes for storage. The Ultimedia's breakthrough in video compression technology makes it possible to store two hours of high-definition video on a tiny, removable, 1 gigabyte flash memory card. Because of its size, the lens is not "broadcast" quality (as with most professional videocams). However, it is not just a video camera. Other types of digital information (music, software, data) can be stored on Ultimedia memory cards—and the Ultimedia can perform many of the functions of a tablet PC or PDA. However, it does not need a keypad or stylus because it responds to spoken commands. Further, the Ultimedia has *automatic indexing*--so the Ultimedia electronically "marks" the beginning of any material stored on the memory card--whether it is video, dictation, music, or data. This allows the user to quickly find and display anything stored on the unit. While some PDAs, cell phones, and digital camcorders already have some of these features, the Ultimedia is the first system to integrate them with high quality digital video.

The Ultimedia also offers several other important benefits. With its revolutionary battery, small case, and light weight the unit is truly portable and can be used anywhere at any time. In addition, it features an innovative system of "user friendly" instructions (an on-screen menu system provides instructions, or will provide spoken guidance) and the controls are so simple that even a child can automatically "program" any of the Ultimedia's functions. For example, it will play back video clips or songs in any order, any number of times.

The Ultimedia also has a unique "digital dubbing" feature and built in microphone. This allows the user to simultaneously watch video and record an audio track. For example, users can make a movie on a trip and then include an audio track later. It can also be used, for example, to record conversations and meetings or to document details of some activity—like the steps to turn off the home security system. It can also be used for simple dictation, or the user can even play an instrumental selection and add in his or her own voice track. In combination, all of these features make the Ultimedia one of the world's most sophisticated multimedia consumer recorders.

The Ultimedia has a manufacturer's suggested list price of $2,595--but it is expected to retail for about $2,295. This price is not out of line when one considers the unique capabilities of the Ultimedia--but the price is much higher than consumers are used to paying for a video camera, MP3 player, PDA, or cell phone. Further, some of the possible uses of the unit will never have occurred to potential customers. For example, the video and narration feature of the Ultimedia makes it easy for the user to create and update an "audio video" diary. Therefore, promotion may be critical for the new unit--which will be distributed through electronics retailers, some computer and camera dealers, and selected electronics equipment mass-merchandisers.

Mediamax, Ltd. managers are not sure what promotion blend to use to introduce this new recorder. One manager has noted that some customers will adopt the Ultimedia faster than others--and therefore the promotion blend may have to vary over time. So, they are asking you to advise them.

Suggested Promotion Blends for Communicating with Potential
Consumers in Each Adopter Group

1.   Innovators

      a)   Market characteristics: _____

_____

_____

_____

      b)   Promotion blend: _____

_____

_____

_____

_____

      c)   Comments: _____

_____

_____

_____

_____

2.   Early adopters

    a)   Market characteristics: _____

          _____

          _____

          _____

    b)   Promotion blend: _____

          _____

          _____

          _____

    c)   Comments: _____

          _____

          _____

          _____

3.   Early majority

    a)   Market characteristics: _____

          _____

          _____

          _____

    b)   Promotion blend: _____

          _____

          _____

          _____

    c)   Comments: _____

          _____

          _____

          _____

4. Late majority

    a)   Market characteristics: _____

                _____

                _____

                _____

    b)   Promotion blend: _____

                _____

                _____

                _____

    c)   Comments: _____

                _____

                _____

                _____

5. Laggards

    a)   Market characteristics: _____

                _____

                _____

                _____

    b)   Promotion blend: _____

                _____

                _____

                _____

    c)   Comments: _____

                _____

                _____

                _____

Which of the adopter categories is probably the most important from the viewpoint of the marketing strategy planner? That is, which is most crucial in launching a successful new product? Why?

Exercise 14-3

Selecting a communications channel

This exercise is based on computer-aided problem number 14--Selecting a Communications Channel. A complete description of the problem appears on page 393 of *Basic Marketing,* 16th edition.

Helen Troy had almost decided to go with advertising on FM radio--given the numbers on the original spreadsheet. This would result in a "cost per buyer" of about $8.65. At that point, the sales rep for the magazine space called and suggested that Troy consider some new information.

1.   First, the rep said it was hard to verify the actual number of readers--but that some of his 200,000 magazines are actually read by two or three people. He stressed that, when this "pass-along circulation" is included, the actual number of readers is greater than 200,000--probably between 230,000 and 250,000. Troy decided to evaluate this new information with her spreadsheet. Do you think it should influence her decision? Briefly explain why.

_____

_____

_____

_____

2.   The magazine's sales rep also told Troy about a new "quantity discount." The magazine has reduced the rate for a one-page ad to $1,500 when an advertiser agrees to place five or more ads in one year. How does the lower ad rate affect the two kinds of costs? (Note: do this analysis and subsequent analyses assuming 240,000 readers--for the reasons described in the question above.)

$ _____ cost per aware prospect $ _____ cost per buyer

3.   As in question 2, companies that do more advertising often get lower advertising rates. Briefly discuss how this might affect their ability to compete with other firms.

_____

_____

_____

_____

4. The magazine's sales rep has also told Troy that the magazine has just started to include a "reader service" card in each issue--so readers can follow up on advertising of interest by simply returning the postage-paid card. Troy will receive all of the names--and her salespeople can follow up with personal phone calls. Troy is optimistic that this could help identify good prospects and increase the percentage of "awares" converted to buyers from a low of the expected 1.5 percent to as high as 2.5 percent. Given the increased number of readers due to pass-along circulation, the rate discount for placing five or more ads, and the reader interest card, evaluate the "new" situation-regarding use of the magazine. How does it compare with the original spreadsheet proposal for the radio campaign? Briefly summarize your conclusions based on your analysis. (Hint: one approach is to do a What If analysis--varying the percent of awares who will buy and comparing these results with the results for the radio ad.)

_____

_____

_____

_____

_____

_____

_____

_____

_____

_____

Chapter 15

Personal selling and customer service

What This Chapter Is About

Chapter 15 is concerned with the strategy decisions in the personal selling area.

It is important to see that not all sales jobs are alike. This is why a good understanding of the three basic sales tasks--order getting, order taking, and supporting--is important. The blend of these tasks in a particular sales job has a direct bearing on the selection, training, and compensation of salespeople.

Making an effective sales presentation is an important part of personal selling. Three approaches are explained. Each can be useful--depending on the target market and the products being sold.

Try to see that the strategy personal selling decisions are a part of the whole marketing strategy planning effort. Our earlier discussion of buyer behavior and communication theory is applied here. Be sure to see how materials are being tied together. This chapter continues the strategy planning emphasis that has been running throughout the text. Note the significant impact of information technologies on personal selling and customer service.

Important Terms

basic sales tasks, p. 399
order getters, p. 399
order-getting, p. 399
order takers, p. 401
order-taking, p. 401
supporting salespeople, p. 402
missionary salespeople, p. 402
technical specialists, p. 402
customer service reps, p. 403
team selling, p. 405
major accounts sales force, p. 405

telemarketing, p. 405
sales territory, p. 406
job description, p. 410
sales quota, p. 413
prospecting, p. 415
sales presentation, p. 417
prepared sales presentation, p. 417
close, p. 417
consultative selling approach, p. 417
selling formula approach, p. 417

True-False Questions

___ 1. Personal selling has declined in importance to the point that there are now more Americans employed in advertising than in personal selling.

___ 2. Professional salespeople don't just try to sell the customer—they try to help him buy.

3.   Some salespeople are expected to act as marketing managers for their own geographic territories and develop their own marketing mixes and strategies.

4.   Three basic sales tasks are found in most sales organizations—although in some situations one salesperson might have to do all three tasks.

5.   Good order getters are essential in sales of business installations and accessory equipment.

6.   Sales representatives for progressive merchant wholesalers often serve as advisors to their customers--not just as order takers.

7.   Unsought consumer products often require order getters--to convince customers of the product's value.

8.   A wholesaler's order takers handle so many items that they usually will not--and probably should not--give special attention to any particular items.

9.   A consumer products manufacturer using an indirect channel system has little need to use missionary salespeople.

10.   A business products manufacturer may benefit considerably by using technical specialists, even though a direct channel of distribution and order getters are used.

11.   Customer service reps are usually involved in helping customers resolve a problem after a purchase has been made.

12.   All types of personal selling help to win customers, but customer service is critical in keeping them.

13.   Customers weigh positive experiences more heavily than negative experiences when deciding to buy the same product (or from the same company) again.

14.   Customer service reps are needed to fix errors—irregardless of whether the error was made by the customer or the company.

15.   A major accounts sales force sells directly to very large accounts.

16.   Telemarketing has none of the benefits of a personal visit.

17.   The big advantage of telemarketing is that it saves time, but a disadvantage is that its costs are high.

18.   A sales territory is a geographic area that is the responsibility of one salesperson or several working together.

19.   The first step in deciding how many salespeople are needed is to estimate how much work can be done by one person in some time period.

20.   The less serious a customer's problem, the more likely digital self-service can fix it.

___ 21. Companies are using new information technology tools to change how sales tasks and responsibilities are planned and handled.

___ 22. Information technology does not change the basic nature of sales tasks, but it does change the way and how well those tasks get done.

___ 23. The only costs associated with new information technology tools in the area of personal selling are price-related.

___ 24. A good job description should not be too specific--since the nature of the sales job is always changing.

___ 25. A written job description can be helpful in setting the level of compensation for salespeople, because it shows whether any special skills or responsibilities are required that will command higher pay levels.

___ 26. All new salespeople should receive the same kind of sales training.

___ 27. A combination compensation plan will usually provide the greatest incentive for a salesperson to increase sales.

___ 28. The most popular compensation method is the straight commission plan.

___ 29. A sales manager's control over a salesperson tends to vary directly with what proportion of his compensation is in the form of salary.

___ 30. Many firms set different sales objectives--or sales quotas--to adjust the compensation plan to differences in potential in each territory.

___ 31. Basically, prospecting involves following all the leads in the target market--and deciding how much time to spend on which prospects.

___ 32. Some kind of priority system is needed to guide sales prospecting--because most salespeople will have too many prospects.

___ 33. The prepared (canned) sales presentation probably would be appropriate for the majority of retail clerks employed by convenience stores.

___ 34. A salesperson's request for an order is called a close.

___ 35. The consultative selling approach requires less skill on the part of the salesperson than the prepared approach.

___ 36. An effective office equipment salesperson might use a selling formula sales presentation.

___ 37. The AIDA sequence is helpful for planning a consultative selling sales presentation--but not for a selling formula sales presentation.

1. F, p. 397	14. T, p. 404	27. F, p. 413
2. T, p. 397	15. T, p. 405	28. F, p. 413
3. T, p. 398	16. F, p. 405	29. T, p. 413
4. T, p. 399	17. F, p. 405	30. T, p. 413
5. T, p. 399	18. T, p. 406	31. T, p. 415
6. T, p. 400	19. T, p. 406	32. T, p. 416
7. T, p. 400	20. T, p. 408	33. T, p. 417
8. T, p. 401	21. T, p. 408	34. T, p. 417
9. F, p. 402	22. T, p. 410	35. F, p. 417
10. T, p. 402	23. F, p. 410	36. T, p. 417
11. T, p. 403	24. F, p. 410	37. F, p. 418
12. T, p. 403	25. T, p. 410	
13. F, p. 403	26. F, p. 411	

Multiple-Choice Questions (Circle the correct response)

1. Which of the following statements about personal selling is *true?*
   a. As a representative of his company, a salesperson's job is to sell the customer rather than to help him buy.
   b. Today's salesperson is really only responsible for "moving products."
   c. The modern salesperson's sole job is to communicate his company's story to customers.
   d. Some sales representatives are expected to be marketing managers in their own geographic territories.
   e. A beginning salesperson could not expect to be responsible for a sales volume as large as that achieved by many retail stores.

2. Which of the following is an accurate description of the sales task listed?
   a. *Supporting:* routinely completing sales made regularly to target customers.
   b. *Order getting:* confidently seeking possible buyers with a well-organized sales presentation designed to sell a good, service, or idea.
   c. *Order taking:* developing goodwill, stimulating demand, explaining technical aspects of product, training the middleman's salespeople, and performing other specialized services aimed at obtaining sales in the long run.
   d. All of the above are correct.
   e. None of the above is correct.

3. Order-getting salespeople would be required for which one of the following jobs?
   a. Helping a buyer plan and install a computer and software for use as a website server.
   b. Helping drug retailers figure out better ways to display and promote their products.
   c. Seeking orders from supermarket buyers for a new brand of high-protein diet supplement that has been added to the company's line.
   d. "Helping" an indecisive consumer in a supermarket select the kind of meat she should buy for dinner.
   e. All of the jobs call for order takers.

4. Chemco, Inc., a three-year-old producer of chemicals, has just hired a manufacturers' agent. The agent
   a. is probably replacing a company order getter who built up the territory.
   b. should assume that Chemco won't ever hire its own sales force for the territory.
   c. may lose the business when the territory gets to the point where it can be handled by an order taker.
   d. All of the above are equally likely.
   e. None of the above is a good answer.

5. A large appliance manufacturer has adequate wholesale and retail distribution--but is concerned that the middlemen do not push its products aggressively enough--because they also carry competitive lines. The manufacturer should hire some:
   a. missionary salespeople.
   b. order getters.
   c. order takers.
   d. technical specialists.
   e. customer service reps.

6. Which of the following is *not* a task associated with customer service reps?
   a. solving the customer's problem after a purchase has been made.
   b. promoting the customer's next purchase.
   c. referring the customer to the company's digital self-service.
   d. dealing with errors irregardless of whether it was the company's error or the customer's error.
   e. advocating for the customer.

7. Which of the following statements is *false?*
   a. Team selling involves different specialists--to handle different parts of the selling job.
   b. A major accounts sales force is used to sell to small retailers who are not covered by wholesalers in the channel.
   c. Carefully selected sales territories can reduce the cost of sales calls.
   d. The first step in deciding how many salespeople are needed is to estimate how much work can be done by one person in some time period.
   e. Telemarketing provides salespeople with many of the benefits of a personal visit--including the ability to modify the message as feedback is received.

8. Which of the following is a good example of a sales technology?
   a. spreadsheet analysis of scanner data.
   b. electronic slide show for a sales presentation.
   c. software for shelf space management.
   d. order status information available over the Internet.
   e. all of the above.

9. With regard to the level of compensation for salespeople, a marketing manager should recognize that:
   a. order takers generally are paid more than order getters.
   b. the appropriate level of compensation should be suggested by the job description.
   c. a good order getter will generally be worth less to a firm than a good technical specialist.
   d. the firm should attempt to pay all its salespeople at least the going market wage for order getters.
   e. salespeople should be the highest-paid employees in the firm.

10. The sales manager of the Retro Butterfly Chair Corp. wishes to compensate his sales force in a way which will provide some security, incentive, flexibility, and control. The company should offer its sales force:
   a.   straight salaries.
   b.   straight commissions.
   c.   a combination plan.
   d.   a value plan.
   e.   a bonus plan.

11. Regardless of the sales volume, the least expensive type of sales force compensation system is always:
   a.   straight salary.
   b.   straight commission.
   c.   a combination plan.
   d.   None of the above.

12. Paige Whaley works as telephone salesperson for a newspaper. She calls new residents in the city to try to get subscriptions for home delivery. Which of the following types of sales presentations should she use?
   a.   Prepared sales presentation.
   b.   Selling formula approach.
   c.   Consultative selling approach.
   d.   Customer service approach.
   e.   Sales quota approach.

13. Dale Jetta sells life insurance. The company provides a list of prospects and Dale starts each sales call by asking the potential customer to explain his or her financial goals. Dale is probably using the
   a.   selling formula approach.
   b.   consultative selling approach.
   c.   canned presentation approach.
   d.   target market approach.
   e.   missionary approach.

Answers to Multiple-Choice Questions

1. d, p. 398
2. b, p. 399
3. c, p. 399-400
4. c, p. 400
5. a, p. 402

6. c, p. 403-408
7. b, p. 405
8. e, p. 409
9. b, p. 412
10. c, p. 413

11. d, p. 414
12. a, p. 417
13. b, p. 417

Exercise 15-1

Analyzing nature of the personal selling task

Introduction

Personal selling may involve three basic tasks: (1) *order getting, (2) order taking,* and (3) *supporting.* Each task may be done by different individuals--or the same person may do all three. While we use these terms to describe salespeople by referring to their *primary* task, it is important to keep in mind that many salespeople do all of the three tasks to some extent.

Consider, for example, a sales rep for a manufacturer of an established consumer good that is distributed through wholesalers. Since the product is established in the marketplace, the sales rep's primary task would probably be order taking--obtaining routine orders from regular wholesale customers. The same rep may also be expected to do other secondary tasks, however. For example, he or she may be expected to get orders from new wholesale customers--and so would also do order getting at times. Further, the rep might also spend part of the time helping the wholesaler's sales force--by informing retailers about the company's product, building special store displays, and so forth. In this case, the sales rep would be doing a supporting task.

This exercise focuses on the basic differences among the three selling tasks. In some cases, these differences may be rather clear. In other cases, the differences may be quite difficult to see. To determine what kind of sales rep is needed to handle a particular personal selling job, we will try to distinguish between the *primary* and *secondary* selling tasks. *Note: the words "primary* n *and "secondary" are used in this way in this exercise only--they do not appear in the text.*

Assignment

Six cases are presented below to show how the selling tasks may vary. In some of the cases, the sales rep will perform both primary and secondary selling tasks, while in others only the primary selling task will be discussed. Read each case and then indicate (a) the *primary* selling task *usually required to effectively carry out the specified job* and (b) any secondary selling task(s) that *may also be described in the case.* Then explain your answer in the space marked "Comments. " The first case is answered for you as an example.

1. Olivia Teton, a sophomore at Midwestern University, works part-time at the Campus Drugstore. During the week, Olivia works afternoons waiting on customers at the lunch counter. On weekends, she usually operates the cash register at the candy and cigarette counter--in addition to handling bills for public utilities. According to her boss, Olivia is a very good worker.

    a)   Primary selling task: *Order-taking*

    b)   Secondary selling task: *Posssibly order-getting*

    c)   Comments: *No order getting is specifically mentioned, but she may do some occasionally. For example: "Would you like to try some of our fresh strawberry pie today? It's delicious!"*

2. The Pinnacle Equipment Company is a large merchant wholesaler that distributes chain saws, lawnmowers, and other outdoor power equipment. Pinnacle sells to retailers and also sells direct to large end-users--such as golf courses and cemeteries. Recently Pinnacle decided to target local government (city and county) buyers--who purchase equipment to maintain parks, roadside areas, and public schools and hospitals. In the past, these buyers often just purchased equipment from local retailers. Brian Jourdan, a sales rep for Pinnacle, was assigned responsibility for identifying who influenced these purchase decisions, and for persuading them either to buy from Pinnacle or at least allow Pinnacle to bid on their next order. In addition, Jourdan has been successful in getting Pinnacle on the state government list of approved vendors. That means that various state agencies can select equipment from the Pinnacle catalog and submit a purchase order without a lot of additional red tape. Jourdan follows up with the warehouse manager to make certain that these orders are shipped promptly.

    a)   Primary selling task: _____

    b)   Secondary selling task: _____

    c)   Comments:

3. Rod Soloman, a marketing major in college, went to work for Frito-Lay as soon as he graduated. While he hopes to become a brand manager some day, Rod is a district sales representative--calling on supermarkets, grocery stores, and convenience stores. His job is to build special displays, inform store managers of new products, provide merchandising assistance, review customer complaints, and occasionally to suggest special orders for the stores he visits. Rod is paid a straight salary--plus a bonus when sales in his district are good. (Note: Frito-Lay uses merchant wholesalers to distribute its products.)

a) Primary selling task: _____

b) Secondary selling task: _____

c) Comments:

4. For twenty years, Josie Langley has been a manufacturers' agent. Based in Baltimore, Maryland, she represents a variety of noncompeting manufacturers of parts and components used in the production of recreational vehicles ("vans") and boats. For example, she calls on the many small producers of boats in the Baltimore area and sells them the special water-resistant fabrics and chrome-plated hardware that they need for boat interiors. Her customers also include the "conversion shops" that customize vans and RVs, as well as large boatyards that repair and renovate older boats. She also calls on a number of very large boating supply wholesalers. Josie has worked at getting to know her customers really well. Because of the variety and complexity of the lines she represents, she spends much of her time checking her customers' parts inventories. This gives her continual customer contact--and provides a useful service. She also finds some time to seek new customers--and is always looking for new producers to represent. Recently, however, the producer of one of Josie's most profitable lines switched to another agent. Apparently, the producer was concerned that Josie had not been aggressive enough in promoting its products; the company was especially concerned that a competing European producer represented by another agent was getting an increasing share of the market. Josie was bitter about losing the account. "I built their Baltimore business from scratch--and now they're dropping me cold," she complained. "I handle too many products to devote all of my time to just one manufacturer's offerings."

a) Primary selling task: _____

b) Secondary selling task: _____

c) Comments:

5. Heather Paterno is a "sales engineer" with Peak Packaging Corporation--which specializes in foam and air "bubble" packaging materials. Producers use these packaging materials to protect their products inside shipping cartons during shipping. Peak Packaging has a line of standard products but also will produce custom packaging materials if that is what a customer needs. The company does advertising in trade magazines, and each ad includes a response card. When a prospect calls to inquire about Peak Packaging products, Paterno is sent out to analyze the customer's packaging needs. She determines how much protection is needed and which packaging product would be best. After finishing her work, Paterno reports back to her sales manager --who assigns another sales rep to handle the rest of the contacts with the customer.

    a)   Primary selling task: _____

    b)   Secondary selling task: _____

    c)   Comments:

6. Grant Scurlock is paying most of his own college expenses by selling Fuller Brush personal care products door-to-door. At first, Grant did not like his job, but lately has been enjoying it more--and doing very well. As Grant puts it, "Once you learn the knack of getting your foot in the door, sales come easily and the commissions add up fast. After all, people like our products and the convenience of in-home buying."

    a)   Primary selling task: _____

    b)   Secondary selling task: _____

    c)   Comments:

Question for Discussion

Three different kinds of sales presentations are discussed in the text: the *prepared, consultative,* and *selling formula* presentations. Which of these three kinds of sales presentations would be most appropriate for each of the sales reps described in Exercise 15-1? Why?

Exercise 15-2

Selecting the appropriate kind of salesperson

Introduction

Many people believe that a good salesperson must always be an aggressive, extroverted type of individual with highly developed persuasive skills. Such is not the case, however. Studies have shown, for example, that middle-class shoppers often prefer salespeople who tend to be passive and impersonal. Thus--like all other ingredients of a firm's marketing mix--the kind of salesperson needed depends on the needs and attitudes of the firm's target market.

In addition, the firm must keep its basic promotion objectives in mind. The selling task is not always one of persuasion--but may involve informing or reminding target customers about the company's products and/or the company itself. Therefore, it is often desirable to use order takers--or supporting salespeople-- rather than order getters. And, when the task is resolving problems after the sale has already been made, a customer service rep may be the appropriate choice.

Selecting the right kind of salesperson is an important strategy decision. Using the wrong kind of salesperson to handle a specific selling situation may do a firm more harm than good.

Assignment

This exercise will give you practice in selecting the appropriate kinds of salespersons. Several situations involving a need for personal selling are described below. For each situation, indicate which of the following kinds of salespeople would be *most* appropriate--and then explain why in the space provided.

A.	Order getter
B.	Order taker
C.	Missionary salespeople
D.	Technical specialist
E.	Customer service rep

The first situation is answered for you as an example.

1. A video rental store needs a person to operate its checkout counter.

   a) Type of salesperson: *Order taker*

   b) Reason: *The chief task is to complete transactions which the customers have begun by coming to the store and making a selection.*

2. A producer of hand soaps--that sells to retail food stores and drugstores through their normal wholesale suppliers--wants to get retailer promotional support and shelf space for a new line of liquid soaps.

   a) Type of salesperson:

   b) Reason:

3. A group of Cisco managers who have taken early retirement want to hire a salesperson to promote their new business which is performing "MIS Audits"--evaluating the expense and effectiveness of firms' current management information systems and offering suggestions for improvement. Some firms do this type of evaluation themselves, but many companies don't have the technical or management expertise to know about all of the alternative ways the MIS might be improved.

   a) Type of salesperson:

   b) Reason:

4. A group of lawyers wants to sell prepaid legal services to unions and other employee groups; although the idea has been popular in other areas of the country, they are the first law firm to offer this service in their city.

   a) Type of salesperson:

   b) Reason:

5. A company that manufactures radio equipment for commercial aircraft wants to add a new salesperson to be responsible for global positioning satellite systems (a type of radio receiver which can compute a plane's position based on satellite signals) with its existing customers, a small number of very large commercial aircraft manufacturers.

   a) Type of salesperson:

   b) Reason:

6. A maker of industrial dishwashing machines (used by institutions and very large restaurants) wants to take advantage of lower freight tariffs to expand the market for its existing product line.

   a) Type of salesperson:

   b) Reason:

7. A manufacturer of specialized light bulbs needs someone to call on automobile companies to determine their needs for new models and to work with the company's engineers and pricing staff to develop new proposals.

   a) Type of salesperson:

   b) Reason:

8. A real estate developer is about to open the model homes for a new subdivision and wants to hire a salesperson who is experienced in new home sales.

   a) Type of salesperson:

   b) Reason:

9.   A new firm that hopes to offer a series of "wellness" programs--including exercise classes, stress-reduction seminars, and diet plans--for employees of large companies needs a salesperson to call on the personnel managers of prospect firms, explain the service, and negotiate contracts.

      a)   Type of salesperson:

      b)   Reason:

10.   A distributor of "stock" steel (steel bars, pipes and so on, used by fabricators to make things out of steel) needs an "inside" counter salesperson. The duties are primarily telephone work, processing orders from existing customers, and helping "walk-in" customers.

      a)   Type of salesperson:

      b)   Reason:

11.   A producer of a line of skin care products--including sun-block lotions, hand creams, and facial cleansers--needs some people to provide free samples and information about new products to dermatologists.

      a)   Type of salesperson:

      b)   Reason:

12.   A company that produces ready-to-assemble furniture needs someone to respond to final consumers who call the firm's toll-free number about parts missing from a package or other problems encountered when assembling the furniture they've purchased from their local home improvement retailer.

      a)   Type of salesperson:

      b)   Reason:

Question for Discussion

What kind of sales compensation plan--straight salary, straight commission, or a combination plan--would be appropriate in the above situations? Why? What factors must be considered in choosing a sales compensation plan?

Exercise 15-3

Sales compensation

This exercise is based on computer-aided problem number 15--Sales Compensation. A complete description of the problem appears on page 421 of *Basic Marketing,* 16th edition.

1.   Franco Welles knows that his estimates of "expected sales" are just that--estimates. He wants to know what the effect will be on the two compensation plans if unit sales are less or more than expected--but otherwise as he initially planned them. Use the Spreadsheet to fill in the blanks in the following tables, and indicate by marking " < " (less than) or " > " (greater than) which plan gives the highest compensation to the rep and the highest contribution to Nanek in each of the situations.

Sales Volume as Planned			
	Commission	< or >	Combination
Units of A	4000		3600
Units of B	1000		1250
Compensation (TC)			
Contribution			

Actual Volume Less than Planned			
	Commission	< or >	Combination
Units of A	3600		3240
Units of B	500		625
Compensation (TC)			
Contribution			

Actual Volume Greater than Planned			
	Commission	< or >	Combination
Units of A	4400		3960
Units of B	1500		1875
Compensation (TC)			
Contribution			

2. From the analysis of the three tables above, how do the two compensation plans perform from the perspective of Nanek?

_____

_____

_____

_____

3. Franco Welles and the new rep agree to start on the combination plan as originally formulated, but the rep points out that Product A is a mature line and unit sales would surely increase if the rep has authority to cut prices. Welles estimates that each $5 price cut might increase sales by 10 percent--that is, 360 more units than his original estimate. To test this idea, Welles constructs the following table to see the effect on total revenue, total compensation and profit contribution.

Price	Unit Sales	Total Revenue	Total Compensation	Profit Contribution
110	3600			
105	3960			
100	4320			
95	4680			
90	5040			

4. Examine the figures you have entered into the table and discuss the implications of what happens to Total Revenue, Total Compensation, and Profit Contribution as the price is lowered.

_____

_____

_____

_____

Chapter 16

Advertising and sales promotion

What This Chapter Is About

Chapter 16 focuses on advertising and sales promotion, and the strategy decisions that must be made.

The importance of specifying advertising objectives is emphasized. Advertisements and advertising campaigns cannot be effective unless we know what we want done.

Next, the kinds of advertising that can be used to reach the objectives are explained. Then, how to deliver the message--via the "best" medium, and what is to be communicated--the copy thrust--is discussed. Advertising on the Internet is a new medium that has grown rapidly--and more growth is expected.

Advertising agencies are also treated. They often handle the mass-selling details for advertisers--under the direction of the firm's advertising manager. Avoiding deceptive advertising is also treated--because the FTC can proceed against both the advertiser and its agency. In most countries, the government takes an active role in deciding what kinds of advertising are allowed.

Try to see how advertising and sales promotion would fit into a promotion blend--and be parts of a whole marketing strategy. Advertising and sales promotion are not isolated topics. They can be vital ingredients in a marketing strategy, but they must work together with the other elements of the marketing mix.

Important Terms

product advertising, p. 429
institutional advertising, p. 429
pioneering advertising, p. 429
competitive advertising, p. 430
direct type advertising, p. 430
indirect type advertising, p. 430
comparative advertising, p. 430

reminder advertising, p. 430
advertising allowances, p. 431
cooperative advertising, p. 431
copy thrust, p. 438
advertising agencies, p. 441
corrective advertising, p. 445

True-False Questions

____ 1. Advertising expenditures grew continuously from World War II until the mid-1980s, but since then the trend has been down.

____ 2. The U.S. has the highest advertising spending of any nation in the world.

____ 3. U.S. corporations spend an average of 20 percent of their sales on advertising--with the largest share of this going to television.

4. Advertising objectives should be very specific--even more specific than personal selling objectives.

5. A firm whose objective is to help buyers make their purchasing decision should use institutional advertising.

6. Pioneering advertising should be used in the market introduction stage of the product life cycle to develop selective demand for a specific brand.

7. The objective of competitive advertising is to develop selective demand--demand for a specific brand.

8. Direct competitive advertising involves making product comparisons with competitive brands, while indirect competitive advertising focuses solely on the advertiser's products.

9. The Federal Trade Commission has banned comparative advertising that involves specific brand comparisons using actual product names.

10. Reminder advertising is likely to be most useful when the firm has achieved brand preference or brand insistence for its products.

11. Advertising allowances are price reductions to firms further along in the channel to encourage them to advertise or otherwise promote the firm's products locally.

12. The main reason cooperative advertising is used is that large manufacturers usually can get lower media rates than local retailers.

13. Regardless of a firm's objectives, television advertising is generally more effective than newspaper or magazine advertising.

14. A major advantage of using "cost per thousand" data to aid in media selection is that this approach is very helpful for target marketing.

15. Some advertising media are "must buys"--meaning that the FTC requires firms to use such media.

16. Some companies know where customers have previously been on the Web and thus can target them more effectively.

17. When a website sets fees based on actual sales, it is using the same method as traditional media does to set fees.

18. A company's website provides much less interactivity than traditional advertising.

19. Copy thrust means what is to be communicated by an ad's words and illustrations.

20. The first job in message planning is to determine how to get attention.

21. Global ads have not been very successful because they emphasize mass marketing instead of target marketing.

___ 22. Advertising agencies are specialists in planning and handling mass selling details for advertisers.

___ 23. With the growth of mega-agencies, it will only be a matter of time before small agencies disappear.

___ 24. Normally, media have two prices: one for national advertisers and a lower rate for local

___ 25. The 15 percent commission system of ad agency compensation is most favored by large national advertisers of consumer products.

___ 26. Advertising effectiveness can be measured quite simply and accurately just by analyzing increases or decreases in sales.

___ 27. The Federal Trade Commission has the power to control deceptive or false advertising.

___ 28. Corrective advertising and affirmative disclosures are methods used by the FTC to control false or deceptive advertising.

___ 29. The effect of most sales promotions is long-lasting.

___ 30. Sales promotion spending has grown, but not at the expense of advertising.

___ 31. One basic reason for increased use of sales promotion by consumer products firms is that they are competing in mature markets.

___ 32. Sales promotion aimed at final consumers usually is trying to increase demand and speed up the time of purchase.

___ 33. Sales promotion aimed at middlemen--sometimes called trade promotion--stresses price-related matters.

Answers to True-False Questions

1. F, p. 426	12. F, p. 431	23. F, p. 441
2. T, p. 426	13. F, p. 432	24. T, p. 442
3. F, p. 426	14. F, p. 433	25. F, p. 442
4. T, p. 428	15. F, p. 436	26. F, p. 443
5. F, p. 429	16. T, p. 437	27. T, p. 445
6. F, p. 429	17. F, p. 437	28. T, p. 445
7. T, p. 430	18. F, p. 437	29. F, p. 446
8. F, p. 430	19. T, p. 438	30. F, p. 447
9. F, p. 430	20. T, p. 439	31. T, p. 447
10. T, p. 430	21. T, p. 441	32. T, p. 449
11. T, p. 431	22. T, p. 441	33. T, p. 450

Multiple-Choice Questions (Circle the correct response)

1. Advertising spending as a percent of sales dollars is largest for:
   a. malt beverages.
   b. soaps and detergents.
   c. soft drinks.
   d. investment advice.
   e. motor vehicles.

2. The largest share of total advertising expenditures in the United States goes for:
   a. Internet advertising.
   b. television advertising.
   c. magazine advertising.
   d. direct-mail advertising.
   e. radio advertising.

3. Regarding "good" advertising objectives:
   a. Given no clearly specified objectives, advertising agencies may plan campaigns that will be of little benefit to advertisers.
   b. Advertising objectives often are not stated specifically enough to guide implementation.
   c. Advertising objectives should be more specific than personal selling objectives.
   d. The objectives should suggest which kinds of advertising are needed.
   e. All of the above are true.

4. Which of the following statements about advertising objectives is *false?*
   a. They should be as specific as possible.
   b. They should be more specific than personal selling objectives.
   c. They should be left to creative ad agencies, not the marketing manager.
   d. They should flow from the overall marketing strategy.
   e. They should set the framework for an advertising campaign.

5. The message "Drink milk every day" is an example of which type of advertising?
   a. Pioneering
   b. Competitive
   c. Indirect action
   d. Reminder
   e. Direct action

6. Thad Gibson developed an innovative machine to make a more effective and less expensive bottle cap. He found a backer, produced a model, photographed it, and placed an advertisement in a food canners' magazine explaining how caps could be made as needed--right in the canner's plant. Much of the ad copy tried to sell the convenience and inventory cost-saving features of in-plant production as needed, rather than purchasing large quantities. Gibson's advertising was trying to develop:
   a. selective demand.
   b. primary demand.
   c. derived demand.
   d. elastic demand.

7. Regarding comparative advertising, which of the following statements is NOT true?
   a. Comparative advertising may actually help the competitor.
   b. The Federal Trade Commission encouraged the use of comparative advertising.
   c. Comparative advertising is intended to stimulate selective demand.
   d. Comparative advertising means making comparisons in which competitors' products are actually named.
   e. Guidelines about the evidence needed to support superiority claims are clear and specific.

8. Comparative ads:
   a. have been encouraged by the Federal Trade Commission.
   b. attempt to develop primary demand.
   c. have been banned on television because of their tendency to deceive consumers.
   d. have consistently pleased consumers.
   e. that actually name the competitor's brand are illegal.

9. A firm that uses advertising that tells customers that the firm focuses on "Better things for better living through chemistry" illustrates:
   a. pioneering advertising.
   b. reminder advertising.
   c. competitive advertising.
   d. institutional advertising.
   e. cooperative advertising.

10. "Cooperative" advertising refers to the practice of:
   a. producers and middlemen sharing in the cost of advertising that is done by the producer.
   b. producers doing some advertising and expecting their middlemen to cooperate by providing the rest of the promotion blend.
   c. the producer paying for all of the advertising which is done by its middlemen.
   d. middlemen doing advertising which is partially paid for by the producer.
   e. middlemen picking up the promotion theme of the producer and carrying it through.

11. The choice of the "best" advertising medium depends upon:
   a. the promotion objectives.
   b. the budget available.
   c. the target markets.
   d. the characteristics of each medium.
   e. All of the above.

12. A media buyer knows that:
   a. the local newspaper will probably be a must buy for a retailer targeting local consumers.
   b. a 30-second commercial on primetime network television is likely to be too expensive for all but large national firms.
   c. a Yellow Pages listing will probably be a must buy for a service firm serving customers in a local market.
   d. website advertising will probably be a must buy for firms targeting business buyers in overseas markets.
   e. All of the above.

13. Regarding Internet advertising, which of the following statements is true?
   a. It is likely that a few portal websites will become for the Internet what the networks once were for television.
   b. As with traditional media, getting lots of exposure for Internet ads doesn't help if viewers are not in the firm's target market.
   c. Search ads know what customers are looking for.
   d. Some advertisers pay only if ads deliver.
   e. All of the above.

14. Advertising agencies
   a. usually specialize in one particular type of work, such as media buying, sales promoion planning, or website design.
   b. were traditionally paid based on a percent of the sales they achieved, but now the trend is toward a commission based on 15 percent of media purchases.
   c. vary in size, but the largest ones account for most of the billings.
   d. All of the above are true.
   e. None of the above is true.

15. Which of the following statements about advertising agencies and compensation methods is *true*?
   a. The 15 percent commission system is no longer required--and some advertisers have obtained discounts or fee increases.
   b. The traditional compensation arrangements between advertisers and agencies might make it difficult for an agency to be completely objective about low cost media.
   c. Some advertisers--especially business products manufacturers--were quite satisfied with the traditional compensation arrangements whereby the agency did the advertiser's advertising work in return for the normal discount allowed by the media.
   d. The agencies earn commissions from media only when time or space is purchased at the national rate (as opposed to local rates).
   e. All of the above are true statements.

16. Which of the following statements about measuring advertising effectiveness is *false?*
   a. The most reliable approach is to check the size and composition of media audiences.
   b. Some progressive advertisers are now demanding laboratory or market tests to evaluate the effectiveness of advertisements.
   c. No single technique or approach has proven most effective.
   d. When specific advertising objectives are set, then marketing research may be able to provide feedback on the effectiveness of the advertising.
   e. Ideally, management should pretest advertising before it is run rather than relying solely on the judgment of creative people or advertising "experts."

17. Advertisers should keep in mind that:
   a. advertisers, but not ad agencies, can be held responsible for false and misleading ads.
   b. only false and deceptive ads can be controlled by the FTC.
   c. the FTC does not have the power to require corrective advertising or affirmative disclosures.
   d. there are very clear-cut guidelines concerning how to substantiate ad claims.
   e. what is seen as "positioning" in one country may be viewed as "unfair" or "deceptive" in another.

18. Sales promotion:
    a. usually lasts for only a limited time period.
    b. spending has grown rapidly in mature markets.
    c. involves a wide variety of activities which often require the use of specialists.
    d. can make the personal selling job easier.
    e. All of the above are true statements.

19. Sales promotion:
    a. to consumers usually is trying to increase demand or speed up the time of purchase.
    b. aimed at middlemen is sometimes called trade promotion.
    c. might include free samples of a product.
    d. used by service firms is often aimed at its employees.
    e. all of the above.

Answers to Multiple-Choice Questions

1. b, p. 426
2. b, p. 427
3. e, p. 428
4. c, p. 428
5. a, p. 429
6. b, p. 429
7. e, p. 430

8. a, p. 430
9. d, p. 431
10. d, p. 431
11. e, p. 432
12. e, p. 436
13. e, p. 436-37
14. c, p. 441

15. e, p. 442
16. a, p. 443
17. e, p. 444-45
18. e, p. 446-47
19. e, p. 449-50

Exercise 16-1

Identifying different kinds of advertising

Introduction

Perhaps because of the high cost of advertising, some companies try to use multi-purpose ads to reach several promotion objectives at the same time. Studies have shown, however, that such ads often fail to produce *any* of the desired effects. On the contrary, several special-purpose ads are much more likely to stimulate positive responses than a single multi-purpose ad. Thus, a marketing manager usually should use different kinds of advertising to accomplish different promotion objectives.

This exercise is designed to show the different kinds of advertising that can be used--and to show the various objectives an advertisement might have. While doing the assignment, you should see that promotion objectives may be only indirectly concerned with increasing sales--and that a firm may have other reasons for advertising. Try to guess what these "other reasons" are--and how they might relate to a company's overall marketing mix.

Assignment

Using recent magazines and newspapers (or, if you wish, the Internet), find advertisements to *final consumers* which illustrate the following kinds of advertising (as defined in the text):

A.	Institutional
B.	Pioneering
C.	Direct competitive
D.	Indirect competitive
E.	Comparative
F.	Reminder

Clip out the ads (or print out any Internet ads)--and for each ad attach a separate sheet of paper indicating:

a) what kind of advertising the ad illustrates.
b) at what target market, if any, the ad appears to be aimed.
c) the general and specific objectives of each ad--e.g., to inform consumers (general) about three new product improvements (specific).
d) the name of the magazine or newspaper in which the ad appeared (or, in the case of ads on the Internet, the a brief description of the website where it appeared).

Question for Discussion

When one overall objective of a company's marketing activities must be to sell its products, why would advertisements have objectives such as those you indicated for your examples?

Exercise 16-2

Determining advertising objectives and the appropriate kind of advertising

Introduction

About 1910 George Washington Hill--president of the American Tobacco Company--is said to have made this now-famous quote: "I am convinced that 50 percent of our advertising is sheer waste, but I can never find out which half." Today, there are many business executives who share Mr. Hill's feelings. Billions of dollars are spent each year creating clever--and sometimes annoying--ads which often appear to be poorly designed and largely ineffective.

Actually, it is extremely difficult to measure the effectiveness of advertising--because companies often lack clearly defined advertising objectives. In hopes of remaining competitive, advertisers often budget some fixed percent of their sales dollars to advertising without any specific objectives in mind--other than to just "promote the product."

Like all business expenditures, however, there is no reason for making advertising expenditures unless the company has some specific purpose in mind. Since the advertising objectives selected will largely determine the kind of advertising that is needed, companies should set specific advertising objectives that are tied to their overall marketing strategies.

Assignment

This exercise will give you some practice determining the kind of advertising that may be needed to obtain some specific advertising objectives. Described below are several situations in which some kind of advertising may be necessary or desirable. For each situation: (a) indicate what *general (i.e.,* inform, persuade, and/or remind) and *specific* objectives the advertising probably would be meant to achieve; and (b) indicate which of the following kinds of advertising would be *most* appropriate to accomplish that objective.

        A.   Pioneering advertising
        B.   Direct competitive advertising
        C.   Indirect competitive advertising
        D.   Reminder advertising
        E.   Institutional advertising

The first situation is answered for you as an example.

1. A print ad shows an insurance adjuster with a clipboard in hand watched by a family with grateful expressions on their face. The only "copy" is a single line: "You're in good hands with Allstate."

   a) Advertising objectives: *Remind. This ad assumes that consumers already know that Allstate is in the domestic casualty insurance market and builds on other advertisements that have given greater details about product benefits.*

   b) Kind of advertising: *Reminder.*

2. Print advertisements for a producer of designer clothing simply feature the designer's "brand name" and a picture of scantily clad models frolicking in romantic situations.

   a) Advertising objectives: _____

   _____

   _____

   b) Kind of advertising: _____

3. Enterprise uses testimonials from satisfied customers to differentiate itself from competing car rental services. In particular, it promotes its service of delivering a car to you--at home, at the office, or on vacation. Its slogan says, "Pick Enterprise. We'll pick you up."

   a) Advertising objectives: _____

   _____

   _____

   b) Kind of advertising: _____

4. In an attempt to reposition its high performance multimedia, laptop computers towards the higher end of the market, Toshiba's print ads include a table comparing product benefits of its multimedia laptops with features and service of IBM and Apple laptop computers.

   a) Advertising objectives: _____

   _____

   _____

   b) Kind of advertising: _____

5. Charter Hospitals' radio advertisement describes the symptoms and serious consequences of depression, and explains that most health insurance policies cover treatment for this condition. At the end, the ad gives a toll-free number for Charter as the announcer encourages the friends and families of depressed people to "seek help today, even if not from Charter."

a) Advertising objectives: _____

_____

_____

b) Kind of advertising: _____

6. For several decades Texaco has sponsored broadcasts of the Metropolitan Opera House on classical music stations. Since many of the stations are public radio stations, there are no formal "pitches" for individual products, but the host uses the line: "You can trust your car to the man with the Texaco star."

a) Advertising objectives: _____

_____

_____

b) Kind of advertising: _____

7. Buick takes out single-page advertisements in national business magazines to tout the amenities of owning its Riviera. Its ads mention, "You can get a supercharged engine, a CD player with six speakers, and an ashtray big enough for two cigars. It's not for carpooling, but then, neither are you. You're due. Definitely due."

a) Advertising objectives: _____

_____

_____

b) Kind of advertising: _____

8. The metropolitan transportation district receives a grant from the coalition of local governments to advertise bus services to promote clean air by switching commuters from single-occupancy cars. Billboards and TV time are too expensive, so the bus company uses the money to purchase placard ads inside its own buses. The copy says: "Save gas--take the bus!"

    a)   Advertising objectives: _____

              _____

              _____

    b)   Kind of advertising: _____

9. British Airways in Hong Kong uses print advertisements that feature one of four Chinese flight attendants and builds on the airline's image as "global and caring in the eyes of Chinese consumers." The emphasis is on its people, not its product or fares.

    a)   Advertising objectives: _____

              _____

              _____

    b)   Kind of advertising: _____

10. A print advertisement for Rolls Royce automobiles features an attractive couple driving a Rolls convertible in front of New York's Plaza hotel. The driver of a Mercedes sedan looks on and there is also a Lincoln in the background. The ad copy is a single line: "Simply the best motor car in the world."

    a)   Advertising objectives: _____

              _____

              _____

    b)   Kind of advertising: _____

Question for Discussion

Would there be difficulties in evaluating the effectiveness of ads for the situations mentioned in Exercise 16-2? Why?

Name: _____   Course & Section: _____

Exercise 16-3

Sales promotion

This exercise is based on computer-aided problem number 16--Sales Promotion. A complete description of the problem appears on page 452-53 of *Basic Marketing,* 16th edition.

1. The PTA likes the idea of the T-shirt promotion, but is concerned about the "front-end" costs. Thus, it has decided to order only 400 T-shirts at $2.40 each, the minimum order from the supplier. In addition, the PTA has decided to evaluate a variation of the president's idea--offering a choice of a regular ticket at $5.00 or a ticket with a T-shirt at $6.50. If the PTA used this approach and sold 400 tickets with T-shirts and 200 tickets without T-shirts, how much money--net--would the PTA earn? How would this compare with what the PTA would earn if it sold the same total number of tickets at $5.00 each--with the first 400 purchasers getting a free T-shirt.

    $ _____ money earned by PTA using 2 prices (with and without T-shirt)

    $ _____ money earned by PTA selling all tickets at $5.00 and giving away 400 T-shirts

2. Another possibility is that the game would attract the "normal" number of ticket buyers at $5.00 a ticket, but that not all of the higher priced tickets with a T-shirt would be sold. If 300 tickets were sold at $5.00 and only 300 people bought the higher priced tickets with the T-shirt, how much money would the PTA earn?

    $ _____ money earned by the PTA.

3. Spreadsheet analysis helped the PTA evaluate various possibilities, but it is still uncertain how to proceed. The group thinks there will be a lot of interest in the T-shirts--but they worry that they will cause dissatisfaction and lose potential ticket sales if they order the minimum and then run out of T-shirts. One member of the group has proposed an idea that might solve the problem.

    He recommends a "sweepstakes" approach. Specifically, he suggests that they sell all the tickets at a regular price of $5.50--but that every person who has a ticket with a winning number will be given a T-shirt at the game. 400 winning numbers will be drawn from a bowl during the game. He thinks this will stimulate the most interest--and allow the PTA to place the minimum T-shirt order.

    If the PTA uses this approach, how many extra tickets will it have to sell to pay for the T-shirt promotion?

    _____ extra tickets to pay for the T-shirt promotion

    If 700 tickets are sold, how much money will be earned for the PTA?

    $ _____ money earned if 700 tickets are sold.

4.   If the PTA earns $3,000 from the game, they will be able to buy new uniforms for the school band. If they use the sweepstakes approach, about how many tickets would they have to sell to be able to buy the new uniforms? (Hint: use the What If analysis to vary the number of tickets sold, and display the amount of money earned.)

_____ number of tickets to sell to be able to buy new uniforms

5.   Based on your analysis of this problem, briefly comment on the following quote: "Companies spend too much money on sales promotion. It just adds to the cost of marketing."

_____

_____

_____

_____

_____

_____

Chapter 17

Pricing objectives and policies

What This Chapter Is About

Chapter 17 talks about the strategy decisions in the Price area. You should see that there is much more to Price than accepting the price set by the interaction of supply and demand forces (as discussed in Appendix A). The actual price paid by customers depends on many factors. Some of these are discussed in this chapter. They include: the trade, quantity, and cash discounts offered; trade-ins; who pays the transportation costs; and what actually is included in the marketing mix.

The chapter begins with a discussion of possible pricing objectives--that should guide price setting. Then, the marketing manager's decisions about price flexibility and price level over the product life cycle are discussed.

The marketing manager must also set prices which are legal. This chapter discusses what can and cannot be done legally. Clearly, there is much more to pricing than the simple economic analysis that we used earlier to understand the nature of competition. Chapter 17 is an important chapter--and deserves very careful study.

Important Terms

True-False Questions

_____ 1. Any business transaction in our modern economy can be thought of as an exchange of money, the money being the Price for something of greater value.

_____ 2. The "something" that Price buys is different for consumers or users than it is for channel members.

_____ 3. A target return objective is often used in a large company to evaluate several different divisions or products.

_____ 4. Profit maximization objectives are undesirable from a social viewpoint, because profit maximization necessarily leads to high prices.

_____ 5. Instead of setting profit-oriented objectives, a marketing manager should follow sales-oriented objectives because--in the long run--sales growth leads to big profits.

_____ 6. Market share objectives provide a measurable objective--but an increase in market share does not always lead to higher profits.

_____ 7. Status quo pricing objectives don't ever make sense if the firm intends to develop an overall marketing strategy that is aggressive.

_____ 8. Instead of letting daily market forces determine their prices, most firms set their own administered prices.

_____ 9. A one-price policy means offering the same price to all customers who purchase products under essentially the same conditions and in the same quantities.

_____ 10. Flexible pricing is seldom used anymore in the United States because it does not aid selling.

_____ 11. A skimming pricing policy is especially desirable when economies of scale reduce costs greatly as volume expands--or when the firm expects strong competition very soon after introducing its new product.

_____ 12. A penetration pricing policy might be indicated where there is no "elite" market--that is, where the whole demand curve is fairly elastic--even in the early stages of the product's life cycle.

_____ 13. Introductory price dealing is the same thing as using a penetration pricing policy.

_____ 14. How much a nation's money is worth in some other nation's currency is called the exchange rate.

_____ 15. Basic list prices are the prices final consumers (or business customers) are normally asked to pay for products.

_____ 16. Discounts from the list price may be granted by the seller to a buyer who either gives up some marketing function or provides the function for himself.

17. Noncumulative quantity discounts apply only to individual orders.

18. Cumulative quantity discounts tend to encourage larger single orders than do noncumulative quantity discounts.

19. The following is an example of a seasonal discount: A local supermarket gives a free half gallon of milk with every order of $10.00 or more, provided the purchases are made on either Monday, Tuesday, or Wednesday--that normally are slow days in the food business.

20. Cash discounts are used to encourage buyers to pay their bills quickly--meaning they are granted to buyers who pay their bills by the due date.

21. The following terms of sale appear on an invoice: 2/10, net 30. A buyer who fails to take advantage of this cash discount offer is--in effect—borrowing at an annual rate of 36 percent a year.

22. A mass-merchandiser that allows government employees to purchase products at 10 percent below the store's normal selling prices is using a trade or functional discount.

23. Common occurrences of sale prices and deals are a signal that the basic marketing strategy is constantly changing.

24. Everyday low pricing starts with a low list price that does not change instead of starting with a high list price that changes frequently.

25. Allowances are typically given only to consumers, not to middlemen customers.

26. Stocking allowances have been around for a long time and are just another way for middlemen to make extra profit.

27. PMs are given to retailers by manufacturers or wholesalers to pass on to their salespeople in return for aggressively selling particular items.

28. Trade-in allowances are price reductions given for used products when similar new products are bought.

29. A retailer is usually willing to redeem a producer's coupons since they increase his sales to consumers and also because he's paid by the producer for handling the coupons.

30. Rebates give the producer a way to be sure that final consumers, instead of middlemen, get an intended price reduction.

31. F.O.B. pricing simplifies a seller's pricing--but may narrow his target market because customers located farther from the seller must pay more for transporting costs and may buy from nearby suppliers.

32. With zone pricing, an average freight charge is made to all buyers within certain geographic areas.

33. Uniform delivered pricing--that is used when the seller wishes to sell his products in all geographic areas at one price--is most often used when transportation costs are relatively high.

34. Freight absorption pricing means absorbing freight cost so that a firm's delivered price will meet the nearest competitor's.

35. Value pricing means setting a fair price level for a marketing mix that really gives the target market superior customer value.

36. Most firms don't operate in perfect competition.

37. Sellers who may appear to emphasize below-the-market prices in their marketing mixes may really be using different marketing strategies--not different price levels.

38. A firm involved in an oligopoly situation can usually increase profits by pricing higher than the market.

39. The practical effect of the unfair trade practices acts is to protect certain limited-line food retailers from the kind of "ruinous" competition that full-line food stores might offer if they sold certain products below cost for long time periods.

40. Phony list prices are prices that customers are shown to suggest that the price they are to pay has been discounted from "list."

41. The Wheeler-Lea Amendment bans price fixing in interstate commerce.

42. Price fixing is illegal if it raises or stabilizes prices--but not if it results in lower prices.

43. Although price fixing is illegal under the Sherman Act and the Federal Trade Commission Act, there are no penalties for managers who ignore these laws.

44. The Robinson-Patman Act makes it illegal--under any conditions--to offer price differences to different buyers of products of "like grade and quality."

45. In the *Borden* case, the U.S. Supreme Court upheld the FTC's position that products are of "like grade and quality" if their physical characteristics are similar--even if sold under different labels.

46. A producer could legally refuse to give a wholesale discount to a large retail grocery chain that buys direct--although the chain might handle a larger volume than small wholesalers.

47. Under the Robinson-Patman Act, it is legal for a firm to provide push money, advertising allowances, or other promotion aids to its customers, as long as such allowances are made available to all customers in equal dollar amounts.

1. F. p. 457	17. T, p. 469	33. F, p. 474
2. T, p. 458	18. F, p. 469	34. T, p. 474
3. T, p. 459	19. T, p. 469	35. T, p. 475
4. F, p. 460	20. F, p. 470	36. T, p. 476
5. F, p. 460	21. T, p. 470	37. T, p. 476
6. T, p. 460-61	22. F, p. 471	38. F, p. 478
7. F, p. 461	23. F, p. 471	39. T, p. 479
8. T, p. 462	24. T, p. 471	40. T, p. 480
9. T, p. 463	25. F, p. 471	41. F, p. 480
10. F, p. 463	26. F, p. 471	42. F, p. 480
11. F, p. 464	27. T, p. 472	43. F, p. 480
12. T, p. 466	28. T, p. 472	44. F, p. 480
13. F, p. 466	29. T, p. 473	45. T, p. 480
14. T, p. 467	30. T, p. 473	46. T, p. 481
15. T, p. 468	31. T, p. 474	47. F, p. 481
16. T, p. 469	32. T, p. 474	

Multiple-Choice Questions (Circle the correct response)

1. Which of the following would be *least likely* to be included in the "something" part of the "price equation" as seen by channel members?
   a. Promotion aimed at customers
   b. Rebates
   c. Price-level guarantees
   d. Sufficient margin to allow chance for profit
   e. Convenient packaging for handling

2. A marketing manager for a large company who wants to compare the financial performance of different divisions of his firm would probably pursue which of the following pricing objectives?
   a. Status quo
   b. Market share
   c. Target return
   d. Profit maximization
   e. Sales growth

3. Profit maximization pricing objectives:
   a. can only be achieved when the producer's price is high.
   b. may be in the interest of both producers and consumers
   c. usually focus on low prices as that is what is required to draw in a larger base of customers.
   d. are never used in combination with penetration pricing
   e. can only be achieved by using cost-plus pricing approaches.

4. With respect to pricing objectives, a marketing manager should be aware that:
   a. profit maximization objectives generally result in high prices.
   b. status quo pricing objectives can be part of an extremely aggressive marketing strategy.
   c. target return objectives usually guarantee a substantial profit.
   d. sales-oriented objectives generally result in high profits.
   e. All of the above are true statements.

5. Prices are called "administered" when:
   a. they are determined through negotiations between buyers and sellers.
   b. they fall below the "suggested list price."
   c. a marketing manager has to change the strategy every time a customer asks about the price.
   d. government intervenes to ensure that prices fluctuate freely in response to market forces.
   e. firms set their own prices for some period of time--rather than letting daily market forces determine their prices.

6. In contrast to flexible pricing, a one-price policy:
   a. means that the same price is offered to all customers who purchase products under the same conditions.
   b. involves setting the price at the "right" level from the start--and holding it there.
   c. generally results in rigid prices which change very infrequently.
   d. means that delivered prices will be the same to all customers.
   e. All of the above.

7. Which of the following factors would be *least favorable* to a skimming price policy?
   a. The firm has no competitors.
   b. The quantity demanded is very sensitive to price.
   c. The product is in the market introduction stage of its life cycle.
   d. The firm follows a multiple target market approach.
   e. The firm has a unique, patented product.

8. The Arrowhead Corp. is introducing a new "me-too" brand of shampoo in market maturity. To speed its entry into the market--without encouraging price competition with other shampoo producers--Arrowhead should consider using:
   a. a penetration pricing policy.
   b. a flexible-price policy.
   c. a skimming price policy.
   d. introductory price dealing.
   e. an above-the-market price-level policy.

9. The Sierra Corporation purchases large quantities of iron castings from a well-known producer. Sierra receives a discount which increases as the total amount ordered during the year increases. What type of discount is involved here?
   a. Seasonal discount
   b. Cumulative quantity discount
   c. Brokerage allowance
   d. Noncumulative quantity discount
   e. Cash discount

10. The terms "3/20, net 60" mean that:
    a. in effect, the buyer will pay a 27 percent interest rate if he takes 60 days to pay the invoice.
    b. the buyer must make a 3 percent down payment--with the balance due in 20 to 60 days.
    c. a 3 percent discount off the face value of the invoice is permitted if the bill is paid within 60 days--otherwise, the full face value is due within 20 days.
    d. the invoice is dated March 20 and must be paid within 60 days.
    e. None of the above is a true statement.

11. A producer of sports equipment offers its retailers a 2 percent price reduction on all purchases if the dealer advertises the products locally. Apparently, the producer is using
    a. "push money."
    b. a brokerage allowance.
    c. a cash discount.
    d. a trade (functional) discount.
    e. an advertising allowance.

12. Some producers give _____ to retailers to pass on to the retailers' salesclerks in return for aggressively selling particular items or lines.
    a. brokerage commissions
    b. advertising allowances
    c. trade discounts
    d. "push money" allowances
    e. cash discounts

13. A producer in North Carolina sold some furniture to a firm in Tulsa. If the *seller* wanted title to the products to pass immediately--but still wanted to pay the freight bill--the invoice would read:
    a. F.O.B. delivered.
    b. F.O.B. seller's factory--freight prepaid.
    c. F.O.B. Baltimore.
    d. F.O.B. seller's factory.
    e. F.O.B. buyer's warehouse.

14. If a buyer purchases a shipment of products from a seller in another city and the invoice reads "F.O.B. shipping point,"
    a. the seller pays the freight bill and keeps title to the products until they are delivered.
    b. the seller pays the freight bill but title to the products passes to the buyer at the point of loading.
    c. the buyer pays the freight but the seller keeps title to the products until delivery.
    d. the buyer pays the freight and gets title to the products at the point of loading.
    e. Both a and c.

15. Which of the following statements about geographic pricing policies is *true*?
    a. Zone pricing penalizes buyers closest to the factory.
    b. Uniform delivered pricing is more practical when transportation costs are relatively low.
    c. Freight absorption pricing may increase the size of market territories.
    d. F.O.B. pricing tends to reduce the size of market territories.
    e. All of the above are true statements.

16. A main purpose of "unfair trade practice acts" is to:
    a.   prevent manufacturers from taking high markups.
    b.   eliminate price competition on manufacturers' brands.
    c.   require some minimum percentage markup on cost.
    d.   permit different types of retail outlets to charge different retail prices.
    e.   guarantee retailers some profit.

17. Price fixing:
    a.   is always illegal.
    b.   is prohibited by the Robinson-Patman Act.
    c.   is illegal if it raises or stabilizes prices--but not if it lowers prices.
    d.   is technically illegal--but there is very little that the federal government can do about it.
    e.   All of the above are true statements.

18. According to the _____ Act, it is unlawful to practice price discrimination between different purchasers of "commodities of like grade and quality" which may tend to injure competition.
    a.   Magnuson-Moss
    b.   Fair-Trade
    c.   Sherman Antitrust
    d.   Robinson-Patman
    e.   Celler-Kefauver

19. A manufacturer might try to defend himself against charges of illegal price discrimination by claiming that:
    a.   the price discrimination occurred as a defensive measure to "meet competition in good faith."
    b.   the price differentials did not actually injure competition.
    c.   the price differentials were justified on the basis of cost differences in production and/or distribution.
    d.   his products were not of "like grade and quality."
    e.   Any of the above could make price discrimination legal.

20. Which of the following price-related actions by a manufacturer *most likely* would be a violation of the Robinson-Patman Act?
    a.   Offering a lower price to only one buyer to match a competitor's price.
    b.   Selling to all its customers at uniform prices.
    c.   Granting a lower price to a buyer because of a large-quantity purchase.
    d.   Giving a special advertising allowance to a retailer that was having difficulty competing in its local market.
    e.   None of the above is a violation.

Answers to Multiple-Choice Questions

1. b, p. 458	8. d, p. 466	15. e, p. 474
2. c, p. 459	9. b, p. 469	16. c, p. 479
3. b, p. 460	10. a, p. 470	17. a, p. 480
4. b, p. 461	11. e, p. 471	18. d, p. 480
5. e, p. 462	12. d, p. 472	19. e, p. 480-81
6. a, p. 463	13. b, p. 474	20. d, p. 481
7. b, p. 464	14. d, p. 474	

Exercise 17-1

Using discounts and allowances to improve the marketing mix

Introduction

Most price structures have a basic list price from which various discounts and allowances are subtracted. *Discounts* (not to be confused with discount selling) are reductions from list price that are given by a seller to a buyer who either gives up some marketing function or provides the function himself. Several types of discounts are commonly used, including:

a) Cumulative quantity discounts
b) Noncumulative quantity discounts
c) Seasonal discounts
d) Cash discounts
e) Trade (functional) discounts

Allowances are similar to discounts. They are given to final consumers, customers or channel members for doing "something" or accepting less of "something." Different types of allowances include:

a) Advertising allowances
b) Push money or prize money allowances
c) Trade-in allowances
d) Stocking allowances

While many firms give discounts and allowances as a matter of custom, they should be viewed as highly useful tools for marketing strategy planning. As outlined in the text, each type is designed for a specific purpose. Thus, some firms offer buyers a choice of several discounts and allowances.

The purpose of this exercise is to illustrate how discounts and allowances can be used in marketing strategy planning. The emphasis will be on recognizing opportunities to improve a firm's marketing mix. In Exercise 17-2, we will discuss various legal restrictions that may affect a firm's policies regarding discounts and allowances.

Assignment

Presented below are five cases describing situations in which a firm *might* want to add or change some discount or allowance--as part of its marketing mix. Read each case carefully and then answer the questions which follow.

1.	Creekside Apartments offers two-bedroom apartments with the same basic "roommate" floor plan that is popular with other student-oriented apartments in the area. In August and early September, there is no difficulty in attracting tenants at the "going rate" of $650 per month rent. Although there is a penalty for breaking the lease, each year a number of unexpected vacancies occur at the end of the first semester when some students graduate or drop out of school, move to a dorm, or find someone new with whom to live. Of course, the same thing happens at other apartments, so in late December and early January there are always more empty apartments than new renters. As a result, competition for tenants is usually intense. In this "buyer's market," student renters look for the best deal--and apartment managers dread the idea of having an empty apartment that brings in no rent for the spring semester.

	a)	What type of discount or allowance would you recommend in this situation? Why?

2.	Prestige Speakers, Ltd. manufactures expensive speakers that are sold through manufacturers' agents to selected retailers who specialize in selling and installing high-quality audio components and home theatre systems. Most of Prestige's audio speakers are sold on credit. In fact, Prestige usually does not get paid until its retailers manage to sell the speakers themselves. While this service is convenient and necessary for most of its customers, it places a heavy financial burden on Prestige. Recently, for example, the company was forced to postpone production of a promising new product due to a lack of cash.

	a)	Should Prestige consider using discounts or allowances to solve its financial problem? Why? If so, what type would be best? Why?

3. Exact-Treat, Inc. manufactures a large assortment of fertilizers, weed killers, plant nutrients, and insecticides. Exact-Treat's products are sold across the Southeast through merchant wholesalers (distributors) who supply not only farmers but also plant nurseries, landscaping services, hardware stores, and lumberyards. Exact-Treat's production manager recently complained to the firm's marketing manager that "the sales force needs to do a better job of smoothing out sales. In the fall and winter--when there is little planting activity--we have extra capacity. Then, in the spring all of the orders come in at once--and we have to pay overtime to get everything produced. It's not just a matter of putting items in our warehouse. We need to get the orders. We have bills to pay."

    a) Could Exact-Treat's problem be due in part to a lack of appropriate discounts or allowances? Why? Is so, what type might be best for the company to adopt? Explain.

4. PowerPro Electrical Supply Company sells a wide assortment of products to electricians, electrical contractors, and general building contractors in the area around Dallas, Texas. PowerPro's line includes almost everything its customers might need--ranging from wire, electrical tape, circuit breaker boxes, conduit, switches, outlet boxes, lighting fixtures, and a wide variety of electrician's tools and equipment. In addition, like most other electrical wholesalers in the area, PowerPro offers free delivery to the construction site. Despite PowerPro's efforts to promote itself as "the most economical source for all your needs," most of its customers split their business among a number of different electrical supply wholesalers. When PowerPro's owner complained about this, one of his counter clerks offered an explanation: "The person having the work done usually doesn't care what electrical supply house gets the business--so the different electricians just call whoever comes to mind first."

    a) Could discounts or allowances be useful to PowerPro Electrical Supply? Why? If so, what type would be best? Explain.

5.	Cape Fear Furniture Co. produces a line of high quality reproductions of Early American style beds, dressers, tables and chairs. Cape Fear's furniture is distributed nationally through a network of carefully selected furniture retailers. When Cape Fear first introduced its line, sales grew rapidly--in part because of its ongoing advertising in national home furnishings magazines. Now, however, sales are flat--and in some areas falling. Other producers have come out with similar lines, and most retailers now carry several competing brands. The company is concerned about what it considers "a lack of adequate promotion support at the retail level."

a)	Could Cape Fear Furniture Company use discounts or allowances to obtain additional promotion support at the retail level? Why? If so, what type would you recommend? Why?

b)	What would be the advantages and limitations of your recommendation relative to other approaches?

6.	Nina's Teen Shop has just purchased $10,000 worth of fashionable accessories for teens from Sassy, Inc. The invoice for the accessories included the terms "3/10, net 60."

a)	What do the terms 3/10, net 60 mean?

b)	Suppose Nina's Teen Shop pays the invoice 10 days after receipt. What amount should it pay Sassy, Inc.?

c)   If Nina's Teen Shop does not pay the invoice until 60 days after receipt, it will in effect be borrowing money at a fairly high interest rate. Calculate what the effective interest rate would be in this case. (Assume a 360 day year.)

d)   What conditions would make it sensible for Sassy, Inc. to offer these terms?

Question for Discussion

Do discounts and allowances really offer marketing managers a great deal of flexibility in varying their marketing mixes? Explain.

Exercise 17-2

How legislation affects pricing policies

Introduction

Pricing legislation is a very complex area. Even legal experts cannot always provide their clients with clear-cut advice in pricing matters. This is due in part to the vague way in which many laws have been written by legislators--and in part to the fact that no two situations are ever exactly alike. It is up to the courts and administrative bodies, such as the Federal Trade Commission, to interpret pricing legislation. And their interpretation of laws has tended to vary a lot, depending on the political environment.

Nevertheless, a marketing manager should try to understand the legal environment--and know how to work within it. Legislation and legal cases often tend to focus on pricing matters, because prices are highly visible elements of the marketing mix. Business managers have a lot of freedom to charge whatever prices they choose--subject to the forces of competition. But they must be aware of and work with the restrictions that do exist. Ignorance of the law is no excuse. The penalties for violating pricing laws are tough--even jail!

This exercise is designed to increase your understanding of the basic federal laws (Sherman Act, Robinson-Patman Act, Federal Trade Commission Act, Wheeler-Lea Amendment) related to pricing matters. The intent is not to make you a legal expert--but rather to be sure you understand the kinds of pricing activities which *might* be illegal.

Assignment

The following five cases describe pricing activities which *might* be judged illegal in certain circumstances. Study each case carefully and then answer the questions that follow. Be sure to identify the law (or laws) that are *most relevant* to each situation *as it is described.*

1.   Lakeside Dairy produces a line of milk products and sells them directly to retailers in a three-state area. Recently, one of Lakeside's major competitors--a large national firm--offered to sell one of Lakeside's retail accounts its brand of white milk for $1.50/half gallon, which was 10 cents less than Lakeside charged for its brand. When the retailer threatened to stop carrying Lakeside half gallons--and instead stock only the national brand--Lakeside offered to sell that retailer its regular white milk for $1.40 per half gallon. When the national firm accused Lakeside of "price discrimination with predatory intent," Lakeside replied that it was simply "meeting competition in good faith."

Who is right in this case--Lakeside or its competitor? What law(s) would apply?

2.   PharmCo, Inc.--a large manufacturer of pharmaceuticals--sells its consumer products exclusively through drug wholesalers--who sell to retail druggists. Wholesalers are allowed a "chain discount" of 35 percent and 10 percent off of the manufacturer's suggested retail list prices. The wholesalers are then expected to pass the 35 percent discount on to retailers. Recently a large retail drug chain approached PharmCo about buying direct. PharmCo agreed to sell direct to the chain--and offered a discount of 35 percent. However, the chain wanted the additional 10 percent usually given to wholesalers. PharmCo felt this would be unfair to those retail druggists who must buy through wholesalers--and refused the chain's request on the grounds that such a discount would be illegal.

Do you agree with PharmCo? Why or why not? Be sure to identify what type(s) of discounts or allowances and which law(s) are involved.

3. The Better Business Bureau (BBB) recently received a telephone call from an angry consumer who wished to complain about Best Deal Electronics--an electronics discount chain with nine stores in the surrounding four-state area. The consumer had gone to Best Deal to buy some items listed in an "inventory clearance sale" advertisement. The first item was a "top-name" color TV marked down from $450 to $200. Upon arrival at the store, he found only one of the featured TVs in stock--a floor model in very poor condition. The salesclerk apologized--and suggested that the customer buy one of the store's other models at "regular everyday low prices" ranging from $199 on up. The consumer then asked to see a video camera that--according to the ad--was "originally priced at $1,295" and "now reduced to only $795." The salesclerk pointed to a dusty camera in a case near the back of the store. On closer inspection, the customer realized that the camera was a three-year-old model that did not have any of the features found on new cameras--even one that regularly sold for less than $795. An official from BBB sympathized with the consumer and said that his agency had received many similar complaints about Best Deal. He went on to say, however, that there was very little anyone could do--other than to avoid shopping at such stores.

    Comment on the Better Business Bureau's analysis of the above situation. Are Best Deal's pricing practices deceptive and/or illegal? Can anything be done in such situations?

4. Libby Corporation produces a wide line of calmed foods--including "Early," one of the leading brands of canned corn. The wholesale selling price for a case (48 cans) of Early corn is $9.60--which includes a 5 percent trade discount for the wholesaler. Libby also gives a 10 percent quantity discount to wholesalers who buy in carload quantities. Wholesalers normally pass the quantity discount along to their customers in the form of lower prices. The identical corn is also sold to a few large food chains for use as dealer brands. The cans are sold under different labels at $8.00 per case (minus the 10 percent quantity discount if earned). Libby allocates 3 percent of its net sales of Early corn toward national advertising.

    Suppose the Federal Trade Commission were to take a close look at Libby's pricing methods to see whether the manufacturer was violating federal pricing legislation. What aspects of Libby's pricing policies do you think the FTC might question based on what is presented above? Why? What laws might be involved?

5.   Mimi Glover, a rising manager at Archer America Corporation (AAC), has just been given responsibility for pricing products sold in AAC's Corn Products division. Because the division's products are based on corn, the firm's costs vary a lot depending on the cost of corn, which is set in the agricultural commodity market. In light of that, Glover has always wondered how the firm has been able to maintain consistently high prices and attractive profits. However, she is told that another executive, Guy Figueroa, will help her to better understand the firm's pricing approaches. Figueroa says that as far as he is concerned the firm's customers are the enemy--they're the ones pushing for low prices. He also argues that competitors in the same industry are friends--because it's in their interest as well as AAC's interest to keep prices high. Figueroa suggests that he and Glover play golf with the pricing manager for a competing firm and make it clear that they have very similar interests in the worldwide market.

What would government lawyers think about Figueroa's comments? If the meeting with the competitor takes place, what law would be most relevant?

Question for Discussion

According to one point of view, the Robinson-Patman Act benefits consumers by prohibiting pricing practices which may tend to injure competition. Another point of view, however, holds that the act only serves to protect inefficient competitors and thus may actually be harmful to consumers. Which view do you agree with? Why? How can we determine which view is "right?"

Exercise 17-3

Cash discounts

This exercise is based on computer-aided problem number 17--Cash Discounts. A complete description of the problem appears on page 483 of *Basic Marketing*, 16th edition.

1.   Tulkin has several variables to consider as he tries to decide what cash discount terms to offer. One thing he has noticed about his current situation (with 90 percent of his customers taking the cash discount) is that his ratio of cash discounts to total invoice amounts is .027--or about 3 percent. It occurred to him that another alternative might be to leave his terms the way they are for the short term, but increase his prices by about 3 percent. If he does this--so that the average invoice is about $927 instead of $900--and everything else stays the same, what will happen to his total <u>net</u> sales (after the cash discounts are taken)?

    For 120 customers:

    Net sales without price increase $ _____

    Net sales with 3.0 percent price increase $ _____

2.   Tulkin realizes that if he increases his list price some price-sensitive retailers will switch to other wholesalers. If he increases the price, how many customers can he "afford" to lose before his net sales are back to the level he had before the price increase?

    Number of customers to earn about the same net sales _____

3. In thinking about price-sensitive customers, Tulkin feels he may be able to promote his favorable invoice terms to attract customers away from other wholesalers who have already changed to less favorable terms. He recognizes that drawing attention to his invoice terms will probably mean that more customers will take the cash discount. He also knows he might still have to change his terms of sale later--but thinks he could hang on to some of the new customers once they become aware of his good service and quality products. If he keeps his invoice terms the same--and 95 percent of the customers take the cash discount--how many new customers will Tulkin have to attract to increase his net sales by about $5,000? What will his expected gross sales and total monthly cash discount amount be in this case?

Net sales with 120 customers, 90 percent taking discount	$ _____
plus target increase in net sales	$ ___5000___
equals, new target for net sales	$ _____
Number of customers required to achieve target net sales, assuming 95 percent take the discount	_____
expected gross sales with that many customers	$ _____
expected cash discount with that many customers	$ _____

4. Tulkin feels this plan may work--so he wants to see how things might look later if and when he reduces his terms closer to what competitors are charging--2/10, net 30. He figures he wouldn't lose customers at that point--since others would already be offering similar terms. He is not certain how many customers will take the cash discount with the new terms--but he estimates that it will be between 40 percent and 60 percent. He is uncertain how his net sales might vary over that percentage range. To help answer this question, prepare a table that shows how his net sales, the total dollar value of cash discounts, and the ratio of cash discounts to invoice face value would change as the percentage of customers that take the discount varies between 40 percent and 60 percent.

Percent Taking Discounts	Total Cash Discounts	Net Dollar Sales	Ratio Discount to Face Value
40			
42			
44			
46			
48			
50			
52			
54			
56			
58			
60			

Chapter 18

Price setting in the business world

What This Chapter Is About

Price setting is challenging--but deciding on the right price is crucial to the success of the whole marketing mix.

Chapter 18 treats cost-oriented pricing in detail--because it is commonly used and makes sense for some firms. But cost-oriented pricing doesn't always work well. You should study this approach carefully, so you can better understand its advantages and disadvantages.

Pay special attention to the relationships of the various cost curves. Notice how costs vary at different levels of operation.

Some business managers have recognized the problems with average-cost pricing and have tried to bring demand into their price-setting. Demand-oriented pricing requires some estimate of demand--and ideally a whole demand curve. But demand curves are not easy to estimate. This is one reason why demand-oriented pricing has not been widely used. But it is possible to *estimate* demand curves. And it is probably better to try to estimate a demand curve than ignore it. Some examples of how this is being done are presented at the end of the chapter.

By estimating demand, it is possible to estimate the likely profit of various quantities--and find the most profitable price and quantity. Although this approach is not as widely used as cost-oriented pricing, it deserves careful study. Demand must be considered when setting price--unless you are willing to leave making a profit to chance. Demand-oriented pricing can be done--and can be very useful in helping to carry out the marketing concept--that is, satisfying customers *at a profit.*

Important Terms

markup, p. 486
markup (percent), p. 487
markup chain, p. 488
stockturn rate, p. 489
average-cost pricing, p. 490
total fixed cost, p. 491
total variable cost, p. 492
total cost, p. 492
average cost (per unit), p. 492
average fixed cost (per unit), p. 492
average variable cost (per unit), p. 492
target return pricing, p. 495
long-run target return pricing, p. 496
break-even analysis, p. 496
break-even point (BEP), p. 496
fixed-cost (FC) contribution per unit, p. 497
marginal analysis, p. 498
marginal revenue, p. 499

marginal cost, p. 499
rule for maximizing profit, p. 500
marginal profit, p. 500
price leader, p. 501
value in use pricing, p. 503
reference price, p. 505
leader pricing, p. 506
bait pricing, p. 506
psychological pricing, p. 506
odd-even pricing, p. 506
price lining, p. 507
demand-backward pricing, p. 507
prestige pricing, p. 508
full-line pricing, p. 508
complementary product pricing, p. 509
product-bundle pricing, p. 509
bid pricing, p. 509
negotiated price, p. 510

True-False Questions

____ 1. Markup (dollars) means the dollar amount added to cost of products to get the selling price--or markup (percent) means a percentage of the selling price that is added to the cost to get the selling price.

____ 2. According to the definition of markup given in the text, a product that a retailer buys for $2.00 would be priced at $3.20 if the retailer applied a markup of 60 percent.

____ 3. Considering the large number of items the average retailer or wholesaler carries--and the small sales volume of any one item--a markup approach to pricing makes sense.

____ 4. A producer--whose product sells for $24--distributes its product through wholesalers and retailers who traditionally use a "markup chain" of 20 percent and 40 percent, respectively. Therefore, the retail-selling price of this product is $50.

____ 5. A wholesaler or retailer concerned with increasing profits should consider using a smaller markup as a way of achieving a substantial increase in turnover.

____ 6. "Stockturn rate" means the number of times a firm's beginning inventory is sold in a year.

____ 7. Producers commonly use a cost-oriented pricing approach--adding a standard markup to obtain their selling price.

____ 8. Because average-cost pricing consists of adding a "reasonable" markup to the average cost of a product, it assures the producer of earning a profit at any level of output.

___ 9. Total fixed cost is the sum of those costs that are fixed in total--no matter how much is produced.

___ 10. Total variable cost would include items such as wages paid to workers, sales commissions, and salaries paid to top executives.

___ 11. The rate of growth of total cost as output increases is not affected by total fixed cost.

___ 12. Average cost is obtained by dividing total cost by the related total quantity.

___ 13. Average fixed cost increases as the total quantity produced increases.

___ 14. Average variable cost is obtained by dividing total variable cost by the number of units produced.

___ 15. Because of economies of scale, all average and total costs tend to decline as the quantity produced increases.

___ 16. Average-cost pricing works best when demand conditions are changing rapidly and substantially.

___ 17. Unlike the average-cost curve approach, target return pricing assures that the target return is achieved--even if the quantity that is actually sold is less than the quantity used in setting the price.

___ 18. Those who use long-run target return pricing assume that short-run losses and above-normal profits will average out in the long run--thus allowing the firm to achieve its long-run target return objectives.

___ 19. Break-even analysis suggests that once a firm reaches its break-even point, profit will keep increasing with every additional unit sold.

___ 20. Although break-even analysis considers the relationship of total revenue and total cost, it may not solve the firm's pricing problem because the assumed price may not be tied to realistic demand estimates.

___ 21. Marginal analysis helps the marketing manager make the best pricing decision by focusing on how selling one more unit will affect total revenue and total cost.

___ 22. Since marginal revenue is the change in total revenue which results from the sale of one additional unit of a product--and since this extra unit will be sold while charging a positive price for all items--marginal revenue can never be negative.

___ 23. To maximize profit--the firm should produce that output where the difference between marginal revenue and marginal cost is the greatest.

___ 24. Marginal analysis indicates that--to maximize profits--a firm should be willing to increase the quantity it will sell until the marginal profit of the last unit is at--or near--zero.

25. Marginal analysis focuses on *the* price that earns the highest profit, but there is usually a *range* of profitable prices.

26. A firm in an oligopoly situation cannot use marginal analysis to maximize its profits because of the "kinked" demand curve facing the firm.

27. A price leader in an oligopoly situation should have a very good understanding of its own and its competitors' cost structures--as well as an estimate of the industry demand curve.

28. When customers can easily compare prices for substitutes, they are likely to be less price sensitive.

29. Customers tend to be more price sensitive the greater the total expenditure.

30. Value in use pricing is setting prices that will capture some of what customers will save by substituting the firm's product for the one currently being used.

31. Auctions are popular for consumer products, but not business products.

32. Sequential price reductions are commonly used with products that have a short life or that are in short supply.

33. Reference prices do not vary from one customer to another for the same basic type of purchase (for example, paperback books).

34. Leader pricing is most common in oligopoly situations—where most firms will raise or lower their price only after the industry leader raises or lowers its price.

35. Items featured in "bait pricing" are real bargains priced low to get customers into the store to buy these and other items.

36. Psychological pricing assumes that some price changes will not affect the quantity sold.

37. Retailers who use "odd-even pricing" seem to assume that they face a rather jagged demand curve--that slightly higher prices will substantially reduce the quantity demanded.

38. Although price lining may result in higher sales, faster turnover, and simplified buying--it also increases the retailer's total inventory requirements and often leads to greater markdowns.

39. Henry Ford's decision to build a car for the "masses"—setting "a price so low as to force everybody to the highest point of efficiency"--is an example of demand-backward pricing.

40. Prestige pricing is possible when target customers think that high prices mean high quality or high status--and the demand curve for this market slopes down for a while and then bends back to the left again.

___ 41. A producer that offers a complete line (or assortment) of products should not be overly concerned about full-line pricing if it is aiming at different target markets for each of its products.

___ 42. Complementary product pricing is setting prices on several products as a group.

___ 43. Firms that use product-bundle pricing usually set the overall price so that it's cheaper for the customer to buy the bundle than to buy each item separately.

___ 44. The major job in bid pricing is assembling all of the costs--including the variable and fixed costs--that should apply to each job.

___ 45. Bargaining may involve the whole marketing mix, not just the price level in arriving at a negotiated price.

Answers to True-False Questions

1. T, p. 486	16. F, p. 494	31. F, p. 504
2. F, p. 487	17. F, p. 495	32. T, p. 504
3. T, p. 487	18. T, p. 496	33. F, p. 505
4. T, p. 488	19. T, p. 498	34. F, p. 506
5. T, p. 489	20. T, p. 498	35. F, p. 506
6. F, p. 489	21. T, p. 498	36. T, p. 506
7. T, p. 490	22. F, p. 499	37. T, p. 506
8. F, p. 490	23. F, p. 500	38. F, p. 507
9. T, p. 491	24. T, p. 500	39. T, p. 507
10. F, p. 492	25. T, p. 500	40. T, p. 508
11. T, p. 492	26. F, p. 501	41. T, p. 509
12. T, p. 492	27. T, p. 501	42. T, p. 509
13. F, p. 492	28. F, p. 502	43. T, p. 509
14. T, p. 492	29. T, p. 502	44. T, p. 510
15. F, p. 493	30. T, p. 503	45. T, p. 511

Multiple-Choice Questions (Circle the correct response)

1. A certain product retails for $100. How much does this product cost the retailer if his markup is 33 1/3 percent?
   a. $25.00
   b. $33.00
   c. $50.00
   d. $75.00
   e. $66.67

2. The markup approach to price setting used by most intermediaries:
   a. makes little sense--given the large number of items carried and the small sales volume of any one item.
   b. is very inflexible because the same markup percent must be applied to all products.
   c. often uses the trade (functional) discount allowed by the manufacturer.
   d. is quite complicated--because each product has a different delivered cost.
   e. All of the above.

3. A certain item is sold at retail for $50. The retailer's markup is 25 percent *on cost*. The wholesaler's markup is 25 percent *on selling price*. What is the manufacturer's selling price?
   a. $30.00
   b. $32.00
   c. $28. 10
   d. $35.11
   e. $25.00

4. With respect to markups and turnover, a marketing manager should be aware that:
   a. a low stockturn rate increases inventory carrying costs.
   b. depending on the industry, a stockturn rate of 2 or 3 may be quite profitable.
   c. high markups don't always mean big profits.
   d. speeding turnover often increases profits because the firm's operating costs are a function of time and the volume of goods sold.
   e. All of the above are true statements.

5. Which of the following statements about average-cost pricing is *true?*
   a. The chief merit of this approach is that it is based on well-researched pricing formulas.
   b. It consists of adding a "reasonable" markup to the average cost of a product.
   c. This method takes into consideration cost variations at different levels of output.
   d. It assumes that the average cost for the next period will be different from that of the last period.
   e. All of the above are true statements.

6. Average-cost pricing:
   a. consists of adding a "reasonable" markup to the average cost of a product.
   b. puts a great deal of emphasis on determining how sensitive consumer demand is at different price levels.
   c. does not consider cost variations at different levels of output.
   d. focuses on the differences between fixed and variable costs.
   e. Both a and c are true.

7. Total cost usually:
   a. is zero at zero quantity.
   b. grows at a rate determined by increases in total variable cost.
   c. is the sum of total fixed and total marginal costs.
   d. grows at a rate determined by increases in total fixed cost.
   e. None of the above is a true statement.

8. The *major* weakness of average-cost pricing is that:
   a. it always leads to losses instead of profits.
   b. costs decline and rise at different levels of output.
   c. demand is ignored.
   d. average fixed cost increases as the quantity increases.
   e. All of the above.

9.	Average-cost pricing will result in *larger* than expected profit:
	a.	most of the time.
	b.	if the average fixed cost estimate is based on a quantity that is smaller than the actual quantity sold.
	c.	if the average total cost is higher than expected.
	d.	only if the manager makes arithmetic errors in computing average variable cost.
	e.	None of the above is correct.

10.	When a firm seeks to obtain some specific percentage return on its investment (or a specific total dollar return), it is using:
	a.	break-even pricing.
	b.	negotiated pricing.
	c.	"what the traffic will bear" pricing.
	d.	target return pricing.
	e.	average-cost pricing.

11.	A manufacturer who uses "target return" pricing sold 1,000 units of his product last year. He wants to earn a profit of at least $20,000 in the coming year. If his fixed costs are $40,000 and his variable costs equal $20 per unit, what price would he charge (assuming that he could still sell 1,000 units)?
	a.	$60
	b.	$40
	c.	$80
	d.	$120
	e.	Cannot be determined with information given.

12.	Break-even analysis assumes that:
	a.	variable cost is constant per unit but varies in total.
	b.	average fixed costs increases as quantity increases.
	c.	the demand curve slopes downward and to the right.
	d.	average variable cost first decreases and then increases as quantity increases.
	e.	All of the above.

13.	Assume that a producer's fixed costs amount to $240,000, its variable costs are $30 per unit, and it intends to sell its portable washer to wholesalers for $50. Given this information, the break-even point is:
	a.	8,000 units.
	b.	12,000 units.
	c.	14,000 units.
	d.	20,000 units.
	e.	almost 50,000 units.

14.	Given the following data, compute the BEP *in dollars:*
		Selling price = $1.25
		Variable cost = $ .75
		Fixed cost = $45,000
	a.	$36,000
	b.	$60,000
	c.	$90,000
	d.	$112,500
	e.	None of the above.

15. Break-even analysis can be used for:
    a. relating prices to potential demand.
    b. comparing various assumed pricing alternatives.
    c. finding the most profitable price.
    d. estimating future sales.
    e. All of the above.

16. Trying to find the *most profitable* price and quantity to produce:
    a. requires average-cost pricing.
    b. requires an estimate of the firm's demand curve.
    c. is easy once the average fixed cost is known.
    d. is only sensible if demand estimates are exact.
    e. All of the above are true.

17. A monopolistic competitor's "marginal revenue":
    a. is always positive.
    b. is always negative.
    c. is the change in total revenue that results from the sale of one more unit of a product.
    d. Only a and c above are true statements.
    e. None of the above are true statements.

18. The change in total cost that results from producing one more unit is called:
    a. average variable cost.
    b. marginal cost.
    c. average fixed cost.
    d. total variable cost.
    e. average total cost.

19. To maximize profit, a firm should:
    a. produce that output where marginal revenue is at a maximum.
    b. produce that output where marginal cost is just less than or equal to marginal revenue.
    c. produce that output where marginal cost is greater than marginal revenue.
    d. try to maximize the difference between marginal revenue and marginal cost.
    e. produce that output where marginal profit is at a maximum.

20. A marketing manager should be aware that the most profitable level of output:
    a. is where total revenue equals total cost.
    b. is where the difference between marginal revenue and marginal cost is the greatest.
    c. is where the vertical difference between total revenue and total cost is the greatest.
    d. is where marginal revenue is at a maximum.
    e. Both b and c are correct.

21. Marginal analysis focuses on the price that earns the highest profit, but:
    a. it is almost impossible to determine the maximum profit point.
    b. there is a profitable operating range which surrounds the point of maximum profit.
    c. there is no such thing as the maximum profit point.
    d. there are usually three profit points that could be referred to as maximum points.
    e. None of the above.

22. Profit-maximizing oligopolists will find that their marginal cost curves intersect:
   a. marginal revenue curves that are horizontal.
   b. marginal revenue curves that appear to drop vertically at some prices.
   c. down-sloping marginal revenue curves.
   d. negative marginal revenue curves.

23. A "price leader" in an oligopoly situation should recognize that:
   a. does not need to understand its competitors' costs.
   b. other firms in the industry are sure to raise their prices if he raises his first.
   c. price cutting may occur if the "followers" are not able to make a reasonable profit at the market price.
   d. marginal analysis is not applicable because of the kinked demand curve.
   e. All of the above are true.

24. Customers are likely to be more price sensitive when:
   a. there are substitute ways of meeting their needs.
   b. it is easy to compare prices.
   c. they have to pay the bill themselves.
   d. the total expenditure is great.
   e. All of the above.

25. An equipment producer is introducing a new type of paint sprayer to sell to automobile body-repair shops. The sprayer saves labor time, gives as good a job with less expensive paint, and requires less work polishing. This seller should probably use:
   a. leader pricing.
   b. bait pricing.
   c. complementary product pricing.
   d. odd-even pricing.
   e. value in use pricing.

26. The manager of Hot Topics Fashion Shop has concluded that her customers find certain prices very appealing. Customers see prices above or below these levels as roughly equal—and price cuts in these ranges don't increase sales. This seems to call for
   a. prestige pricing.
   b. bait pricing.
   c. leader pricing.
   d. psychological pricing.
   e. odd-even pricing.

27. The practice of setting different price levels for different quality classes of merchandise--with no prices between the classes--is called:
   a. full-line pricing.
   b. prestige pricing.
   c. price lining.
   d. odd-even pricing.
   e. psychological pricing.

28. "Demand-backward" pricing:
   a. is like leader pricing.
   b. has been called "market-minus" pricing.
   c. requires no demand estimates.
   d. is usually performed by retailers.
   e. All of the above are true statements.

29. Setting relatively high prices on products with perceived high status is known as:
   a. price lining.
   b. odd-even pricing.
   c. leader pricing.
   d. prestige pricing.
   e. bait pricing.

30. Which of the following statements is *true?*
   a. Prestige pricing is used to target government buyers.
   b. With full-line pricing, all products in the company's line must be targeted at the same market.
   c. Demand-backward pricing is used to target industrial buyers.
   d. Value pricing can only be used by mass-merchandisers.
   e. None of the above is true.

31. With regard to bid pricing, a marketing manager should be aware that:
   a. the customer is always required to accept the lowest bid.
   b. since it costs very little to submit a bid, most firms try to bid for as many jobs as possible.
   c. the same overhead charges and profit rates usually apply to all bids.
   d. a big problem is assembling all the costs--including the variable and fixed costs that apply to a particular job.
   e. All of the above are true statements.

Answers to Multiple-Choice Questions

1. e, p. 487
2. c, p. 488
3. a, p. 488
4. e, p. 488-89
5. b, p. 490
6. e, p. 490
7. b, p. 492
8. c, p. 493
9. b, p. 493
10. d, p. 495
11. c, p. 495

12. a, p. 497
13. b, p. 497
14. d, p. 497
15. b, p. 498
16. b, p. 493,498
17. c, p. 499
18. b, p. 499
19. b, p. 500
20. c, p. 500
21. b, p. 500
22. b, p. 501

23. c, p. 501
24. e, p. 501-502
25. e, p. 503-504
26. d, p. 506
27. c, p. 507
28. b, p. 507
29. d, p. 508
30. e, p. 507-508
31. d, p. 510

Exercise 18-1

Elements of cost-oriented price setting

Introduction

This exercise is designed to familiarize you with the arithmetic of cost-oriented pricing. Because most firms use cost-oriented methods to set prices, it is important that you understand these methods. Retailers and wholesalers, for example, use traditional markups that they feel will yield a reasonable rate of profit. You should be aware of how markups are figured. And you should know how stock turnover is calculated. Further, you should understand how the various types of costs differ, how they relate to each other, and how they affect profits as the sales volume varies.

Note: It is highly recommended that you review Appendix B: Marketing Arithmetic on pages 631-42 of the text before starting this exercise.

Assignment

Answer the following set of problems. Show your work in the space provided.

1. The usual retail price of an item is $100.00. The manufacturer's cost to produce the item is $40.00. Retailers take a 50 percent markup and wholesalers take a 10 percent markup. (Note: markup is calculated on selling price, unless otherwise indicated.)

   a) What is the retailer's markup in dollars? _____

   b) What is the wholesale price? _____

   c) What is the manufacturer's price? _____

d) What is the manufacturer's markup percentage? _____

e) What is the manufacturer's markup percentage *on cost*? _____

2. The Sycamore Manufacturing Company is trying to set its price on an item that will sell at retail for $80.00.

 a) For retailers to earn a markup of 25 percent, what should the wholesale price be?

 _____

 b) For the wholesalers in 2a to earn a markup of 10 percent, what should the manufacturer's price be?

 _____

3. Complete the following table by filling in the blanks. *Hint:* start with the first column and work to the right, column by column.

| Item | *Quantity produced* | | | | |
	0	*1*	*2*	*3*	*4*
Total Cost	____	____	____	____	$400
Total fixed cost	$120	____	____	____	____
Total variable cost	____	____	$140	____	____
Average cost	N/A*	____	____	$110	____
Average fixed cost	N/A*	____	____	____	____
Average variable cost	N/A*	$70	____	____	____

* Note: N/A means not applicable (because at zero output there is not an average cost per unit).

4. a) Using the data from Question 3, plot the total cost, total fixed cost, and total variable cost curves on the following graph.

b) Using the data from Question 3, plot the average cost, average fixed cost, and average variable cost curves on the following graph.

5.   SturdyBuilt Corp. has fixed costs of $2,000,000 and average variable costs of $100 per unit at all levels of output. It wishes to earn a profit of $300,000 this year--which is an increase of 10 percent over last year when SturdyBuilt sold 5,000 units of its product.

   a)   Use the average-cost pricing method to determine what price SturdyBuilt should charge for its product.

   b)   Suppose SturdyBuilt were only able to sell 4,000 units this year because of increased competition. What would its profit (or loss) be?

   c)   Suppose SturdyBuilt's sales increased to 7,000 units this year. What would its profit (or loss) be?

   d)   Based on your answers to parts a, b, and c, what do you conclude about the effectiveness of average-cost pricing?

6.   Suppose in Question 5 that SturdyBuilt had decided to use "target return" pricing instead of average-cost pricing. Suppose further that it wished to earn a 20 percent return on its investment of $500,000.

a)   What price should SturdyBuilt charge for its product?

b)   What would SturdyBuilt's return on investment be if it were only able to sell 4,000 units?

c)   What would SturdyBuilt's return on investment be if its sales increased to 7,000 units?

Question for Discussion

Why do so many firms use cost-oriented pricing methods when such methods have so many obvious shortcomings?

Exercise 18-2

Using break-even analysis to evaluate alternative prices

Introduction

Break-even analysis can be a very useful tool for evaluating alternative prices--especially when the prices being considered are fairly realistic from a demand point of view. Break-even analysis shows how many units would have to be sold--or how much dollar volume would have to be achieved--to just cover the firm's costs at alternative prices. A realistic appraisal of the likelihood of achieving the break-even point associated with each alternative price might show that some prices are clearly unacceptable--that is, there would be no way that the firm could even reach the break-even point, let alone make a profit.

The mechanics of break-even analysis are relatively simple--once you understand the concepts and assumptions. This exercise reviews these ideas and then has you apply them to a fairly common decision-making situation.

Assignment

Read each of the following problems carefully--and fill in the blanks as you come to them. Where calculations are required, make them in the space provided--and show your calculations to aid review.

1. Study the break-even chart in Figure 18-2a on the next page and answer the following questions:
   a) According to Figure 18-2a, at what quantity, total revenue, and price will the firm break even?

   Quantity _____ Total Revenue _____ Price _____

   b) The firm's total fixed cost in this situation is: _____

   c) The firm's average variable cost (AVC)is: _____

   d) Using the information in Figure 18-2a, plot the firm's *demand curve (D), average fixed cost curve* (AFC), and *average variable cost curve* (AVC) in Figure 18-2b on the next page. Label each curve and both axes.

FIGURE 18-2a
Break-Even Chart

FIGURE 18-2b

e) Using Figure 18-2a, draw the total revenue curve that would be relevant if the firm were considering a price of $50 per unit. Given this price of $50 per unit, at what quantity and total revenue would the firm break even?

Quantity _____ Total Revenue _____

f) What price should the firm charge to maximize profits--the price you calculated in (a) or $50? Why?

2. a) Suppose you were considering going into the car-washing business and investing in a new kind of car-washing unit which is more mechanized than the usual ones--but also has higher fixed costs. Calculate the break-even point in dollars and units if the usual price of $4.00 per car were charged. The variable cost per car is estimated at $2.00. The total fixed cost per year (including depreciation, interest, taxes, fixed labor costs, and other fixed costs) is estimated at $320,000.

BEP in $ _____ BEP in units _____

b) There is some possibility that there will be increased price cutting in your proposed market in the near future. Calculate the BEPs for the situation in (a) if the retail price drops to $3.50 per car.

BEP in $ _____ BEP in units _____

c) There is also a possibility that the new washing unit will deliver a better job for which some people will be willing to pay more. Calculate the new BEPs if it were possible to raise the retail price to $4.50.

BEP in $ _____ BEP in units _____

d) Should you go into the car-washing business in *any* of the above situations? Explain.

Question for Discussion

Looking at Figures 18-2a and 18-2b, what does break-even analysis assume about the nature of demand and about the competitive environment? Is break-even analysis relevant for monopolistic competition?

Exercise 18-3

Setting the most profitable price and quantity to produce

Introduction

Demand must be considered when setting prices. Ignoring demand curves does not make them go away. Usually, a market will buy more at lower prices--so total revenue my increase if prices are lowered. But this probably won't continue as the price gets closer to zero. Further, total cost--and perhaps average costs--will increase as greater quantities are sold.

So, if a firm is at all interested in making a profit (or avoiding losses), it should consider demand and cost curves *together*. This exercise shows how this can be done--and emphasizes that not all prices will be profitable.

Assignment

Figure 18-3 shows the Touchdown Manufacturing Company's estimated total revenue and total cost curves for the coming year. Study this figure carefully and answer the questions which follow.

FIGURE 18-3

1.   Complete the following chart by referring to Figure 18-3--the graph of Touchdown's total costs and revenues.

Quantity	Total Cost	Average Cost	Total Revenue	Price*	Total Profit (Loss)
1,000	____	____	____	____	____
2,000	____	____	____	____	____
3,500	____	____	____	____	____
4,500	____	____	____	____	____

* Remember: Total Revenue = Price x Quantity

Total Profit = Total Revenue – Total Cost

Using the information from Question 1, and Figure 18-3, answer Questions 2-11.

2.   The maximum amount of profit Touchdown can earn is: $ _____

3.   Touchdown has total fixed costs of: $ _____

4.   Given that Total Revenue = Price X Quantity, what should Touchdown's price be if it wants to get the most total revenue it can and plans to sell:

a.   1,000 units: _____

b.   2,000 units: _____

c.   3,500 units: _____

d.   4,500 units: _____

5.   What would Touchdown's average cost per unit be at:

a.   1,000 units: _____

b.   2,000 units: _____

c.   3,500 units: _____

d.   4,500 units: _____

6.   To maximize its *total revenue*, Touchdown should sell (check the correct response):

___a.   1,000 units.

___b.   2,000 units.

___c.   3,500 units.

___d.   4,000 units.

___e.   more than 4,500 units.

7.   Figure 18-3 indicates that Touchdown's demand curve is (check the correct response):

___a.   horizontal.

___b.   vertical.

___c.   downward-sloping from left to right.

___d.   upward-sloping from left to right.

8.   Touchdown's demand curve is (check the correct response):

___a.   elastic.

___b.   inelastic.

___c.   unitary elastic.

___d.   elastic up to 3,500 units and inelastic beyond 3,500 units.

___e.   inelastic up to 3,500 units and elastic beyond 3,500 units.

9.   Touchdown's *average* cost curve is (check the correct response):

___a.   horizontal.

___b.   U-shaped.

___c.   vertical.

___d.   upward-sloping from left to right.

10. Touchdown will *lose money* if it sells (check the correct response):

   ___a. less than 1,000 units.

   ___b. less than 4,500 units.

   ___c. more than 3,500 units.

   ___d. more than 4,500 units.

   ___e. both a and d are correct.

11. Touchdown will *break even* if it sells (check the correct response):

   ___a. 1,000 units.

   ___b. 2,000 units.

   ___c. 3,500 units.

   ___d. 4,500 units.

   ___e. both a and d are correct.

12. To *maximize profit,* Touchdown should sell (check the correct response):

   ___a. 1,000 units.

   ___b. 2,000 units.

   ___c. 3,500 units.

   ___d. 4,500 units.

   ___e. more than 4,500 units.

Question for Discussion

Should a firm in monopolistic competition try to sell as many units as it can produce? Why or why not? State your assumptions.

Exercise 18-4

Using marginal analysis to set the most profitable price and quantity to produce

Introduction

Too many firms seem to ignore demand--depending almost blindly on cost-oriented pricing. A firm might operate quite profitably using cost-oriented pricing--but could it earn larger profits by charging a different price? The firm has no way of answering this question unless it also takes demand into consideration. When both costs and demand are known (or estimated), marginal analysis can be used to determine the most profitable price and the most profitable quantity to produce. Of course, in the short run the firm's objective may *not* be to maximize profit. In this case, marginal analysis can be used to show how much profit is "lost" when the firm pursues some other objective--such as maximizing sales.

This exercise gives you practice in working with the concepts of marginal analysis by applying them to the graph (Figure 18-4) on the next page. This graph shows curves for demand (D), average cost (AC), marginal revenue (MR), and marginal cost (MC) at different price and quantity combinations. (Review the discussion of marginal analysis on pages 498-501 of the text). Note that the graph in this exercise is different from the graph (Exhibit 18-10, page 500) used to illustrate marginal analysis in the text. Thus, this exercise gives you an opportunity to look at marginal analysis issues from a different point of view. However, you will see that you can answer the questions in this exercise by applying the concepts discussed in the text.

Assignment

Use Figure 18-4 on the next page to answer the following questions:

1.   At what price would 184 units be sold? _____

2.   How many units would be sold if the firm priced its product at $24? _____

3.   At what output (quantity) _____ and price _____ would the average cost per unit be *minimized?*

4.   At what output _____ and price _____ would the firm break even?

5.   At what output _____ and price _____ would the firm maximize its *total revenue?*

6.   At what output _____ and price _____ would the firm maximize its *total profit?*

7.   What will the average profit per unit be when the firm maximizes its total profit? _____

8.   What is the maximum amount of profit this firm can earn? _____

FIGURE 18-4

Question for Discussion

Why do so few firms use demand-oriented pricing? Is it an impossible task?

Name: _____   Course & Section: _____

Exercise 18-5

Break-even/profit analysis

This exercise is based on computer-aided problem number 18--Break-Even/Profit Analysis. A complete description of the problem appears on page 513 of *Basic Marketing*, 16th edition.

1. The marketing manager is interested in how the break-even point--in both units and sale dollars-- changes as fixed costs vary. Do a What If analysis (using the break-even column on the left side of the spreadsheet) to vary fixed costs between $27,000 and $33,000 (that is, plus or minus 10 percent from the initial $30,000 level). See how the break-even point changes and fill in the missing numbers in the table below. Then, briefly explain the pattern you observe.

Fixed Cost Level	Break-Even (Units)	Break-Even ($ Sales)
$ 27,000		$
$	72,000	$
$ 30,000		$
$		$ 95,400
$ 33,000		$

Explanation: _____

_____

_____

_____

_____

2. The marketing manager is also interested in how variable cost changes affect break-even. If fixed cost remains at $30,000 and price and other variables stay the same, what happens to the break-even points (units and dollar sales) as the variable cost varies between $.72 and $.88--that is, plus or minus 10 percent from the initial value of $.80 a unit? As you did above, fill in the missing values in the table on the next page, and briefly explain the pattern you observe.

Average Variable Cost	Break-Even (Units)	Break-Even ($ Sales)
$ .72		$
$	68,182	$
$ .80		$
$		$ 105,882.00
$ .88		$

Explanation: _____

_____

_____

_____

_____

3. The marketing manager is also considering what happens if fixed costs and variable costs change at the same time. For the two combinations of fixed cost and variable cost shown below, what are the break-even points in units and dollars?

Fixed Cost	Variable Cost	Break-Even (Units)	Break-Even ($ Sales)
$ 27,000	$ 0.84		$
$ 33,000	$ 0.76		$

In the first situation above, fixed cost decreased and variable cost increased from the original (spreadsheet) situation. In the second, fixed cost increased and variable cost decreased. Once the break-even point is achieved, which of these combinations would earn profits the fastest as additional units are sold? Briefly explain why.

_____

_____

_____

_____

Chapter 19

Implementing and controlling marketing plans: evolution and revolution

What This Chapter Is About

Chapter 19 shows that a wealth of information may be available from a firm's own records. But it will be useless unless the marketing manager knows how it can be obtained and used--and then asks for it!

This is an important chapter. Marketing plans are not always easy to implement. The marketing manager must know how to use these control-related tools. They help keep a plan on course--and point to situations where a new plan is needed.

We discuss ways to build quality into the implementation effort. Total quality management means more than offering customers products that don't have defects. Because marketing is dynamic, managers must seek ways to continually improve the marketing strategy and how it is implemented. Total quality management approaches--ranging from application of techniques such as fishbone diagrams and Pareto charts to empowerment and training of service employees--are proving to be important ways to implement quality marketing programs. Benchmarking performance and getting a return on quality are part of the evaluation process.

Various sales and cost analysis techniques are presented in this chapter. They can be useful for evaluating and controlling the marketing activities of a firm. These techniques are not really complicated. They require only simple arithmetic, and perhaps a computer if a large volume of adding and subtracting is required.

Be sure to distinguish between straightforward sales or cost analysis and performance analysis. Also, be sure to distinguish between the full-cost approach and the contribution-margin approach to cost analysis. Each can be useful in certain situations. But uncritical use of either method might lead to the wrong decision.

Important Terms

control, p. 517
total quality management (TQM), p. 522
continuous improvement, p. 523
Pareto chart, p. 523
fishbone diagram, p. 524
empowerment, p. 526
benchmarking, p. 527

sales analysis, p. 529
performance analysis, p. 530
performance index, p. 531
iceberg principle, p. 534
full-cost approach, p. 536
contribution-margin approach, p. 536
marketing audit, p. 540

True-False Questions

____ 1. Control is the feedback process that helps the marketing manager learn how ongoing plans and implementation are working and how to plan for the future.

____ 2. For most firms, one of the biggest obstacles to fast feedback is that the data is not in a form that can be quickly sorted and analyzed by computer.

____ 3. New information technologies help speed decision-making within the company and the implementation process outside the company.

____ 4. Total quality management works because everyone in the firm is concerned about quality to better serve customers' needs.

____ 5. The commitment to constantly make things better one step at a time is called continuous improvement.

____ 6. In a Pareto chart, problem causes are ordered from least frequent to most frequent.

____ 7. The fishbone diagram is a visual aid that helps managers figure out why things go wrong.

____ 8. A company may benchmark each of its sales reps against its other sales reps or against a competitor's sales reps.

____ 9. Because of the 80/20 rule--traditional accounting reports are usually of great help to marketing managers in controlling their plans and programs.

____ 10. Routine sales analyses are best done by manually reviewing data stored in sales invoice files.

____ 11. The best way to analyze sales data is to break it down by geographic region and customer type.

____ 12. Sales analysis provides a detailed breakdown of company sales records, but with no attempt to compare them against standards. Performance analysis seeks exceptions or variations from planned performance.

____ 13. A performance index is a number--such as a baseball batting average--that shows the relation of one value to another.

____ 14. A well-designed performance analysis will not only solve marketing problems--but may also be used to forecast sales.

____ 15. The "iceberg principle" suggests that--while averaging and summarizing data can be helpful to managers--these summaries sometimes hide more than they reveal.

____ 16. The full-cost approach requires that difficult-to-allocate costs be split on some basis.

_____ 17.   Although the contribution-margin approach focuses management attention on variable cost--rather than total cost--it is likely to lead to the same marketing decisions as the full-cost approach.

_____ 18.   While full-cost analysis is especially useful for evaluating alternatives, the contribution-margin approach does a better job of showing individuals within the firm how much they have actually contributed to general overhead and profit.

_____ 19.   Ideally, a marketing audit should not be necessary because a good manager should continually evaluate the effectiveness of his operation—but, in practice, a marketing audit is probably needed because too many managers are "so close to the trees that they can't see the forest."

Answers to True-False Questions

1. T, p. 517
2. T, p. 518
3. T, p. 518
4. T, p. 522
5. T, p. 523
6. F, p. 523
7. T, p. 524

8. T, p. 527
9. F, p. 528
10. F, p. 529
11. F, p. 529
12. T, p. 530
13. T, p. 531
14. F, p. 532

15. T, p. 534
16. T, p. 536
17. F, p. 536
18. F, p. 538
19. T, p. 540-41

Multiple-Choice Questions (Circle the correct response)

1.   Total quality management:
   a.   requires that everyone in the organization be concerned with improving quality.
   b.   means more than just using statistical controls to reduce manufacturing defects.
   c.   views the cost of lost customers as an important result of quality problems.
   d.   applies to service producers as well as manufacturers.
   e.   all of the above are correct.

2.   Using total quality management to improve the implementation of a marketing program is likely to include:
   a.   the use of Pareto charts to determine the critical path for scheduling marketing activities.
   b.   the use of fishbone diagrams to show which problems are most important.
   c.   an emphasis on treating routine customer problems and unusual ones in the same way--because every problem is equally important.
   d.   training and empowerment of employees to identify and solve customer problems.
   e.   all of the above are correct.

3.   According to the "80/20 rule":
   a.   marketing accounts for 80 percent of the consumer's dollar.
   b.   only 20 out of every 100 firms use formal marketing control programs.
   c.   about 20 percent of a typical firm's customers are unprofitable to serve.
   d.   even though a firm might be showing a profit, 80 percent of its business might be coming from only 20 percent of its products or customers.
   e.   none of the above is correct.

4. A marketing manager who wants to analyze his firm's sales should be aware that:
   a. sales invoice files contain little useful information.
   b. the best way to analyze sales data is according to geographic regions.
   c. sales analysis involves a detailed breakdown of a company's sales forecasts.
   d. sales analysis may not be possible unless the manager has made arrangements for the company to capture identifying information about each sale.
   e. a manager can never have too much data.

5. Performance analysis differs from sales analysis in that performance analysis involves:
   a. detailed breakdowns of a company's sales records.
   b. analyzing only the performance of sales representatives.
   c. comparing performance against standards--looking for exceptions or variations.
   d. analyzing only people--not products or territories.
   e. budgeting for marketing expenditures on the basis of contribution margins.

6. If Salesperson X had a performance index of 80 and Salesperson Y had a performance index of 120, then:
   a. Salesperson X may be having some problems and his sales performance should be investigated.
   b. the two would average out to 100--and this would suggest that "all is well."
   c. Salesperson X's performance should be investigated as a guide to improving everyone's performance.
   d. Salesperson Y probably should be fired.
   e. Salesperson Y obviously had higher sales than Salesperson X.

7. Which of the following statements best describes the "iceberg principle"?
   a. Problems in one area may be offset by good performances in other areas--and thus the problems may not be visible on the surface.
   b. Ten percent of the items in inventory usually account for 80 percent of the sales.
   c. Within a company's sales force there are usually one or two sales reps who don't carry their weight.
   d. Many sales reps do not make their quotas because they ignore certain clients.
   e. Airfreight is less risky than shipping by boat.

8. If one were using the "full-cost" approach to marketing cost analysis, then allocating fixed costs on the basis of sales volume would:
   a. make some customers appear more profitable than they actually are.
   b. not be done--because only variable costs would be analyzed.
   c. make some products appear less profitable than they actually are.
   d. decrease the profitability of the whole business.
   e. Both a and c are true statements.

9. Which of the following statements about the contribution-margin approach is *false?*
   a. It is concerned with the amount contributed by an item or group of items toward covering fixed costs.
   b. This approach suggests that it is not necessary to consider all costs in all situations.
   c. Top management almost always finds this approach more useful than full-cost analysis.
   d. This approach frequently leads to data that suggest a different decision than might be indicated by the full-cost approach.
   e. It focuses on controllable costs--rather than on total costs.

10. Which of the following statements about a "marketing audit" is *true?*
    a. A marketing audit should be conducted only when some crisis arises.
    b. It probably should be conducted by someone inside the marketing department who is familiar with the whole program.
    c. A marketing audit should evaluate the company's whole marketing program--not just some parts of it.
    d. A marketing audit should be handled by the specialist most familiar with each of the marketing plans in the program.
    e. All of the above are true statements.

Answers to Multiple-Choice Questions

1. e, p. 522-25
2. d, p. 525
3. d, p. 528
4. d, p. 529

5. c, p. 530
6. a, p. 531
7. a, p. 534
8. e, p. 539

9. c, p. 539
10. c, p. 540

Exercise 19-1

Total quality management

Introduction

Marketing strategy planning is important to the success of every firm. Yet, a firm that doesn't do a good job implementing its strategy is likely to find itself losing customers and profits.

Many firms are finding that *total quality management* can help them not just with reducing defects in production but also in implementing all aspects of a marketing program. As discussed in the text, total quality management approaches can be adapted to firms of any size and for all classes of products.

There are many technical details on how to use statistical techniques as part of a total quality management process. In the text, you get an introduction to a few of these--fishbone diagrams and Pareto charts. But, even more than the techniques is the basic philosophy that motivates quality management. In that regard, learning about and understanding the basic ideas and concepts (see pages 522-27) of quality management is an important first step to using the approaches.

The purpose of this exercise is to give you practice analyzing different marketing problems from a total quality management perspective.

Assignment

In each of the following situations, a firm is having difficulty in reliably satisfying customer needs. In each situation, identify the most important problem (or problems) and make recommendations for how the firm can improve the implementation of its marketing plan. Be specific in relating your diagnosis and recommendations to the quality management concepts and techniques discussed in the text. The first question is answered for you as an example.

1. Century Bank is interested in shifting its emphasis from commercial lending to lending to consumers--especially in the area of residential mortgages. The bank has the "back office" capacity to handle the business and, with interest rates coming down, there is growing demand for new mortgages. Century's ad agency developed an effective series of radio and TV ads, and the bank president was pleased to learn that the new thrust seemed to be working. At the end of two months, mortgage applications were up 300 percent over the same period the year before. It wasn't long, however, before there were signs of trouble. Several customers complained about the slow turnaround time for loan approvals and the problems the delays had caused them. When the president checked on the matter, she found that there were many such cases--and she was even more surprised to find that the number of loans actually completed had decreased relative to the previous year. When she asked the head of the loan-processing group for an explanation, he said "It's no one single bottleneck. Sometimes the appraisal is late coming in. Other times there's some problem with the credit report or customers haven't completed the forms correctly. Sometimes the title insurance company holds us up on some detail. So, it's hard to say." The bank president said, "Well, I'm not happy about it. We'll just have to work harder until we can catch up. In the meantime, I hope it doesn't hurt our reputation."

a)   Problem: *Neither the head of the loan-processing group nor the president is coming to grips with the problem. They are not actively looking for ways to make continuous improvements. To make real improvements and do a better job of meeting customer needs, they will need to sort out the causes and effects for the things that have gone wrong (the delays in processing.) Some of the delays are interrelated because parts of the process depend on completion of work by other people--the applicants, the title company, the appraisers.*

b)   Solution: *Century can begin to get a handle on the delays by developing a simple fishbone diagram to understand which parts of the system are causing delays. Then after some simple data collection, a Pareto Chart would help to identify which problems should be attacked first--for example, improving the application forms so consumers don't have trouble filling them out, and developing closer coordination with the appraisers and title insurance companies. Satisfying the customer is--or at least should be--important to them too.*

2.   Excel Skates, Inc. manufactures recreational roller skates. Its new in-line design has turned out to be much more popular than expected--and demand far exceeds production capacity. The only glitch is that there have been some problems with the wheels on some of the skates; after a short period of use, the bearings in the wheels break and skates don't roll properly. The chief of production wants to change to a new assembly procedure that will eliminate the problem altogether, but he acknowledges that it will reduce output somewhat. The sales manager doesn't think that makes sense, however, because "the problem isn't very common, and it will be cheaper and easier to fix any problem skates under warranty."

    a)   Problem:

    b)   Solution:

3.   The University Cashier's office is open from 8 until 5 every day and students can come to pay their tuition and fees, take care of campus parking tickets, get a bus pass, sign up to rent a dorm room, and handle just about everything else that involves money. There are two service windows that work on a "first come, first serve" basis and most of the time students only need to wait in line a few minutes to get help. However, sometimes there are long delays. As one student recently complained, "All I wanted to do was pay a fine for a lost library book, and it took nearly an hour because the computer had accidentally unenrolled the guy in front of me--and they couldn't get it straight. The line at the other window wasn't moving either--they couldn't figure out how much to refund a student who had to drop out of school because of an accident. There must have been 20 people behind me in the line."

    a)   Problem:

    b)   Solution:

4.   High Point Lake is a well known summer camp for girls. Many campers return year after year and most of the promotion is handled by direct-mail responses to word-of-mouth referrals. The camp has a unique lake location and special boating facilities, and its superior reputation means that each year the camp has a waiting list. The camp has been owned by Lance Fisher's family for three generations. Prices at High Point Lake have always been set by the Fisher family by "what seems fair," and there has never been any customer resistance to price raises. This summer Mr. Fisher has received two notes and one phone call from parents complaining that the college and high-school age counselors don't seem quite as involved with the campers. When asked for specifics, parents find it hard to define their complaints, but one notes: "Nowadays, they all seem to bring cars with them to High Point Lake and, as soon as they have time off, they're out of there." When Mr. Fisher asked the head counselor, Sandi Running Deer, about the parents' complaint, Running Deer responded, "That's true. A lot of them have boyfriends back in the city and they're commuting back to see them every chance they get. I guess we've just got a bad crop this year. Next year we'll get a better group of counselors--and be back to the old High Point Lake!"

a)   Problem:

b)   Solution:

5.   SportRover Automobile Co. has a reputation for producing elegant--but notoriously unreliable--sports sedans. One writer in the automotive press suggested that there was nothing finer than a Sunday afternoon spin in a SportRover--as long as you could afford a "chase car" to follow behind with a mechanic and spare parts. In the face of aggressive new competition from Japanese and German manufacturers of luxury sedans, SportRover has been losing market share. To counter this trend, Sebastian Lott, SportRover's director of marketing, announces to a convention of SportRover dealers that the marketing mix will be adjusted. "For the new model year, leather upholstery and lambswool carpets will no longer be extra-cost options, but instead will be included in the base price of the car. We have also increased the horse power of the engine and made a number of other changes that will make it clear to customers that we have improved the quality of our cars."

a)   Problem:

b)   Solution:

6.   Tess Zimmerman's objective is to build a profitable chain of bookstores, so she's pleased that a literary critic for a local paper has written a very favorable review of the selection of books in her first store. However, while Tess was out to lunch a young woman approached the checkout counter at the store and told the salesclerk, "I don't have my receipt with me, but I bought this book here yesterday and, as you can see, one whole section is just blank pages. I've checked the shelf and the other two copies have the same problem. I'd like my money back." The clerk replied, "I'm very sorry for the problem, but the store policy is that only the manager can approve a refund without a receipt--and she's on her lunch break. Can you come back in a couple of hours?" The irritated customer replied, "I came here on my lunch break just to get this straight." The clerk responds, "I really regret the inconvenience. Would it be helpful if I had the manager call you when she comes back?"

a)   Problem:

b)   Solution:

Question for Discussion

If a firm has really adopted the marketing concept, why should it need to worry about having some sort of total quality management program?

Exercise 19-2

Sales and performance analysis

Introduction

This exercise shows how sales analysis and performance analysis might be used to help plan and control marketing programs. *Sales analysis* begins with a detailed breakdown of the company's sales records and can take many forms--since there is no one best way to analyze sales data. As outlined in the text, any one of several sales breakdowns may be appropriate--depending on the nature of the company, its products, and which strategies are being evaluated.

Performance analysis seeks exceptions or variations from planned performance. In contrast to simple sales analysis--where facts and figures are merely listed--performance analysis involves the use of predetermined standards against which actual results are compared. Here, the purpose is to determine where--and why--performance was better or worse than expected.

Sales analysis and performance analysis can be useful in pinpointing operating problems which may require corrective action--or in identifying areas in which the company may be performing exceptionally well. Such analyses will *not* reveal *what* is causing a given problem--nor will they provide a *solution* to the problem. This requires sound management judgment--both in interpreting the data and in developing solutions. By using sales and performance analyses, however, marketing managers can rely on factual evidence--rather than guesswork--when problems do arise--and thereby improve the quality of their decision making. Better yet, by continually auditing their marketing programs--by analysis of well-chosen data--they may be able to anticipate problems and take action *before* they become serious.

Assignment

Assume you are the marketing manager for a small manufacturer of electrical products. Your company's products are sold by five sales reps--each serving a separate territory--who earn a straight commission of 10 percent of sales. The company's accountant has just given you the data shown on the next page describing last year's sales. Actual sales were less than expected, so you decide to analyze the data further to help you decide what to do.

TABLE 19-2a

Sales Territory	Sales Quota	Actual Sales	Total Calls	Total Orders	Total Customers
A	960,000	480,000	1,200	360	420
B	600,000	600,000	1,320	780	300
C	720,000	360,000	480	300	240
D	900,000	1,080,000	1,560	1,200	480
E	360,000	540,000	720	360	120
Total	$3,540,000	$3,060,000	5,280	3,000	1,560

1. a) Calculate a *sales performance index* for each sales territory. Show your work. One answer is provided as an example:

Territory A:

Territory B:

Territory C:

Territory D: ($1,080,000 / 900,000) X 100 = 120.0

Territory E:

b) What do the performance indexes indicate about the relative selling performance of each salesperson? One answer is provided as an example.

Territory A:

Territory B:

Territory C:

Territory D: This salesperson's actual sales were much higher than expected for some reason. We should try to find out why.

Territory E:

2. Some additional sales analysis would be desirable to help you decide why the sales reps performed as they did. Therefore, using the data in Table 19-2, make the necessary calculations to complete the following table. Some answers have been provided as a check on your work.

TABLE 19-2b

Sales Territory	Order/Call Ratio	Average Sale per Order	Average Sale per Customer	Sales Commission
A	30.0			
B				$36,000
C			$2,000	
D		$900		
E				
Average for All Territories	56.8			

3. On the basis of your sales and performance analyses, what do you conclude about the sales performance of each salesperson? What factors would you want to investigate further before taking any corrective action?

Territory A:

Territory B:

19-15

Territory C:

Territory D:

Territory E:

Question for Discussion

Does the above analysis suggest any specific management action that was not clearly indicated by a review of Table 19-2a? How does this illustrate the "iceberg principle"?

Exercise 19-3

Marketing cost analysis

This exercise is based on computer-aided problem number 19--Marketing Cost Analysis. A complete description of the problem appears on page 543 of *Basic Marketing,* 16th edition.

Tapco's marketing manager is considering changing the price of one or both products. He has decided to use the spreadsheet to analyze his idea more carefully.

1. At present, Tapco is selling 5,000 units of Product A for $10.00 each and 4,000 units of Product B for $6.00 each. Based on the full-cost approach, what is Product A's allocated administrative expense and allocated advertising expense? How much profit does Product A contribute to the company?

    Administrative expense-Product A $ _____

    Advertising expense-Product A $ _____

    Net profit or loss-Product A $ _____

2. The marketing manager is considering raising the price of Product A to $12.00. He estimates that the quantity demanded will be only 3,725 at $12.00--but he is not certain how that will affect profits from Product A. Given his price and quantity estimates, use the full-cost approach column of the spreadsheet to compute the following information for this situation (a price increase).

    Administrative expense-Product A $ _____

    Advertising expense-Product A $ _____

    Net profit or loss-Product A $ _____

3. Based on these two analyses (1 and 2 above), is it a good idea to increase the price of Product A to $12.00? Briefly explain your answer.

    _____

    _____

    _____

    _____

    _____

4. Now, evaluate the same pricing change using the contribution-margin approach. What happens to the contribution margin for Product A at the higher price and lower quantity?

Contribution margin with 5,000 units at $10 each $ _____

Contribution margin with 3,725 units at $12.00 $ _____

5. Based on the change in the contribution margin, is it a good idea to increase the price of Product A to $12.00? Briefly explain your answer.

_____

_____

_____

_____

_____

6. Briefly explain why the effect of the price increase appears to be attractive using the full-cost approach--but unattractive using the contribution-margin approach. Be specific. (Be sure to consider Tapco's total profitability before answering.)

_____

_____

_____

_____

_____

7. Based on this analysis, Tapco's marketing manager decided not to increase the price of Product A. But he is also considering lowering the price of Product B to $5.50--because he thinks that the lower price will stimulate increased unit sales. But he is not certain exactly how much the quantity sold would increase. What (minimum) quantity should Tapco expect to sell to make a price reduction on Product B a good idea?

a minimum of _____ units of Product B at $5.50 each

Chapter 20

Managing marketing's link with other functional areas

What This Chapter Is About

Chapter 20 discusses some of the most important ways that marketing strategy planning is linked with other areas in the firm. For example, the funds to pay for a marketing plan come from capital, and managing a firm's capital is usually the job of a chief financial officer. Similarly, firms need something to sell; they either have to have their own internal production capacity or they have to work with other firms that can provide it. The type of production capacity that a firm has may create great flexibility to pursue new opportunities as they arise, or it may limit the firm and the type of business it can conduct.

Most marketing activities involve costs, and it's necessary to be certain that those costs are less than revenue or the firm won't earn a profit. So, marketing managers need to understand costs and how to work with them. Unfortunately, data from traditional accounting reports often isn't very useful for understanding the costs or profitability of particular customers, products, or markets. However, a number of progressive marketing managers are finding that they can work with accountants--and marketing cost analysis--to improve the quality of their decisions.

Of course, no plan is going to be effective if there is no one who can implement it. Yet, new strategies often require new people, new ways of looking at things, and new skills. So, marketing managers often turn to human resource experts for help to be sure that the people and skills needed to get the job done are there when the plan calls for them.

Everyone in the firm should work together to satisfy customers--that's basic to the marketing concept. But that doesn't mean that marketing people are always in control. Rather, managers from different areas must work together as a team to be certain that the firm's marketing plans are really feasible--and will result in a strategy that offers a true competitive advantage.

Important Terms

capital, p. 547
working capital, p. 548
stock, p. 550
debt financing, p. 550
cash flow statement, p. 553
production capacity, p. 553

virtual corporation, p. 555
task transfer, p. 556
mass customization, p. 557
natural accounts, p. 559
functional accounts, p. 559

True-False Questions

____ 1. Marketing's link with the other functional areas of a firm (financing, production, accounting, human resources, etc.) affects strategy planning.

____ 2. Capital is the money to pay for short-term expenses such as employee salaries, advertising, and storing.

____ 3. In most large companies, there is a separate chief financial officer who works with the chief executive to make major financial decisions.

____ 4. Once the decision is made to fund a marketing plan, the marketing manager usually doesn't have to worry about budget constraints.

____ 5. Working capital is the money to pay for short-term expenses such as employee salaries, advertising, marketing research, storing, etc.

____ 6. Capital is the money used to pay for short-term expenses and working capital is the money used to pay for long-term expenses.

____ 7. Marketing managers in most American firms face intense pressure to develop plans that will generate profits quickly.

____ 8. Debt financing is borrowing money based on a promise to repay the loan, usually within a fixed time period and with a specific interest charge.

____ 9. A firm's selling price must cover the interest charge on borrowed money as well as the marketing expenses and the other costs of doing business.

____ 10. A cash flow statement is a financial report that forecasts how much cash will be available after paying expenses.

____ 11. Direct distribution usually requires less investment capital than indirect approaches.

____ 12. Production capacity is the ability to produce a certain quantity and quality of specific goods or services.

____ 13. Problems of matching supply and demand are likely to be greatest when a marketing plan calls for quick expansion into many different market areas all at once.

____ 14. When a firm is a virtual corporation, it acts primarily as a coordinator--with a good marketing concept.

____ 15. Task transfer is using unskilled workers to do the jobs formerly done by skilled workers.

____ 16. Mass customization is tailoring the principles of mass production to meet the general needs of all customers.

____ 17. Producing products in large batches usually requires maintaining large inventories.

18. Marketing managers and accountants should work together to improve analysis of the costs and profitability of specific products and customers.

19. Because most marketing expenditures are made for the general purpose of "increasing sales," detailed marketing cost analysis is all but impossible--and most marketing expenditures should be treated as general overhead costs.

20. While *functional* accounts are the categories to which various costs are charged in the normal accounting cycle--*natural* accounts are set up to indicate the *purpose* for which the expenditures are made.

21. The first step in marketing cost analysis is to reclassify all the dollar cost entries in the functional accounts into natural accounts.

22. Marketing cost analysis can be used to analyze not only total company profitability-- but also the profitability of territories, products, customers, salespeople, or any other breakdowns desired.

23. People are one of a company's most important resources.

24. Human resource issues are often critically important both in a marketing manager's choice among different possible marketing opportunities and in the actual implementation of marketing plans.

25. Communication is very important because you can't expect people to pull together in an companywide effort if they don't know what's going on.

26. Rapid growth strains human resources (because new employees must be trained), but slow growth also strains human resources (because jobs may be cut or reassigned).

Answers to *True-False Questions*

1. T, p. 546	10. T, p. 553	19. F, p. 559
2. F, p. 547	11. F, p. 553	20. F, p. 559
3. T, p. 547	12. T, p. 553	21. F, p. 560
4. F, p. 547-48	13. T, p. 555	22. T, p. 560
5. T, p. 548	14. T, p. 555	23. T, p. 564
6. F, p. 547-48	15. F, p. 556	24. T, p. 564
7. T, p. 550	16. F, p. 557	25. T, p. 565
8. T, p. 550	17. T, p. 558	26. T, p. 565-66
9. T, p. 551	18. T, p. 559	

Multiple-Choice Questions (Circle the correct response)

1. Working capital would be used to pay for:
    a.   employee salaries
    b.   marketing research
    c.   advertising
    d.   storing
    e.   all of the above

2. There are a number of different possible sources of capital, but
    a.   the sale of stock or bonds is considered to be an internal source of capital.
    b.   debt financing is now illegal in the U.S.
    c.   they are all likely to have the same effect when it comes to the time horizon within which a marketing manager's plan is expected to be profitable.
    d.   a firm that is not yet profitable is likely to need to use external sources.
    e.   a firm isn't likely to be able to sell stock unless its marketing plan is a sure thing.

3. Which of the following statements is FALSE in regard to borrowing money?
    a.   In general, the greater the risk associated with a loan the greater the interest rate charge will be.
    b.   Interest expense on a loan may impact prices and profits.
    c.   Borrowing money is usually less expensive than reinvesting cash generated from operations.
    d.   A company with a successful marketing strategy has its own internal source of fund--profits.
    e.   None of the above is false.

4. A virtual corporation
    a.   has strong capital, but it can only survive if it develops a close relationship (i.e., a partnership) with another firm that has developed a good marketing plan.
    b.   looks for capable suppliers who can meet the specs it lays out.
    c.   handles all of its sales using the Internet.
    d.   all of the above
    e.   none of the above

5. Overseas production
    a.   generally makes distribution more complicated.
    b.   may be very economical.
    c.   sometimes brings concerns over nationalism to the forefront.
    d.   can apply to services as well as physical goods.
    e.   all of the above.

6. Production flexibility should help a supplier support its business customers with:
    a.   just-in-time delivery
    b.   EDI
    c.   rapid response replenishment of inventories
    d.   computerized reorder capabilities
    e.   any of the above

7. Firms now using mass customization to give their customers more or better choices include:
   a. Lands' End.
   b. Andersen.
   c. Nike.
   d. ChemStation.
   e. All of the above.

8. Firms that use mass customization
   a. may target either business customers or final consumers.
   b. may be able to take advantage of the Internet for orders.
   c. may be able to give their customers more or better choices.
   d. are likely to have higher costs than do firms who produce more standardized products, but may earn better profit margins.
   e. all of the above.

9. Marketing cost analysis
   a. just uses the same "natural" accounting categories commonly used for financial analysis.
   b. allocates costs to products or customers to focus on the purpose for which marketing money is spent.
   c. is not very accurate, since it is almost impossible to link marketing costs to specific sales.
   d. is done more frequently than analysis of manufacturing costs.
   e. None of the above is true.

10. Which of the following statements regarding marketing cost analysis is *false?*
    a. Functional accounts include items such as salaries, wages, supplies, raw materials, and advertising.
    b. The costs allocated to the functional accounts will be equal in total to those in the natural accounts.
    c. Functional accounts can be used to show the profitability of territories, products, customers, sales representatives, and so on.
    d. Cost analysis is not performance analysis.
    e. Traditional accounting methods do not show the purpose for which marketing expenditures are made.

11. A good marketing manager knows that:
    a. the costs allocated to functional accounts during a marketing cost analysis should equal-- in total--those in the natural accounts.
    b. functional accounts usually are needed for determining the profitability of customers.
    c. functional accounts usually are needed for determining the profitability of products.
    d. All of the above are true.
    e. Only b and c are true.

Answers to Multiple-Choice Questions

1. e, p. 548
2. d, p. 550
3. c, p. 552
4. b, p. 555

5. e, p. 556-57
6. e, p. 557
7. e, p. 557-58
8. e, p. 557

9. b, p. 559
10. a, p. 559
11. d, p. 560

Exercise 20-1

Cross-functional influences on marketing mix planning

Introduction

Marketing managers don't plan strategies in a vacuum. In selecting target markets and blending the 4Ps, it's crucial to consider the firm's objectives and its overall resources as well as the external market environment. Understanding the firm's marketing resources and objectives is an important part of such thinking. However, its resources and capabilities in some other area--such as production, finance, or human resources--may be what gives a firm a real advantage by enabling it to pursue a marketing strategy that is hard for a competitor to follow.

Alternatively, some possible strategies may not even be feasible for a firm that doesn't have some needed resource. For example, a really innovative new product usually requires informative promotion to be successful. However, a small firm that is trying to pioneer the market for such a product may not have enough money to pay for advertising or enough people to work in sales jobs and recruit middlemen.

Sometimes it's a challenge for the marketing manager to decide how to blend the overall marketing mix so that it appropriately accounts for links with other functional areas--because there are often both advantages and disadvantages that must be balanced when selecting a strategy. For example, a small firm might want to set up its own sales force--to have more control--but using a manufacturer's representative might require less capital. One approach for choosing among different alternatives starts by identifying the major advantages and disadvantages of each alternative. This exercise gives you some practice doing that.

Assignment

In each of the following questions, a manager must decide between several different alternatives. Think carefully about each decision and then concisely list the major advantages and disadvantages of each alternative.

1. A retired U.S. Marine Corps officer is interested in setting up a business on the Internet. He is certain that his idea will ultimately be very profitable, but it may take a while for it to catch on. He doesn't want to risk what little money he has saved, so he is trying to decide how to finance his marketing plan. He thinks that he would be able to finance the business by selling stock to some other investors. Alternatively, it might be possible to start with a small investment from his savings and then finance growth through cash flow.

    a. *Sell stock to investors*

        Advantages:

        Disadvantages:

    b. *Finance growth by relying on cash flow*

        Advantages:

        Disadvantages:

2.   A fast-growing firm has been expanding its sales force as rapidly as it can recruit and hire qualified people. Until now, the sales manager and several of the district managers have been doing most of the training of the new sales reps. However, the training job keeps getting bigger at the same time that their other responsibilities are expanding. Thus, the sales manager is thinking about hiring an assistant who would work as a sales training specialist. Alternatively, there are a number of good human resources consultants who specialize in sales training; thus, the sales manager could pay one or more of them to help out on an "as needed" basis. What are the major advantages and disadvantages of the two alternatives?

a.   *Hire the sales training expert*

Advantages:

Disadvantages:

b.   *Use a part-time consultant*

Advantages:

Disadvantages:

3.   A firm is interested in expanding into international markets, but at present it does not have enough capacity to produce much more than it is currently selling. The firm might be able to increase its capacity by (a) expanding its current factory or (b) arranging to have a supplier produce to its specifications on a contract basis. The president of the firm has said that he is going to make the final decision, but he's interested in the marketing manager's inputs about the major advantages and disadvantages of each approach.

a.   *Expand the current factory*

Advantages:

Disadvantages:

b: *Rely on a supplier*

Advantages:

Disadvantages:

Question for Discussion

The marketing mix often needs to change over the different stages of the product life cycle. Do you think that the effect of other areas (finance, production, human resources) on marketing strategy planning is also likely to change over the different stages in the product life cycle? Why or why not.

Exercise 20-2

Marketing cost analysis for controlling marketing plans and programs

Introduction

This exercise shows the importance of marketing cost analysis in controlling marketing plans and programs. Our focus will be on analyzing the profitability of different *customers*--but marketing cost analysis could also be used to determine the profitability of different *products*. (Try it!)

The first step in marketing cost analysis is to reclassify all the dollar cost entries in the natural accounts into functional cost accounts. This has already been done for you in this exercise--to simplify your work. The next step is to reallocate the functional costs to those customers (or products) for which the expenditures were made. Here, careful judgment is required--because although no single basis of allocation is "correct," in some cases one may be better (i.e., make more sense) than others. Further, the basis of allocation selected can have a very significant effect on the profitability of a customer (or product).

Assignment

1.   Using the data in Tables 20-2a and 20-2b, calculate profit and loss statements for each of three customers. Show your answers in Table 20-2c. Where you must make allocations of costs to products or customers, indicate under "Comments" the basis of allocation you selected and why. (See the example on pages 559-64 of the text for suggestions.)

TABLE 20-2a
Sales by Product

Product	Cost/Unit	Selling Price per Unit	Number of Units Sold	Items/Unit	Items Packaged
A	6	12	10,000	3	30,000
B	10	17	6,000	2	12,000
C	$11	$22	5,000	1	5,000

TABLE 20-2b
Sales by Customer

Customer	Number of Sales Calls	Number of Orders	Number of Units of Each Product Ordered		
			A	B	C
1	20	10	4,000	1,000	500
2	25	20	3,500	3,000	2,000
3	15	10	2,500	2,000	2,500
Total	60	40	10,000	6,000	5,000

Other expenses from functional cost accounts:

Sales salaries	$48,000
Clerical expenses (order and billing)	12,000
Advertising	33,000
Packaging expenses	11,750
Administrative expenses	36,000

Comments:

TABLE 20-2c
Profit and Loss Statement by Customer

	Customer 1	Customer 2	Customer 3	Whole Company
Net Sales:				
Product A:	_____	_____	_____	_____
Product B:	_____	_____	_____	_____
Product C:	_____	_____	_____	_____
Total Sales	_____	_____	_____	_____
Cost of Sales				
Product A:	_____		_____	_____
Product B:	_____	_____	_____	_____
Product C:	_____	_____	_____	_____
Total Cost of Sales	_____	_____	_____	_____
Gross Margin	_____	_____	_____	_____
Expenses:				
Sales Salaries	_____	_____	_____	
Clerical Expenses	_____	_____	_____	_____
Advertising	_____	_____	_____	_____
Packaging Expense:				
Product A	_____	_____	_____	_____
Product B	_____	_____	_____	_____
Product C	_____	_____	_____	_____
TOTAL EXPENSE	_____	_____	_____	_____
Net Profit (or loss)	_____	_____	_____	_____

2.   What do you conclude from your analysis? Should any of the customers be dropped? Why or why not? What factors must you consider in answering this question?

Question for Discussion

Which of the two basic approaches to cost analysis--full cost or contribution margin--was used in the above exercise? Would your conclusions have been different if the other approach had been used? If so, which approach is "correct"?

Chapter 21

Developing innovative marketing plans

What This Chapter Is About

Chapter 21 emphasizes that marketing strategy planning requires creative *blending* of all the ingredients of the marketing mix. And, eventually, a marketing manager must develop a time-related *plan* that spells out the implementation details for a strategy. Then, since most companies have more than one strategy, marketing managers should develop a whole marketing *program* that integrates the various plans.

Since Chapter 9, we have been discussing various aspects of the four Ps. The product classes and the product life cycle are integrating themes that have been running through these chapters. This chapter highlights these ideas. A product's class and stage in the life cycle can suggest some "typical" marketing mixes, but typical is not always desirable.

You need an estimate of potential sales to know if a marketing plan will be profitable. So this chapter explains different methods for forecasting sales. You should become familiar with the different methods and their likely accuracy--because each has advantages *and* disadvantages. Some firms make several forecasts on the way to developing one final estimate of future sales.

Sales forecasting must consider not only market potential but also the firm's (and competitors') marketing plans--and how customers might respond to those plans.

Following selection of a firm's marketing program, use of project scheduling and related techniques can help the implementation effort. Finally, Chapter 21 also highlights the types of opportunities that are available in international marketing. The typical evolution of corporate involvement in international marketing is explained. It is noted that some corporations become so deeply involved with international marketing that they become "multinational corporations."

Important Terms

___ 1. A marketing strategy is a "big picture" of what a firm will do in some target market--while a marketing plan includes the time-related details for that strategy--and a marketing program is a combination of the firm's marketing plans.

___ 2. There are often more different strategy possibilities than a firm can pursue.

___ 3. A S.W.O.T. analysis is one way to zero in on a marketing strategy that is well-suited to the firm.

___ 4. Even if you don't know as much as you would like about potential customers' needs and attitudes, knowing how they would classify your product--in terms of the product classes--can give you a starting point in developing a marketing mix.

___ 5. When marketers fully understand the needs and attitudes of their target markets, they may be able to develop marketing mixes that are obviously superior to "competitive" mixes.

___ 6. Typically, marketing variables should change during a product's life cycle.

___ 7. Market potential is an estimate of how much a whole market segment might buy.

___ 8. National economic forecasts available in business and government publications are often of limited value in forecasting the potential of a specific market segment.

___ 9. A major limitation of trend extension is that it assumes that conditions in the past will continue unchanged into the future.

___ 10. The factor method of sales forecasting tries to find a relation between a company's sales and some other factor that is readily available.

___ 11. A factor is a variable that shows the relation of some other variable to the item being forecasted.

___ 12. The main problem with the "buying power index" (BPI) is that it is based on just one factor--population.

___ 13. A leading series is a time series that, for some reason, changes in the opposite direction but ahead of the series to be forecasted.

___ 14. Indices are statistical combinations of several time series.

___ 15. "Trend-projecting" forecasting techniques should probably be supplemented by a "jury of executive opinion" or some other type of judgmental approach.

___ 16. Instead of relying heavily on salespeople to estimate customers' intentions, it may be desirable for a firm to use marketing research techniques such as surveys, panels, and market tests.

_____ 17. The best approach for estimating the costs of various parts of a marketing strategy is the task method.

_____ 18. A spreadsheet analysis is a useful tool for demonstrating how sales and profits change over a range of prices.

_____ 19. The marketing plan serves as a blueprint for what the firm will do, including the time-related details.

_____ 20. Planning the time-related details of a marketing plan can be greatly aided by use of PERT--that stands for Product Evaluation and Rating Techniques.

_____ 21. A marketing plan should contain the marketing mix decisions, but not the reasons for those decisions because that would make the plan too long.

_____ 22. Finding the best marketing program requires some juggling among the various plans-- comparing profitability versus resources needed and available.

_____ 23. When a manufacturer moves into exporting, it usually is primarily concerned with selling some of what the firm is currently producing to foreign markets.

_____ 24. Licensing is a relatively easy--but risky--way to enter foreign markets.

_____ 25. Management contracting--in international marketing--means turning over production to others, while retaining the marketing process.

_____ 26. A domestic firm wishing to enter international marketing can use a joint venture-- which simply involves entering into a partnership with a foreign firm.

_____ 27. If a foreign market looked really promising, multinational corporations might set up a wholly owned subsidiary--which is a separate firm owned by a parent company.

_____ 28. A multinational company is one that earns over 30 percent of its total sales or profits by exporting domestic production to foreign markets.

Answers to True-False Questions

1. T, p. 572	11. T, p. 581	21. F, p. 592
2. T, p. 574	12. F, p. 583	22. T, p. 593
3. T, p. 575	13. F, p. 585	23. T, p. 593
4. T, p. 575-76	14. T, p. 585	24. F, p. 594
5. T, p. 576	15. T, p. 585	25. F, p. 594
6. T, p. 579	16. T, p. 586	26. T, p. 594
7. T, p. 579	17. T, p. 586	27. T, p. 595
8. T, p. 580	18. T, p. 587	28. F, p. 595
9. T, p. 581	19. T, p. 588	
10. T, p. 581	20. F, p. 589	

Multiple-Choice Questions (Circle the correct response)

1. The main difference between a "strategy" and a "marketing plan" is:
   a. that a plan does not consider the firm's target market.
   b. that a plan includes several strategies.
   c. that time-related details are included in a plan.
   d. that resource commitments are made more clear in a strategy.
   e. There is no difference.

2. Developing a "marketing plan":
   a. means selecting a target market and developing a marketing mix.
   b. involves nothing more than assembling the four Ps better than your competitors.
   c. is easy--and profits are virtually guaranteed--provided that a firm fully understands the needs and attitudes of its target market.
   d. All of the above are true statements.
   e. None of the above is a true statement.

3. A manufacturer of a consumer product is trying to establish brand recognition and preference in monopolistic competition. The firm places considerable emphasis on channel development and is becoming somewhat less selective in its choice of middlemen. Promotion is both informative and persuasive--as the firm is seeking to increase both primary and selective demand. Prices in the industry are competitive--but there has been little price-cutting to date. What stage of the product life cycle is this firm's situation characteristic of?
   a. Market introduction
   b. Market growth
   c. Market maturity
   d. Sales decline

4. As defined in the text, market potential is:
   a. what a market segment might buy (from all suppliers).
   b. how much a firm can hope to sell to a market segment.
   c. how much the firm sold to a market segment in the last year.
   d. the size of national income for the coming year.

5. A good marketing manager knows that:
   a. market potential is an estimate of how much a firm can hope to sell to a particular market segment.
   b. sales forecasts should be developed BEFORE marketing strategies are planned.
   c. a firm's sales forecast probably will be less than the estimated market potential.
   d. sales forecasts are estimates of what a whole market segment might buy.
   e. All of the above are true.

6. You have been asked to develop a sales forecast for one of your company's major products. What would be the most logical *starting point?*
   a. Determine why the company's sales fluctuate the way they do.
   b. Consider the prospects for the economy as a whole.
   c. Determine your industry's prospects for the near future.
   d. Analyze regional sales for this product for last year.
   e. Perform marketing research into consumer buying habits.

7. The trend-extension method often can be useful for forecasting annual sales, but it depends upon the assumption that:
   a. the forecast is for a new product.
   b. sales during the coming period will be about the same as the previous period.
   c. there will be big changes in market conditions.
   d. the general growth (or decline) which has been seen in the past will continue in the future.
   e. the firm will continue to improve its marketing mixes.

8. *Sales & Marketing Management* magazine's "Buying Power Index" is based on:
   a. each market's share of the total U.S. population.
   b. each market's share of the total income in the United States.
   c. each market's share of the total retail sales in the United States.
   d. All of the above.
   e. Only a and b above.

9. Given the complexity of buyer behavior, sales forecasts for established products are likely to prove more accurate if based on:
   a. market tests.
   b. trend extension.
   c. a single factor.
   d. several factors.

10. Sales forecasters often try to find business indicators that change before sales and thus will help predict future sales. These indicators are called:
    a. correlation coefficients.
    b. time series.
    c. leading series.
    d. trend extenders.
    e. input-output measures.

11. Forward Solutions, Inc., has developed a new product about which it is quite excited. Which of the following sales forecasting methods would be *least appropriate?*
    a. Market tests
    b. Sales force estimates
    c. Trend extension
    d. Jury of executive opinion
    e. A survey of customers

12. Which of the following sales forecasting techniques would be most useful for the marketing manager of a business products manufacturer that already faces intense competition?
    a. Sales force estimates
    b. Jury of executive opinion
    c. Use of a national economic forecast
    d. Trend extension of past sales
    e. Multiple-factor method

13. A company that wants to *objectively* estimate the reaction of customers to possible changes in its marketing mix should use:
    a.   trend extension.
    b.   jury of executive opinion.
    c.   sales force estimates.
    d.   surveys, panels, and market tests.
    e.   None of the above.

14. Flow-charting techniques such as CPM and PERT:
    a.   require that all marketing activities must be done in sequence.
    b.   do not indicate how long a project will actually take to complete.
    c.   identify the tasks which must be performed to achieve predetermined objectives.
    d.   require complex mathematical tools and analysis.

15. A marketing program can be best described as consisting of several:
    a.   marketing plans.
    b.   advertising campaigns.
    c.   marketing mixes.
    d.   operational decisions.
    e.   target markets.

16. When a business firm in one country sells a firm in another country the right to use some process, trademark, or patent for a fee or royalty--this practice is called:
    a.   exporting.
    b.   contract manufacturing.
    c.   joint ventures.
    d.   licensing.
    e.   management contracting.

17. To minimize its own risks, the Boomtown Petroleum Corp. of Houston, Texas, operates a South American oil refinery that is wholly owned by residents of that country. Boomtown is engaged in an activity known as:
    a.   management contracting.
    b.   a joint venture.
    c.   exporting.
    d.   licensing.
    e.   contract manufacturing.

18. A multinational corporation:
    a.   is any U.S.-based corporation with direct investments in several foreign countries.
    b.   is one that sells the right to use some process, trademark, patent, or other right for a fee or royalty to foreign firms.
    c.   is a worldwide enterprise that makes major decisions on a global basis.
    d.   is any firm that earns over 30 percent of its sales and profits in foreign markets.
    e.   All of the above are true statements.

1. c, p. 572,589
2. e, p. 572-78
3. b, p. 578
4. a, p. 579
5. c, p. 579
6. b, p. 579

7. d, p. 580
8. d, p. 583
9. d, p. 583
10. c, p. 585
11. c, p. 585
12. a, p. 585-86

13. d, p. 586
14. c, p. 592
15. a, p. 572,593
16. d, p. 594
17. a, p. 594
18. c, p. 595

Exercise 21-1

Using the "Survey of Buying Power" to estimate market and sales potential

Introduction

All marketers are faced with the ongoing problem of forecasting market and sales potentials. Forecasting is as much an art as a science--and many different forecasting methods can be used. Regardless of which method is used, the forecast should be based on data that is as accurate, reliable, and up-to-date as possible.

Many forecasters rely very heavily on data published in *Sales and Marketing Management's* annual "Survey of Buying Power" (see pages 582-83 of the text). The "Survey" provides data on three important market characteristics--population, retail sales, and "Effective Buying Income." Population is reported by age group. Retail sales are shown for five store categories. "Effective Buying Income" (similar to disposable income) is broken down into median household and three income groups. Further, the data is broken down geographically according to Metropolitan Statistical Areas, counties, and cities.

While similar U.S. census data is published every 10 years, the "Survey of Buying Power" data is published each year. Moreover, "Survey" estimates have been shown to do a good job of updating the census data on which they are based. A disadvantage, however, is that "Survey" data, like all published data, may not be available in the exact form a particular firm desires. Most firms find it necessary to modify the data or supplement it with other data--before making their forecasts.

Probably the most widely used part of the "Survey" is the "Buying Power Index" (BPI), a weighted index of three variables--population, retail sales, and Effective Buying Income--that measures a market's *ability* to buy as a percentage of the total U.S. potential. The BPI is calculated by giving a weight of 2 to its percent of the U.S. population, a weight of 3 to its percent of U.S. retail sales, and a weight of 5 to the market's percent of the U.S. Effective Buying Income. The sum of those three weighted percents (population, retail sales, and effective buying income) is then divided by 10 to arrive at the BPI--as shown in the formula below:

$$BPI = \frac{2(\% \text{ U.S. Population}) + 3(\% \text{ U.S. Retail Sales}) + 5(\% \text{ U.S. Effective Buying Income})}{10}$$

For example, suppose Hometown, U.S.A., had about 1 percent of the U.S. population, about 4 percent of U.S. retail sales, and about 5 percent of the total U.S. Effective Buying Income. Then the BPI for Hometown is found by substituting these percentages into the formula above:

$$\frac{2(1)+3(4)+5(5)}{10} = 3.9$$

Thus Hometown's market potential--relative to the entire United States--would be 3.9 percent. So if Americans were expected to buy $10,000,000 worth of "gadgets" during the coming year, the population of Hometown might be expected to buy 3.9 percent X $10,000,000, or $390,000 worth of gadgets.

There is nothing sacred about the weights used to calculate the BPI. Many firms tailor the index to their own needs by applying a different set of weights or adding additional variables to the index based on their past experience. A manufacturer of snowmobiles, for example, might add a weather variable, such as average inches of snowfall, to the BPI. A potential pitfall in applying the BPI is that because it is broadly based, the BPI is said to be most useful for "mass products sold at popular prices." Thus, for more expensive products, or for products that are used regionally, the BPI may need to be modified by taking additional buying factors into account. For example, a simple BPI calculation won't help to predict the number of snow shovels we could expect to sell in Tucson, AZ and Buffalo, NY. But including an additional variable--such as average number of inches of snowfall each winter--might help to make reliable estimates.

Assignment

The purpose of this exercise is to familiarize you with the Survey of Buying Power and the Buying Power Index--and to show how they are used in forecasting market and sales potential. Before examining a sample table from the *Survey*, we'll begin with a review of the calculations used to produce the standard BPI. Answer each of the following questions and show your work in the space provided.

1.   Suppose that Green Pastures accounts for 3 percent of the U.S. population, 3 percent of U.S. retail sales, and 4 percent of the nation's Effective Buying Income. Calculate Green Pastures' "Buying Power Index."

2.   Look at the sample table from the *Survey of Buying Power* reproduced on the next page. The table summarizes population information, retail sales by store group, information about effective buying income, and shows the BPI. Next, study the headings carefully to learn the format for listing by Metropolitan area (in bold print), counties that make up that Metropolitan area (indented and listed under each Metropolitan area) and finally cities in that county. Now, reading from Figure 21-1, provide the following information:

For the Boulder-Longmont Metropolitan area:

       the total population: _____

       the total Effective Buying Income: _____

       the Buying Power Index: _____

For Boulder County in the Boulder-Longmont Metro area:

       the total population: _____

For Longmont (the city):

       the Buying Power Index: _____

Figure 21-1
Sample of Pages from *Sales & Marketing Management's* Survey of Buying Power: Metro and County Totals

COLORADO
METRO & COUNTY TOTALS

METRO AREA COUNTY City	Total Population (000s)	% of Population by Age Group 18-24	25-34	35-49	50+	House-holds (000s)	Total Retail Sales	Food & Beverage Stores	Food Service & Drinking Establish-ments	General Merchan-dise	Furniture & Home Furnish. & Electron. & Appliances	Motor Vehicle & Parts Dealers	Total EBI ($000)	Median Hsld. EBI	A $20,000-$34,999	B $35,000-$49,999	C $50,000 & Over	Buying Power Index
BOULDER-LONGMONT	**303.7**	**13.6**	**15.5**	**25.6**	**22.4**	**119.6**	**5,081,227**	**1,001,555**	**556,377**	**448,453**	**247,484**	**1,220,087**	**7,716,546**	**51,714**	**17.8**	**17.1**	**51.6**	**0.1360**
BOULDER	303.7	13.6	15.5	25.6	22.4	119.6	5,081,227	1,001,555	556,377	448,453	247,484	1,220,087	7,716,546	51,714	17.8	17.1	51.6	0.1360
• Boulder	97.1	26.4	18.8	20.0	20.1	40.7	2,147,663	439,133	267,970	121,357	117,520	447,464	2,480,204	43,427	21.5	15.8	43.1	0.0479
• Longmont	74.6	8.7	14.6	25.3	23.6	28.0	1,126,804	250,483	122,965	125,103	40,068	272,449	1,531,271	47,526	19.4	20.1	46.8	0.0290
COLORADO SPRINGS	**537.3**	**10.7**	**14.4**	**24.7**	**22.6**	**200.1**	**7,883,675**	**819,826**	**647,101**	**984,753**	**465,488**	**2,031,112**	**10,259,019**	**42,082**	**24.7**	**21.0**	**38.7**	**0.1994**
EL PASO	537.3	10.7	14.4	24.7	22.6	200.1	7,883,675	819,826	647,101	984,753	465,488	2,031,112	10,259,019	42,082	24.7	21.0	38.7	0.1994
• Colorado Springs	373.1	10.5	14.8	24.5	23.7	146.5	6,786,693	628,690	549,107	858,048	443,063	1,848,219	7,353,670	41,212	24.9	20.9	37.5	0.1515
DENVER	**2199.5**	**9.2**	**16.2**	**25.0**	**23.8**	**858.0**	**33,750,880**	**4,700,116**	**3,232,590**	**3,615,646**	**2,518,616**	**9,368,057**	**52,585,220**	**49,109**	**18.8**	**19.0**	**48.9**	**0.9282**
ADAMS	382.9	10.5	16.7	23.3	21.1	134.3	4,558,882	670,017	371,810	416,956	385,657	1,466,781	6,459,840	42,802	22.5	22.4	38.7	0.1253
Thornton	87.3	9.7	17.5	24.9	18.0	30.6	707,386	152,812	68,679	122,478	40,099	150,769	1,594,293	48,053	19.4	22.4	46.8	0.0270
Westminster	105.4	9.9	17.1	26.0	20.3	40.1	1,052,771	153,993	114,177	292,678	100,304	88,416	2,368,971	51,512	17.0	21.6	51.9	0.0384
ARAPAHOE	505.4	8.8	15.1	25.7	23.9	197.5	9,846,119	1,160,676	872,314	963,885	595,477	4,049,257	13,314,002	52,887	18.2	18.6	53.1	0.2422
Aurora	286.8	10.4	17.2	24.0	21.0	109.0	3,889,713	531,245	378,269	566,186	225,882	1,236,463	5,874,943	47,398	20.7	21.5	46.0	0.1076
DENVER	568.5	11.1	19.9	22.1	25.1	243.7	9,287,630	1,235,129	1,270,413	730,810	755,362	1,701,220	13,899,851	42,540	21.6	18.4	41.0	0.2474
• Denver	568.5	11.1	19.9	22.1	25.1	243.7	9,275,551	1,224,988	1,269,426	730,810	755,362	1,700,815	13,899,851	42,540	21.6	18.4	41.0	0.2474
DOUGLAS	200.7	4.9	15.9	29.6	18.0	69.6	2,725,601	517,182	250,871	294,714	289,389	355,394	5,147,699	59,715	10.9	18.2	64.7	0.0851
JEFFERSON	542.0	8.3	13.2	26.8	26.5	212.9	7,332,648	1,117,112	467,182	1,209,281	492,731	1,795,405	13,763,828	54,470	16.4	18.6	55.1	0.2282
Arvada	104.0	8.0	11.9	25.9	28.1	40.0	1,007,245	224,707	79,597	133,524	60,181	74,965	2,332,241	51,557	18.1	19.3	51.8	0.0376
Lakewood	148.0	9.9	15.2	24.1	28.8	62.3	2,065,827	297,529	149,068	292,832	124,879	567,796	3,451,207	46,782	20.8	21.1	45.2	0.0599
DENVER-BOULDER-GREELEY CONSOLIDATED AREA	***2695.8***	***10.0***	***15.9***	***24.9***	***23.6***	***1044.7***	***40,882,936***	***5,939,206***	***3,929,714***	***4,267,775***	***2,809,610***	***11,246,398***	***63,170,157***	***48,397***	***19.2***	***19.0***	***47.9***	***1.1216***

3.   Based on the Buying Power Index, if total U.S. annual sales for a consumer product are predicted to be 6,000,000 units next year, how many would you estimate will be sold in the Boulder-Longmont *Metro Area* (show your work):

_____ units

4.   Based on the Buying Power Index, how many of the units above in question 3 would you expect to be sold in the city of Longmont (show your work)?

_____ units

5.   If your firm has about a 25 percent share of the market for the product in questions 3 and 4 above, how many units would your firm expect to sell in Longmont?

_____ units

6.   Suppose that a producer of a new luxury car was trying to determine the sales potential in Longmont--to determine whether or not to establish a dealership there. Would the BPI be useful for this purpose? Why or why not?

Question for Discussion

Would the "Survey of Buying Power" data be more useful to "mass marketers" or "target marketers"? Why?

Exercise 21-2

Adjusting marketing strategies over the product life cycle

Introduction

A marketing manager must take a dynamic approach to marketing strategy planning. Markets are continually changing--and today's successful strategy may be tomorrow's failure. Competitive advantages are often achieved and maintained by firms who are best able to anticipate and respond positively to changes in their marketing environment. Some changes may be completely unpredictable, of course--but other changes may be somewhat predictable and should be planned for in advance. Otherwise, by the time the planner realizes that some important changes have taken place, it may be too late to adjust an existing strategy or, if necessary, to plan a new strategy.

Among the changes that are more predictable--and should be considered when developing marketing plans--are the typical changes in marketing mix variables that are often made over the course of a product life cycle. Exhibit 21-4 on page 578 of the text shows some of these typical changes.

Assignment

This exercise stresses how marketing strategies may need to be adjusted over the product life cycle. Read the following case and follow the instructions.

CREATEQUIP FREEZE-DRY APPLIANCE FOR FOOD

Createquip, Inc. manufactures a broad line of electric equipment for industrial buyers. Its sales and profits have stopped growing in recent years--and the firm's top executives are anxious to diversify into the consumer products market. However, they do not want to enter a new market with just another "me too" product. Instead, they hope to discover a real "breakthrough opportunity"--an unsatisfied market with large profit potential.

For several years, Createquip's marketing research and product planning departments have been working together in search of an innovative new product for the firm's entry into the consumer market. Now, the top executives believe that they have finally found such a product. The new product is a "freeze-dry appliance" for food. The unit makes it easy for consumers to make instant versions of just about any food--just as freeze-dried coffee makes great instant coffee. The unit can process almost any type of food (ranging from eggs and hamburger to oatmeal, rice, and fruits) which are available at any supermarket. It has the capacity to cook up to two-pound batches of a food product and convert it to freeze-dried

Figure 21-2
Planned Changes in Marketing Strategy for Createquip
Over the Course of Its Product Life Cycle

Item	Market Introduction Stage
Target Market Dimensions	
Nature of Competition	
Product	
Place	
Promotion	
Price	

Market Growth Stage	Market Maturity Stage

"pellets." Whenever the consumer is ready, the freeze-dried pellets can be put in a microwave oven with water and heated to produce fresh-tasting soups, sauces, gravy, drinks--and hundreds of other items which are otherwise time consuming to cook in small quantities. With the unit, a gourmet cook would be able to make fancy sauces on an impulse, an office worker could create a favorite type of homemade soup to take to work without the mess, and busy singles could keep pellets ready for when there's no time to go to the store or cook something from scratch. At first the new product idea seemed strange--perhaps even hard to believe--but in tests with consumers it has generated a very favorable response. Moreover, the freeze-dry unit is inexpensive and easy-to-operate, and it is expected to retail for about $100.

Createquip's marketing manager believes the new product will appeal to convenience-oriented families-- and also health-conscious people who want to make their own "instant" foods but with more nutritious ingredients and without the preservatives typically found in packages at the store. The marketing manager feels the product has almost unlimited potential--citing the rapid growth of prepared and instant foods and the wide use of microwave ovens. Further, the firm's research and development staff is sure that it will take any potential competitors at least two years to introduce a similar product.

The electric freeze-dry unit is really a revolutionary new concept--and will probably require a major promotion effort to gain consumer acceptance. Moreover, Createquip has no established channels of distribution in the consumer products market--and middlemen may be reluctant to handle an unproven product which lacks a well-known brand name. Also, the firm is not sure what pricing policies to adopt, because it has no previous experience in the consumer products market.

To further complicate the strategy planning efforts, Createquip's marketing manager recognizes that the marketing strategy will need to be modified over time--as the new product passes through the various stages of its life cycle. So that the firm will be in a position to adjust quickly to changing market conditions, the president has asked the marketing manager for an overview of future marketing strategies for the freeze-dry unit--as well as the beginning strategy.

1.   Assume the role of marketing manager for Createquip, Inc. and fill in Figure 21-2 to show how your marketing strategy for the electric freeze-dry unit would vary over the stages of its product life cycle. (See Exhibit 21-4 on page 578 of the text for some general ideas about what you might include in your answers.) Be specific.

Question for Discussion

What kind of product will the "freeze-dry" unit be--that is, what product class--and what type of marketing mix would be typical for such a product? Are there any other factors that should be taken into account in planning the marketing mix for this product?

Chapter 22

Ethical marketing in a consumer-oriented world: appraisal and challenges

What This Chapter Is About

Chapter 22 provides an evaluation of the effectiveness of both micro- and macro-marketing. The text explains the authors' views, but their answers are far less important than their reasoning. It is extremely important to understand the arguments both pro and con--because the effectiveness of marketing is a vital issue. How well you understand this material--and how you react to it--may affect your own feelings about the value of business and the contribution you can make in the business world. Do not try to memorize the "right" answers. Rather, try to understand and evaluate the authors' reasoning. Then, develop your own answers.

When you have studied this chapter, you should be able to defend your feelings about the worth of marketing--using reasoned arguments rather than just "gut feelings." Further, you should have some suggestions about how to improve marketing--if you feel there are any weaknesses. Perhaps you yourself--as a producer and/or consumer--can help improve our market-directed economy.

True-False Questions

___ 1. Although our economic objectives may change in the future, at the present time marketing probably should be evaluated according to the basic objective of the American economic system--which is to satisfy consumer needs--as *consumers see them.*

___ 2. Since individual consumer satisfaction is a very personal concept, it probably does not provide a very good standard for evaluating macro-marketing effectiveness.

___ 3. At the micro-level, marketing effectiveness can be measured--at least roughly--by the profitability of individual marketers.

___ 4. According to the text, macro-marketing does not cost too much, but micro-marketing frequently does cost too much, given the present objective of the American economic system--consumer satisfaction.

___ 5. One reason why micro-marketing often costs too much is that many firms are still production-oriented and not nearly as efficient as they might be.

6. Marketing inefficiencies are generally due to a lack of interest in the customer, improper blending of the four Ps, or a lack of understanding of the marketing environment.

7. According to the text, the ability to identify new target markets would result in better, more efficient, micro-marketing decisions.

8. Despite the fact that the marketing concept is now applied universally, marketing does cost too much in most firms.

9. Despite its cost, advertising can actually *lower* prices to the consumer.

10. Unfortunately, firms can usually manipulate consumers to buy anything the firms choose to produce.

11. Marketing caters to materialistic values, but doesn't create them.

12. A good business manager might find it useful to follow the following rule: "Do unto others as you would have others do unto you."

13. Because of the consumerism movement, the majority of consumers are now socially responsible.

14. Given the role that business is supposed to play in our market-directed economy, it seems reasonable to conclude that a marketing manager should be expected to improve and expand the range of goods and services made available to consumers.

15. The text suggests that socially responsible marketing managers should try to limit consumers' freedom of choice for the good of society.

Answers to True-False Questions

1. T, p. 601	6. T, p. 603-604	11. T, p. 607
2. T, p. 601-602	7. T, p. 604	12. T, p. 610
3. T, p. 603	8. F, p. 605	13. F, p. 613
4. T, p. 603	9. T, p. 606	14. T, p. 614
5. T, p. 603	10. F, p. 606	15. F, p. 614

Multiple-Choice Questions (Circle the correct response)

1. Consumer satisfaction:
   a. is the basic objective of all economic systems.
   b. is easier to measure at the macro-level than at the micro-level.
   c. depends on one's own expectations and aspirations.
   d. is hard to define.
   e. is totally unrelated to company profits.

2. Which of the following statements about marketing does the text make?
   a. Micro-marketing never costs too much.
   b. Macro-marketing does not cost too much.
   c. Marketing is not needed in all modem economies.
   d. Micro-marketing always costs too much.
   e. Macro-marketing does cost too much.

3. Micro-marketing may cost too much because:
   a. firms fail to identify new target markets.
   b. prices are frequently set on a cost-plus basis.
   c. promotion is sometimes seen as a substitute for product quality.
   d. All of the above are true statements.
   e. None of the above--marketing never costs too much!

4. Which of the following does NOT support the idea that "MICRO-marketing often DOES cost too much"?
   a. Many firms focus exclusively on their own internal problems.
   b. Distribution channels may be selected on the basis of personal preferences.
   c. Product planners frequently develop "me-too" products.
   d. Costly promotion may try to compensate for a weak marketing mix.
   e. Many firms try to maximize profits.

5. In conditions of monopolistic competition, marketing:
   a. may result in lower consumer prices in the long run.
   b. may contribute to higher profits for successful firms.
   c. may spur economic growth.
   d. All of the above are true.
   e. None of the above is true.

6. The text concludes that:
   a. advertising is a poor use of resources.
   b. advertising can actually lower prices to the consumer.
   c. marketing makes people buy things they don't need.
   d. marketing makes people materialistic.
   e. marketing's job is just to satisfy the consumer wants which exist at any point in time.

7. An objective of our MACRO-marketing system should be to:
   a. eliminate monopolistic competition.
   b. eliminate materialism.
   c. satisfy only the minimum material requirements of life.
   d. eliminate advertising, which will lower prices.
   e. continually seek more satisfying solutions to consumer problems.

8. Which of the following is not a current trend affecting marketing strategy planning?
   a. popularity of the Internet and intranets.
   b. less use of single source data and scanner panels.
   c. more attention to quality.
   d. greater use of rapid response, JIT, and ECR.
   e. move toward integrated marketing communications.

9. The future poses many challenges for marketing managers because:
   a. new technologies are making it easier to abuse consumers' rights to privacy.
   b. the marketing concept has become obsolete.
   c. it is marketing managers who have full responsibility to preserve our macro-marketing system.
   d. social responsibility applies only to firms--not to consumers.
   e. ultimately it is marketing managers who must determine which products are in the best interests of consumers.

10. By developing and implementing more effective marketing strategies, a marketing manager can:
   a. improve the profits of a firm.
   b. provide more consumer satisfaction.
   c. reduce the costs of wasted effort by a firm.
   d. contribute to the effectiveness of the MACRO-marketing system.
   e. all of the above.

Answers to Multiple-Choice Questions

1. c, p. 602
2. b, p. 603
3. d, p. 604
4. e, p. 604-605

5. d, p. 606
6. b, p. 606
7. e, p. 607
8. b, p. 609

9. a, p. 610
10. e, p. 614

Exercise 22-1

Does micro-marketing cost too much?

Introduction

One reason that managerial (micro) marketing often *does* cost too much is that some production-oriented firms insist on clinging to their traditional ways of doing things--ignoring new marketing mixes and strategies. In a dynamic market, this can lead to higher than necessary costs--and perhaps even to the bankruptcy of the firm.

This can easily be seen in channels of distribution--where many inefficient and high-cost channels exist even today. High-cost channels are not *necessarily* evidence of inefficiency, however. If some target markets really do want some special service which is relatively expensive--then perhaps that is the best channel system for them. But this possible reason for "high-cost" channels of distribution does not explain all such systems. Some do appear to be more expensive than necessary because the established firms insist on buying from and selling to their usual sources and customers--even though other available channels would do as good a job (or maybe better), at lower cost.

This exercise shows how the use of alternative channels of distribution might lead to different--and in some cases higher--prices to final consumers. You are asked to calculate the probable *retail* prices that would result if a manufacturer were to use several different channels to distribute its product.

Assignment

1.   A manufacturer of a new shampoo is planning to use several different channels of distribution, as listed below. Each middleman in each of the alternative channels uses a cost-plus approach to pricing. That is, each firm takes a markup on its selling price to cover operating expenses plus profit. The manufacturer sells the shampoo to the *next* member of each channel for $1.00 per six-ounce plastic bottle.

Using the data shown on the next page for markup estimates, calculate the *retail-selling* price in each channel of distribution. Show your work in the space provided. The price for the first channel is calculated for you as an example.

	Operating Expenses*	Profit Margin*
Retail		
Small drugstores	39%	2%
Supermarkets	20%	1%
Chain drugstores	33 %	3 %
Mass-merchandisers	29 %	2 %
Wholesale		
Merchant wholesalers	13%	2%
Rack jobbers	18%	2%

*Note: operating expenses and profit margin are given as a percentage of sales

a)   Manufacturer to merchant wholesalers who sell to small drugstores:

13% + 2%   =   15%   =   Merchant wholesalers' markup on selling price

$$\frac{\$1.00}{100\% - 15\%} = \$1.18 = \text{Price to retailers}$$

39% + 2%   =   41%   =   Retailers' markup on selling price

$$\frac{\$1.18}{100\% - 41\%} = \$2.00 = \text{Retail price}$$

b)   Manufacturer directly to a national chain of drugstores:

c)   Manufacturer to merchant wholesalers who sell to supermarkets:

d)   Manufacturer directly to a regional chain of mass-merchandisers:

e)   Manufacturer to rack jobbers who sell to supermarkets:

2.   Consider the different retail prices that you calculated for Question 1. Assuming that it wanted to maximize profit, which channel(s) should the manufacturer choose to develop an effective marketing strategy or strategies? Why?

3. Assume that each of the five channels in Question 1 were to survive in the marketplace. From a *macro* viewpoint, should the "high-cost" channels be made illegal to "protect" consumers--and develop a "fair and efficient" marketing system? Why or why not?

Question for Discussion

What other reasons besides "tradition" help explain why managerial (micro) marketing often *does* cost too much? What can (should) be done to make sure that managerial marketing (by individual firms) does *not* cost too much in the future?

Exercise 22-2

Does macro-marketing cost too much?

Introduction

All economies *must* have a macro-marketing system. The economies may take many forms, but all must have some way of deciding *what* and *how much* is to be produced and distributed by *whom, when,* and *to whom.*

Our macro-marketing system is basically a market-directed economy. The key decisions are made fairly automatically and democratically--through the micro-level decisions made by individual producers and consumers. Together these individual decisions determine the macro-level decisions--and provide direction for the whole economy.

Does our macro-marketing system work in an efficient and fair way that achieves our social objectives? This question is very subjective, and we usually analyze the performance of our marketing system in terms of how well it satisfies consumer needs--as consumers see them. But remember that not all consumers have the same needs!

The marketing concept suggests that a firm should try to satisfy the needs of *some* consumers (at a profit). But, what is "good" for some producers or consumers may not be "good" for the whole society. This is the "micro-macro dilemma." It means that in running our macro-marketing system, some compromises must be made to balance the needs of society and the needs of individual producers and consumers. Making these compromises and still protecting individual freedom of choice is not easy. This exercise will help you understand the difficulty of resolving micro-macro dilemmas.

Assignment

Listed below are several imaginary situations that might be classified as "micro-macro dilemmas." For each situation, identify both sides of the dilemma--i.e., who benefits and who suffers in each situation-- and state what action you would recommend.

1. The release of chlorofluorocarbons into the atmosphere may be causing long-term damaging changes in the protective ozone layer--and plans are underway to stop producing fluorocarbons. As a result, manufacturers are trying to find other gases to use in products such as refrigerators and automobile air-conditioners. Although reputable scientific authorities disagree on the matter, some are arguing that any man-made gas may disrupt the environment, and thus manufacturers should only use gases "harvested" from the atmosphere, so accidental release would just return the environment to the status quo. But legislation banning the use of man-made gases might increase the cost of an average household refrigerator by more than $1,000.

2. Large hospitals often end up treating "uninsureds"--people who do not carry health insurance and who are not covered under any government program. To make up this loss, hospitals routinely increase the fees charged to patients who *do* have insurance, a process known as "cost shifting." Cost shifting increases the prices of medical insurance by 15 percent or more.

3. A study by a highway traffic safety commission reveals that anti-lock brakes on automobiles—in combination with air bags--reduce traffic fatalities by about 30 percent. A senator is drafting legislation that would require ALL new cars to be equipped with these items. Manufacturers estimate that the cost of the average car would increase by $800.

4. The Food and Drug Administration is considering a proposal to stop all television advertising for beer. Critics charge that the ads are primarily targeted at young people, including those under legal drinking age, and that the ads portray beer drinkers as living more interesting, exciting lives.

5. Wanting to protect domestic jobs, Congress is considering a bill which would limit any imported product to a maximum market share of 10 percent--requiring foreign firms with larger market shares to either move production to the U.S. or to find other markets.

6. Eager for new sources of revenue to reduce the federal deficit, but equally eager to avoid the appearance of raising tax rates, some legislators are interested in eliminating certain "allowable business expenses." One proposal argues that advertising expenses should no longer be tax deductible. This would have the net effect of making advertising much more expensive.

7. The Consumer Product Safety Commission is considering legal action that would force manufacturers of blow-type hair dryers to add a special safeguard to prevent electrical shocks if the dryer is accidentally dropped in a sink or tub full of water. The proposed safeguard would double the cost of most blow dryers.

8. A state is considering a law that would ban the sale of "fortified" (high alcohol content) wines. Studies reveal that the potent, low-cost wines are sold primarily to alcoholics--especially homeless "winos."

9.   Americans pay for the costs of trash disposal, often indirectly through municipal taxes that are assessed annually. To make people more aware of the problems associated with landfilling trash, some environmental advocates have proposed taxing "disposables" at the time they are purchased, according to the estimate of the anticipated trash. Paper diapers would attract a large fee, a banana would rate a small fee (for the inedible skin) and tomatoes would attract no fee (because all of a tomato can be eaten.)

10.   Americans no longer take cheap energy costs for granted. Nevertheless, gasoline in the U.S. still costs as little as 20 percent of the price in other developed nations. To encourage Americans to purchase more fuel efficient cars, Congress enacted legislation setting up the "Corporate Average Fuel Economy" (CAFE) Standards. Each manufacturer is responsible for selling a mix of models, which, on average, should achieve a lower fuel-consumption target in miles per gallon. An alternative is to abandon the CAFE Standards and raise the tax on gasoline--by as much as $1.00 per gallon.

Question for Discussion

Can "micro-macro dilemmas" such as those discussed above be resolved in any workable way? How? Be specific. Would "micro-macro dilemmas" be better resolved in a market-directed economy or a command economy? What implication does this have for answering the question: "Does macro-marketing cost too much?"

Appendix A

Economics fundamentals

What This Chapter Is About

Appendix A is important to understanding how buyers and sellers look at products and markets. Some of the economist's tools are shown to be useful. In particular, demand and supply curves, and their interaction are discussed. Also, elasticity of demand and supply are explained. They help us understand the nature of competition. Three kinds of market situations are discussed: pure competition, oligopoly, and monopolistic competition.

The material in this Appendix is not easy--but it is very important. A good marketing manager does not always "win" in every market because consumers' attitudes are continually changing. But an understanding of the nature of demand and competition in different markets will greatly increase your chances for success. Careful study of this appendix will build a good economics base for this text (especially Chapters 3, 4, 17, and 18).

Important Terms

law of diminishing demand, p. 618
demand curve, p. 619
inelastic demand, 620
elastic demand, p. 620
substitutes, p. 622
supply curve, p. 623
inelastic supply, p. 624

elastic supply, p. 624
equilibrium point, p. 625
consumer surplus, p. 625
pure competition, p. 626
oligopoly, p. 627
monopolistic competition, p. 628

True-False Questions

____ 1. Economists usually assume that customers evaluate alternatives in terms of whether they will make them feel better or in some way improve their situation.

____ 2. "The law of diminishing demand" says that if the price of a product is raised, a greater quantity will be demanded--and if the price of a product is lowered, a smaller quantity will be demanded.

____ 3. A demand schedule may indicate that as prices go lower, the total unit sales increase, but the total revenue decreases.

____ 4. A demand curve is a graph of the relationship between price and quantity demanded in a market.

___ 5. Most demand curves slope upward.

___ 6. Unitary elasticity of demand means that total revenue remains the same when prices change, regardless of whether price is increased or decreased.

___ 7. If total revenue would decrease if price were raised, then demand is said to be elastic.

___ 8. If total revenue would increase if price were lowered, then demand is said to be inelastic.

___ 9. A demand curve must be entirely elastic or inelastic; it cannot be both.

___ 10. Whether a product has an elastic or inelastic demand depends on many factors including the availability of substitutes, the importance of the item in the customer's budget, and the urgency of the customer's need in relation to other needs.

___ 11. When only a small number of good "substitutes" are available, demand tends to be quite inelastic.

___ 12. A supply curve shows the quantity of products that will be offered at various possible prices by all suppliers together.

___ 13. An extremely steep or almost vertical supply curve is called elastic because the quantity supplied would not change much if the price were raised.

___ 14. The intersection of demand and supply determines the size of a market and the market price.

___ 15. A market is at the equilibrium point if the quantity and the price that sellers are willing to offer are equal to the quantity and the price that buyers are willing to accept.

___ 16. "Consumer surplus" is the difference between the value of a purchase and the price the consumer has to pay.

___ 17. In pure competition, both the industry demand curve and the individual firm's demand curve are horizontal.

___ 18. Except for oligopolies, most markets tend to become more competitive--that is, move toward pure competition.

___ 19. Oligopoly situations develop when a market has a few sellers of essentially homogeneous products and a fairly elastic industry demand curve.

___ 20. In oligopoly situations, individual firms are faced with a "kinked" demand curve.

___ 21. In monopolistic competition, there is only one seller and that seller has complete control over the price of its unique product.

1. T, p. 618	8. F, p. 621	15. T, p. 625
2. F, p. 618	9. F, p. 621-22	16. T, p. 625
3. T, p. 618-19	10. T, p. 622	17. F, p. 626
4. T, p. 619	11. T, p. 622	18. T, p. 627
5. F, p. 619	12. T, p. 623	19. F, p. 627
6. T, p. 621	13. F, p. 624	20. T, p. 627-28
7. T, p. 621	14. T, p. 624	21. F, p. 628

Multiple-Choice Questions (Circle the correct response)

1.   The "law of diminishing demand" says that:
   a.   if the price of a product were lowered, a greater quantity would be demanded.
   b.   if the price of a product were raised, a greater quantity would be demanded.
   c.   the demand for any product will tend to decline over time.
   d.   if the price of a product were lowered, a smaller quantity would be demanded.
   e.   the more of a product a person buys, the less utility that particular product offers him.

2.   A demand curve:
   a.   is generally up-sloping from left to right.
   b.   is formed by plotting the points from a supply schedule.
   c.   shows what quantities would be demanded by potential customers at various possible prices.
   d.   shows how total revenue increases as prices decrease.
   e.   All of the above are true statements.

3.   If a firm's total revenue increases when the price of its product is reduced from $15 to $10, the demand for this product is:
   a.   elastic.
   b.   inelastic.
   c.   unitary elastic.
   d.   cannot be determined without looking at the demand curve.

4.   Study the following demand schedule:

PRICE	QUANTITY DEMANDED	TOTAL REVENUE
$500	1,000	$500,000
400	2,000	800,000
300	3,000	900,000
200	4,000	800,000
100	5,000	500,000

This demand schedule shows that the demand for this product is:
   a.   elastic.
   b.   inelastic.
   c.   unitary elastic.
   d.   both elastic and inelastic.
   e.   This demand schedule cannot be correct because it violates the "law of diminishing demand."

5. The elasticity of demand for a particular product does *not* depend upon:
   a. the availability of substitutes.
   b. the importance of the item in the customer's budget.
   c. the urgency of the customer's need.
   d. how much it costs to produce the product.
   e. All of the above affect the elasticity of demand.

6. Which of the following products would have the most *inelastic* demand for most potential customers?
   a. A home computer
   b. A vacation trip to France
   c. A one-pound package of salt
   d. A pair of designer jeans
   e. A "Big Mac" hamburger

7. A supply curve:
   a. is generally flatter than its supply schedule.
   b. is not affected by production costs.
   c. is generally up-sloping from left to right.
   d. is a picture of the quantities of goods that would be demanded at various possible prices.
   e. All of the above are true statements.

8. Which of the following statements about elasticity of supply is *true?*
   a. If a product's demand curve is elastic, then its supply curve also must be elastic.
   b. A product's elasticity of supply determines its elasticity of demand.
   c. In the short run, the supply curve for most agricultural products is highly elastic.
   d. In the long run, the supply curve for most products is highly inelastic.
   e. None of the above statements are true.

9. Which of the following statements about demand and supply interaction is *true?*
   a. Demand is the sole determiner of price.
   b. A market is said to be in equilibrium when the elasticity of demand equals the elasticity of supply.
   c. The interaction of supply and demand determines the size of the market and the market price.
   d. For a market to be in equilibrium, the price and quantity that buyers are willing to accept must be greater than the price and quantity that suppliers are willing to offer.
   e. All of the above statements are true.

10. Given a situation where there is elastic demand and elastic supply, an *increase* in the quantity suppliers are willing to supply at all possible prices will:
    a. decrease price, but not change quantity demanded.
    b. increase price and decrease quantity demanded.
    c. lower price and increase quantity demanded.
    d. increase price and increase quantity demanded.

11. The term "consumer surplus" means that:
    a. consumers never get their money's worth in any transaction.
    b. there are more needs than there are products to satisfy them.
    c. consumers don't consume all the products they buy.
    d. some consumers would be willing to pay more than the market equilibrium price if they had to.
    e. there are more consumers than there are producers.

12. Which of the following is *not* a factor affecting competition?
    a. the number of the firm's competitors.
    b. the uniqueness of the firm's marketing mix.
    c. the size of the firm's competitors.
    d. the elasticity of the firm's demand curve.
    e. All of the above are factors that do affect competition.

13. In which of the following situations would an individual firm be most likely to face a flat demand curve?
    a. Oligopoly
    b. Pure competition
    c. Monopoly
    d. Monopolistic competition
    e. None of the above--demand is always downward sloping.

14. Oligopoly situations are generally characterized by:
    a. essentially heterogeneous products.
    b. relatively few sellers, or a few large firms and perhaps many smaller firms.
    c. fairly elastic industry demand.
    d. a and b above--but not c.
    e. All of the above.

15. In an oligopoly situation:
    a. an individual firm's demand is inelastic above the "kink" and elastic below the kink.
    b. the market price is usually somewhere above the "kink."
    c. price wars usually increase profits for all competitors.
    d. price fluctuations may occur despite the kinked demand curve faced by each firm.
    e. All of the above are true statements.

16. A particular market is characterized by different (heterogeneous) products in the eyes of some customers and sellers who feel they do face some competition. This product-market is an example of:
    a. oligopoly.
    b. monopoly.
    c. monopolistic competition.
    d. pure competition.
    e. It could be any of the above.

17. Which of the following statements about the competitive environment is *true'*
   a. The industry demand curve in a pure competition situation is horizontal
   b. Monopolistic competition is characterized by downsloping demand curves due to the lack of any substitute products.
   c. In a pure competition situation, an individual firm is faced with a very inelastic demand curve.
   d. Since a monopolistic competitor has a downsloping demand curve just like a pure monopolist, it has some control over its price.
   e. All of the above are true statements.

Answers to Multiple-Choice Questions

1. a, p. 618
2. c, p. 619
3. a, p. 621
4. d, p. 621
5. d, p. 622
6. c, p. 622

7. c, p. 623
8. e, p. 623-24
9. c, p. 624
10. c, p. 625
11. d, p. 625
12. e, p. 625

13. b, p. 626-27
14. b, p. 627
15. d, p. 627-28
16. c, p. 628
17. d, p. 628

Exercise A-1

Estimating and using demand elasticity

Introduction

"Demand elasticity" is a very useful concept for analyzing the nature of demand and competition in markets. As explained in Appendix A in the text, demand elasticity can be defined in terms of what happens to total revenue when the price of a product is lowered.

a.   If total revenue would increase if the price were lowered, then demand is said to be *elastic*.

b.   If total revenue would decrease if the price were lowered, then demand is said to be *inelastic*.

c.   If total revenue would stay the same if the price were lowered, then we have a special case called *unitary elasticity of demand*.

Different products have different demand elasticities because of factors such as the availability of substitutes, the importance of the item in the customer's budget, and the urgency of the customer's need in relation to other needs.

The elasticity of a firm's demand curve is extremely important to a marketing strategy planner. It provides a shorthand description of the nature of competition and demand facing a firm--often suggesting necessary changes in strategies. For example, a firm with a highly elastic demand curve might have many competitors and would have very little control over the price it could charge for its product. In this case, perhaps the firm should plan a new strategy--one aimed at a different target market with fewer competitors and less elastic demand.

Assignment

This exercise has three parts and is designed to increase your understanding of demand elasticity. The first part focuses on the relationship of demand elasticity to changes in total revenue. The second part shows how demand elasticity can vary in different market situations. The third part shows how product and price are related through demand elasticity.

1.   Demand elasticity was defined above in terms of what happens to total revenue when price is lowered. Now complete the following table--showing what happens to total revenue (TR) when price is *raised* instead of lowered.

	Elastic demand	Inelastic demand	Unitary elasticity of demand
Price lowered	TR increases	TR decreases	TR remains the same
Price raised	_____	_____	_____

2. Figure A-1 shows three demand curves--each with a different degree of elasticity. Each of the demand curves represents *one* of the following situations:

a)   The demand for airline fuel during a holiday season.
b)   The demand for an individual farmer's blueberry crop.
c)   The demand for one firm's "quality" CD player.

In the space provided, state which of the three situations each demand curve most likely represents. Then briefly explain each answer in terms of the factors that can cause demand elasticity to vary in different market situations.

FIGURE A-1

Graph (i) Situation: _____

Explanation: _____

_____

_____

Graph (ii) Situation: _____

    Explanation: _____

_____

_____

Graph (iii) Situation: _____

    Explanation: _____

_____

_____

3.   Read the following paragraph and then answer questions (a) through (c).

Centrex Instruments Plus, Inc. produces and sells quality control instruments that are used by industrial firms to control the production process. The firm's management is seeking a larger share of the market. Thus, its objective for the coming year is to increase both its dollar sales volume and its market share for the instruments--which are currently priced at $1,600. Centrex's estimated demand curve for the next year is shown in Figure A-2.

FIGURE A-2

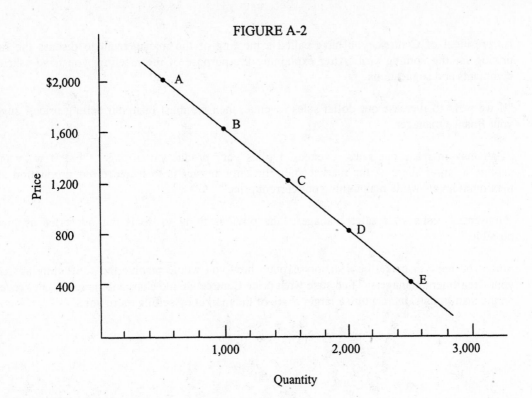

a)   Use Figure A-2 to complete the following table:

Demand Schedule of Centrex's Quality Control Instruments

Points on Graph	Price per unit	Quantity Demanded per unit	Total Revenue per year
A	$2,000	500	$1,000,000
B	1,600	_____	_____
C	1,200	_____	_____
D	800	_____	_____
E	400	_____	_____

b)   Looking at Centrex's demand curve and demand schedule, would you describe the demand for the firm's instruments as (a) elastic, (b) inelastic, (c) unitary elastic, or (d) both elastic and inelastic? Explain your answer.

_____

_____

c) As president of Centrex, you have called a meeting of top management to discuss the firm's pricing for the coming year. After explaining the purpose of the meeting, you have asked for comments and suggestions.

"If we want to increase our dollar sales revenue, then we must raise our selling price," suggest your finance manager.

"That may increase our sales revenue," replies your production manager, "but if we want to capture a larger share of the market, then the only answer is to increase our production to its maximum level--while maintaining our current price."

"Nonsense," yells your sales manager, "the obvious thing to do is cut our price as low as possible."

Since you have to make the decision, explain how you would resolve the conflicting advice of your department managers. Then state what price Centrex should charge to increase sales revenue on the instruments *and* capture a larger share of the market by selling more units.

Question for Discussion

Consider the three market situations in Question 2. If a firm's demand curve is elastic, does the demand curve for the industry also have to be elastic? What if the firm's demand curve is inelastic?

Exercise A-2

Analyzing the competitive environment

Introduction

Marketing managers do not always enjoy a full range of alternatives when planning a marketing mix. Their choices may be limited--or largely determined--by the nature of the competitive environment.

For example, a firm might be able to use almost any marketing mix in a *pure monopoly* situation, while a firm's mix might be entirely determined by market forces in *a pure competition* situation. In an *oligopoly* situation, a firm would have some control over its marketing mix, but it might find it difficult to differentiate its product and any price-cutting could lead to a "price-war." Of course, most firms find themselves in a *monopolistic competition* situation where their control over their marketing mix can range from a lot to a little--depending on how competitive the monopolistic competition is.

It is not always easy to identify the nature of a firm's competitive environment. In general, one must consider many factors--besides just the number and size of competitors. Other factors that should be considered include: (a) the similarity of competing products and marketing mixes--as seen by the target customers, (b) barriers to entry for new firms, and (c) seller concentration--(i.e., the extent to which a few large sellers control the bulk of industry sales).

Assignment

This exercise will give you some practice in analyzing the competitive environment. Read the following cases carefully and for each of them:

a)   Indicate the nature of the competitive environment, taking into consideration the probable target market.

Use the following terms to identify the nature of competition: pure competition, monopolistic competition, monopoly, and oligopoly.

Note: The term "monopolistic competition" can be used to describe situations ranging from near-monopoly to almost pure competition. Try to distinguish between "moderately competitive monopolistic competition" situations and those that may be "extremely" or only "slightly" competitive--by labeling the latter as either "monopolistic competition approaching pure monopoly" or "monopolistic competition approaching pure competition."

b)   Briefly explain your answer, taking into account the various factors which were discussed above.

The first case has been answered for you as an example.

1.   Long Haul Truck Stop is a combination gasoline station-restaurant-motel that caters to long-distance truck drivers. It is located at the intersection of two major highways near a city of about 150,000 people. There are no other truck stops in the immediate area.

    a)   Nature of competition: *Monopolistic competition approaching pure monopoly.*

    b)   Explanation: *Although Long Haul Truck Stop probably gets a large share of the long-distance truckers' business, it does not have a pure monopoly because truckers can go into the city or on to the next truck stop. Further, there is nothing to prevent a potential competitor from locating nearby--that may very well happen if Long Haul is enjoying unusually high profits.*

2.   Snow Camp Ski Area is one of five ski resorts in Provo County, Utah, one of the most popular ski destinations in the U.S. All five resorts set their base price for a one-day ticket in advance of the season--with the different resorts settling on about the same "going rate" that most skiers are prepared to pay. When Utah prices are too high, destination skiers can choose Colorado, California, or New England resorts for their vacations. Like destination skiers, day skiers (who drive from Salt Lake City and other towns for a day of skiing without purchasing lodging) are attracted by each area's unique trails, terrain, and facilities. Depending on the snowfall and the level of bookings by destination skiers, the number of special "deals" and promotions offered by the ski areas can be quite large.

    a)   Nature of competition: _____

    b)   Explanation: _____

    _____

    _____

    _____

    _____

    _____

3. Delightfully Clean specializes in dry cleaning of clothing and other household items--as well as operating a shirt laundry. It operates a central processing plant and 10 conveniently located branches where dry cleaning can be dropped off and picked up a day or two later. This company is located in a city of 400,000 where there are about 80 other dry cleaners (some of whom also have multiple-outlet operations). All these cleaners charge approximately the same "low" prices for basically the same services--because a steady influx of new dry cleaners has tended to keep prices at a fairly low level. Further, some firms have not been able to attract enough business to cover their rising labor costs and have been forced out of business.

a) Nature of competition: _____

b) Explanation: _____

_____

_____

_____

_____

_____

4. Racket World, Inc. operates the only privately-owned indoor racket ball court facility in Colorado Springs--a western city with a population of 340,000. It runs a full program of racket ball lessons, tournaments, and public play. It is also the "sponsor" of local "high school racket ball"--trading practice time for a share of the gate. Its only "indoor" competition is from the state university courts--which are only three miles away. The university athletic department does not run competing programs--because its primary role is to serve the students and intramural teams. However, it does have a large amount of "extra time" and regularly sells blocks of time to groups (for example, businessmen who come to town for conferences at local hotels). The athletic department usually charges such groups prices that are below Racket World's prices (by 10-40 percent) and probably way below its variable costs of operating the facility.

a) Nature of competition: _____

b) Explanation: _____

_____

_____

_____

_____

_____

5. The Windy City metropolitan area is supplied by five regional manufacturers of bricks. The bricks are used in constructing homes and office buildings as well as for other purposes (decorative walls, patios). Three of these firms account for more than 80 percent of all the bricks sold in the area. The bricks are purchased either in standardized sizes or according to buyer specifications, and all five firms charge almost identical prices. When bricks are in short supply, a few buyers have purchased some bricks from other firms located outside the region, but high transportation costs make this an extremely expensive alternative. Two manufacturers have announced plans to boost their production capacity, and all five manufacturers have announced price increases of at least six percent for the coming year.

    a) Nature of competition: _____

    b) Explanation: _____

    _____

    _____

    _____

    _____

6. The trend toward cholesterol-free diets has been a problem for Tilly Flannery, who owns a chicken farm in southern Virginia. Like thousands of other chicken farmers in the United States, Flannery produces the eggs that end up on the breakfast tables of America, that are used by restaurants in preparing meals, and that are used in producing a variety of packaged foods. Flannery's chicken flock has always been a very small portion of the 500,000,000 egg-laying hens in the United States. But like most other egg producers, she has had to decrease the size of her flock in recent years as consumer demand for eggs has declined.

    a) Nature of competition: _____

    b) Explanation: _____

    _____

    _____

    _____

    _____

Question for Discussion

Have the firms described in the above cases achieved any "competitive advantage" over their competitors? If not, what steps might they take in the future to achieve some competitive advantage?

Appendix B

Marketing arithmetic

What This Appendix Is About

Appendix B provides a brief introduction (overview) of some important accounting terms that are useful in analyzing marketing problems.

The content of an operating statement (profit-and-loss statement) is reviewed first. Accounting terms are used in a technical sense--rather than a layman's sense--and should be studied with this in mind. Accountants try to use words precisely--and usually try to place the same kinds of data in the same places in their statements. So try to capture the "model" which they are using. Basically, it is: sales minus costs equals profit.

It is also useful to be able to calculate stockturn rates, operating ratios, markups, markdowns, and ROI and ROA--to fully understand some of the concepts in the text chapters.

This material should be "easy review" for those who have had some accounting. But regardless of your background, it probably will be helpful to study this material--to deepen your understanding of accounting statements and tools. Familiarity with these ideas is assumed in the text!

Important Terms

operating statement, p. 632
gross sales, p. 634
return, p. 634
allowance, p. 634
net sales, p. 634
cost of sales, p. 634
gross margin (gross profit), p. 635
expenses, p. 635
net profit, p. 635

purchase discount, p. 635
stockturn rate, p. 637
operating ratios, p. 638
markup, p. 638
markdown ratio, p. 639
markdown, p. 640
return on investment (ROI), p. 640
balance sheet, p. 640
return on assets (ROA), p. 641

True-False Questions

____ 1. An operating statement is a simple summary of the financial results of a company's operation over a specified period of time.

____ 2. The three basic components of an operating statement are sales, costs, and return on investment.

____ 3. Net sales equals gross sales minus returns and allowances.

___ 4. The "cost of sales" is the total value (at cost) of the sales during the operating period.

___ 5. Gross margin (or gross profit) equals net sales minus operating expenses.

___ 6. Net profit equals net sales minus the cost of sales minus operating expenses.

___ 7. To calculate the net profit accurately, purchase discounts and freight charges should be added to the cost of sales.

___ 8. Expenses do not include the cost of sales.

___ 9. The stockturn rate is a measure of how long it takes a certain inventory of goods to be sold.

___ 10. Stockturn rate may be calculated as the cost of sales divided by the average inventory at cost.

___ 11. The various components of an operating statement should always be expressed in absolute numbers rather than in percentages.

___ 12. If a store takes a 50-cent markup on a certain product, then its net profit for that item is also 50 cents.

___ 13. A 25 percent markup on cost equals a 20 percent markup on selling price.

___ 14. Markdowns are generally shown on a firm's operating statement.

___ 15. A markdown ratio equals dollar markdowns divided by net sales; returns and allowances are not included.

___ 16. Return on investment is not shown on the firm's operating statement.

___ 17. To increase return on investment, a firm *must* increase sales.

___ 18. Although return on investment is calculated in the same way as return on assets, the two ratios are trying to show different things about the company's use of resources.

Answers to True-False Questions

1. T, p. 632	7. F, p. 635	13. T, p. 639
2. F, p. 632	8. T, p. 635	14. F, p. 639
3. T, p. 634	9. F, p. 637	15. F, p. 640
4. T, p. 634	10. T, p. 637	16. T, p. 640
5. F. p. 635	11. F, p. 638	17. F, p. 641
6. T, p. 635	12. F, p. 638-39	18. F, p. 641

Multiple-Choice Questions (Circle the correct response)

1. The primary purpose of the operating statement is:
   a. to determine which products or customers are most profitable.
   b. to determine the net profit figure for the company.
   c. to present data to support the net profit figure.
   d. to indicate the source of the firm's assets.
   e. both b and c above.

2. The essential components of an operating statement are:
   a. gross sales, gross margin, and net profit.
   b. net sales, cost of sales, and profit or loss.
   c. sales, costs, and profit or loss.
   d. gross sales, gross margin, expenses, and net profit.
   e. sales, markdowns, and ROI.

3. Which of the following statements is *true*?
   a. "Gross sales" is equal to revenue actually received and kept.
   b. "Cost of sales" means the cost value of goods on hand at any given time.
   c. Expenses are included in the "Cost of sales" section of the operating statement.
   d. "Gross margin" less the "Cost of sales" equals "Net profit."
   e. None of the above statements is true.

4. Given the following data for the OnTarget Company for the year 200X, calculate OnTarget's net profit.

Gross sales	$157,000
Returns	3,000
Allowances	4,000
Purchases	60,000
Beginning inventory	50,000
Freight-in	3,000
Cost of sales	100,000
Expenses	30,000

   a. $10,000
   b. $12,000
   c. $17,000
   d. $20,000
   e. $27,000

5. Which of the following statements is *false*?
   a. Stockturn rate equals cost of sales divided by average inventory at cost.
   b. Stockturn rate equals gross sales divided by average inventory at selling price.
   c. Stockturn rate equals net sales minus gross margin divided by average inventory at cost.
   d. Stockturn rate equals sales in units divided by average inventory in units.
   e. Stockturn rate equals net sales divided by average inventory at selling price.

Use the following data to answer questions 6 and 7.

Gross sales	$1,020,000	
Markdowns	50,000	
Cost of sales		50%
Beginning inventory	150,000	
Returns and allowances	20,000	
Expenses		30%
Purchases	400,000	

6. Calculate the net profit (or loss) for the firm described above.
    a. $150,000
    b. $190,000
    c. $204,000
    d. $200,000
    e. Cannot be determined without more information.

7. Assume that the average stockturn rate for this industry is 4. How does this firm compare to its competitors?
    a. The firm has an above-average turnover rate.
    b. The firm has a below-average turnover rate.
    c. The firm has an average turnover rate.
    d. Cannot be determined.

Use the following data from a company's last accounting period to answer questions 8-10.

Sales returns	$ 10,000	
Sales allowances	15,000	
Expenses		25 %
Closing inventory at cost	50,000	
Markdowns	45,000	
Freight-in	5,000	
Purchases	150,000	
Net profit	30,000	10%

8. The cost of sales is:
    a. $225,000
    b. $105,000
    c. $145,000
    d. $195,000
    e. $ 75,000

9. The stockturn rate is:
    a. 6.0
    b. 3.9
    c. 4.3
    d. 2.8
    e. 1.5

10. The markdown ratio is:
    a.   20 percent
    b.   11 2/3 percent
    c.   18 1/3 percent
    d.   10 percent
    e.   15 percent

11. Rosemary's Florist Shop uses a traditional markup of 25 percent for all of its long-stem roses. If a rose costs her $6, what should Josie *add* to this cost to determine her selling price?
    a. $1.50
    b.   33 1/3 percent of $6.00
    c.   125 percent of $6.00
    d. $3.00
    e.   25 percent of $6.00

12. Knowledge of departmental markdown ratios for a given period would be useful in:
    a.   preparing an operating statement for that period.
    b.   determining the value of goods on hand.
    c.   measuring the efficiency of the various retail departments.
    d.   computing the stockturn rate for that period.
    e.   All of the above.

13. To increase its return on investment (ROI), a firm could:
    a.   increase its profit margin.
    b.   increase its sales.
    c.   decrease its investment.
    d.   increase its leveraging.
    e.   All of the above.

14. *Given the following information, calculate the FirstChoice Company's ROI.*

Net sales	$1,000,000
Gross margin	200,000
Markdowns	200,000
Assets	300,000
Net profit (after taxes)	10,000
Owner's investment	100,000

    a.   3.3 percent
    b.   1,000.0 percent
    c.   10.0 percent
    d.   2.5 percent
    e.   5.0 percent

15.   In Question 14, the FirstChoice Company's ROA was:
    a.   3.3 percent.
    b.   2.5 percent.
    c.   30.0 percent.
    d.   150.0 percent.
    e.   Some negative number--because the assets were larger than the owners' investment.

Answers to Multiple-Choice Questions

1. e, p. 632   6. d, p. 635   11. b, p. 639
2. c, p. 632   7. a, p. 637   12. c, p. 639
3. e, p. 633-34   8. d, p. 634   13. e, p. 641
4. d, p. 635   9. d, p. 637   14. c, p. 640-41
5. b, p. 637   10. a, p. 640   15. a, p. 641

Exercise B-1

Marketing arithmetic

Introduction

A firm's financial records contain much useful information for a marketing manager. An effective marketing manager will make regular use of them in his planning. This exercise is designed to improve your understanding of the operating statement and the information it contains.

Assignment

Answer each of the following questions about the financial records of FastTrack Corporation.

1.   Complete FastTrack's operating statement (on the next page) by filling in the blank lines and then use the information in the financial statement to answer the following questions.

2.   Calculate the stockturn rate (using cost figures).

3.   Calculate the following operating ratios. (Round each answer to one decimal place.)

   a)   Net sales   100%

   b)   Cost of sales   _____

   c)   Gross margin   _____

   d)   Expenses   _____

   e)   Net profit   _____

FASTTRACK CORPORATION
Operating Statement
For the Year Ending December 31, 200X

Gross sales $62,000

Less: Returns and allowances

Net sales   a) _____

Cost of sales   58,000

     Beginning inventory at cost $12,000

     Purchases at billed cost $26,000

         Less: Purchase discounts   3,000

     Purchases at net cost   b) _____

     Plus freight-in   3,000

     Net cost of delivered purchases   c) _____

Cost of goods available for sale   d) _____

         Less: Ending inventory at cost.   8,000

Cost of sales

Gross margin (gross profit)   e) _____

Expenses   f) _____

     Selling expense

         Sales salaries   7,000

         Advertising expense   2,200

         Delivery expense   3,300

         Total selling expenses   g) _____

     Administrative expense

         Office salaries $ 3,800

         Office supplies   900

         Miscellaneous   1,300

         Total admin. expense   h) _____

     General expense

         Rent expense   1,100

         Miscellaneous   100

         Total general expense   i) _____

         Total expense   j) _____

Net profit from operation   k) _____

Question for Discussion

What additional financial information would help the marketing manager of FastTrack Corporation to improve his operation?